CITY LIVES AND CITY FORMS: CRITICAL RESEARCH AND CANADIAN URBANISM

Edited by Jon Caulfield and Linda Peake

Focusing on a series of pivotal issues confronting Canadian cities and city-dwellers today, this volume addresses key themes in urban studies: the interaction between social relations and urban landscapes, the status of the city in the new world economy, and the sociocultural complexity of urban populations. The fifteen essays presented here reflect the current preoccupations and perspectives of critically oriented urban researchers in Canada. The essays in Part 1, 'People, Places, Cultures,' examine the nature of urban space and the links between this space and social relations, illustrating the fundamental principle that urban spaces are 'built values' and 'built politics' – physical expressions of social process. Part 2, 'The Economy of Cities,' explores recent fundamental shifts in the economic character of Canadian cities, whose effect on the social and physical landscapes has been as dramatic as the explosive onset of industrialism was in the last century. Part 3, 'Urban Social Movements,' focuses on the practices of social movements, including those oriented to gender, race, and the environment.

Consisting largely of applied case studies, rather than broad thematic essays, *City Lives and City Forms* presents an overall argument for focused critical research in the urban field and suggests possible directions for the future.

JON CAULFIELD is a member of the Division of Social Science, York University, and author of *City Form and Everyday Life: Toronto's Gentrification and Critical Social Practice.* LINDA PEAKE is a member of the Division of Social Science, York University.

EDITED BY
JON CAULFIELD AND LINDA PEAKE

City Lives and City Forms: Critical Research and Canadian Urbanism

UNIVERSITY OF TORONTO PRESS
Toronto Buffalo London

Toronto Buffalo London
Printed in Canada

ISBN 0-8020-0514-4 (cloth)
ISBN 0-8020-6950-9 (paper)

Printed on acid-free paper

Canadian Cataloguing in Publication Data

Main entry under title:

City lives and city forms : critical research and Canadian urbanism

ISBN 0-8020-0514-4 (bound) ISBN 0-8020-6950-9 (pbk.)

1. Cities and towns – Canada. 2. Sociology, Urban – Canada. I. Caulfield, Jon. II. Peake, Linda, 1956–

HT127.C57 1997 307.76'0971 C96-931443-2

University of Toronto Press acknowledges the financial assistance to its publishing program of the Canada Council and the Ontario Arts Council.

Contents

Acknowledgments

The editors are grateful to the Faculty of Arts, to the Office of the Vice-President–Research, and to the Urban Studies Programme at York University, whose funding helped make this book possible; to Stephen Bell, Valerie Preston, and Margaret Rodman, whose advice and support helped secure this aid; to two anonymous reviewers at University of Toronto Press, whose comments were very useful in revising the text; to Virgil Duff and Anne Forte at University of Toronto Press for their patience and counsel; to Kate Baltais for her thorough and able copy-editing; and to our colleague Engin Isin, for valuable editorial aid.

Contributors

Agnes Calliste
Department of Sociology and Anthropology, St Francis Xavier University

Jon Caulfield
Division of Social Science, York University

Michael Goldrick
Department of Political Science, York University

Franz Hartmann
Department of Political Science, York University

Jeffrey Hopkins
Department of Geography, University of Western Ontario

Engin F. Isin
Division of Social Science, York University

Robert Lewis
Department of Geography, University of Toronto

David Ley
Department of Geography, University of British Columbia

Warren Magnusson
Department of Political Science, University of Victoria

Beth Moore Milroy
School of Urban and Regional Planning, Ryerson Polytechnic University

Linda Peake
Division of Social Science, York University

Evelyn Peters
Department of Geography, Queen's University

Damaris Rose
Institut national de la recherche scientifique – Urbanisation, Université du Québec

Rob Shields
Department of Sociology and Anthropology, Carleton University; Culture and Communications Programme, University of Lancaster

Alan Smart
Department of Anthropology, University of Calgary

Josephine Smart
Department of Anthropology, University of Calgary

Graham Todd
Department of Political Science, York University

Gerda Wekerle
Faculty of Environmental Studies, York University

CITY LIVES AND CITY FORMS

Introduction

JON CAULFIELD

This book addresses a series of pivotal issues confronting Canadian cities and city-dwellers at present. It has two objectives.

First, *City Lives and City Forms* is meant as a resource for critically oriented urban studies curricula. Towards this purpose, a selection of key current themes in the urban field are explored through a representative cross-section of the preoccupations and perspectives of 'critical' urban researchers in Canada. The focus is especially on the interaction between social relations and urban landscapes, on the status of Canadian cities in the new world economy, on the sociocultural complexity of Canada's urban populations, and on urban social movements oriented to altering existing patterns of power and privilege. A few of the chapters are more general in scope; others closely examine particular topics in specific cities, placing these topics in their wider historical and global framework. Some authors work their themes through economic, political, or statistical analysis. Others explore 'narratives' with which city-dwellers often make sense of urban life and which may sometimes buttress patterns of social prejudice and skewed opportunity. Still others *create* narratives, recounting untold stories of city-dwellers who have acted together as urban citizens.

Second, this book is directed to our colleagues in urban study across Canada's regions and within the various disciplines of social science. A great deal of critical research is currently in progress about the economics, politics, and cultures of Canadian cities in the contexts of both larger processes that affect the urban realm and the intimate stage of everyday urban life. But it has seemed to the editors – and to colleagues with whom we have conferred – that, amid the complexity of academic institutions and the dense volume of scholarly work in constant production, critically oriented urban researchers are sometimes less conversant than they prefer with the breadth of interests and activity in the field. *City Lives and City Forms* is meant to help address this predicament by seeking to familiarize researchers in different branches of urban study with at least a fragment of the work of their colleagues.

The latter audience is generally familiar with the idea of critical urban research and debates about its nature. For students, however, a brief introduction may be useful. Viewed most broadly, the critical perspective in urban study is characterized by some degree of serious discomfort with the urban realm as it is. In its more felicitous forms, this may involve focused critique of a specific facet of cities or city life. At its most acerbic, it may bitterly assault a whole urban fabric. In some cases, it is animated by a particular interest – for example, 'a commitment to a more egalitarian and democratic society' (Hansen and Muszynski 1990: 2), objectives shared by most of the authors represented here. Other researchers have no prescriptive agenda but seek simply to call serene or angry attention to contradictions, deceits, or barbarisms they perceive in the urban field that surrounds them. Some – again, including most authors here – share at least some degree of optimism about the possibilities for more humane cities; others are more darkly skeptical about our ability to exert influence over prevailing social structures and institutions, or even about human nature itself.

Amid these differences, however, critical urban researchers generally have at least two common interests. First, they are usually in some way concerned either to expose ways in which social institutions suppress human possibility, or to uncover forms of social resistance to such institutions, or to explore alternative institutions people have devised to amplify their social freedoms and life chances (or some combination of these three themes). Second, they have an interest in denaturalizing the urban realm as it is; in other words, their objective is to undermine the idea that urban life in any given situation is a 'normal' state of affairs that has evolved by a 'natural' process. The critical perspective views social fabrics not as analogous to physical ecosystems – the outcome of fundamental natural laws and unyielding chains of cause and effect – but as willed human constructions. It sees any given city as one of innumerable possible cities that might have been produced and as having innumerable possible futures. The notion that there is anything 'natural' about even the smallest detail of a social fabric is a myth, because societies do not 'evolve' but are created by their members.

Critical urban study is a subset of critical social research more generally; a number of writers have sought to define what the critical approach may mean in the context of Canadian society. Alberta sociologist Raymond Morrow associates it with the perspective of the Frankfurt school of social inquiry that arose in Germany in the 1920s and believed that 'analysis [should] not take the form of an indifferent value-free contemplation of social reality but ... be engaged consciously with the process of its transformation' (1994: 14). In other words, Morrow rejects the notion of 'objective' or disinterested social science in favour of research based in the desirability of social change and oriented to helping define the character of this change and to bringing it about. From this perspective, 'objective' social science is a seductive fiction, because research which is not grounded in the possibility of social change but imagines it is outside the web of ordinary social life effectively works, for better or worse, to sustain social relations as they are.

Two Saskatchewan researchers, Philip Hansen and Alicja Muszynski, approach the question by describing social life 'as a field of complex and contradictory possibilities for social actors who could in principle assume command of these possibilities and produce new social realities' (1990: 3). In this context, 'the task of critical research involves identifying these possibilities and suggesting what social actors might do to bring their lives under their conscious direction' (1990: 3). Hansen and Muszynski stress their commitment to democratic and 'progressive' change oriented to social equality, and they explicitly distance themselves from perspectives that view human beings as helpless flotsam in a tide of overwhelming institutions – perspectives in which 'people who experience crisis are rendered passive, and thus powerless in the face of superior structural determinations' (1990: 3, 5). Quebec geographer Damaris Rose echoes the latter view, clearly demurring from the attitude that people are 'mere bearers of a process determined independently of them' (1984: 56).

In a vein parallel to Hansen and Muszynski, Quebec sociologist Marcel Rioux identified the work of critical research as 'clarify[ing] and promot[ing] the self-creation by human beings of their own society' (1984: 4). Rioux viewed this not as an abstract, theoretical exercise but as a job requiring careful fieldwork, with close attention to people's everyday lives and aspirations and, 'above all, [to] the ... historical situations held by social agents' (1984: 4). In other words, it is essential to understand human activity in the context of the specific social settings where it occurs and to identify directions for social change from the vantage point of human actors in those settings; it is not the critical researcher who defines what 'should' occur. This perspective is shared by two British

Columbia writers who advise that, in critical research, 'it is essential to *listen*' to the ongoing practices of people in their everyday lives 'rather than specify the ... object of history in advance' according to an a priori theoretical scheme (Magnusson and Walker 1988: 59). Based on his research and reflections, Rioux identified a series of social realms – that among others include the workplace, gender and the family, the environment, and 'the large bureaucratic machine[s]' of corporations and the state (1984: 12) – as key possible sites for resistance and social change; urban researchers would add the city to this list.

Michael Goldrick has sketched a further key dimension of the critical perspective with specific reference to the urban field. He challenges the commonly promoted view of city-building as 'a random, haphazard process propelled by a constellation of private decisions ... mediated by government intervention' and observes that the contemporary city must instead be viewed as 'a particular spatial expression of [the] production, reproduction, circulation and organization of ... capital' (1978: 30). That is, Goldrick calls attention to the crucial role played in the construction of urban fabrics and ways of life by modes and institutions of economic production that lie beneath the surface of everyday experience. Some critical researchers view these economic forces as *the* crucial building blocks of urban life; others treat the workings of the state, as an agent in its own right, as equally important in shaping the city; still others locate economic relations within a wider context of 'human desires expressed ... in everyday culture' (Caulfield 1994: 45). For most critical researchers, however, clarifying the influence of the economic realm is a fundamental aspect of denaturalizing urban landscapes and social relations.

These short paragraphs identify a few Canadian texts about critical research and some key ideas of their authors. The chapters that follow illustrate several ways that individual researchers have translated these ideas into specific research agendas in the urban field.

Part 1 of this book focuses on aspects of the social and physical fabric of everyday life in Canadian cities. Its chapters examine the nature of urban space and links between this space and social relations, illustrating the fundamental principle that urban places are 'built values' and 'built politics' – physical expressions of social process. It includes two case studies whose most immediate concern is the issue of 'race' in urban life but whose authors identify a more general and subterranean process: the manner in which myths are fabricated and play themselves out in the social relations of cities.

Chapter 1, by David Ley, considers a group of city-dwellers who have been at the heart of recent processes of urban change, well-to-do beneficiaries of the corporate/service economy who have settled into and dramatically altered many formerly working-class districts in Canada's inner cities. Ley identifies the roots and implications of this pattern, closely tracing the relationship between social fabric and urban form. He explores the construction of the 'convivial city' – part of the pastiche of images and disguises that characterize 'postmodern' urbanism – and he examines ways that the 'gentrification' of city neighbourhoods may exacerbate the polarization of advantage and disadvantage that are currently being bred by processes of urban economic restructuring.

The chapters by Alan and Josephine Smart and by Evelyn Peters explore 'narratives' that are told by established urban society about two groups at its cultural borders. One group is made up of newcomers, affluent immigrants from Hong Kong whose recent influx into Canadian cities has had a decisive influence on the social composition and landscapes of many urban neighbourhoods. The other group consists of Canada's original people, the natives whose societies have been overwhelmed by history – and by the breathtaking cultural brutality of their conquerors – and many of whom now live at the social margins of cities in the Prairie provinces. Peters and the Smarts explore how 'stories' that are told about these groups, that is, ways in which they are commonly perceived and understood, influence their fit within Canada's urban mosaic.

Jeffrey Hopkins reports on research about Toronto's underground city, the network of commercial spaces beneath the city's downtown core that is daily crowded by shoppers and by white-collar workers who descend from the towers above. The underground city is one example of a wider process at work in the corporate city, the 'malling' of urban life in commodified space. Hopkins's concern is how the ambiguous legal nature of such places – semi-public in appearance, but privately owned – differs from that of traditional urban space and may influence the everyday lives of city-dwellers, particularly those who may be left outside the new enclosed urban sphere.

Rob Shields also reflects on people's experience of urban space. He is preoccupied, though, less with 'practical' issues than with the sensual relationship of the body both to the places through which it moves and to other bodies moving through the same places. Shields explores what it means to find everyday enjoyment and pleasure in urban environments and considers some of the ways in which people interact with and 'consume' urban fabrics that surround them.

In the final chapter of Part 1, Engin Isin returns to the theme of 'narratives' in the context of a crucial issue for contemporary urbanism, urban 'sprawl' and the political, economic, and environmental dilemmas it raises. Isin documents the emergence of a new urban form he designates the 'cosmopolis.' Then, based in an interpretation of 'modern' and 'postmodern' intellectual stances, he argues that sprawl is ill-understood both by the policy-makers who seek to curtail it – and promote urban intensification – and by apologists for sprawl who characterize it as merely the legitimate outcome of the workings of a free market.

As noted above, one key area of critical research involves economic and political analysis of the complex, deeply embedded relationships between the marketplace, the state, and people's everyday lives, the theme of the second section of this book. In recent decades, there has been a fundamental shift in the economic character of Canadian urbanism whose effect on the social and physical landscapes of cities has been as dramatic as the explosive onset of industrialism in the last century. The workings of the corporate global economy have created a 'postindustrial' city whose livelihood is anchored in its white-collar and service sectors and whose demography is increasingly characterized by a split between privilege and disadvantage. The authors in Part 2 approach these dilemmas and related issues from a variety of vantage points.

In her chapter Damaris Rose is concerned with a much broader reality than solely the economic realm. But a key dimension of Rose's analysis is the effect of larger processes of economic change on Canadian cities, a question which she places in the context of particular Montreal neighbourhoods and the lives of their residents. In this respect, she illustrates a focal concern of critical research, seeking to understand the relationship between the global and the local – how overarching structural and institutional processes play themselves out in the streets of the city and the everyday lives of city-dwellers. Rose stresses the importance of exploring specific cases, arguing that urban study too often frames general theories that are ill-connected to what fieldworkers observe on the ground in the course of their research.

The chapters by Graham Todd and by Michael Goldrick explore in different ways the issue of how much real power Canadian city-dwellers have to shape the economic futures of their communities amid the institutions of capitalism and the global economy. Neither Todd nor Goldrick is wholly 'structuralist' in his outlook; that is, neither argues that the fates of Canadian cities are intractably linked to institutional processes utterly beyond their control. But they do sketch powerful structural forces that sharply limit the current options for urban communities. This focus on wider contexts of political economy in which urban citizens and policymakers act illustrates another central preoccupation of critical urban research in Canada.

Beth Moore Milroy redefines our understanding of the economic realm by excavating the meaning and nature of 'work' in the context of the changing lives of women in Kitchener-Waterloo. Milroy observes that community-building is not just a matter of constructing the economic and physical fabrics of cities but also involves less visible, more subtle kinds of work that require close appreciation at a time when women's roles are undergoing key changes and the state is 'privatizing' once-communal systems of social support. Like Rose, she directs our attention to the importance of studying the social relations of cities in the context of people's everyday rounds of life in specific local places.

Robert Lewis further illustrates this approach, in a historical study of Hamilton during the depression of the 1930s when many working people were cut adrift by the machinations of the labour market from the economic resources that had sustained them and were forced to develop strategies to cope with the crisis they faced. This effort exhausted their energies, leaving them unable to organize collectively in opposition to the institutions that constrained their lives. Lewis concludes by drawing a stark parallel between the circumstances of urban working people sixty years ago and those in which they often find themselves today.

Part 3 focuses on urban social movements. This is a notion with a specific status in contemporary social theory. It emerged in response to a key inadequacy found by many researchers in orthodox Marxian thought, for which meaningful social conflict occurs solely within the frameworks of class and economic production. Social-movement theorists argue that effective social practices oriented to democratic and egalitarian objectives may also be mounted in the context of other dimensions of social life besides only the economic realm. These may include gender, 'race,' subculture, or simply shared values, for example, values relating to ecological issues or to 'good' urban planning. In this way, social movements are conceived as critical social formations that may transcend class structures and interests; and one key issue that researchers often examine in relation to social-movement activity, illustrated by some of the chapters here, is the interaction between the economic realm and the composition and practices of movement participants.

Gerda Wekerle and Linda Peake explore ways that women in cities have organized across an array of social realms and constructed new institutions that address specific forms of gendered disadvantage and suppression. Their account is grounded in the context of a more general understanding of the intersection of feminism, the urban field, and the rise of urban social movements.

Agnes Calliste has a parallel interest, the endeavours of black city-dwellers in urban Canada to organize and resist racism in such sites as the workplace, educational institutions, and the spaces of everyday life, and the extent to which their endeavours can be understood as an example of an urban-based social movement. Calliste sketches the history of black activism in recent decades, identifying its roots, some of the strategies through which it has opposed racism, and some key conflicts in which it has played itself out.

Franz Hartmann considers a third social movement, environmentalism, arguing that a sound understanding of the dire ecological circumstances faced by Canada's cities today requires careful analysis of the modes and institutions of capitalist economic production that create the urban landscape. Hartmann then illustrates some of the objectives and activities of urban environmental activists in Toronto and argues that, while the environmental movement does generally not confront capital directly, it may affect the production of urban space in ways that impair the logic of capital.

Finally, Warren Magnusson calls attention to the abstract and cybernetic dimension of the contemporary urban space within which social movements act. He argues that, in looking at any urban 'place' – he uses the example of Victoria – we are looking at one expression of a global reality spawned by 'the greatest but in many ways most pernicious "social movement" of modern times: capitalism.' Social movements that would resist capital are required to break the boundaries of political space as it has traditionally been understood. In this context, while cities are centres of the hierarchical concentration of capital, they are also sites of unpredictable complexity offering new possibilities for effective critical practice, and thus potential nodes for social movements that may disrupt capital's hierarchies.

Overall, *City Lives and City Forms* identifies an urban system on the verge of crisis. Large segments of Canada's metropolitan population are now marginal workers employed part-time in low-paid service labour or on unstable short-term contracts (when they can find jobs at all), a very different situation from forty or fifty years ago when many working people were frequently at least able to find steady, full-time and – with union contracts – reasonably well-paid work. The state's apparent lack of control of Canada's economic future and its strategy, both federally and provincially, for addressing this dilemma, by sharply cutting its investment in such resources as health care, social services, education, and urban infrastructure, bode singularly ill for the future of Canadian cities. Urban governments, meanwhile, gut their planning and environmental codes in competitive pursuit of economic development, often falling back on tourism-oriented investments in spectacle. It is neither too soon nor overwrought to imagine a future in which the social morphology of Canadian urbanism is composed of fragile enclaves of privilege amid an increasingly disadvantaged majority. This is not a scenario which will foster enlightened social and urban policies, political civility, or cultural and racial harmony.

In this milieu, there is clear need for focused critical research in the urban field, activity for which this book suggests several directions. The excavation of urban history, for example, is not an academic luxury but a key aspect of understanding the present circumstances of cities and their social relations; as Harold Chorney has observed, a kind of 'amnesia' affects our memory of past social and political movements and of working-class history in urban Canada (1981). Another area for research are myths – about gender, 'race,' and unemployment, for example, or about human nature, about how urban economies work, and about 'what people want' – that sustain patterns of social inequity in cities. It is also essential to continue exploring the workings of social movements and of community organizations committed to devising alternatives to existing institutional structures, work that is necessary in order for critical research to remain closely linked to the activities and aspirations of human actors in their specific social settings. As well, much research is required about the physical form of cities and city-regions – for example, about the genesis and meanings of 'sprawl' – and about the wantonly destructive ecological character of the contemporary urbanism. Finally, among the most fundamental fields for research are the current economic trajectories of cities and the possibilities for wresting control of urban economies from the abstract institutions of global capital; in this context, the viability of community-based economic development requires immediate and careful fieldwork.

In seeking to suggest directions for further research amid the present problematic circumstances of Canadian cities, *City Lives and City Forms* is a signpost. Much work needs to be done.

REFERENCES

Caulfield, J. 1994. *City Form and Everyday Life.* Toronto: University of Toronto Press

Chorney, H. 1981. 'Amnesia, integration and repression: The roots of Canadian urban political culture.' In M. Dear and R. Scott, eds., *Urbanization and Urban Planning in Capitalist Society*, 535–63. New York: Methuen

Goldrick, M. 1978. 'The anatomy of urban reform in Toronto.' *City Magazine* 3(4/5): 29–39. Reprinted in D. Roussopoulos, ed., *The City and Radical Social Change*, 260–82. Montreal: Black Rose Books, 1982

Hansen, P., and A. Muszynski. 1990. 'Crisis in rural life and crisis in thinking: Directions for critical research.' *Canadian Review of Sociology and Anthropology* 27(1): 1–22

Magnusson, W., and R. Walker. 1988. 'Decentring the state: Political theory and Canadian political economy." *Studies in Political Economy* 26: 37–71

Morrow, R. 1994. *Critical Theory and Methodology.* Thousand Oaks: Sage Publications

Rioux, M. 1984. 'Remarks on practices and industrial societies in crisis.' *Canadian Review of Sociology and Anthropology* 21(1): 1–20

Rose, D. 1984. 'Rethinking gentrification: Beyond the uneven development of marxist urban theory.' *Environment and Planning D: Society and Space* 1: 47–74

PART 1

PEOPLE, PLACES, CULTURES

1

The New Middle Class in Canadian Central Cities

DAVID LEY

The 1960s were an era of massive landcape change in many Canadian cities. The full force of postwar economic growth led to significant development pressures, including new construction in the suburbs and the reshaping of the central city, with an expansion of office growth downtown and the private redevelopment of inner city blocks into low- and high-rise apartments. This was the period when high-density redevelopment forever transformed the face of residential districts like Vancouver's West End and St Jamestown in Toronto. State intervention was also at a high point with major infrastructure additions, notably freeways that sliced through pre-existing neighbourhoods, removing land from the city's tax base; Montreal under the pro-growth regime of Mayor Jean Drapeau built no less than seven expressways through the urban fabric between 1960 and 1976. Vast clearances were also proposed for aging inner city districts. Vancouver's council anticipated the massive clearance of 2500 acres of developed land around the downtown in an urban renewal plan dating from the 1950s, while a Toronto report of the same vintage designated almost half the city's residential districts for renewal, redevelopment, or major improvement. Other urban administrations were equally committed to major change, empowered by federal urban renewal policy which authorized ninety projects across Canada between 1964 and the program's effective termination in 1972. At the ideological level, government, like the private sector, was fully committed to what Joseph Schumpeter had called the creative destruction of the market process; to such an ideology, change and progress were inseparable. They were undoubtedly confirmed in this mentality by the utopian visions of the modern movement in planning and architecture, with its heroic narrative of the new, its surgical imagery of the dissection and removal of aged and (implicitly) infirm urban members to be replaced by prostheses marked by their functionality and universality.

The slash-and-build policy of the 1960s ran into severe difficulties at the end of the decade. The massive destruction of the city's body parts, and their replacement by large, anonymous projects, were resisted in city after city both by neighbourhood groups and newly elected reform councillors who spoke and voted on their behalf. Major reorientations of government policy at the federal and local levels encouraged the emergence of a softer city, one that gave a new prominence to the *quality* of the built environment and not merely the quantitative tally of the value of new building permits, the boast of virtually every urban politician up to the late 1960s. Downzoning in some neighbourhoods limited the scale of physical change in the built environment (but not, as we shall see, social change); a fresh commitment after 1972 to renovation and service enrichment policies in older neighbourhoods had the same effect of preserving the landscape. Heritage preservation was an important part of the new planning lexicon that also included incentives for design improvements, parks and public space enhancement, an active arts and cultural policy, more humane forms of social housing, and renewed attempts to establish a public transportation alternative to the voracious appetite of the automobile for urban space.

Every land use plan and every development scenario has a sociology of stakeholders. If the slash-and-build policies of the 1960s were the 'natural' outworking of a belief in progress as change held by a business class that dominated local politics in cities across Canada, who was the patron of the soft city? Which social groups were associated most closely with the liveable city, and the quality of urban life, the planning slogans of the 1970s and 1980s, the expressions of an urban perspective that sought to broaden out the one-dimensional goals of postwar regime politics? Among these stakeholders was a generation closely identified with the critical values of the 1960s, a rapidly growing new middle class that included social and cultural professionals in the arts and media, education, the design professions, and others such as social workers and lawyers working within the public sector. Well educated, and aware in general terms of the arguments of the 1960s concerning the limitations of life as *One-Dimensional Man* (Marcuse 1964), the alienations of a *Society of the Spectacle* (Debord 1967), this group was active in neighbourhood politics that were resistant to massive change and were centrally involved in mobilizing to renew older political options (notably a municipal version of the New Democratic Party) or to establish a new set of political reform parties, including the Montreal Citizens' Movement (MCM) and, in Vancouver, the left-wing Committee of Progressive Electors (COPE) and, at the centre-left, The Electors Action Movement (TEAM). Replacing the earlier hegemony of business people and business ideas, over a quarter of TEAM's membership of several hundred in the early 1970s were drawn from just four professions, while two-thirds of candidates for the major left-liberal parties in the twelve civic elections between 1968 and 1990 held professional occupations (Ley 1980, 1994). In 1984 a councillor for the MCM descibed a typical supporter in the following terms: 'Well-educated, 25–45 years old, a professional, probably in the public sector, but not necessarily career-oriented ... has other goals instead.' Even more explicitly, a prominent NDP councillor in Toronto interviewed at the same time acknowledged, 'Reform leadership consisted of first-wave gentrifiers. What they shared in common was a concern for neighbourhoods and the quality of life.'

The new middle class in the central city, in important respects the sponsor of the soft city, is the subject of this chapter. We have already seen its contribution to a reshaping of urban politics. But more familiar is its role in reshaping older residential districts in the city through the process known as gentrification, where a social transition occurs as lower-income groups are progressively replaced in inner city neighbourhoods by middle-income groups. The chapter will begin by examining the pattern of social change in six Canadian cities between 1971 and 1991. Second, I shall briefly review some of the explanations offered to account for this changing social geography. Finally, we shall consider some of the consequences of both gentrification and of a broader *embourgeoisement* of the central city for the quality of citizenship in the Canadian city in the 1990s.

Patterns of Social Change in Canadian Inner Cities

Historically, the inner city has been the zone of older and affordable housing adjacent to the central business district, the point of arrival for consecutive waves of working-class immigrants. It has been home to a population who often walked to work in the factories and warehouses around the principal railway and port facilities, or undertook construction work and a range of labouring jobs associated with the growth and infrastructure development of the emergent metropolis. This pattern held into the postwar period, when, for example, the Fairview Slopes in Vancouver still contained households of South and East Asian origin who worked in the adjacent sawmills and metalworking plants of False Creek. At the same time Don Vale in Toronto was the home of a working-class population that originated in large measure from Britain and Ireland and found work in the manufacturing belt near the lakeshore and in a range of service jobs. For example, in 1967, near the end of this era, on one stretch of adjacent houses on Amelia Street in the more respectable northern section of Don Vale, lived a punch press operator, a city parks employee, a Toronto Transit Commission operator, a rigger for Canadian General Electric, and a steel fitter. In both neighbourhoods the social transition over the next twenty years was virtually complete. The Fairview Slopes were rapidly transformed as the old rooming houses were replaced by condominiums for professional and managerial households (Mills 1988). In Don Vale renovation was the dominant transition process, but the outcome was the same, for by 1986 the working-class households on Amelia Street had been largely replaced by residents who included two ballet dancers and a writer, a social worker and a minister, someone in advertising, three teachers, two physicians, and two barristers (Ley 1996; Lorimer and Phillips 1971).

Fairview Slopes and Don Vale represent two of the most dramatic examples of inner city gentrification in Canadian inner cities, but their experience is far from unique. In the six metropolitan areas of Toronto, Montreal, Vancouver, Ottawa-Hull, Edmonton, and Halifax there was a net gain of some 160,000 people employed in professional, managerial, administrative, or technical occupations living in inner city districts between 1971 and 1991; this so-called quaternary workforce rose from 18 per cent to 38 per cent as a share of the employed inner city population. Simultaneously, the deindustrialization of the inner city led to the rapid diminution of working-class jobs, at the same time as inflating housing costs severely eroded the affordability of shelter. These trends are reflected in the net loss of almost 230,000 inner city residents with non-quaternary jobs in the same six inner cities over the same period. As a consequence, and reversing the historic condition of the industrial inner city, non-quaternary workers are now *under*represented in the inner city relative to the metropolitan region as a whole, while professional and managerial workers are *over*represented in the inner cities of these six metropolitan areas.

The geography of social class transition for the six cities is recorded in Figure 1.1. Social status change between 1971 and 1991 was measured by assessing the variation in the value of an index, derived from occupational and educational variables, at each of the two dates (see Ley 1988,

1992).[1] The inner city was defined from a government study that employed two criteria, the age of housing and, to include redeveloped areas near downtown, proximity to the central business district (CBD) (Brown and Burke 1979). This demarcation of the inner city was satisfactory, although it may have inflated somewhat local perceptions of the inner city's spatial extent. The more than 460 census tracts included in the six inner cities are classified by quintile, permitting a comparison of social change to be made both between cities and within cities. The range of the index is considerable; while the social status of a few tracts declined over the twenty-year period, the dominant movement was upwards, and some tracts rose markedly. It is this latter group, in the top quintile of social change, that contains many of the more celebrated gentrified districts in urban Canada.

In inner Toronto (Figure 1.1a) social status gains have occurred in a broad swath of tracts around the CBD. East of downtown, renovation of Don Vale (tracts 67 and 68) has spilled over east of the Don River into Riverdale (tracts 69, 70, 71). A mix of middle-class renovation and redevelopment connects this core with the new structures on the Toronto Harbour (tract 13), and on the former industrial land of the municipally built St Lawrence district (tract 17). North of downtown, gentrification has transformed Yorkville (tract 89), as well as moving west along Bloor and south along Spadina from the middle-class base of the Annex (tract 91). Middle-class North Toronto contains nodes of further upgrading through infill and condominium intensification. In the west end an island of upgrading tracts (49, 51, 99) is clustered around the regional amenity of High Park, and a similar cluster occurs in the lakeshore community of the Beaches in the east end, and beyond the range of the inner city as described here. Aside from concentrations of public housing like Regent Park (tract 31) or austere apartment areas, notably St Jamestown (tract 65), the districts of limited upgrading, and in some cases downgrading, are on the edges of the inner city, particularly in the outer west end.

The concentration of gentrification in central districts is even more evident in Montreal (Figure 1.1b). For a number of reasons, the city has the largest number of tracts in the top quintile of social status gains. Most self-evidently, inner Montreal as defined covers the largest area and therefore contains the greatest stock of available tracts. But, more significantly, Montreal has experienced a severe collapse of its former inner city industrial base. The old manufacturing region in the southwest, along the Lachine Canal, was the site of perhaps the most concentrated manu-

FIGURE 1.1

The Geography of Social Class Transition in Toronto, Montreal, Vancouver, Ottawa, Halifax, and Edmonton

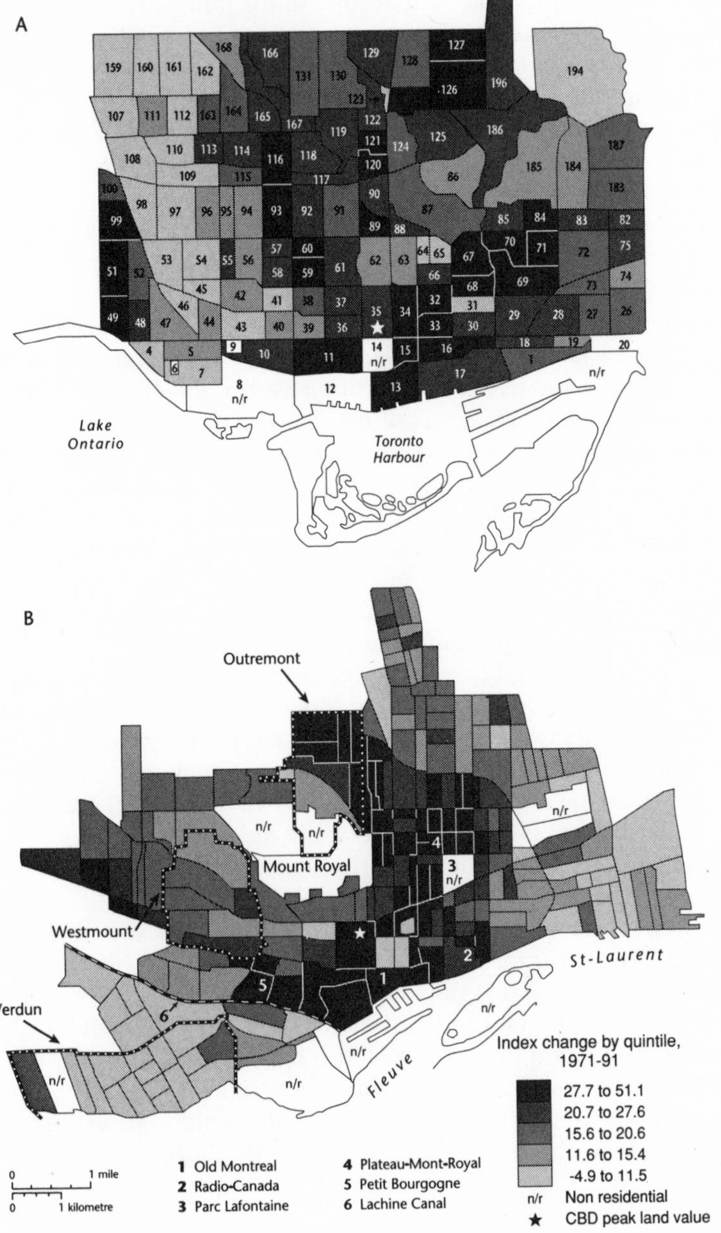

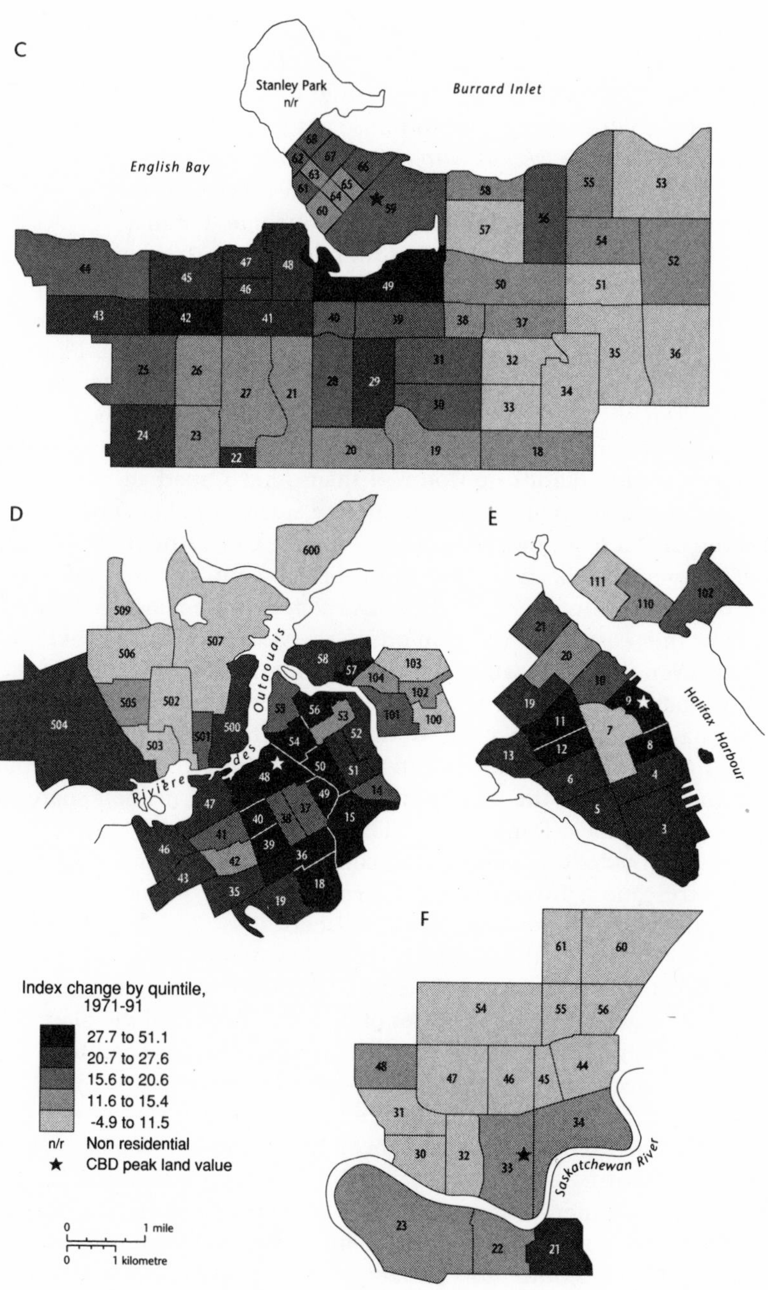

C
Stanley Park
n/r
Burrard Inlet
English Bay
D
Rivière des Outaouais
E
Halifax Harbour
F
Saskatchewan River
Index change by quintile, 1971-91
27.7 to 51.1
20.7 to 27.6
15.6 to 20.6
11.6 to 15.4
-4.9 to 11.5
n/r Non residential
★ CBD peak land value
0 1 mile
0 1 kilometre

facturing district in Canada in the immediate postwar period. Deindustrialization has ravaged the area. Between 1959 and 1988, 21,000 jobs were lost; in twenty-five years over 50,000 people left the district, halving its population (DeVerteuil 1993). In response to such devastation, the City of Montreal launched its *Opération 10,000* [later *20,000*] *Logements* program in 1979, with the intent to repopulate such districts and 'offer a larger variety of housing to young and middle income families' (Ville de Montréal 1984). Petite Bourgogne, north of the canal, has been substantially rebuilt through this initiative and registered some of the sharpest upgrading of any district in the six cities. Between 1976 and 1986 property assessments for duplexes and triplexes in Petite Bourgogne and Plateau-Mont-Royal increased by between 90 and 125 per cent in *real* terms, the highest increment in the Montreal Urban Community (Sénécal et al. 1990). More generally, the process of publicly stimulated gentrification has greater manifestations in Montreal than other Canadian cities. The warehouse conversions of Old Montreal were aided by public funds, while east of the CBD a new downtown campus for the Université du Québec is part of a larger revitalization effort to establish a Latin Quarter of francophone cultural institutions. Like the construction of the Maison de Radio-Canada further east, it has had spin-offs in reinvestment in adjacent housing stock. Even the remarkable middle-class colonization of Plateau-Mont-Royal has benefited from public infrastructure, in this case the subway line that has brought the plateau within easy reach of downtown and particularly the east-side cultural institutions. Significantly in this respect, the gentrifying *quartiers* of the plateau are overrepresented in their share of cultural professionals (Dansereau and Beaudry 1985, Rose 1987).

Montreal provides one other lesson concerning the locational specificity of gentrification. Invariably the districts of choice include attractive older architectural forms with vibrant streetscapes. The greystones of Shaughnessy Village on the western edge of downtown, the warehouses of Old Montreal, the mansard roofs of the St-Denis corridor in the Latin Quarter, the external metal staircases of the old triplexes of the plateau – each architectural form offers a mark of distinction, separating the dweller from more recent periods of mass construction.

Vancouver offers some informative contrasts to Montreal (Figure 1.1c). Because its economic base has never been as dependent on manufacturing as has Montreal's, deindustrialization has had much less severe impacts. Indeed inner Vancouver gained 8,500 residents in non-quaternary jobs between 1981 and 1991, while inner Montreal lost over 42,000. However, inner Vancouver also gained 18,000 quaternary workers during this period, almost as many as the 25,000 recorded in inner Montreal with four times as many census tracts. But Vancouver's *embourgeoisement* is understated on the map of social status change because the social status index is based on the relative, not the absolute, number of quaternary workers, and is thereby affected by changes in the numbers of the non-quaternary workforce. The increased *share* of higher-status workers is therefore considerably lower in Vancouver than in Montreal, and far fewer tracts appear in the top quintile of social change. Social upgrading has transformed tract 49, with publicly managed redevelopment of the industrial lands of False Creek helping to spur on the subsequent redevelopment of Fairview Slopes above. Westward, the formerly countercultural district of Kitsilano, adjacent to the west-side beaches and enjoying ocean and mountain views, has experienced appreciable upgrading. In Vancouver more generally, environmental amenity has played a significant role in directing the course of gentrification. The west side is also the higher income sector of the city, so that gentrification has repeated a tendency observable in other cities. Reinvestment, at least in its early stages, has favoured proximity to existing higher status districts; gentrification has often represented a wavelike advance on the downtown side of existing middle- or upper-class distincts. During the 1970s the best predictor in all six cities of whether or not a census tract would move upmarket was its proximity to an elite district (Ley 1988).

Middle-class reinvestment in Vancouver has more often taken the form of condominium redevelopment than renovation of heritage properties. But matching the elements of distinction offered by older homes is a mannered postmodern styling that includes design complexity and a broad architectural repertoire, feeding the desire for eminence. The Fairview Slopes, for example, provide a museum of design styles with inspiration drawn from Toronto, London, San Francisco, the Mediterranean, and classical architecture. The district has won more design awards that any other in the province – a striking parallel to the distinction offered by a heritage plaque beside the front door in renovated areas like Don Vale.

We can move more speedily through the three smaller cities. With its strong orientation to government services, Ottawa's economic base is amenable to the production of gentrifiers (Figure 1.1d). Social upgrading has occurred in a set of central tracts, with more than half of them adjacent to the amenity of the Rideau Canal, and two others bordering the Rideau River. These tracts are close to existing middle-class, anglophone areas, and little upgrading has occurred on the Hull side of the

Ottawa River. Halifax (Figure 1.1e) is also a government centre, and the existence of federal regional offices, the provincial legislature, several universities, and a number of hospitals on a small peninsula, along with a stock of older heritage houses, parks, and waterfront views, has encouraged considerable middle-class infill in the established areas of the South End (tracts 3, 4) and the West End (tracts 5, 6). Reinvestment on the edges of these districts has extended the middle-class presence towards downtown and the lower status North End. Edmonton (Figure 1.1f) challenges any hasty generalizations about the incidence of middle-class reinvestment in Canadian cities. Despite its status as a service-dominated city and its population boom in the 1970s, two-thirds of inner city tracts fall into the bottom quintile, indicating very limited upgrading. Indeed, more than half of Edmonton's inner city tracts registered a decline in social status between 1986 and 1991. A pro-growth political culture that continued into the 1980s permitted largely unconstrained apartment redevelopment with few amenities and contributed to an unattractive downtown environment. The problem has become serious enough that the city has been obliged to establish a downtown revitalization program to attempt to correct these image problems and, perhaps too late, to try to restore a more liveable and human-scale environment. Indeed, the only areas where any marked upgrading occurred in the 1980s included the small communities in the Saskatchewan River valley and the old Strathcona townsite which successfully resisted repeated efforts at clearance (tracts 22, 21).

Accounting for Gentrification

Gentrification is a complex phenomenon. As we have seen, social transition in the inner city can involve either renovation or redevelopment of the housing stock. The gentrification submarket has diffused beyond the young urban professional to include a growing number of families with children as well as a significant share of empty nest households who particularly favour new centre city condominium structures. Accounting for such a multifaceted phenomenon presents considerable challenges, and it seems certain that a range of processes have converged to make the inner city attractive to the middle class (Hamnett 1991, Hamnett and Butler 1994). Fundamental is an economy that supports the production of gentrifiers. A national or regional service centre with a large assembly of downtown white-collar workers is an essential prerequisite, particularly if the quaternary labour force includes a substantial body of professionals and managers working for government and for universities, hospitals, and other institutions. Gentrification is limited or absent in such cities as manufacturing centres, where advanced white-collar services are weakly established. No less significant than the economic base is the changing definition of the family, with the deferral or abandonment of child-raising, as women as well as men pursue demanding professional careers. For such career-oriented small households the large suburban home is unnecessary and the long commute to work an aggravation. A further factor is the existence of available housing opportunities in the inner city for purchasers and developers alike. At least initially, some inner city sites may be devalued because of the obsolescence of buildings or the price-depressing effects of adjacent non-residential land uses or poverty populations, making the sites attractive for do-it-yourselfers or for risk-taking developers.

Valid as these explanations are, they omit the fact that gentrifiers are not simply produced but are also self-produced. The selection of the central city is also about the enlargement of identity, the consummation of desire (Caulfield 1989). That desire has shown some evolution through time. The origins of gentrification around 1970 coincided with the demographic bulge of the baby boom entering the housing market, and there is considerable evidence that an inner city address represented a counter-cultural act, or at least an expression of an alternative cultural politics, for a particular fragment of the new class. This fragment was often well educated and rich in cultural capital but, as pre-professionals or at an early stage in a career as a social or cultural professional, may not have been well endowed with economic capital (Ley 1996). The perception of this cultural new class counterposed the world of the conformist suburbs unfavourably against the more diverse opportunities of the inner city. The diversity, community, and non-conformist nature of old urban neighbourhoods were highly valued in contrast to the disparaged blandness of suburbs. The inner city offered the opportunity for a critical cultural politics, an affirmation of a way of life that was simultaneously a negation of the inauthenticity of modern urban landscapes (Caulfield 1994). But more recently this initially critical disposition has been steadily (though not finally) undercut, as it has been aestheticized and incorporated into a distinctive niche submarket by the development industry.

In Toronto, an especially noteworthy example of this process was the imagineering of 'Cabbagetown Victoriana' by the Darrell Kent real estate agency in the late 1970s. Kent was one of the early middle-class settlers in Don Vale in 1968 and did not move into real estate sales until 1975. Then, with remarkable flair and discernment, he was a central figure in the commodification of Cabbagetown and a key beneficiary, as his own firm grew from a couple of agents in 1978 to more than forty in less than two years, during a period of inflationary frenzy in the Don Vale housing market (Tsimikalis 1983). Later middle-class arrivals into Don Vale paid a high entry fee, were more protective of their investment, and were less inclined to support policies that might bring social housing or social-agency transition houses into the neighbourhood (Dineen 1974). Though the neighbourhood still endorses lifestyle liberalism and such middle-class reform values as environmental and heritage protection, the commitment to policies advancing social justice is more muted than in the early days of gentrification. The pursuit of liveability, or the quality of life, may be subtly redefined to devalue redistributive and socially inclusive objectives while continuing to uphold middle-class causes.

Gentrification: A Critical Assessment

No comprehensive inventory of the costs and benefits of the *embourgeoisement* of the central city has been undertaken, though one author set out the scale of the challenge, identifying twenty-nine costs and thirty-one benefits that would need systematic attention (Cicin-Sain 1980). Some of the gains have been achieved by the *Opération 20,000 Logements* program in Montreal: the construction of middle-range housing on underutilized inner city land, the addition to the city tax base, the environmental and human benefits of a reduction in the journey to work for central city employees, job creation in the construction industry, and a market for local and downtown businesses.

While these gains are real and should not be minimized, attention should also be directed to the dysfunctional, often less visible, aspects of gentrification. The most apparent is the reduction of the historic inner city role of providing affordable housing. House price data indicate the extent of this transformation. Changes in the assessed values of dupexes and triplexes in the Montreal Urban Community showed uneven trends across the five concentric zones of the region between 1976 and 1986, with the highest increment by far registered in the central core, an average rise of 65 per cent in constant dollars (Sénécal et al. 1990). In Toronto, as well, price inflation in the inner city during the 1970s and the 1980s far outstripped gains in the suburbs; inflation of ten- to twelvefold in many inner city districts was twice the rate of suburban increases. By 1985 the Social Planning Council was noting 'the very real possibility ...

that much of the housing within the City of Toronto will soon be hopelessly beyond the means of even middle-class families' (Social Planning Council of Metro Toronto 1985). Accompanying house price increases, wealthier households have been moving into the central city. During the 1970s and 1980s, some two-thirds of census tracts in Metro Toronto where *real* household incomes rose by at least 20 per cent were in the City of Toronto. These tracts included all of the familiar gentrifying districts: Don Vale (35 per cent real household income growth, 1981–91), Riverdale (33 per cent), the Beaches (31 per cent), and the west Annex (23 per cent).

These trends have inevitably been linked to the displacement of poorer households. A City of Toronto report on income change reached the conclusion that 'renovation activity is continuing throughout east end neighbourhoods and may develop momentum in some west end neighbourhoods. Therefore, further displacement of low-income households may be expected as the trend towards a more middle-income character continues in Toronto' (City of Toronto 1984: 12). The report was based on income change in the 1970s; during the following decade middle-class reinvestment did indeed include a block of tracts in the west end, south of Bloor Street. Not surprisingly, there has been a dramatic reduction of rental units in the city, with gentrification a principal cause of the loss of a thousand dwellings a year in properties of six or more units between the mid-1970s and mid-1980s. *Additional* erosion of affordable housing resulted from the deconversion of joint owner–tenant properties to owner occupancy alone, displacing an estimated 54,000 people over the ten-year period (City of Toronto 1986).

There is not space here to report similar trends in other cities, notably Vancouver and Ottawa, but one submarket does demand further attention. Rooming houses have proven exceedingly vulnerable to the restructuring of residential space in the central city. Ottawa planners recorded a two-thirds contraction of inner city rooming house units in only seven years between 1976 and 1983, with the most severe losses in wards experiencing the highest incidence of gentrification (Peter Barnard Associates 1984). A case study in Shaughnessy Village on the western edge of Montreal's downtown revealed a precipitous decline in rooming houses as reinvestment took hold; tenants were evicted from the seventy-two listed rooming houses in the district in 1977, and by 1982 only sixteen such properties remained, as the structures were converted into middle-class flats and single-family dwellings (Corral 1986). There is undoubtedly a connection between the loss of dwelling units at the bottom end of the housing market and the growth of homelessness over the same period. While social housing has helped offset some of these losses, even in the best years of the 1970s the supply of new assisted housing fell far below the demand, and the gap has widened with the downsizing of social housing allocations through the 1980s and 1990s.

While *embourgeoisement* is widespread in the inner city, it remains far from complete. Areas with less desirable rental units like St Jamestown or Parkdale in Toronto, or with concentrations of public and social housing, contain populations with high levels of unemployment and incomes far below the city mean. In the interstices of the middle-class central city lives a population of the working poor engaged in personal services, an economic sector that has experienced rapid growth and comprises the only occupational category, outside the professional–managerial cohorts, that is disproportionately concentrated among central city residents in the six metropolitan areas. Saskia Sassen (1989) has observed in New York that personal services often provide entry-level positions for immigrants, and it is the same in major Canadian cities, where non-English-speaking immigrants are segregated in such occupations as the restaurant business, home help, and cleaning and janitorial services. Sassen has also observed that a symbiotic relationship exists between gentrification and the personal service sector, for the new middle-class household commonly subcontracts a range of household services to others: nannies and other kinds of domestic helpers; cleaners and gardeners; non-unionized trades people; and specialty stores, restaurants, and leisure venues. Many of these workers are employed at the minimum wage, and personal services overall have the lowest income level among major occupational groups. The outcome of this co-existence of islands of unemployment, the working poor, and the new middle class in Canadian central cities is a growing level of social polarization. Toronto, for example, has experienced a widening gulf between rich and poor in recent years (Bourne 1993).

Housing displacement and income polarization are two aspects of a broader restructuring of the central city at the level of meaning. The political reform initiatives of the early 1970s introduced a more complex set of objectives to urban policy. Replacing the one-dimensional attention to economic growth, they involved a more nuanced commitment to managed growth, social justice, cultural policy, and environmental quality. The harvest of such an ideology is evident in some of the planning successes of the 1970s, such as the socially mixed St Lawrence Project in Toronto, the False Creek Redevelopment in Vancouver, municipal transportation and social housing policies that promoted transit use and grassroots management, and in many successful local projects such as park expansion, public space enhancement, heritage preservation, and neighbourhood land use stabilization, often achieved in a participatory planning process with neighbourhood committees.

But recession, public debt, and the emergence of neo-conservativism fundamentally disrupted the reform program. The slogans of the quality of life and the liveable city have remained, but they have been significantly emptied of their redistributive content. While Toronto's Cityplan '91 claims to be 'promoting social equity, improving the quality of life, and managing growth' (City of Toronto 1991: 11), the discourse of the 1970s is retained largely as a rhetorical gesture. Not only has social justice been devalued, but also a subtle but profound rejigging has occurred in the presentation of cultural and environmental policies. While these elements were conceived of as independent from, if not in opposition to, the forces of growth in the early 1970s, they have now been harnessed as part and parcel of a growth strategy, nicely captured in the arts policy report published by the City of Vancouver under the title *Arts Mean Business.* The links between such arts policy and inner city reinvestment are direct: 'While the cultural industry plays a key role in the city's economy,' notes the report, 'its real impact and effect can be in the less tangible aspects of its activities – by bringing suburban residents back to the city core and drawing people to redeveloped downtown neighbourhood districts' (City of Vancouver 1983: 16). Audience surveys indicate that arts patrons are highly educated, more likely to be single or childless than the general population, and hold incomes at or above the metropolitan average. Not surprisingly, the existence of a vital arts and cultural complex has been shown to be correlated with the incidence of gentrification (Zukin 1989, Ley 1996).

Arts policy is one example of a broader trend towards urban entrepreneurialism, where quality-of-life arguments are commodified in economic development policy. The pursuit of *the convivial city* has become a municipal objective, reflected in arts, leisure, and tourism initiatives, and public expenditures for sports stadia, convention centres, palaces for the arts, and tourist attractions. In Montreal, for example, over $300 million were spent on the development of fourteen tourist sites in 1992 (Broadway 1993). In Toronto in recent years the stakes have been even higher, with the city simultaneously bidding for the spectacles of both the 1996 Olympics and Expo 2000, at a combined estimated cost of $4 billion in 1990. In a period of recession, high unemployment, and reduced social services, the opportunity costs of such expenditures raise some fundamental questions about the meaning of the central city in the 1990s. Citizens who are not waged, middle-income consumers are becoming much less visible in public policy. Has the epigram of bread and circuses become an accurate description of the entitlements of citizenship in the soft city? This is certainly how matters appear to an anti-poverty group in Toronto: 'At a time when as many as 100,000 people are lined up every month at food banks, when as many as 20,000 are homeless, when 100,000 or more tenants are trapped in the housing crisis, when our beaches are polluted, when our child care services can take no more children – this city's largest corporations and their political friends want to spend billions of dollars in public and private funds on a series of super-expensive events ... The people want bread, and we get circuses' (Bread Not Circuses Coalition 1989).

Conclusion

The gentrification of the inner city is far from the only manifestation of growth and change in Canadian metropolitan areas, and it is certainly not the most widespread. Its numbers pale against the rate of continuing suburbanization, or the influx of immigrants from outside Europe who have made Canadian cities not only multicultural but also genuinely multiracial. But while suburbanization and immigration are old stories, albeit with some new inflections, gentrification is a process which, although it has now lost its novelty, nonetheless does represent a reversal of how the inner city has been perceived for most of the twentieth century. *Embourgeoisement* and aestheticization are major departures from the working-class and industrial connotations of the inner city popularized and reproduced in textbook models of urban structure. But as this essay has pointed out, this restructuring has not treated all groups equally. It represents a polarization of closely integrated housing and labour markets, where the growth of a new class of professional and managerial workers has been accompanied by inflating inner city land values, while the simultaneous growth of poor-paying service jobs and higher unemployment rates are associated with diminishing bidding power in the housing market for less privileged citizens. This bifurcation in fortunes occurs in a context where growing numbers fall through the fraying safety net of the welfare state. Among the many questions raised by gentrification, critical scholarship cannot escape a consideration of how the process reflects a changing and less egalitarian definition of citizenship.

NOTE

1 Specifically, the percentage of the workforce employed in administrative, managerial, professional, and technical jobs, plus the percentage of the population with some university education, were computed for each census tract. These values were added and divided by two to arrive at a social status index for each tract. Various checks confirmed the validity of this index as an indicator of social status; see the discussion in Ley (1996). This exercise was repeated for different census dates, and the variation in social status between dates was interpreted as revealing the presence (or absence) of gentrification.

REFERENCES

Bread Not Circuses Coalition. 1989. *Stop Playing Games with Toronto.* Toronto: Brief submitted to City of Toronto

Broadway, M. 1993. 'Montreal's changing tourist landscape.' *Canadian Journal of Urban Studies* 2: 30–48

Brown, P., and D. Burke. 1979. *The Canadian Inner City 1971–1976: A Statistical Handbook.* Ottawa: Central Mortgage Housing Corporation

Bourne, L. 1993. 'Close together and worlds apart: An analysis of the changes in the ecology of income in Canadian cities.' *Urban Studies* 30: 1293–1317

Caulfield, J. 1989. '"Gentrification" and desire.' *Canadian Review of Anthropology and Sociology* 26: 617–32

– 1994. *City Form and Everyday Life: Toronto's Gentrification and Critical Social Practice.* Toronto: University of Toronto Press

Cicin-Sain, B. 1980. 'The costs and benefits of neighborhood revitalization.' In D. Rosenthal, ed., *Urban Revitalization,* 49–75. Beverly Hills: Sage

City of Toronto. 1984. *Toronto Region Incomes.* Toronto: Planning and Development Department, Research Bulletin 24

– 1986. *Trends in Housing Occupancy.* Toronto: Planning and Development Department, Research Bulletin 26

– 1991. *Cityplan: The Citizens' Guide.* Toronto: Planning and Development Department

City of Vancouver. 1983. *Arts Mean Business.* Vancouver: Social Planning Department

Corral, I. 1986. *Inner City Gentrification: The Case of Shaughnessy Village, Montreal.* Montreal: School of Urban Planning, McGill University

Dansereau, F., and M. Beaudry. 1985. 'Les mutations de l'espace habité montréalais: 1971–1981.' *Les Cahiers de l'ACFAS* 41: 283–308

Debord, G. 1967. *La Société du Spectacle.* Paris: Buchet-Chastel

DeVerteuil, G. 1993. 'Evolution and impacts of public policy on the Canadian inner city: Case study of southwest Montreal, 1960–1990.' Master's thesis, School of Planning, University of British Columbia

Dineen, J. 1974. *The Trouble with Coops.* Toronto: Green Tree Press

Hamnett, C. 1991. 'The blind men and the elephant: The explanation of gentrification.' *Transactions, Institute of British Geographers* NS 16: 173–89

Hamnett, C. and T. Butler. 1994. 'Gentrification, class and gender.' *Society and Space* 12: 477–93

Ley, D. 1980. 'Liberal ideology and the postindustrial city.' *Annals, Association of American Geographers* 70: 238–58

– 1988. 'Social upgrading in six Canadian inner cities.' *Canadian Geographer* 32: 31–45

– 1992. 'Gentrification in recession: social change in six Canadian inner cities, 1981–1986.' *Urban Geography* 13: 230–56

– 1994. 'Gentrification and the politics of the new middle class.' *Society and Space* 12: 53–74

– 1996. *The New Middle Class and the Remaking of the Central City.* Oxford: Oxford University Press

Lorimer, J., and M. Phillips. 1971. *Working People: Life in a Downtown Neighbourhood.* Toronto: James Lewis and Samuel

Marcuse, H. 1964. *One-Dimensional Man.* Boston: Beacon Press

Mills, C. 1988. 'Life on the upslope: The postmodern landscape of gentrification.' *Society and Space* 6: 169–89

Peter Barnard Associates. 1984. *City of Ottawa Strategic Housing Study: Phase 1 Report.* Toronto

Rose, D. 1987. 'Un aperçu féministe sur la restructuration de l'emploi et sur la gentrification: le cas de Montréal.' *Cahiers de Géographie du Québec* 31: 205–24

Sassen, S. 1989. New trends in the socio-spatial organization of the New York City economy. In R. Beauregard, ed., *Economic Restructuring and Political Response,* 69–113. Newbury Park: Sage

Social Planning Council of Metro Toronto. 1985. Housing affordability in Metropolitan Toronto. *Social Infopac* 4 (2)

Sénécal, P., C. Tremblay, and D. Teufel. 1990. *Gentrification or Urban Sprawl?* Montreal: Société d'Habitation du Québec

Tsimikalis, S. 1983. 'The gentrification of Don Vale: The role of the realtor.' Master's thesis, School of Environmental Studies, York University

Ville de Montréal. 1984. *Opération 20,000 Logements.* Montreal: CIDEM

Zukin, S. 1989. *Loft Living,* 2nd ed. New Brunswick, NJ: Rutgers University Press

2

Monster Homes: Hong Kong Immigration to Canada, Urban Conflicts, and Contested Representations of Space

ALAN SMART AND JOSEPHINE SMART

Hong Kong migration in recent years has upset standard stereotypes of migrants as predominantly composed of low-income groups, who keep to their own ethnic areas in less desirable parts of the city, or who participate in processes of ethnic succession in the 'zone of transition.' Instead, a considerable number of migrants from Hong Kong have purchased homes in the most expensive parts of Canadian cities, often areas which previously were neighbourhoods dominated by Anglo[1] upper-middle or upper-class populations. The processes by which this 'incursion' has taken place seem to have threatened the 'sense of place' of the social groups associated with these communities, and led to protests, criticism, and even changes in urban planning rules. The new dwellings that are constructed are often referred to as 'monster homes,' and this essay will focus on the meaning of this characteristic of 'monstrosity' and its implications for our understanding of processes of change in Canadian cities.

The Hong Kong migrants have selected these locations and redeveloped them partly because of a bundle of social meanings attached to place, meanings which are partially at odds with those held by elite Anglo-Canadians. In 1993 a 1000-square-foot apartment in a desirable area in Hong Kong could be sold for C$800,000 (*South China Morning Post,* 23 June 1993: 2), which would allow the outright purchase of a property in almost any of Canada's elite residential areas. Given the experience of Hong Kong migrants with high profits from real estate, it is not surprising that much of their savings should be parked in Canadian real estate. As well, residences are chosen in areas where it is possible to minimize potential disruptions caused by more complex ethnic diversity and tension, higher crime rates, 'unruly' youth, and an uncertain educational system. Ideas of status are certainly involved in the desire to live in the best neighbourhoods, but just as important is the wish to place children in the best schools.

This chapter will primarily draw on the analysis of media reports of disputes to highlight these conflicting senses of place. This procedure has the disadvantage of media emphasis upon precisely what is contested, unusual, newsworthy as opposed to the mundane, the unexceptional, the uneventful flow of daily life. However, such media accounts have an important advantage in that they draw attention to practices of representation. Representations draw on a stock of narrative themes which recur again and again, not only among participants and journalists, but also within urban studies. The attention paid to affluent Hong Kong migrants is partially a result of the way the encroachment of non-white immigrants into elite enclaves does not easily fit within standard narrative themes, and in the land use disputes considered here such narratives are drawn on selectively to engage in tasks of persuasion, particularly with regard to planning officials. Examining these processes may also lead to a greater awareness of the possible conflicts among master narratives used in studies of Canadian cities.

Representation, Contestation, and Sense of Place

As well as having stories told about them, places *are* stories, stories that we tell each other about spatial locations and their social meanings. In telling these stories, we constitute the places, or at least we try to. Places, or their representations, always have multiple and ambiguous meanings (Rodman 1992), and when we tell stories we are often denying or erasing the stories that others propose. It is often precisely to counter such other possible accounts that we tell stories about places that we constitute *as* places through our representations of them. For example, we say that this place is 'a decaying slum,' and as with other such places we project a tragic plot with endings of 'crime, middle-class flight, dysfunctional families, disease and despair' (D.T. Goldberg 1993: 197). Alternatively, the same place is instead a 'vibrant working-class inner-city community, caught up in a drama where the downtrodden struggle against the odds to preserve their homes and prevent their neighbourhood from becoming a sterile institutional wasteland' (see, for example, Gans 1962). Work on the experience of place has partly been motivated by recognition that distinctive areas within cities cannot be understood 'only by objective empirical studies of their content,' but that people's social and discursive construction of urban places is also critical in the process of urban differentiation (Davies and Herbert 1993: 85).

Place has three interconnected but distinct aspects. There is, first, place as location, a specific spot in the world, where some things and people are near and others are far. Second, there is place recognized by participants as a distinct locale or setting (the men's house or the private bedroom). Third, there is the *sense* of place, the meanings caught up with specific spaces, which users hold (Agnew and Duncan 1989: 2). These aspects are multiple, since location, locale, and sense of place may all vary according to the social position and daily undertakings of different users.

Conflicts over the meanings of particular spaces have received a great deal of attention in urban studies. For example, there is a large literature on urban protests about conflicting projects for neighbourhoods, usually low-income ones, which are seen as efficient sites for a transportation corridor or some other redevelopment (Logan and Molotch 1987). However, a limitation in much of the literature on place is that images or representations of place are seen as either shared properties of the residents of an area, or are examined as purely individual, psychological properties (Shields 1991: 12). Missing is the publicly contested element of such representational work: by labelling a particular location we are making certain claims of inclusion, exclusion, or evaluation that not everyone will agree with. As Shields (1991: 18) suggests, 'Place-images ... are produced historically, and are actively contested.'

The phenomenon that we are discussing here cuts across most conventional ways of thinking about the contestation of place. First, it reverses the common assumption in discussions of 'racial change' that the in-movers are socially subordinate to those being invaded, and that a major interest in resisting race change is the fear of a drop in property values. Second, it complicates the standard story about entrepreneurs seeking profit in opposition to residents striving to preserve use values. Logan and Molotch see the conflict between exchange values and use values, profit and sentiment, as fundamental to urban processes: 'The city is a setting for the achievement of both exchange values and use values; and the neighborhood is the meeting place of the two forces, where each resident faces the challenge of making a life on a real estate commodity' (1987: 99). 'Money' becomes opposed to 'community,' a placeless search for the highest profits in contrast to a grounded and emplaced network of social ties and common values. In this context, Hong Kong migrants can be easily vilified by placing them within the role of the 'ruthless developer.'

In disputes about the transformation or preservation of places, narrative themes are a set of resources with which we can organize our observations and ideas. There are a small number of narrative themes which recur again and again in urban studies – for example, the opposition between developers and communities. The difficulty, but also the opportunity for innovation, arises when standard narrative themes no longer work, or when elements of intertwined stories are given twists that are at odds with each other. In such circumstances, decisions are made about which narratives are stressed and which are ignored, and the resulting stories may be mobilized to engage in persuasion and contestation over the fate of particular places.

The implementation of land use and building controls can be seen as involving authoritative forms of representation that choose between or mediate contesting place-narratives. Planning outcomes are expected to be presentable, as being in conformity with such controls. In the planning process, claims are made about desired places, the way we want places to become, or remain, or what we do not want them to change into. Sometimes we resist imposed plans or projects, and in doing so we may change or modify outcomes. The issue of monster homes concerns changing controls to try to maintain architectural and landscape conformity with 'community traditions,' and adds in, for increased complexity, questions of intercultural (mis)communication.

These contending visions and practices come into play particularly through the medium of official discourse and practices such as those which authorize, scrutinize, and discipline what can be built or destroyed in particular places and how these practices can be undertaken and with what results: only certain kinds of representations can be admitted into or be effective within the decision-making process. Thus, explicit rejection of Hong Kong and other migrants is illegitimate within official discourse, and should such concerns be involved, they must be recast and recoded within a language of universality and of public interests. As Blomley (1993: 5) indicates, there is a critical link between locale and law which becomes most evident in the 'complex interpretive practices of local legal officials, such as police officers or planning officials.'

Stories describe, but every description is a culturally creative act. Stories can create spaces, but they can also defend them. The stories which are told in Kerrisdale (a formerly Anglo middle-class neighbourhood in Vancouver) or Willowdale (a North Toronto upper-middle-class Anglo enclave) tell of a mythical, green Arcadia and cast the Hong Kong people as the devils 'who paved paradise.' Stories in this case have been used to convince government officials to create new authoritative narratives of place, narratives that dictate what can be where, and how it can be put there.

In discussing a comparable but very different issue of power, place, and ethnic identity, Crenshaw and Peller (1993: 59–60) suggest that 'law, in general, and the courtroom, in particular, are arenas where narratives are contested, and the power of interpretation exercised ... But it would be a mistake to see narratives simply as some after-the-fact story about events concocted after the *real* power has already been exercised; the story lines developed in law "mediate" power in the sense that they both "translate" power as nonpower ... and they also *constitute* power, in the sense that the narrative lines shape what and how events are perceived in the first place.' We shall use these ideas to explore representations of monster homes and Hong Kong migration to Canada.

Hong Kong and Migration to Canada

A British colony since 1841, located on the edge of the last great agrarian empire, while China has undergone its tortuous integration into a Western and capitalist-dominated world system, Hong Kong is now an intensely capitalist enclave on the margin of the last important communist nation. It has constantly been affected by the upheavals in China, but its entrepreneurs have also constantly turned adversity into opportunity, and eventually into prosperity. In 1994 per capita gross domestic product was higher than Australia's or Britain's (and only US$550 below Canada's at US$18,350), and life expectancy was higher than in Canada, while infant mortality was lower (*Asiaweek* 1994: 58–62).

The negotiated handover of Hong Kong to China in 1997 has raised great concern about whether its 'economic miracle' can be maintained. One response has been high levels of emigration. Canadian cities, particularly Vancouver and Toronto, have experienced large inflows of immigrants from Hong Kong who do not fit established narratives of immigration – they are not usually the 'wretched refuse of your teeming shore' (Lazarus, quoted in Funk and Wagnalls 1986: 99), but are more frequently affluent or at least 'comfortable,' skilled, and educated. Their frontiers and most attractive economic opportunities are in China or Southeast Asia; Canada is a 'safe haven' or 'political insurance.'

Until the 1960s immigrants to Canadian cities primarily came from the classes of landless or poor peasants and unemployed or underemployed labourers in Europe. With some exceptions, most immigrants came with few resources beyond their labour power, skills, and the willingness to work hard and long. Now immigrants are often more likely to be from the middle or privileged classes and from the countries of Asia and Latin America. Hong Kong accounted for 13.6 per cent of all immigrants to Canada in 1990, 33.6 per cent of whom entered under the Business and Independent categories, the conditions of which would exclude the vast majority of the poor or working class. Of the 29,261 Hong Kong migrants to enter Canada in 1990, 53.2 per cent entered as business immigrants or as independents (J. Smart 1994).

In Hong Kong, the recent large-scale emigration of economic elites, professionals, and members of the 'middle class' to Canada, Australia, and the United States is rooted primarily in political worries. The attraction for Hong Kong migrants is almost always the desire for a safe haven, or a passport guaranteeing access to one, and not an economic motive (J. Smart 1995). This politically motivated emigration is in direct opposition to the economically and socially based desires to remain in, or return to Hong Kong.

One of the outcomes of this experience of being pulled between two different places is the fairly common emergence of a dual-household arrangement in which one of the spouses returns to work and live in Hong Kong, while the other spouse and children remain in Canada. This may produce 'astronauts,' transnational commuters so named because they are said to 'spend more time in the air than on the ground.' Such arrangements naturally have an effect on the experience that Hong Kong migrants have of their home and neighbourhood in Canada.

Because of these contrasts with the classic immigrant experience, these 'newcomers' are not 'keeping in their place'; instead they are buying, and often demolishing and rebuilding, houses in the most established and exclusive neighbourhoods, often enclaves of the 'Anglo' elite.

Hong Kong is one of the most densely crowded cities in the world, and housing has always been extremely expensive in relation to average incomes. Even dual-career professional households may only be able to afford to live in a three-hundred square-foot apartment. Almost all forms of housing are crowded, and private housing is expensive as well as being congested (A. Smart 1992).

The irony is that, in Canada, many Hong Kong migrants shift from being dramatic under-consumers of urban space to dramatic over-consumers. It is unlikely that this occurs because they need that much additional space for physical or psychological reasons (E.N. Anderson 1972). Instead, this heavy consumption of housing space results because large houses are an affordable luxury after selling a Hong Kong apartment and are seen as good investments given the available alternatives in a period when Canada is experiencing prolonged slow or negative growth. Furthermore, such houses provide access to desired values of safe neighbourhoods and good schools and are socially desirable as status symbols.

Hong Kong Migrants and Conflicts in Canadian Cities

The story of 'race' and 'place' has generally been one of segregation and exclusion. Kay Anderson demonstrates that 'Chinatown was something of a "counter-idea" (Voegelin, 1940; cited in Anderson 1988: 137) into which were herded things held to be in opposition to mainstream society. It was "their" home away from home, "their" doing, "their" evil. So in the late 1910s, when some ambitious Chinese merchants attempted to breach the moral order of race and place with moves to the suburbs, the disturbance was a particularly jarring one.' In response came official strategies that 'attempted to seal the limits of Chinese entitlement in Vancouver' within Chinatown (K. Anderson 1991: 107).

Can current phenomena be seen as more modern and less explicitly racist attempts to accomplish the same end of 'keeping the Chinese in their place'? Duncan and Duncan argue that in the neighbourhoods of Shaughnessy in Vancouver and Westchester near New York City, an anglophile elite had constructed residential landscapes which reflected a preference for an 'English style of landscape,' in which 'symbols of the English landed gentry are ... considered prestigious' (1984: 2 62). Until the 1960s the uniformity of landscape could be maintained through minimum lot sizes and high land values that kept out people not sharing the same values (Logan and Molotch 1987: 120). This assumption was threatened by the emergence of a new elite drawn from non-Anglo backgrounds. An 'influential member of the Vancouver old elite' was quoted as saying that the people they did not want in their area were 'those awful *nouveau riche* people who build monstrosities' (Duncan and Duncan 1984: 266).

The answer to this dilemma in Shaugnessy was successful political lobbying to create an area plan that would 'institutionalize English landscape tastes' (Duncan and Duncan 1984: 271). The design guidelines are 'simply the latest and most thorough attempt to exert a kind of cultural control over those who move into the area. They cannot keep the new elite out, but the design guidelines can maintain the old elite's taste, forcing newcomers' housing and landscaping to look like their own' (Duncan and Duncan 1984: 272). However, this portrayal of these events as a cultural struggle between the old and new elites is suppressed in the public arena in order to present cultural control as being in the public interest by mobilizing themes of 'historical preservation' and 'livability' and stressing community participation and distinctive neighbourhood character. In addition, the old elite represented their cause 'as a struggle between the interests of residents and those of developers' (Duncan and Duncan 1984: 271, 273).

These accounts make it clear that narratives of place are not just a reflection of underlying forces in the political economy of Canada but are also resources used in waging urban conflicts (D.T. Goldberg 1993). The decisions and justifications of the development approval process have been mediated by reference to such narratives. However, only certain types of narrative are effective or admissable within the public planning process. It is fascinating, for example, that an article entitled, 'How we saved Shaughnessy from monsters' can omit any reference to 'immigrants' or 'newcomers' (Ohannesian 1990), while another article asserts that 'Those monster houses – massive, lavish, new or renovated homes that often seem out of scale and style with their neighborhoods, along with soaring real estate prices, have caused friction between residents and newcomers' (Fennell 1992: 32). Is there another, unvoiced, meaning behind the 'monsters' of the first article? Who are the 'monsters' of this narrative, only the houses themselves, or those who produce and occupy them? The demons of such a morality tale can safely be presented as 'developers' or 'speculators,' but is that the only meaning read into the discourse by those who are affected? Why do newspaper articles in Hong Kong emphasize the dramatic potential impact of racism on the economy of Australia, but also Canada[2]?

Michael Goldberg (1990: 249) suggests that Vancouver received a great deal of media attention in the late 1980s because it is 'a metaphor for the dawning Pacific Rim reality,' and this is clearly a central narrative theme. Illustrating this theme, Donald Gutstein argues that the impact of Asian investment has been to strengthen an already existing tendency for real estate to be seen as a source of profit rather than sentiment: 'Despite the flipping that does occur, Canadians generally tend to regard their home more as the place they live and less as an investment. East Asians, on the other hand, are "much more inclined to think of property as an investment to be bought or sold many times, like stocks, bonds or gold"' (1990: 162).

The narrative theme that associates cities with the money nexus and with instrumental rather than solidary interactions is an old one in urban studies, harkening back to Tönnies, Simmell, and Wirth (see Smith 1979). This theme of 'profit versus sentiment' has been merged with that of the 'developer versus the community' and here becomes associated with the East Asian/Canadian dichotomy.

In 1989, International Trade Minister Pat Carney commented on the monster house problem: 'Monster homes are not an immigration problem, they are a zoning problem and they can be dealt with through the zoning process. Similarly, empty houses and guard dogs can be dealt with by the appropriate municipal bylaws, as can chopping down trees and paving back yards. We need to return to the concept of neighbourhood planning which has fallen out of fashion in the past few years, and encourage local residents to turn out and talk about the kind of neighbourhood they wish to live in' (quoted in Gutstein 1990: 210). This statement suggests a vocabulary and strategy in which a 'cultural struggle' could be recoded more legitimately.

Gutstein agrees with Carney that monster houses are a zoning problem, but adds that it is not as easily resolved as Carney suggests. Changing the zoning laws 'has proved difficult indeed to put into practice' because municipal councillors are indebted to the development industry for campaign support (Gutstein 1990: 210).

In addition to this developers-against-community plot-line, Gutstein also clearly illustrates the Pacific Rim/globalization theme, suggesting that the result of these trends will be that 'Canada's urban property will become a global commodity and municipal governments may lose their ability to regulate the use of land in their communities. Decisions affecting the future of neighbourhoods like Agincourt and South Granville will increasingly be made in Hong Kong, Taipei, Tokyo and Seoul' (1990: 214).

Returning to Michael Goldberg's suggestion of Vancouver as a metaphor for the Pacific Rim, a number of positive and negative developments are attributed, usually in an overly simplified manner, to this Asian influence. Such 'myths,' to use Goldberg's term, are most widely circulated with regard to property markets. Asian immigrants and/or investors are accused 'of being responsible for our house price spirals, for destroying the city, for "Manhattanizing" it with Hong Kong densities' (1990: 258). He concludes that there is no evidence to support these claims other than media accounts which 'give them the illusion of legitimacy' (1990: 258).

Regardless of their truth value, though, it is clear such claims are having an impact on the Vancouver urban scene. Speculation that Hong Kong investment in Vancouver property will continue has helped drive housing prices to record levels, an average $278,000 in June 1993. Concerns about monster homes and the loss of neighbourhood character have prompted the legislation of new building codes, guidelines, and neighbourhood-specific design guidelines in both Vancouver and Toronto. A proposed neighbourhood zoning amendment for Shaugnessy in 1992, which would have included stricter architectural design controls, made apparent divisions 'between long-standing residents, who favoured the downzoning amendment, and more recent residents, many from Hong Kong, who opposed it' (Mitchell 1994: 11; see also Ley 1995). Long-term residents argued that the neighbourhood character was being threatened. In this case, however, 'newer Hong Kong immigrants' worried that the zoning plans contain assumptions 'having to do with questions of ethnicity as well as those of landscape and house design. Is the appropriate community "character" of Shaughnessy one that is predicated on notions of Anglo-Canadian identity? Are the zoning amendments directed at excluding large houses or at excluding the people arriving from Hong Kong' (Mitchell 1994: 11)? Li indicates that these restrictive building codes in Vancouver, along with high lot prices, resulted in many Chinese developers turning their interest to the suburban municipality of Richmond (1992: 132).

What is distinctive about the most affluent Hong Kong migrants is that they 'have even penetrated, the city's – and therefore, Canada's – old-money establishment' (Demont and Fennell 1989: 112). The use of terms like 'penetrated' in this and other accounts suggests a kind of 'violation' of formerly pristine retreats. The authors go on to suggest that 'the two disparate cultures do not mix easily. Among the Tudor manors, French *chateaux* and 1960s geometric experiments now stand ornate marble-and-stucco structures with snarling Oriental stone lions at the gates' (Demont and Fennell 1989: 112). A female resident of The Bridle Path (an elite neighbourhood in Toronto) for twenty years worried about the impact of the increased number of Chinese buyers in recent years, suggesting that there 'are perfectly charming homes that have been trashed by them to put up great abortions. I have no racist feelings, but they have so much money it is kind of scary' (quoted in Demont and Fennell 1989: 113). Here, racism is explicitly denied, and a concern about the impact of the lack of taste of the 'nouveau riche' affirmed instead.

The prevalence of themes such as 'money versus sentiment,' 'developers versus the community,' and 'the powerful versus the (minority) disadvantaged' within our discourse of the city means that the 'Asianization' of certain elite Anglo enclaves attracts a great deal of attention because it is unusual and therefore 'newsworthy.' The terms of narratives which have been commonly entwined are given distinct twists, and we can no longer associate developer/money/Anglos versus community/sentiment/minorities. The problem of 'monster homes' is that the assumption of Suttles (in Logan and Molotch 1987: 12) that the rich choose to live 'where the character of fellow residents is assured by the costs of living there' no longer holds.

A central term in these stories is the 'monster house.' A Vancouver lawyer is reported to have made what he considers a very good investment since 'it has a big lot, on a flat street that does not have many trees. The Chinese love that. It is perfect for a monster house' (Fennell 1992: 32). The link between Hong Kong migrants and monster houses is made even more explicit in Margaret Cannon's book *China Tide*: 'Hong Kong families are buying houses on pleasant, shady streets, then tearing them down and throwing up "monster" houses that destroy the streetscape and block neighbors' gardens from the sun' (Cannon 1989: 14).

One main theme in the discussion of Hong Kong property investment is simply that of money and its connection with the emerging Pacific Rim economy. Hong Kong is important for funnelling a share of that money to Canada and for creating a much tighter linkage between local property markets and emergent global property markets. Hong Kong is thus seen as the leading edge of globalization, dramatic change, and the erosion of local and national sovereignty. In Canadian cities, this loss of control becomes represented by 'monster homes.'

Another prevalent theme is that those who build monster houses put less value on the public and the open, which undermines 'the streetscape' (Li 1994). Trees, especially mature ones, seem to receive a particularly large amount of attention (Ley 1995). When Hong Kong migrants are specifically discussed in this regard, attention is frequently paid to the practice of *feng shui* or geomancy, the manipulation of the geographic positioning of man-made objects to improve the owner's fortunes. Discussions of Chinese geomantic practices sound very reminiscent of what Said (1978) calls the 'orientalist gaze' and which Anderson (1991: 92) shows was operating in Chinatown to make it represent 'a collection of essences that seemed to set the Chinese fundamentally apart.' Such emphases on the exotic differences of Hong Kong migrants, represented by such concerns as avoiding the number '4' or homes at the junction of 'T' intersections, may be used to support the arguments of those who, while claiming to support immigration, argue for attention to the limits on the 'absorptive capacity' of Canadian society for those from 'drastically different cultures' (Anderson 1991: 240–1).

Conclusion

A number of narrative themes have emerged in this examination of stories people utilize as resources in representing their thoughts and words about what a place is, what it is becoming, and what it should be. Particularly important among these themes are:

1 Hong Kong migrants as the source of commodification of place and of the threat of the dominance of profit over sentiment and community;
2 Hong Kong migrants as the leading edge of a vibrant and innovative Asian Pacific Rim, constructing links which will bring Canada into the bright future of the 'Pacific Century';
3 Hong Kong migrants as the source, intentionally or as the inadvertent victims of 'developers,' of threats to highly desired elements of the streetscape and of the sense of place of communities with a coherent design and landscape;
4 Hong Kong migrants as the source of an orientalizing culture, typified by geomancy and 'stone lions,' cultural influences that can be alternatively narrated as expressions of diversity and vibrant cultural expression, or as a threatening Otherness which must be 'kept in its place.'

These narratives are powerful, but their plot-lines do not run in accordance with some of the conventional fields of discourse with which we are familiar in urban studies, and, therefore, they raise some interpretive difficulties. These distinct narratives have varying advantages and disadvantages which lead to their differential presentation in different arenas of public or private discourse. Effective mobilization of narrative story-lines which can persuade those in authority to intervene in desired ways can lead to significant changes in Canadian cities, and one important task for the future will involve more detailed examination of precisely how this is accomplished.

Just as the narratives fit awkwardly with each other, the implications of cultural struggles around monster homes raise difficult questions for the critical urban scholar and practitioner. Do we support local communities in their efforts to control their local sense of place? Or is this simply an unacceptable smokescreen for excluding people who are not seen as fitting in with the dominant culture? How can the simultaneously attractive ideals of community control, ethnic tolerance, and equality be reconciled in a situation like this? We have no answers here, but will conclude simply by suggesting that one value of the attention paid to contested representations of place is precisely the way in which it can make apparent the conflicts between our conventional social science master narratives and indicate the need for attempts to reorganize them rather than simply selectively apply them in different contexts.

NOTES

1 We are using the term 'Anglo' here as a shorthand phrase to refer not only to white Canadians with roots in Great Britain and Ireland, but also to native-born anglophones who do not have a strong alternate ethnic self-identity.

2 Analysis of media representation of these issues in the Hong Kong press is an important additional task which is not possible here, but see Ley (1995).

REFERENCES

Agnew, J.A., and J.S. Duncan. 1989. 'Introduction.' In J. Agnew and J. Duncan, eds., *The Power of Place*, 1–8. London: Unwin Hyman

Anderson, E.N. 1972. 'Some Chinese methods of dealing with crowding.' *Urban Anthropology* 1: 141–50

Anderson, K.J. 1988. 'Cultural hegemony and the race-definition process in Chinatown, Vancouver: 1880–1980.' *Environment and Planning D: Society and Space* 6: 127–49

– 1991. *Vancouver's Chinatown.* Montreal: McGill-Queen's University Press

Asiaweek. 1994. 'The bottom line.' *Asiaweek*, 9 Feb., 58–62

Blomley, N. 1993. 'Editorial: Making space for law.' *Urban Geography* 14(1): 3–6

Cannon, M. 1989. *China Tide.* Toronto: Harper and Collins

Crenshaw, K., and G. Peller. 1993. 'Reel time/real justice.' In R. Goodin-Williams, ed., *Reading Rodney King/Reading Urban Uprising*, 57–70. New York: Routledge

Davies, W., and D. Herbert. 1993. *Communities within Cities.* London: Belhaven Press

DeMont, J., and T. Fennell. 1989. *Hong Kong Money.* Toronto: Key Porter

Duncan, J.S., and N.G. Duncan. 1984. In J. Agnew and J. Duncan, eds., *The City in Cultural Context*, 255–76. Winchester: Allen and Unwin

Fennell, T. 1992. 'The right stuff?' *Maclean's*, 24 Aug. 32–3

Funk and Wagnalls. 1986. *Funk and Wagnalls New Encyclopedia.* New York: Rand McNally

Gans, H. 1962. *The Urban Villagers*. New York: Free Press

Goldberg, D.T. 1993. *Racist Culture*. Cambridge: Blackwell

Goldberg, M. 1990. 'Vancouver: A Pacific Rim city in the making.' *Transactions of the Royal Society of Canada* 1(1): 249–61

Gutstein, D. 1990. *The New Landlords*. Victoria: Porcepic Books

Ley, D. 1995. 'Between Europe and Asia: The case of the missing sequoias.' *Ecumene* 2

Li, P. 1992. 'Ethnic enterprise in transition: Chinese business in Richmond, B.C., 1980–1990.' *Canadian Ethnic Studies* 24: 120–38

– 1994. 'Unneighbourly houses or unwelcome Chinese: The social construction of race in the battle over "monster homes" in Vancouver, Canada.' *International Journal of Comparative Race and Ethnic Studies* 1(1): 14–33

Logan, J., and H. Molotch. 1987. *Urban Fortunes*. Berkeley: University of California Press

Mitchell, K. 1994. 'Zoning controversies in Vancouver.' *Canada and Hong Kong Update* 11: 11

Ohannesian, P. 1990. 'How we saved Shaughnessy from monsters.' *Vancouver Sun*, 23 June, D10–11

Rodman, M. 1992. 'Empowering place: Multilocality and multivocality.' *American Anthropologist* 94(3): 640–56

Said, E. 1978. *Orientalism*. London: Routledge and Kegan Paul

Shields, R. 1991. *Places on the Margin*. London: Routledge

Smart, A. 1992. *Making Room: Squatter Clearance in Hong Kong*. Hong Kong: Centre of Asian Studies

Smart, J. 1994. 'Business immigration in Canada: Deception and exploitation.' In R. Skeldon, ed., *The Reluctant Exiles*, 98–119. Armonk, NY: M.E. Sharpe

– 1995. 'The changing selective pressure in international migration: A case study of Hong Kong immigration to Canada before 1997.' In J. Ong, K. Chan, and S. Chew, eds., *Asian Transmigration, 187–208*. New York: Prentice-Hall

Smith, M. 1979. *The City and Social Theory*. New York: St Martin's Press

3

'Urban' and 'Aboriginal': An Impossible Contradiction?

EVELYN PETERS

In recent years the question of how space is implicated in the construction and reproduction of minority groups has become an important focus for social and cultural geographers (Jackson 1987). Researchers have noted that groups socially constructed as 'other' are assigned to spaces which express their marginalization, and that spatial arrangements contribute to the reproduction of racial and minority group categories over time (see, for example, Anderson 1991; Sibley 1981, 1992; Smith 1989; Western 1981). However, recognizing the entanglement of space and the definition of minority groups does not explain the connection for any particular group. The content of the social construction of 'the Oriental' (Said 1978) is different from that concerning 'the indigene' (Goldie 1989) or 'the gypsy' (Sibley 1981). It is this content which provides the rationale for associating minority group members with particular places and spaces.

The writing on aboriginal people which has emerged out of colonial history has created a tradition whose presence shapes any attempts to analyse the situation of contemporary aboriginal people. It is in this context that this chapter addresses the social construction of aboriginal[1] people in relation to the city. It begins by identifying important components of the definition of aboriginal people and then explores how this system of meaning has structured writing about aboriginal urbanization.

A number of researchers have explored European images and definitions of aboriginal people and 'aboriginality' in literature (Berkhoffer 1979, Francis 1992, Goldie 1989, Monkman 1981). Although these authors address different bodies of literature and employ different methods, there is a significant degree of convergence in their analysis.[2] Two recurring and inter-related themes in this work form the framework for the analysis here. The first has to do with conceptions of where 'authentic' aboriginal cultures belong in space and time. The second has to do with the motives underlying dichotomous and often contradictory images of aboriginal people.

Authentic Aboriginal Culture in Time and Space

How aboriginal people are defined in Western thought sets up a fundamental tension between the idea of aboriginal culture and the idea of modern 'civilization.' Goldie (1989) identifies a number of themes which define aboriginal people in non-aboriginal writing. He argues that 'the natural' is central. Aboriginal people are seen as the power of nature in human form, distinguished from whites representing civilized order. The natural is often linked with orality and mysticism. Orality incorporates the idea that cultures without writing have a completely different system of understanding, linked to their direct association with nature. The mystical represents spiritual consciousness linked to the power of the land. Together these elements create a contradiction between 'aboriginality' and civilization. Berkhoffer notes that 'since Whites primarily understood the Indian as an antithesis to themselves, then civilization and Indianness as they defined them would forever be opposites' (1979: 29).

The image of 'aboriginality' in European thought requires distance or separation in both time and space as a prerequisite for the 'authenticity' of aboriginal culture. Although the analysis of ideas about where aboriginal cultures are seen to belong in space is not very well developed, Goldie points out that in non-aboriginal writing 'true' aboriginal people continue to live far away from major population centres (1989: 165). He argues that the shift to distance or history is necessary because it is impossible to maintain the exotic image of the local, contemporary aboriginal person. Contrasting the image of aboriginal people with 'orientalism' as this is depicted in Said's work, Goldie indicates that 'orientalism ... has an important spatial dimension ... The mystical exotic element of the orient is quickly lost in simplistic racism when the oriental becomes an immigrant ... In the case of indigenous peoples the contradiction between exotic image and immediate experience remains but it slips ... [L]ocal indigenes ... cannot be simply floated as exotics. Instead the spatial split usually becomes temporal ... [which] shapes the indigene into an historical artifact, a remnant of a golden age that seems to have little connection to anything akin to contemporary life' (1989: 16–17).

Motives Underlying Images of Aboriginal People

Like other conceptualizations of 'the other' in Western thought, images of aboriginal people are structured around positive and negative elements. In his examination of 'the white man's Indian' in U.S. history, Berkhoffer emphasizes the fundamental but contradictory conceptions of the 'good' and the 'bad' Indian found in literature, art, and policy (1979). Francis (1992) and Monkman (1981) make similar observations about the Canadian context.

Goldie (1989) argues that the motives of fear and temptation underlie these contradictory images. The way in which a particular component is valorized as positive or negative is determined by whether a particular text views aboriginal culture as tempting or fearful. Thus, for example, aboriginal violence can signify freedom and evoke temptation, or it can signify fear and evoke horror. Aboriginal mysticism can offer insights not accessible through non-aboriginal religions, or it can represent an uncontrollable threatening and fearful power. The dichotomous images of aboriginal people are a function of the fear and temptation which accompanies Europeans' construction of aboriginal people and aboriginal cultures.

Fear and temptation, however, are only associated with 'authentic' aboriginal cultures which are assigned to history or distance. A third category has emerged to describe contemporary and local aboriginal people, which evokes neither emotion. Berkhoffer describes this category: 'If there is a third major White image of the Indian, then this degraded, often drunken, Indian constitutes the essence of that understanding. Living neither as an assimilated White nor an Indian of the classic image, and therefore neither noble nor wildly savage but always scorned, the degraded Indian exhibited the vices of both societies' (1979: 29–30).

Sources

If the social construction of 'aboriginality' maintains that the 'authentic' aboriginal is historic and non-urban, this raises serious questions about how aboriginal cultures are depicted in relation to cities. The analysis which follows focuses on four non-fiction books written by non-aboriginal people which attempt to present and analyse the nature of the urban experience for aboriginal people in particular Canadian cities.

Mark Nagler's (1970) *Indians in the City*, set in Toronto, and Edgar Dosman's (1972) *Indians: The Urban Dilemma*, set in Saskatoon, appeared

TABLE 3.1
Location of Residence, Aboriginal Identity Population,[1] 1991.

	Total aboriginal[2]	Registered North American Indian[3]	Non-registered North American Indian[4]	Métis[5]	Inuit
Total	625,710	351,590	104,260	135,260	36,215
On-reserve	183,600 (29.3%)	173,655 (49.4%)	3,600 (3.5%)	4,535 (3.4%)	620 (1.7)
Off-reserve	412,105 (70.7%)	177,940 (50.6%)	100,660 (96.5%)	130,725 (96.6%)	35,590 (98.2%)
Urban,[6] off-reserve	309,940 (49.5%)	143,910 (40.9%)	72,150 (69.3%)	87850 (64.9%)	7,151 (21.9%)

Source: Royal Commission on Aboriginal Peoples, February 1994: 20–21
1 These data have not been adjusted for non-enumeration or under-counting.
2 Because some respondents (approximately 1 per cent) gave multiple aboriginal identities, summing identity categories will result in overcounting. The 'Total Aboriginal' category does not double count those giving multiple aboriginal identities.
3 The North American Indian population registered according to the Indian Act of Canada. This category excludes: 4,830 North American Indians with registration status not stated in the APS; 17,060 Métis who reported being registered according to the Indian Act (they are counted as Métis); 2,080 Inuit who reported being registered according to the Indian Act (they are counted as Inuit); an estimated 58,000 persons residing on unenumerated Indian reserves or settlements.
4 Those who identified themselves as North American Indian, who were not registered according to the Indian Act.
5 Those who identified themselves as Métis.
6 This number does not include urban reserves.

when the prospect of the rapid migration of aboriginal peoples to cities challenged academics, citizens' groups, and policy-makers to formulate what the 'urban experience' meant for the migrants. Only a few studies appeared in the early 1980s, including Larry Krotz's (1980) *Urban Indians: The Strangers in Canada's Cities,* with material from Winnipeg, Regina, and Edmonton.

In the early 1990s aboriginal people in urban areas received renewed attention in the context of the Royal Commission on Aboriginal Peoples, established in 1991, and the Charlottetown Accord. The Aboriginal Peoples Survey, a post-censal survey conducted in 1991 (Royal Commission on Aboriginal Peoples 1994), showed that the majority of those who identified themselves as aboriginal people lived off a reserve, and approximately half lived in cities (Table 3.1). Lynda Shorten's (1991) *Without*

Reserve: Stories from Urban Natives, largely focused on Edmonton, appeared as the situation of urban aboriginal people had been brought to public attention again, although not with the same force as during the 1960s and 1970s.

These four references comprise the only published books by non-aboriginal people which focus on aboriginal urbanization in Canada, and they have become 'classics' in this field.[3] A broader survey of written materials would be interesting, but it is beyond the scope of this essay. Here I am interested in the underlying ideology which informs work on aboriginal urbanization, and I argue that the system of meaning which comprises the idea of 'aboriginality' in Canada is represented in these books.

I do not analyse all the important themes in this literature. For example, interpretations of what urban life means for aboriginal people have shifted in the context of changing social and political climates and of aboriginal peoples' attempts to redefine the nature and content of the discourse about them (Peters, 1996). Moreover, I do not address the question of gender biases. This is a significant issue, and I wish to make a note of it here. Women are largely absent from analyses of 'images' of aboriginal people[4] and they are almost invisible in the literature on cities, despite their disproportionate representation in the urban aboriginal population. Both of these issues are important, but they are not treated here. The focus here is how the authors of four books on aboriginal urbanization conceptualize the relationship between aboriginal culture and urban life.

Aboriginal Culture and Urban Life

The impact of urban life on aboriginal cultures is a theme which threads through all four of the books.

Nagler: Indians in the City

Nagler's objectives in *Indians in the City* are to examine the processes through which 'Indians become urbanized and assimilated, if not integrated' into Canadian cities (1970: 1–2). His analysis assigns true or authentic aboriginal culture to history. 'True' aboriginal culture has been largely destroyed, according to Nagler. 'While Indian culture was once a finely patterned mosaic, today it appears to be nothing more than a patchwork of meaningless and unrelated pieces' (1970: 20).

Nagler also appears to believe that aboriginal culture is incompatible with urban life:

> While urban living is not foreign to most European immigrants, it is a completely new way of life for the Indian. The highly generalized characteristics described as 'being Indian' affect the Indian's ability to urbanize. Their 'degree of Indianess' affects the various patterns of adjustments the Indians make to the urban scene ... [They] experience difficulty in adjusting to a new environment because their conceptions of living do not involve punctuality, responsibility, hurry, impersonality, frugality, and the other social practices which are a part of the urban environment. (1970: 25)

Nagler asserts that extended family ties which are useful for aboriginal people in non-urban settings create financial strains in the city; that traditional aboriginal concepts of time are not easily adapted to an industrial work week; and that saving, delaying gratification, and work as a source of prestige are essential in the city, but are not part of aboriginal value systems.

For Nagler, culture change is a prerequisite to adaptation to the city for aboriginal people. When Nagler makes some recommendations to this goal in his final chapter, he illustrates the kind of paralysis which emerges from the way in which aboriginal people have been defined. First, he states that, while change is essential, urban aboriginal people do not appear to desire it. Although he admits that many aboriginal people are suspicious of government initiatives, he asserts, almost with a tone of irritation, that 'Indians must attain the realization that change is worthwhile and that it can take place though [*sic*] concerted efforts on their part in conjunction with government agencies and private organizations' (1970: 90).

According to Nagler, the direction of change must be to create urban adaptations based on a model of ethnic group behaviour – the establishment of neighbourhoods, urban institutions, urban leadership, and a 'pan-Indian' identity. These initiatives must build on aboriginal culture (1970: 90). Yet Nagler has stated earlier both that aboriginal cultures have largely been destroyed and that aboriginal cultures work against successful adaptation to urban life. He also notes that there is no shared culture on which to build urban adaptations, and therefore group formation will 'have to evolve from other elements' (1970: 89)

The result is a sense of complete futility in formulating any response to aboriginal peoples' migration to the city. Every initiative is either internally contradictory or doomed to failure.

Dosman: Indians: The Urban Dilemma

A sense of the contradiction between urban life and aboriginal[5] culture is very strong in Dosman's *Indians: The Urban Dilemma*. Whereas he indicates that aboriginal culture has been destroyed (1972: 13, 42) and is therefore irrelevant in explaining the contemporary situation (1972: 13), aboriginal culture plays an important role in his analysis.

Dosman identifies three groupings of aboriginal people in the city: 'affluent,' 'anomic,' and 'welfare.' The 'affluent' group is successful in maintaining employment and a middle-class standard of living. Dosman argues that the 'affluent' group comes from families which Indian agents on reserves considered successfully assimilated. Although they demonstrate some aspects of aboriginal culture – ties to their extended family and an interest in aboriginal religion, culture, language, and art – Dosman characterizes these elements as rejection rather than a continuation of previously held values. In other words, Dosman sees these not as reflections of aboriginal culture but as contemporary adaptations and therefore not 'authentic.'

For Dosman, the 'welfare' group represents the most complete rejection of urban/industrial values: 'The *Welfare* segment of the native population in Saskatoon is defined by its basic opposition to the urban value system as a whole, particularly its emphasis on "middle class" thrift ... [T]he rejection of industrial life is total' (1972: 68). This state, however, is not generated by exposure to the city. Indeed, the 'welfare' group lives a similar life on the reserve as in the city (1972: 76).

It is the 'anomic' group which faces the greatest challenge in the urban setting. Although Dosman does not detail the contradictions between urban life and aboriginal culture, attachment to aboriginal culture is, in his view, a major source of difficulty: 'The adjective 'anomic' best describes their condition, for in the city they suffer personal disorientation, anxiety and social isolation of such magnitude that they either are forced into the *Welfare* or return dejectedly to the reserve. *They aspire to preserve their Indian heritage and to adapt it to urban life*' (1972: 84, emphasis added).

Dosman recommends that non-aboriginal organizations support the creation of a separate aboriginal community in the city, in order to facilitate the adaptation of the 'anomic' group: 'A well-designed, native, residential community inside the city is one concept which could meet many of the requirements of the urban *Anomic* Indians and Metis ... The enclave would allow the *Anomic* to safeguard a racial heritage different from that of the larger society, and to construct meaningful alternatives that respond to the historical imperatives of a widely different cultural tradition and a heritage of conflict with the settler culture' (1972: 184, 185).

In summary, according to Dosman, aboriginal people who have been assimilated face little difficulty in the city. For those who have rejected urban values, the question of adapting is irrelevant. It is those aboriginal people who attempt to combine aboriginal culture and urban life who face insurmountable difficulties. Dosman's solution betrays his assumptions about the irreconcilable nature of aboriginal culture and urban life. His recommendation is based on distancing, but this time within the city – the creation of a separate urban community until aboriginal residents have adapted their culture to urban life.

Krotz: Urban Indians

Krotz's book is a collection of stories about urban aboriginal people 'selected randomly, as I met them and as they were willing to share with a reporter' (1980: 11). All of the people Krotz presents have employment – they are professionals, artists, caretakers, or factory workers. Even the 'Three Men on Skid Row in Edmonton' (1980: 105–9) have trades, income from employment, and a place to sleep at night which is not a hostel or the street.

Unlike Nagler or Dosman, Krotz presents aboriginal culture neither as having been destroyed nor as a barrier to adaptation to life in the city. Instead, he views aboriginal people as successfully integrating urban and aboriginal culture: 'The urban Indian is identified not by his reserve affiliation or by his treaty status or by his socio-economic position. He or she is identified by ethnicity and heritage and by the fact of having made a conscious choice to maintain and reinforce that ethnicity and heritage, even (or especially) while living in the city' (1980: 156).

Krotz demonstrates the maintenance of aboriginal culture in the city in a number of ways. The people Krotz describes maintain contact with their reserve or community of origin, and many would prefer to live there; extended family ties are cultivated and positive; urban residents hunt for bear, elk, and rabbit, pick blueberries, and make bannock; individuals make a living through Native art or by working in Native organizations; they participate in pow-wows or Native celebrations; many are taking or have taken steps to enhance their knowledge of cultural traditions. Aboriginal identity is reinforced by the attention Krotz pays to origins.

The people in Krotz's book are not homogeneous groups of 'Indians' or 'Natives.' Instead, they are Cree, Chipewyan, Blackfoot, or Métis, from the Peepeekisis or the Lake Manitoba or the Hobbema reserve or the Métis town of Bacon Ridge.

Krotz's work, then, does not depict aboriginal culture as presenting a barrier to successful urban life, and it does not suggest that urban culture destroys aboriginal people's ties with their communities or cultures of origin.

Shorten: Without Reserve

Shorten's book *Without Reserve* is an edited version of tapes containing nine 'autobiographical stories told by Native people living in a mid-size Canadian city,' interspersed with observations from the writer (1991: ix). Although Shorten argues that she simply served as a conduit through which these stories are told (1991: vii), she also indicates that 'it was my white fingers on the computer, editing these stories down from hundreds of hours of tapes and hundreds and hundreds of transcribed pages. I had feelings about what I saw and heard, and it would be dishonest to pretend that my editing was in any way "pure"' (1991: ix).

Because of this editing process, Shorten's work is included here in the category of non-aboriginal writing. A major challenge in analysing this book is that a substantial portion of the text comprises quotations from aboriginal people. But the underlying themes, whether they are the author's observations or edited quotes from the interviews, are Shorten's. They emerge from what is included, what is not, and which gaps are unfilled.

Like other authors, Shorten associates 'authentic' aboriginal culture with history. The switch to history is most explicit in the treatment of 23-year-old Jimmy Mix, whose story is interwoven with vignettes about 'The Famous Ancestor,' an 'Indian scout for the North West Mounted Police in the late 1800's' (1991: 4). The vignettes compare Jimmy's life with the scout's, and the effect is to anchor elements of Jimmy's 'Indianness' in history.

Historicity is also emphasized in the relationship of different generations to aboriginal culture. Two teenage Métis, Lisa, sixteen, and Casey, fourteen, explicitly state that they do not identify with Métis culture. There is no discussion of cultural identity in the presentation of Kicker, a 22-year-old Métis. All of the middle-aged characters, 40-year-old Jane Ash Poitras, 36-year-old Helen, 35-year-old Sky, and 47-year-old Maggie have rediscovered and are relearning their cultural roots. In contrast, 68-year-old Grace is strongly anchored in Cree culture with her language, her crafts, and her role in her extended family. In other words, older people 'have' their aboriginal culture, the middle generation is attempting to regain it, but the younger generation has lost it.

Aboriginal culture is also firmly rooted in places outside the urban milieu. Shorten's description of the experience of Sky, an ex-convict, most clearly demonstrates this theme: 'Sky moved out to the reserve to work with one of the elders, sickened by the concrete, sickened by the sight of his people picking through garbage for food. Over the three years I know him he moves farther and farther away from the city, finding even the reserve too much in the end. After ten years in federal penitentiaries and five years of struggling to stay out, of relying on his pipe, the sweats, the Sun Dances, the company of elders to keep his anger at bay, the only escape for Sky is the bush. The animals. The ancestors' (1991: 263). Helen, born and raised in Edmonton, builds 'a traditional way of life' for herself and her children on a reserve outside of the city (1991: 250). Jane Ash Poitras found her identity with her reserve community (1991: 111–12). In contrast, Shorten does not link the practice and enhancement of aboriginal culture to urban life.

At the same time, Shorten presents aboriginal culture as essential for survival in the city. Maggie describes her culture as a source of strength (1991: 161). Reclaiming her cultural heritage allows Jane to paint and provides others with the strength to come to terms with childhood neglect, discrimination, sexual and physical abuse, and to overcome alcoholism and substance abuse. Life on the streets, prostitution, drug and alcohol addiction, fights, and arrests characterize the young people who are least linked to their culture. In other words, aboriginal people who face the most difficulty in the city, according to Shorten, are those who fail to maintain or enhance their culture, rather than those who attempt to maintain it in contemporary society.

Shorten's analysis, like Nagler's, leaves readers with a sense that it is futile to look for solutions. While her portrayal of 'authentic' aboriginal culture places it in history or at a distance, she also presents the process of regaining that culture as the key to coping and wholeness in urban life. The result is that most of the aboriginal people in the city are faced with an essential but impossible challenge – regaining a damaged and non-urban culture in order to survive as healthy people in the city.

Fear and Temptation

Goldie (1989) has argued that 'authentic' aboriginal cultures evoke fear or temptation in non-aboriginal writing. This section turns to the motives or emotions that appear to underlie writing on aboriginal people and cities in an attempt to provide another lens through which to examine the underlying structure of ideas about aboriginal and urban culture.

Nagler: Indians in the City

Nagler indicates that aboriginal people are 'entering the city at an unprecedented rate' and that many, 'unfamiliar with the ways of the city, experience difficulties adjusting to urban life'(1970: 7). Yet the level of concern for both aboriginal people and cities is relatively low in this work. Although this may be because Nagler's study took place when migration levels were low, and in Toronto where the aboriginal population is relatively small, his perspective on the relationship between aboriginal and urban cultures also affects his analysis. Nagler is certain that aboriginal culture does not belong and cannot survive in cities. In his last chapter he almost appears impatient with aboriginal people who migrate to cities but resist 'change.' Aboriginal people who attempt to maintain their traditions cannot survive in the urban milieu. According to Nagler, aboriginal culture is neither a threat nor an alternative to non-aboriginal urban culture: it evokes neither fear nor temptation.

Dosman: Indians: The Urban Dilemma

The element of 'fear' in Dosman's work has to do primarily with the creation of a large poverty-stricken population: 'The majority of the Indian population will inexorably shift to cities. The appearance of Indian poverty in Canadian cities has produced unprecedented problems. Native people form the hard core of the urban dispossessed: almost the entire minority lies outside the socio-economic structure of the city. The Indian sub-culture is not merely low in status and income; it is not merely at the bottom of the pile; its situation is becoming increasingly worse' (Dosman 1972: 8). Dosman indicates that 'logic, humanity and [white] *self-interest*' demand that the problems of urban Indians should receive immediate attention (1972: 188, emphasis added).

While aboriginal poverty is seen as problematic for cities, aboriginal culture is not. Dosman puts forward four options for aboriginal people in urban areas: assimilate and become part of the 'affluent'; reject urban culture and be part of the 'welfare' group; attempt to integrate aboriginal culture and urban life and fail; or create a separate area and culture within the city which contains and 'distances' aboriginal culture from the rest of the urban community. Each option maintains the separation or distance between aboriginal culture and urban life, and none, therefore, challenges the values and cultural premises on which urban life is seen to be organized.

Krotz: Urban Indians

Fear is most explicit in Krotz's work. Two paragraphs in his Introduction set the tone:

> For two hundred years the Indian has been the mythic skeleton in the collective white European-North American closet ... He always had to be dealt with ... while the Europeans engineered their path of 'progress' across the continent. He would never go away. The Indians lurked both physically and symbolically at the periphery of North American life, at the edge of consciousness; like some constant reminder of sins and of the European's fundamental failure to come to terms with the environment of the New World. For a century they haunted society from the distance of their reservations ... Now they have the ill manners not only to haunt from the distance of the reservation, but to move to the cities and haunt from within. Perhaps the final justice. (1980: 11)

The result of this migration is fear and confusion: 'We continue as two worlds, the Indians and the other city-people; we/they. We are frightened and suspicious of one another ... [F]ew human movements so confront our history; so confront our private fears and stereotypes; so confront our myths; and so leave us confused and paralyzed' (Krotz 1980: 10–11).

Fear is also reflected in Krotz's estimates of the size of urban aboriginal populations. 'Large numbers' states Krotz 'appear threatening' (1980: 50). According to Krotz, Winnipeg in 1976, a city with a population of approximately 578,000, had an aboriginal population of forty to sixty thousand. Edmonton, at approximately 600,000, had an aboriginal population of thirty to forty thousand people. Regina's aboriginal population was projected as 17 per cent of the total metropolitan population by 1981 (Krotz 1980: 10). In contrast, the 1981 Census counted 16,100 aboriginal people in Winnipeg, 11,995 in Edmonton, and 6,410 people – or 4 per cent of the population – in Regina.[6] Krotz quotes a Winnipeg cultural anthropologist's theory that 'when a minority group gets to be twenty percent or more of a city's population, trouble is at hand' (1980: 42). Concern about cities' capacity to 'absorb' aboriginal people, to 'cope,' and to 'integrate native people into the fabric of the city' surface again and again.

The population Krotz presents is not the indigent, welfare-dependent segment highlighted in other studies. It is also not a population which has had its culture destroyed or must abandon this culture in order to survive in the city. The majority of the people Krotz describes are integrated into the urban labour force and are continuing to practice their cultures. If these people are not threatening because of their poverty, then it must be their culture which threatens the urban fabric. Krotz does not elaborate on how or why aboriginal cultures present this threat. I suggest the threat derives from the fear and temptation which accompany European constructions of 'aboriginality.'

Indeed, Krotz suggests that aboriginal people have migrated in order to reclaim cities and indicates that their presence will not be passive but will reshape urban life: 'The native people are not in the cities as guests or as tourists. The cities, too, are part of their birthright. As the reserves and the land once was theirs, *so will the cities be theirs.* Their growing presence will very much decide the shape of those cities' (1980: 157, emphasis added). In other words, aboriginal people challenge cities, not through their poverty, but through their birthright.

Shorten: Without Reserve

There is no undertone of fear in Shorten's book. This is almost certainly related to the overwhelming sense, from her presentation, that aboriginal people in the city are destroying themselves. Every person whose story appears in the book has suffered from physical and/or sexual abuse. Many are overwhelmed by personal problems and family responsibilities. These are not people whose values and aboriginal heritage threaten the cultural fabric of urban life. Instead, these are people whose entire energy as individuals and as families is focused on surviving from day to day.[7] By presenting the challenge of regaining aboriginal culture as essential for survival but impossible, Shorten erases any threat aboriginal culture could have for urban life.

Conclusion

What is striking about writing on aboriginal urbanization is this dichotomy. Where urban life is seen to require the adaptation of aboriginal culture to the extent that 'authenticity' is destroyed, fear is muted and primarily associated with the drain a poverty-stricken minority places on urban economies and service institutions. Where aboriginal culture is presented as strong and authentic in an urban setting, aboriginal people are seen as a threat to cities as we know them.

The social construction of aboriginal peoples incorporates a sense of where they 'belong' as peoples with vital and authentic cultures. In European thought, aboriginal culture is incompatible with urban life. In this context, two of the authors, Nagler and Dosman, assume that in order for Aborginal people to survive in the city, aboriginal cultures must adapt to urban life and in the process become something other than 'authentic.' On the other hand, Shorten and Krotz assume (rightly, I believe) that an affirmation and enhancement of aboriginal culture is essential for the well-being of aboriginal people in urban areas. Yet the system of meaning which defines 'aboriginality' will not allow this to happen. Shorten's characterization of aboriginal culture allows it to flourish only in non-urban places. Krotz reflects, accurately I believe, the almost irrational apprehension with which aboriginal urbanization is viewed in Canadian history.

If the structures of thought identified in these four books represent underlying systems of meaning as they apply to aboriginal people in Canadian cities, they must have implications for all aspects of aboriginal people's lives in urban areas – from day-to-day contact with neighbours and acquaintances to the nature of federal and provincial policies for urban aboriginal people. Aboriginal people are confronted again and again with explicit or implicit messages that cities are not where they belong as people with vibrant and living cultures.

My intent here is not to suggest solutions or alternatives. These are not easily come by, and they will have to emerge through dialogue with aboriginal people. Instead, I have attempted to contribute to a basis for constructive change by exploring the implications of the social construction of aboriginal people for ideas about their 'place' in the city.

NOTES

1 The term 'aboriginal' is not the term used by most of the authors to whom I refer. I use it because, although the image is most often attached to the term 'Indian' in popular conception, the attitudes extend to all the aboriginal peoples of Canada – First Nations, Métis, and Inuit. At the same time, I recognize that this term is rejected by many aboriginal people who associate it with Euro-

pean attempts to homogenize their cultures and who prefer to identify themselves by their nation of origin. As Francis notes, 'It is part of the legacy of the Imaginary Indian that we lack a vocabulary with which to speak about these issues clearly' (1992: 9).

2 While there are persistent and recurring themes in the social construction of minority groups, the details of content and construction of racist images vary historically (Sivanandan 1983: 2; Hall 1978: 179) and, by extension, must vary spatially. Failure to acknowledge this variation is a major omission in existing analyses of images of aboriginal people.

3 This selection leaves out a variety of primarily statistical reports on urban aboriginal people, government studies, articles in journals and chapters in books, and a large 'grey literature' of unpublished studies, graduate theses, and published documents with a relatively small circulation. I chose to omit Hugh Brody's (1970) *Indians on Skid Row* because it focused on only one segment of the urban aboriginal population. I have not included books written by aboriginal people. Available works are fiction or autobiography and their focus is not explicitly on the relationship between aboriginal people and cities.

4 Goldie (1989) addresses women primarily on his chapter on sexuality. Other authors often write about aboriginal people in general, without acknowledging that the image they refer to is specific of male aboriginal people. For work on images of aboriginal women, consult Emberly (1993) and Godard (1987).

5 Dosman uses the term 'Indian' and focuses primarily on First Nations people.

6 The Census probably undercounts urban aboriginal people, but it is unlikely that this number of people would have been missed.

7 It must be noted that there are many urban aboriginal people whose lives do not fit this mould, and they are not featured by Shorten. Second, it is possible to present the same characteristics in a different way. When Lee Maracle's (1992) *Sundogs*, describes an urban aboriginal family, alcoholism and family violence are presented in a very different light – as challenges which are met through strong family ties and effectively dealt with according to aboriginal cultural values.

REFERENCES

Anderson, K.J. 1991. *Vancouver's Chinatown: Racial Discourse in Canada, 1875–1980.* Montreal and Kingston: McGill-Queen's University Press

Berkhoffer, R.F. 1979. *The White Man's Indian: Images of the American Indian from Columbus to the Present.* New York: Vintage Books

Brody, H. 1970. *Indians on Skid Row.* Ottawa: Department of Indian Affairs and Northern Development

Dosman, E.J. 1972. *Indians: The Urban Dilemma.* Toronto: McClelland and Stewart

Emberly, J.V. 1993. *Thresholds of Difference: Feminist Critique, Native Women's Writings, Postcolonial Theory.* Toronto: University of Toronto Press

Francis, D. 1992. *The Imaginary Indian: The Image of the Indian in Canadian Culture.* Vancouver: Arsenal Pulp Press

Godard, B. 1987. 'Listening for the silence: Native women's traditional narratives.' In T. King, C. Calver, and H. Hoy, eds., *The Native in Literature,* 133–58. Oakville: ECW Press

Goldie, T. 1989. *Fear and Temptation: The Image of the Indigene in Canadian, Australian, and New Zealand Literature.* Kingston and Montreal: McGill-Queen's University Press

Hall, S. 1978. 'Racism and reaction.' In Commission for Racial Equality, eds., *Five Views of Multi-Racial Britain,* 23–35. London: Commission for Racial Equality

Jackson, P. 1989. 'Geography, race, and racism.' In R. Peet and N. Thrift, eds., *New Models in Geography: The Political Economy Approach,* 176–95. London: Unwin Hyman

Krotz, L. 1980. *Urban Indians: The Strangers in Canada's Cities.* Edmonton: Hurtig

Maracle, L. 1992. *Sundogs.* Penticton: Theytus Books

Monkman, L. 1981. *A Native Heritage: Images of the Indian in English-Canadian Literature.* Toronto: University of Toronto Press

Nagler, M. 1970. *Indians in the City: A Study of the Urbanization of Indians in Toronto.* Ottawa: Canadian Research Centre for Anthropology, Saint Paul University

Peters, E.J. 1996. 'Aboriginal people in urban areas.' In D. Long and O. Dickason, eds., *Visions of the Heart: Contemporary Aboriginal Issues in Socio-Historical Perspective.* Toronto: Harcourt, Brace

Royal Commission on Aboriginal Peoples. 1994. *Customized Data from the 1991 Aboriginal Peoples Survey.* Ottawa: Research Directorate, Royal Commission on Aboriginal Peoples

Said, E. 1978. *Orientalism.* London: Routledge and Kegan Paul

Shorten, L. 1991. *Without Reserve: Stories from Urban Natives.* Edmonton: NeWest Press

Sibley, D. 1981. *Outsiders in Urban Societies.* New York: St Martin's Press

Sibley, D. 1992. 'Outsiders in society and space.' In K. Anderson and F. Gale, eds., *Inventing Places: Studies in Cultural Geography,* 107–22. Melbourne: Longman Cheshire

Sivanandan, A. 1983. 'Challenging racism: Strategies for the '80s.' *Race and Class* 25: 1–11

Smith, S.J. 1989. *The Politics of 'Race' and Residence.* Cambridge: Polity Press

Western, J. 1981. *Outcast Capetown.* Minneapolis: University of Minnesota Press

4

Excavating Toronto's Underground Streets: In Search of Equitable Rights, Rules, and Revenue

JEFFREY HOPKINS

Sharing the Sidewalk

Canada's sidewalks are changing; they are moving indoors onto private property. During the past several decades, Canadians have witnessed the erosion of traditional streets where public life transpired. The automobile, the skyscraper, the dispersed residential suburb, and the shopping mall have contributed to the demise of a pedestrian-oriented, outdoor street life in our city cores by introducing vehicular noise and air pollution, undue shade and wind, automobile dependency, and the desire, if not necessity, for pedestrian/vehicle segregation. Much of the country's civic life now occurs indoors on privately owned, publicly used, pedestrian places in the form of above-ground 'skywalks' between buildings, ground-level office and retail complexes, atriums and shopping malls, and below-ground, shop- lined tunnels. The privatization of public places has heightened concern about excessive surveillance of pedestrians by private security guards, potential discrimination by property owners against so-called undesirables (for example, the homeless, leafleteers, loiterers, protestors, youths, visible minorities), the degree of accessibility provided to the physically challenged, and the level of environmental safety provided to the public users (for example, in terms of air quality, fire precautions, visible exit routes). Concomitantly, the publicization of private places has intensified anxieties about controlling public users whose volume, activities, and demands may interfere with the operation and management of private business premises. Achieving a just balance between public and private rights and obligations, while promoting and maintaining both commercial and community interests, is a challenge that must be met if it is to be ensured that neither the animation, flexibility, and freedoms conventionally associated with the street, nor the economic livelihood of shopkeepers, are to be left outside. This search, for equitable public and private rights, reasonable rules of social conduct, and viable economic revenues at the public/private space interface is the focus of this chapter; Toronto's 'indoor' and 'underground' streets are at the forefront of the public/private space debate and are, consequently, the site of this geographic excavation.

The underlying supposition, which both inspires the author and provides the basis for the critique to follow, is the ideal of a truly public place: a spatially unrestricted communal meeting ground for all members of a pluralistic society, a shared site where people of various classes, ethnicities, religions, and cultures mingle to create what Harvey calls the 'heterogeneity of open democracy' (1992: 591). This kind of place is threatened by the move indoors and onto private property unless the existing social and legal relationships between private property owners and public users are challenged, alternative modes of spatial control are implemented, and a more balanced distribution of power is realized.

Sharing an 'indoor street' raises a multitude of issues for businesses, community groups, the courts, governments, urban planners, and a variety of scholars. For urban studies, the crux of the problems arising from the public/private space interface may be viewed as a territorial conflict: a power struggle among numerous agents with varying interests over the boundaries demarcating spatial control. From this perspective, access is the key issue. Access structures the degree of publicness and privateness of a place which plays a major role in its social organization (Benn and Gaus 1983: 5). In order to critique both the accessibility of Toronto's underground city and the possible avenues available for renegotiating the distribution of power over its public/private corridors, it is necessary to identify precisely how, why, and by whom spatial control is currently exercised and contested. Although Toronto's underground city is unique in the sense that it is at the centre of the public/private space debate in Ontario, it is representative of a growing trend in Canada and other industrialized countries towards indoor cities and the privatization of civic space.

Toronto's Underground

No satellite image, no air photograph, no intense scrutiny from atop the CN Tower or traverse upon a downtown city street will reveal Toronto's underground city; the ten kilometres of tunnels beneath the core, lined with some 1,100 shops and services, and used daily by 100,000 pedestrians (City of Toronto 1993; Fulford 1993: 29). From above ground it is a hidden geography, but it is by no means a geography exclusive to Toronto: Montreal has in excess of twenty-nine kilometres of underground city with access to over 1,600 shops and services (Besner 1991: 11–12; Boivin 1991: 83); Calgary boasts thirty-eight skywalks (Robertson 1987: 207); Edmonton has seventeen skywalks and the world's largest shopping mall (City of Edmonton 1989). There are at least eighty-two other cities in North America with some form of above- or below-ground pedestrian networks within the central core (Maitland 1992: 162). Asia and Europe also possess large expanses of publicly used, underground space. Japan, for example, has over 800,000 square metres of publicly accessible underground space (Ishioka 1992: 337), including more than seventy-six underground shopping malls (Tatsukami 1986: 19). Tokyo alone had more than fifty underground space projects proposed or in progress by the early 1990s (Wada and Sakugawa 1990: 33). Finland, Germany, The Netherlands, and Norway, for instance, also have underground projects, ranging from a 1,000–seat concert hall, sports facilities, and swimming pools, to a central bus terminal.[1] Toronto's underground city is certainly unique given its size, scale, and intensity of pedestrian use, but it is part of an indoor geography that is international in scope and is fast becoming an integral part of the contemporary urban fabric of major cities. Why the global move underground?

Although the origin of the contemporary underground city is considered to have occurred in 1957 with the completion of the first underground street in Japan (Xueyuan and Yu 1988: 200), humans since antiquity have dug into the earth in search of useful materials, to make tunnels for roads, aqueducts for water, space for storage, and shelter from wars and weather.[2] This has not changed in the twentieth century but our technologies and the demands on, and the lifestyles within, city space have. The introduction of electrical lighting and air ventilation systems, and new developments in construction materials and engineering and mining techniques, have provided the option of working, traveling, and living underground. High urban densities and increased land costs in recent decades have also made the maximum utilization of space in some city cores a priority.[3] The meteoric rise to dominance of the automobile, the skyscraper, and the shopping mall, and the corporations and consumers which promote and sustain them, have created an urban way of life – a culture – whose members are both receptive and conditioned to an indoor, shop-lined, mode of spatial organization. Once acculturated to an indoor way of life – be it within a subway system or an apartment, office, or windowless shopping complex – the move underground is a not-so-taxing extrapolation of the accepted norm. The move underground in Toronto and elsewhere has come about because it has become technologically feasible, spatially advantageous, economically attractive, and a socially accepted cultural norm.

Most chronologies of Toronto's underground city commence in the late 1950s when the Planning Department published a report on the downtown which included proposals for sheltered walkways and enclosed malls (Dudley 1989: 23; Goodman 1984: 2–4). Although this marks the onset of Toronto's underground expansion, its origins lay in the early 1900s with the retail sector and public transportation.[4] The T. Eaton Company initiated the underground at the turn of the century when it connected its main department store, bargain annex, catalogue store, and stable with under-street tunnels. By 1917 a total of five underground corridors had been built. Seven years later, Union Station – a train depot – was erected which connected above- and below-grade levels with stairwells and gently sloping ramps. Although a pedestrian corridor connecting Union Station to the Canadian Pacific Railway Company's Royal York Hotel was later opened in 1929, and remains in use today, no other publicly used underground projects were implemented for over three decades.

Not until the construction of the downtown subway loop in 1954 did proposals for underground developments begin again. The subway stations provided numerous opportunities for below-grade expansion and interconnected spaces in the dense, financial district of Bay Street. In the late 1960s and early 1970s this was exploited by four major Canadian banks which erected large towers in close proximity to one another; each included underground shopping concourses and, ultimately, linkages to subway stations.[5] Other tower and plaza developments followed during the unprecedented growth of the 1970s, many of which, like the new Eaton Centre, included subsurface retail malls and links to the subway. By the early 1980s almost half of the current underground city had been built, but it was not entirely connected. Since then, there has been an in-filling of underground corridors – most shop-lined, others purely functional – linking existing and new buildings to form one large, interconnected, underground walkway.

The pedestrian walkway, illustrated in Figures 4.1 and 4.2, now extends the equivalent of twelve city blocks in length, from the CN Tower at Front Street in the south to the bus terminal on Edward Street in the north, and spans six blocks in width, from One Financial Place on Yonge Street in the east to its western edge at the Metro Hall on John Street. It connects

FIGURE 4.1

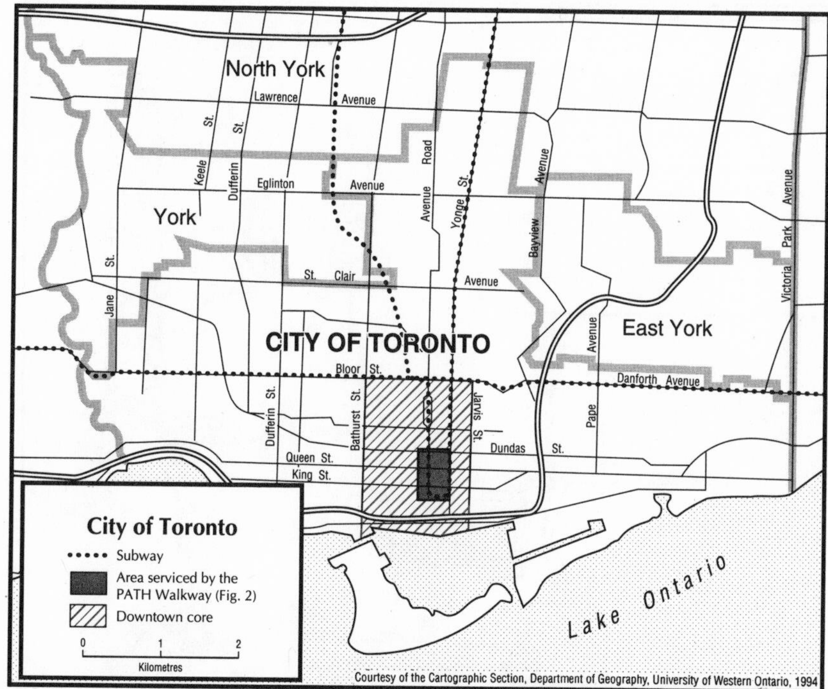

at least sixty-three different buildings,[6] including more than twenty parking garages, nineteen shopping malls, five subway stations, four hotels, the Stock Exchange and City Hall (Jones et al. 1990: 17). The rapidity of its growth over the past three decades and the plans for future extensions would suggest the underground is a success, but for whom? There are pressing questions about precisely who benefits, who does not, and how Torontonians in particular, and Canadians in general, might equally share the benefits and burdens of moving civic life inside and underground.

The Advantages and Disadvantages of an Urban Underground

The advantages – aside from the spatial and economic efficiency noted above – are numerous for both the proprietors and users of the premises (Carmody and Sterling 1987). For the former, there are potential monetary savings through reduced energy and maintenance costs relative to above-ground structures by virtue of occupying space that is enclosed, sub-

Figure 4.2

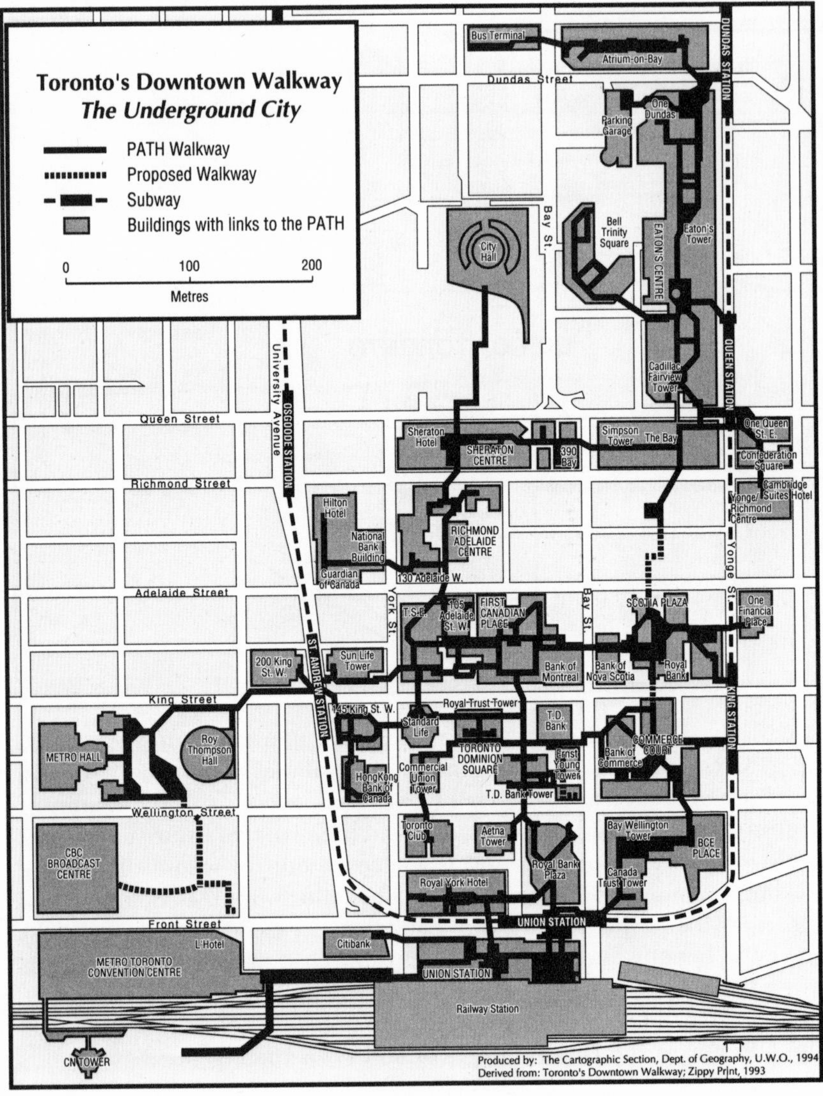

Toronto's Downtown Walkway
The Underground City
PATH Walkway
Proposed Walkway
Subway
Buildings with links to the PATH
0
100
200
Metres
Bus Terminal
Atrium-on-Bay
Dundas Street
DUNDAS STATION
One Dundas
Parking Garage
Bay St.
Bell Trinity Square
EATON'S CENTRE
Eaton's Tower
City Hall
University Avenue
QUEEN STATION
Cadillac Fairview Tower
OSGOODE STATION
Queen Street
Sheraton Hotel
SHERATON CENTRE
390 Bay
Simpson Tower
The Bay
One Queen St. E.
Confederation Square
Cambridge Suites Hotel
Yonge/Richmond Centre
Richmond Street
Hilton Hotel
National Bank Building
RICHMOND ADELAIDE CENTRE
Guardian of Canada
130 Adelaide W.
Yonge St.
Adelaide Street
York St.
T.S.E.
105 Adelaide St. W.
FIRST CANADIAN PLACE
Bay St.
SCOTIA PLAZA
One Financial Place
200 King St. W.
Sun Life Tower
ST. ANDREW STATION
Bank of Montreal
Bank of Nova Scotia
Royal Bank
King Street
KING STATION
145 King St. W.
Royal Trust Tower
Standard Life
T.D. Bank
METRO HALL
Roy Thompson Hall
TORONTO DOMINION SQUARE
Bank of Commerce
COMMERCE COURT
Ernst Young Tower
Commercial Union Tower
HongKong Bank of Canada
T.D. Bank Tower
Wellington Street
Toronto Club
Aetna Tower
Bay Wellington Tower
BCE PLACE
CBC BROADCAST CENTRE
Royal Bank Plaza
Canada Trust Tower
Royal York Hotel
UNION STATION
Front Street
L'Hotel
Citibank
METRO TORONTO CONVENTION CENTRE
UNION STATION
Railway Station
CN TOWER
Produced by: The Cartographic Section, Dept. of Geography, U.W.O., 1994
Derived from: Toronto's Downtown Walkway; Zippy Print, 1993

sumed in earth, and insulated from the natural weathering elements of sun, wind, precipitation and seasonal and daily temperature fluctuations. Security is both enhanced and simplified by the limited number of access points and their perpetual surveillance by video cameras.[7] The passageways are, most importantly, a major source of revenue. In the tunnels, or 'cashacombs' as Relph calls them (1990: 80), pedestrians are quite literally a captured market. These monetary reasons alone are incentive for developers to build indoor and underground sidewalks, and are, in a market-driven, capitalist society, the primary reason for their construction.[8]

For the pedestrian, the conveniences are profuse: ease of mobility on the tiled, well-lit, and climate-controlled corridors; direct access to public transit; proximity to hundreds of stores, services, and workplaces; insulation from the traffic, noise, exhaust, and potential physical harm from motor vehicles; a clean environment with innumerable plants, fountains, benches, pay phones, and rest rooms.[9] There is, for some, the sense of security generated from being indoors, a space guarded by video cameras and removed from the panhandlers, leafleteers, and tumultuous crowds of the streets outside. The convenience, protection, and amenities of such an enclosed and controlled space are sufficient to entice pedestrian use. But despite these and other advantages for both proprietor and pedestrian, such built environments come with qualities both troublesome and dubious.

For the operators there are responsibilities to both tenants and the public users. These premises, like all businesses, need to operate in a safe, functional, and pleasing environment to promote and sustain their economic viability. Ensuring the safety of property, patrons, and employees, maintaining acceptable levels of cleanliness and building maintenance, conforming to various municipal, provincial, and federal laws (such as building codes, fire safety standards, and human rights legislation) present challenges for even the smallest business establishments. Successfully fulfilling these obligations in a private place of business that, by virtue of its position in a large, interconnected network of pedestrian corridors, is a public thoroughfare presents a problem that, although familiar to all businesses, is unequaled in scale: how to delimit, promote, and maintain acceptable behaviour from the public to ensure the proper functioning of the privately operated business premises?

For the public user there are a host of drawbacks, ranging from concerns with personal health and well-being to inconvenient design amenities and the potential loss of civil liberties. Being indoors and underground may generate negative psychological and physiological effects for some people, particulary those who work inside on a regular basis (Carmody and Sterling 1987: 59–60). Lack of exposure to natural sunlight may encourage depression, and the absence of an exterior view may generate a sense of isolation, oppressive feelings of enclosure, phobias of confinement, and perceived or substantiated fears of entrapment during fire or other potential calamities (Wada and Sakugawa 1990). The very notion of descending 'underground' has disturbing connotations of dampness, death, or burial for some, including perhaps, the owners of Toronto's underground city (TUC) who chose to call their corridors not the underground but the 'PATH: Toronto's Downtown Walkway' (Fulford 1993: 31; Ringstad 1994). Indoor air pollution, whether particulate from synthetic materials, radon gas released from the stone and concrete building materials, or simply mould from air conditioning, may induce fatigue or illness if ventilation systems are incompetent. Indoor noise pollution, created by the presence of people, piped 'muzak,' and water fountains reverberating down the hard, tiled, and shiny surfaces of the tunnels, may induce temporary or permanent hearing loss, negative physiological and psychological reactions, and impede social interaction by way of speech interference.[10] The design of Toronto's underground has, like other underground cities, been criticized for being inaccessible to the physically challenged because of a dearth of ramps and elevators; difficult to orient oneself relative to the world above because of few direct, visible, vertical links with the outdoors; and confusing for lack of adequate directional signage (Brown 1989: 81; Fulford 1993: 29–31; Relph 1990: 83). Visibly stated rules of conduct are also sparse and limited to notices of hours of operation and 'no soliciting.' This latter sign is the only declaration, implicit as it is, that the corridors are under predominantly private control; codes of conduct, dress, and assembly are dictated and enforced primarily at the discretion of the property owners. This poses a potential threat, as discussed below, to civil liberties. Although the public's submission to private authority upon entry into a privately owned place of business is a culturally accepted, legally sanctioned, and everyday occurrence, the domination by private interests of such a large and intensely used site of civic life is unprecedented.

Spatial Control and Territorial Justice

Moving indoors and underground clearly has differing advantages and disadvantages for proprietors and users, but they do share a common problem: spatial control. The proprietors must maintain an atmosphere conducive to business, which necessitates prohibiting those members of the public and activities they perceive as detracting from this objective. Given the high intensity of public use in these corridors, maintaining the desired level of spatial control may be problematic. This level of control over the public's activities and composition in a civic thoroughfare by private agents may be perceived by some members of the public as itself problematic if access is discriminatory and rules of conduct unduly restrictive.[11] The corridors have become a site of territorial conflict because they are both a public and a private space. The boundaries demarcating private space from public space have become blurred: privately owned business corridors have become publicly used civic thoroughfares; publicly used civic thoroughfares have come to occupy privately owned business premises. Control over this public/private interface has become a complex question.

At issue is the division of control over the corridors between private and public agents, specifically over the power of exclusion exercised by the former. The dynamics of the conflict are immediately compounded by the number of competing private and public agents involved with differing opinions, varying concerns, and disparate levels of political influence. Among the 'private' agents are, to name only a few, the thirty-six principal corporations who own the major buildings comprising the underground city (J. Morgan, personal interview, 9 June 1994), the hundreds of businesses which rent shop space inside these premises, and the Toronto Transit Commission and GO Transit, which operate the subway stations and regional train and bus depots. The 'public' is everyone else, ranging from a homeless teenager to members of the Metropolitan Toronto Police, as well as the three levels of government and their agencies which, in theory, act in the interests of society or 'the public' at large. To speak of private and public interests, then, is to amalgamate a multifarious collection of individuals and institutions into two broad camps. For the sake of simplicity, the rudimentary dynamics of the conflict over exclusion may be reduced to questions of private and public rights, obligations, and interests, which necessarily leads one into the realm of law and the quest for territorial justice.

Fundamental to this territorial conflict is the ideal of private property and the rights and obligations this embodies. Under Canadian law, a public place is 'a place where the public goes, a place to which the public has or is permitted to have access and any place of public resort' (Vasan 1980: 302). The corridors of TUC are legally public places, but they are not public property. On private property – regardless of the intensity of the public's use of the premises – rules of access and conduct may be determined and enforced in part by the owner as prescribed by private property rights (Martin 1987: 39–50). The government establishes these property rights with the advice and consent of federal and provincial legislative assemblies, and may, at any time, rescind those rights, or vary and fix limitations or conditions on those rights. With the possession of property comes, consequently, obligations. These restrictions are founded on the principle that there is an inherent public interest in private land. This tenet provides the basis for instituting legislation that regulates and limits private property rights – for example, building codes, taxation, and zoning by-laws. In short, this bundle of obligations imposed by governments is a formal recognition that public space – a place to which the public has or is permitted to have access – is a shared space.

The public, in kind, has its bundle of rights and obligations, ranging from those which are constitutionally entrenched to those implicitly understood as cultural norms. Canadians, for instance, have the constitutionally guaranteed freedoms of 'expression,' 'peaceful assembly,' and 'association' which may be used to challenge private codes of conduct on the grounds they violate these freedoms (Charter of Rights and Freedoms 1982). There are also numerous liberties that are sanctioned and maintained by traditional social norms, such as the freedoms of use and action, temporary claim, and presence (Lynch 1981: 205–20; Carr et al. 1992: 137–86). One can, for instance, use the facilities of a public place as long as one does not appropriate them for exclusive personal use or deny others the same freedoms. One may walk along a conventional outdoor sidewalk, but one may not obstruct others from doing so. People may temporarily appropriate part of a public setting for themselves to fulfil various personal needs – solitude, intimacy, anonymity, passive engagement – as long as the duration is not unreasonably long and does not impinge on the personal needs of others. People also have the right simply 'to be,' simply to partake in civic life, as long at they conform to the legally entrenched rules of public conduct and the culturally specific civilities of social intercourse. In order 'to be,' however, to participate in public life, one has to have access to public places; this is fundamental to the fulfilment of spatial rights and associated democratic freedoms.

Rights and privileges for both the private property owner and the public come with controls or limitations in the form of obligations. The primary obligation of both parties is to exercise their respective spatial freedoms without infringing upon or abusing those of others. Conflict has arisen over Toronto's underground city because the spatial rights and freedoms of individuals, groups, and institutions within each camp are perceived as a real or potential threat to the spatial rights or freedoms of the others. Impeding conflict resolution is the current lack of clarity concerning the appropriate division and just exercise of these freedoms, rights, and obligations.

Negotiating the Public and the Private

The rapid growth of the underground city in Toronto and of indoor space in Canada in general has surpassed the pace at which society has been able to address the issues of spatial control and spatial rights and obligations, but progress is being made. There are several modes available for legitimately challenging the existing spatial power distributions within the underground city, and these have been exercised with varying degrees of success. Although the specific examples that follow by no means exhaust the numerous possibilities for resisting and negotiating the existing power relations between the private and public agents, they do illustrate the principal avenues for change and resolution: (1) acquisition, (2) litigation, (3) legislation, and (4) consultation.

Acquisition

If ownership of the disputed corridors is transferred from the private to the public realm, then the blurred distinction between public and private space desists, as does the conflict over control. The tunnels could be policed, serviced, maintained, and regulated like any other publicly used, publicly owned outdoor city street (Brown 1989: 79). Although governments could acquire these lands through expropriation or purchase on the open market, the costs involved – both in terms of public expense and political fallout – make this an extremely unlikely, unfeasible, and perhaps naive solution to the problem. This also assumes, of course, that municipalities wish to acquire the premises, a responsibility Toronto City Hall has expressed no desire to undertake (J. Morgan, personal interview, 9 June 1994). Acquisition of private property by the public sector is one possibility for resolving the problems of spatial control, but an unlikely route because of its Draconian nature and the costs entailed.

Litigation

Challenges to the existing division of power may be undertaken through the courts. For example, a dispute arose in 1984 between Cadillac Fairview Corporation – part owner of Toronto's Eaton Centre – and the Retail, Wholesale, and Department Store Union over the union's right to distribute to Eaton employees information about joining the union (*Globe and Mail* 1989). According to one witness, union members merely stood in the publicly used corridors, greeted employees with a 'good morning,' and handed out leaflets informing them of a forthcoming meeting; there were no placards or boisterous activities (Layton 1989: 9). Cadillac Fairview called the police and had the union members – the 'undesirable' leafleteers – charged with trespassing on private property. The union challenged this charge, and five years later the Supreme Court of Ontario ruled 'the right of workers to meet union organizers is more important than a company's right to protect its private property from trespassers' (*Globe and Mail* 1989). But although this may be regarded as a victory of public rights over private rights, such case law may be so specifically tailored to particular situations – in this instance the Eaton Centre and the right to organize unions – that the rulings hold little, if any, relevance for other cases and places. In addition to this problem, judicial proceedings are expensive and time consuming. Unlike unions, few individuals – particularly the most marginalized, such as a homeless person – have the time and resources to mount a successful legal challenge against private agents in the courts. These drawbacks aside, litigation does provide an opportunity to resolve specific issues between public and private agents.

Legislation

Governments, as noted above, wield an immense amount of authority over the allocation of spatial power and may consequently be very effective instruments of social and spatial change through passing new statutes or modifying existing ones. For example, as Ontario's Trespass to Property Act (TPA) currently stands, private property owners have, in effect, the right to expel others 'at any time, for any reason, or for no reason at all' (Anand 1987: iii). The owner has absolute discretion over who gets expelled, the grounds for expulsion, and the duration of the ban, be it a day, a year, or in perpetuity. Failure to leave immediately and abide by the ban is an offence punishable by a $1,000 fine; failure to pay may result in a jail term. In other words, those deemed 'undesirable' by virtue of appearance, conduct, or assembly – a group of adolescents in unconventional dress chatting while standing about a corridor bench, for example

– may be expelled for no other reason than simply being there. Security guards, acting on behalf of the private property owners, are within their rights, as outlined in the TPA, to regulate and enforce rules of their own design with little, if any, accountability. Such authority gives them a broad range of interpretations over who is or is not 'desirable' and what is or is not acceptable patron behaviour. The potential for abuse – unwarranted restrictions on public conduct; excessive surveillance; or discriminatory expulsion based on real or perceived age, economic position, ethnocultural heritage, race, or sexual orientation – is considerable and comes with little, if any, effective accountability.

As a direct outcome of concerns initiated by the public over unduly restrictive and discriminatory enforcement of the Trespass to Property Act by owners of Toronto's underground city, the attorney general of Ontario appointed a task force in 1986 to investigate this allocation of power (Anand 1987). This probe reached several conclusions, among them that some private property owners discriminate against visible minorities, youth, and other individuals deemed undesirable; that the current law does not distinguish different types of private property and the intensity of the public's use; and that invocation of the Canadian Charter of Rights and Freedoms as a defence from expulsion only addresses symptoms of the problem and not the cause: unrestricted authority to exclude people. As a result the government of Ontario proposed amendments to the provincial Trespass to Property Act that would, if enacted, have limited the expulsionary powers of private property owners while providing a mechanism for defining 'reasonable use' by the public in a case-by-case, space-by-space fashion. This bill failed to pass for a variety of reasons, including lack of political will on the part of subsequently elected provincial governments, intense opposition from the shopping mall industry and small businesses, and a lack of consultation among the parties most effected by the proposed amendments (S. Fram, personal interview 10 June 1994). Nonetheless, legislation remains one of the most effective ways of redistributing power by mandating access and codes of conduct in civic places.[12]

Consultation

Finally, the immediate parties involved may talk directly with each other to solve a specific mutual problem. The Metropolitan Toronto Police – a public agent – and the owners of the Eaton Centre – a private agent – are currently experimenting with a new model of sharing spatial control inside the shopping centre.[13] Because of the high number of requests for police in the Yonge-Dundas district, which includes the Eaton Centre, the police have recently introduced foot-patrol officers to the area. With permission of the landowners, the police located an office inside the shopping mall in a position of high visibility. They service the immediate corridors of the Eaton Centre, have close proximity to a neighbourhood in need of their presence, and, in theory, both the public and private sectors gain. Eaton's gets to supplement its private security force, and the public – mall users and neighbourhood residents alike – receive added police protection. In practice, however, problems may arise over precisely how the patrons, the police, and private security – acting as servants of the landowners – interact. The presence of publicly funded police officers on privately-owned property may, for example, lead the layperson to conclude the general corridors are truly public property and behave accordingly, only to be informed otherwise by private security guards. Altercations might develop from the misunderstandings generated by this enhanced blurring of the public and private domains. Although it is premature to evaluate this particular joint public/private venture, such a process of consultation and cooperation puts into practice ideals that are vital for the creation and sustenance of successful public places: community participation, negotiation, and the sharing of obligations and responsibilities.

Conclusions: The Need Just To Be

The search for an equitable distribution of rights, rules, and revenue in Toronto's underground streets is, on excavation, a quest for territorial justice. How Canadians choose to distribute the benefits and burdens of spatial control inside the corridors of our emergent indoor cities is a morally charged, ideologically laden question of social justice, the resolution of which has immense economic, legal, political, and social consequences.[14] The answer will not come easily. Clearly the emergence of large expanses of publicly used, privately owned space is modifying the spatial structure of our cities, but changes to the balance of power that both dictate and constitute the social relationships within these civic places – whether achieved through acquisition, litigation, legislation, and/or consultation – are lagging behind.

To maintain the current distribution of spatial control is socially unjust insofar as the needs of the public are not being served adequately. Notwithstanding the necessity of private enterprise for premises conducive to business, the power of exclusion currently held and exercised by the private sector impedes and seriously weakens the development, operation, and preservation of the successful and unconditionally public civic place. The right simply 'to be,' to partake in civic life – regardless of one's appearance, perceived 'desirability,' or spending potential – is a prerequisite for the creation and sustenance of shared experiences, a feeling of belonging, and a sense of attachment to, and respect for, public places and the community of friends, neighbours, and strangers who bring them to life. To lose a communal meeting ground – the pedestrian sidewalk, indoors or out – on the basis of private property rights, market forces, and the desire of certain classes to associate with their own kind, is to lose the very site which embodies, perhaps, the best of Western culture: a truly public place where the democratic ideals of tolerance and equality are openly practised and sustained through the inclusion and interaction of all members in our diverse society on the streets and sidewalks of our cities. During the years to come, as our indoor geographies expand, Canadians should not become passive witnesses to yet another erosion of the traditional street: the civil liberty conventionally associated with public life itself – the freedom just to be, to have a place in public. As we move indoors and underground, dare we bury this?

NOTES

1 The Retretti Art Centre, in Punkaharju, Finland, contains a 1,000-seat concert hall built underground in rock (Anttikoski et al. 1989: 17). In Bonn, Germany, there is an underground canteen and numerous below-ground shopping arcades such as those in Cologne and Dusseldorf (Kind-Barkauskas 1993: 25). In an effort to reduce traffic congestion in Amsterdam, there is a proposal to build an underground bus terminal that would accommodate up to fifty buses (Sikkel 1993: 33). Underground sports halls and swimming pools have been constructed and are widely used in Norway (Brook and Collins 1990: 8).

2 Williams (1990) provides a very thorough overview of humanity's relationship with the underground, particularly since the eighteenth century.

3 Over 95 per cent of the cost to erect a building in central Tokyo may be attributed to the cost of land acquisition (Brook and Collins 1990: 8). At these prices, going underground to avoid purchasing more surface space is attractive.

4 Contemporary, publicly used, underground urban space is considered to have commenced with the construction of the first subway in London, England, in 1863 (Xueyuan and Yu 1988: 200). The development of the underground in

both Toronto and Montreal owe much of their growth to subway systems and the desire for direct links between above-ground office/retail buildings and subway stations (Barker 1986: 145; Boivin 1991: 83). The history of TUC development presented here is based primarily on the works of Barker (1986), Williams (1984), and Goodman (1984).

5 For a succinct chronology of the entire development of TUC, see Dudley (1989: 23). For a more in-depth discussion, see Goodman (1984).

6 The number of buildings will vary depending on the classification scheme employed. This value was calculated by counting the number of buildings displayed on the City of Toronto map of the downtown walkway (Toronto 1993).

7 Of the 2.5 million calls for service received by Metropolitan Toronto Police in 1993, only 67 criminal offences or serious occurrences (i.e., suicide) were investigated by the force in the underground city (M. Dear, personal communication, 22 June 1994).

8 A 1991 survey of North American municipalities with an indoor city indicated commercial advantage was the single largest factor driving its construction (Maitland 1992: 165).

9 Although the vast majority of the underground resembles a suburban shopping mall corridor, there are parts that have no stores or services, such as the link between Union Station and the Royal York Hotel, and sections that are murky, such as the underground parking garage which links City Hall to the rest of the underground city.

10 For a case study of the potential auditory, physiological, psychological, and social effects of ambient noise on indoor-city patrons, see Hopkins (1994).

11 One youth services agency estimated that 90 per cent of its clients had been charged with trespassing by mall owners (Anand 1987: ix). These users perceived that mall owners and their security agents labelled them gang members by virtue of their numbers, youth, clothing, and/or race, and expelled them because of it (Anand 1987: ix).

12 For an in-depth discussion of the now defunct proposed amendments to Ontario's Trespass to Property Act, see Hopkins (1993). For a critique of a newly proposed category of quasi-public property ownership, which recognizes the essentially public nature of mall space while retaining reasonable rights for property owners, see Krushelnicki (1993).

13 This account is based on an interview with Sgt. Cocksedge (14 June 1994) and correspondence with the Director of Corporate Planning, M. Dear (22 June 1994), both with Metropolitan Toronto Police.

14 For a succinct overview of social justice, see Smith (1994a). For an in-depth review of the topic as it relates to geography, see Smith (1994b).

REFERENCES

Anand, R. 1987. *Task Force on the Law Concerning Trespass to Publicly-Used Property as it Affects Youth and Minorities.* Toronto: Ministry of the Attorney General's Office

Anttikoski, U., V. Gron, A. Halme, M. Juhola, M. Palmu, O. Parkkamaki, T. Tuisku and O. Ayravainen. 1989. 'Subsurface public assembly spaces in Finland.' *Tunnelling and Underground Space Technology* 4(1): 17–22

Barker, M.B. 1986. 'Toronto's underground pedestrian system.' *Tunnelling and Underground Space Technology* 1(2): 145–51

Benn, S.I., and G.F. Gaus. 1983. 'The public and private: Concepts and action.' In S. Benn and G. Gaus, eds., *Public and Private in Social Life,* 3–27. Beckenham [Australia]: Croom Helm

Besner, J. 1991. 'Montreal underground: Historical perspective.' *Actualité Immobilière* (Autumn): 4–11

Boivin, D.J. 1991. 'Montreal's underground network: A study of the downtown pedestrian system.' *Tunnelling and Underground Space Technology* 6(1): 83–91

Brook, D., and M. Collins. 1990. 'Underground space and planning.' *The Planner* 23: 8–12

Brown, D. 1989. 'The indoor city: From organic beginnings to guided growth.' In B. Demchinsky, ed., *Grassroots, Greystones and Glass Towers,* 70–82. Montreal: Véhicule

Carmody, J.C., and R.L. Sterling. 1987. 'Design strategies to alleviate negative psychological and physiological effects in underground space.' *Tunnelling and Underground Space Technology* 2(1): 59–67

Carr, S., M. Francis, L. Rivlin, and A. Stone. 1992. *Public Space.* Cambridge: University of Cambridge Press

Charter of Rights and Freedoms: A Guide for Canadians. 1982. Ottawa: Ministry of Supply and Services

Cocksedge, Sgt. 1994. Corporate Planning, Metropolitan Toronto Police. Telephone interview with author, 14 June

Dear, M. 1994. Criminal Statistics and Policing Policy Pertaining to the Underground City. Personal letter to the author from the Director of Corporate Planning, Metropolitan Toronto Police, 22 June

Dudley, G. 1989. 'An overview of the retail structure of Toronto's underground pedestrian system.' *Operational Geographer* 7(2): 22–7

Edmonton, City of. 1989. *Downtown Pedway Network Review.* Edmonton: Planning and Development

Fram, S. 1994. Counsel, Ministry of the Attorney General, Policy Development Division. Personal interview with author, 10 June

Fulford, R. 1993. 'Tunnel vision.' *Toronto Life* 27(1): 29–31

Globe and Mail. 1989. 'Union had right to try organizing in public areas of mall, court says,' (21 December)

Goodman, L. 1984. *Streets beneath the Towers: The Development of Toronto's Downtown Underground Pedestrian Mall System.* Toronto: Discussion Paper No. 31, York University

Harvey, D. 1992. 'Social postmodernism and the city.' *International Journal of Urban and Regional Research* 16(4): 588–601

Hopkins, J. 1994. 'Orchestrating an indoor city: Ambient noise inside a mega-mall.' *Environment and Behaviour* 26(6): 785–812

– 1993. 'A balancing act? Trespass amendments for public/private places. *Urban Geography* 14(2): 114–18

Ishioka, H. 1992. 'Security management for underground space.' *Tunnelling and Underground Space Technology* 7(4): 335–8

Jones, K., H. Jacobs, and G. Dudley. 1990. *The Toronto Underground Mall Study.* Toronto: Department of Planning and Development

Kind-Barkauskas, F. 1993. 'Creative aspects of and uses for underground structures: Examples for Germany.' *Tunnelling and Underground Space Technology* 8(1): 25–30

Krushelnicki, B. 1993. 'Shopping centres: Public agora or privileged place?' *Winter Cities* 10(4): 31–3

Layton, J. 1989. 'Vaticans of commerce.' Montreal: Canadian Broadcasting Corporation

Lynch, K. 1981. *Good City Form.* Cambridge: MIT Press

Maitland, B. 1992. 'Hidden Cities.' *Cities* 9(3): 162–9

Martin, S. 1987. *Real Estate Appraising In Canada.* Winnipeg: Appraisal Institute of Canada

Morgan, J. 1994. Senior Economic Development Officer, Economic Development Division, Planning and Development, City of Toronto. Personal interview with author, 9 June

Relph, E. 1990. *The Toronto Guide.* Toronto: Association of American Geographers

Ringstad, A. 1994. 'Perceived danger and the design of underground facilities for public use.' *Tunnelling and Underground Space Technology* 9(1): 5–7

Robertson, K. 1987. 'Pedestrian skywalks in Calgary, Canada.' *Cities* 4(3): 207–14

Sikkel, H. 1993. 'An underground bus terminal in Amsterdam.' *Tunnelling and Underground Space Technology* 8(1): 31–6

Smith, D.M. 1994a. 'Social Justice.' In R.J. Johnston, D. Gregory, and D.M. Smith, eds., *The Dictionary of Human Geography,* 563–6. Cambridge: Blackwell

– 1994b. *Geography and Social Justice.* Cambridge: Blackwell

Tatsukami, T. 1986. 'Case study of an underground shopping mall in Japan.' *Tunnelling and Underground Space Technology* 1(1): 19–28

Toronto, City of. 1993. *PATH: Toronto's Downtown Walkway*. Toronto: Planning and Development

Vasan, R.S. 1980. 'Public place.' In *The Canadian Law Dictionary*, 302. Don Mills: Law and Business

Wada, Y., and H. Sakugawa. 1990. 'Psychological effects of working underground.' *Tunnelling and Underground Space Technology* 3(1/2): 33–7

Williams, M. 1984. 'The underground city.' *City Planning* (Fall): 24–9

Williams, R. 1990. *Notes on the Underground*. Cambridge: MIT Press

Xueyuan, H., and S. Yu. 1988. 'The urban underground space environment and human performance.' *Tunnelling and Underground Space Technology* 3(2): 193–200

5

Feel Good Here? Relationships between Bodies and Urban Environments

ROB SHIELDS

Pleasure, of whatever kind, and no matter who experiences it, is the essential element of all conceptions of modernity. It is a form as necessary to moral intuition as space is to intellectual intuition.

Herbert Spencer, *What Is Morality?*

Simple Enjoyment and the City

When we wander around our town or city, we encounter so many opportunities for fun, for enjoyment, and for straightforward pleasure. However, urban environments are studded with signs forbidding just such activities: 'Do Not Walk on the Grass'; 'No Skateboarders'; 'Children Only in the Playground'; 'Walk Don't Run.' We read 'Keep Off' on the sculptures; 'No Swimming' in the fountains, and 'No Loitering' on the shopping mall doors.

Such notices are evidence that enjoyment and taking pleasure in the urban environment is a cultural problem for society, for planners, and for the administrators of public sites. This problem extends beyond maintaining the grass; it relates to fears that large numbers of people with hedonistic goals will become an uncontrollable mass. Pleasure has historically been considered a danger to social order. However, moments of festival in which entire cities were given over to pleasure such as Mardi Gras, harvest festivals, and feast days were the most important days of the European calender until the early 1800s. And, in comparison with non-European societies throughout history, we live in one of the most thoroughly anti-pleasure societies of all time.

More recently, in the 1960s, the liberation of the city from the tyranny of seriousness, work, and rationality has been equated with a true revolution in everyday life (Debord 1957). With the relaxation of rational order would go the organization of work. It was hoped that the result would be akin to a 'permanent festival' (Lefebvre 1976). If one recalls that the abolition of work in its alienated, modern form was also one of Karl Marx's objectives, then it can be understood how merely turning away from work towards urban play and pleasure could be mistaken for a total social revolution.

This essay has a slightly different focus. I want to emphasize the question of pleasure and the types of interaction that have come to illustrate our understanding of the public 'crowd practice' in streets, squares, malls, and pedestrian districts. This chapter thus assesses the problem of enjoyment and its relationship to the body and social interaction in urban crowds. A definition of what pleasure is will be presented. The key argument, or thesis, is that the bodily pleasure underlying that enjoyment can be taken into account in good urban design at the levels of planning (for example, of pedestrian areas) and design (for example, in street landscaping: benches, lighting, paving textures, plantings), and administration (such as policies on skateboarding). Unfortunately, it is easier to come up with bad examples such as the raised forecourt and amphitheatre in the front of the Mississauga City Hall project. Once built, however, signs forbidding skateboarding were posted and the gates to the amphitheatre were locked. In a study of Mississauga City Hall, Jill Delaney (1996) has shown that such public spaces are crucial to the presentation of a 'serious' image of an 'edge-city' (Garreau 1991) trying to build up its identity as something more than a suburb of Toronto.

Design for Pleasure

We are so well educated to detach ourselves from paying attention to most bodily sensations that it proves a major intellectual exercise to get back to any comprehension of how simple and basic pleasure is to our everyday lives. Could it be that pleasure is 'felt' by bodies much more than thought by minds? While psychological desires may or may not exist, the simple pleasures of the city can be understood in more straightforward terms of *the coordination of the body with itself, with others, and with the environment.* This is a simpler and empirical definition of pleasure at the level of embodied interaction. The conception of pleasure in terms of the fulfilment of desire stops research in its tracks because it leads inexorably back to a psychoanalytic postulate of unconscious drives and urges. Operating with a clearer conception of the body and the opportunities for its multiple coordinations, pleasure and the body can be integrated into urban design practice.

In order to understand the mundane and simple pleasures of being in 'good' urban spaces, we need exactly such a materialist definition of pleasure. Pleasure is a physical, tactile experience. It is related to the body; it is quite different from disembodied 'happiness.' We speak of pleasure in terms of bodily sensations, and even when we talk of abstract 'intellectual' pleasures, such as reading a good book, we use metaphors of bodily pleasure. These indicate the basic primacy of bodily sensations. Thus, we evoke specific sensations which are as much *felt* as thought – sweating, a raised pulse, the excitement of adrenaline, shifting our body around in our chairs with impatience of suspense.

Pleasure as a sensuous and tactile phenomenon is tied directly to the body and to bodily practices of sitting, walking, struggling through a crowd, negotiating obstacles, keeping an appropriate distance between oneself and another person. While cultural norms of proximity were widely studied under the term 'proxemics' in the 1960s and 1970s, little was said about the 'art' of proxemics at the level of the body itself. Similarly, many ergonomic studies have been conducted of the physical capabilities of bodies. (For example, how far up can a person of a certain height reach? And thus, how high up on the wall should builders locate the top shelf in a kitchen cupboard?) Yet there were few analyses of crowds. Thus, understandings of the body and of coordination are open to further cultural analysis. As such, the body can be deconstructed as cultural, as gendered and sexed, as dependent on age and physique, and as *dependent on its context* (what is pleasurable in one situation may well not be in another). This is to say that pleasure is contingent on both the body and the situation (for example, ethnic or class relations) in which the body is positioned, and on its involvement and implication – its inscripted performance in a situation. The body is *not* a constant concrete object or an objective phenomenon on which an empirical theory of subjectivity can be built because the body itself is socially defined and fixed – most typically in North American societies according to a visual logic; its limits are circumscribed at the surface of the skin which is taken for granted as an impermeable boundary. Yet, if it is understood finally as a contingent synthesis of these variables, pleasure escapes determinism because of its personal yet socially unfixed and pre-codified nature. It disturbs overly simplistic, 'averaged-out' notions of the body, for human bodies are different both physically (height, weight, sex) and defined differently in different cultures and settings.

Bodies at Play

Despite this wrinkle, to understand pleasure requires a theoretical inclusiveness which admits the body. Crowd practices such as loitering or hanging-out, looking on, meandering through a crowd, or searching out those who might be its leaders, foreground a flexible, popular understanding of the body in the mundane spaces of everyday life, commerce, and social order.

With the introduction of the body as a factor in the design of public spaces, touch (or the *tactile*) supplements the more typical resort to visual definitions of good urban design: interesting building facades or nostalgic retro-Victorian street furniture such as benches and lights. The tactile should also allow us to avoid the resort to functional definitions of good urban design which prioritizes traffic flows, the satisfaction of needs, and visibility. As a result we will have a better understanding of the attractiveness of 'good spaces' in the city. The tactile experiences which relate to our 'embodiedness' in urban spaces and situations includes rubbing shoulders with others or instead avoiding contact; it includes how we interact with the built environment, and how we use the objects of the urban environment, such as benches and railings, as 'props' for our own bodily comportment and physical conduct.

The coordination of the body with itself, with others, and with the environment is a basic component of experience. Wherever one draws the limits of the body, this is not a form of physical essentialism: even someone whose movement is restricted has some opportunity for some form of coordination of their body parts and for the correlation of their (still) body to others in motion. Moreover, such a coordination is not necessarily experienced directly but can be witnessed, as in the cases of someone who 'watches the world go by,' or watches dance or the choreography of large-scale pageants. One also attempts to choose forms of interaction by which to distance oneself from or engage with others and the environment. In several of his works, French philosopher Michel Foucault (1973) examined the inscription of relations of power on bodies and the control of population forms of discipline and zoning, such as the partitioning of cities into quarantined 'quarters' during times of plague and through exercises (not just athletic exercises such as workouts but military manoeuvres and ritual movements), and other forms of human 'dressage' in bodily and in spatial terms (and I take this term from equestrian training quite deliberately). Foucault's argument is that social control is often implemented by controlling the physical movement of bodies: by teaching certain types of comportment and controlling the coordination of bodies. Minds, he argued, are trained and outlooks formed through regimens of bodily discipline (see Foucault 1973, 1979). With their regulations concerning circulation and their detailed by-laws on bodily interaction of people as individuals or members of crowds, urban environments are key systems of spatial discipline.

The purposive aspects of everyday activities need to be separated from their intrinsic pleasures of movement and interaction. Socially legitimized forms of bodily comportment limit the 'simple pleasures' of sociability and of the urban environment to socially circumscribed modes of interaction which are in turn linked back to socially legitimated forms of leisure. Thus, the pleasures of sitting on a park bench and observing people or 'nature,' or feeding the birds, are proscribed at certain times and places as idleness, 'bench-warming,' or 'sitting around.' Standing still in a place people usually move through is forbidden as 'loitering' or 'hanging around,' although at other times it is perfectly acceptable to 'check out the crowds.' Strolling was a legitimate past-time in nineteenth-century European shopping arcades, but at other times it has been condemned as aimless wandering. The contested quality of the body extends to the norms of comportment and to attempts to define norms of 'coordination' and regulate the everyday motions of the body. 'Walk! Don't run!' is one example which continues to be often shouted in the corridors of primary and elementary schools. Slowing the body down to a dignified – but above all socially uniform – pace is one aspect of this training and of delimiting what types and forms of physical coordination and movement can legitimately be called 'beautiful' or pleasurable.

Both contemporary public spaces (such as a small plaza at the main door of an office building) and consumption sites (such as a pedestrian area or a shopping mall) share one common factor: their provision of the free 'public good' of contact with other people. This is an experience of social centrality, and the possibility of crowd sociality, however anonymous. This 'crowd practice' is one of the untheorized points of orientation amid rapid institutional change, economic restructuring, and shifts in political arrangements.[1]

Whether one considers a site such as Covent Garden in London, the Byward Market in Ottawa, Le Jardin des Halles in Paris, Faneuil Hall in Boston, or the corner of Spencer and Centre Streets in a small town like, say, Spencerville, Ontario (population 260), the activities and the basic attraction are similar. These are urban sites of simple public pleasures such as meeting others, walking, sitting out, being part of a crowd, attending a community event, or simply pausing to pass the time of day with someone. Such basic acts of sociality (Simmel 1950) are the basic building blocks of a more political public sphere. Such simple activities and the very elementary pleasure that goes along with them continue to serve as the models of our 'enactment' of community when we come together as individuals (Jacobs 1984).

There is considerable nostalgia for the almost non-existent architectural form of the veranda on which one can sit out and view and even participate in the public life of the street while remaining 'at home' (see Rybczynski 1988). There is either no significant public life on the street or the veranda is reduced to an architectural 'citation' of the traditional form in the shape of a discrete overhang or narrow pseudo-portico with a steel post or two. Furthermore, such simple interactions remain the models which we use to make sense of the more abstract and complex notions of a 'public sphere' or community on a city-wide scale, which is presented to us through the media (Anderson 1983). Whether in front of Toronto City Hall, along the Kingston waterfront, in the squares of Vieux Montreal, during 'public skating night' on the rink of a small town, or along Robson Street in Vancouver, people sit for a moment on benches or linger if they can in 'good' urban areas. Some determinedly 'hang-out.' Others collide while gawking at the mix of people, products in store windows, and the 'theatre' of the streetscape itself. Some prowl through the crowd; others seem to drift, drawn by the attraction of interesting objects of events taking place.

Each of these activities is quite different from the others. Each involves a different mode of being in the body and in the crowd. Simply put, each involves a different sense and degree of either participation or withdrawal from the scene or 'situation' (Bech 1993), including the action taking place, the possibilities and ambiance of the site, its balance of strict functionality and opportunities for transformation and indolent 'hijackings' of the place, and the obstacles of other bodies in the crowd. There is a continuum which runs from being outside a crowd, through an alienated 'being in' in the city, to being submerged as an integral 'part of' the crowd. Involvement itself is thus subject to different representations and can be coded and manipulated. The crowd – at a fair, on the street, at the beach – is not unified. It is heterogeneous. Crowds are composed of many people; each person following their own agenda and participating in a different and highly personal manner. But the crowd is not just an atomized mass of 'lonely individuals' either (Riesman 1950). To better respond to the crowd, planners must think in terms of strategies for choreographing bodies in crowded urban spaces, at times as a mere part of a crowd (when one hardly thinks of individual bodies at all but just of a mass) and at other times as self-contained individuals.

At the same time as types of behaviour and bodily abilities (for example, climbing stairs, walking certain distances without stopping, and so on) are assumed to take place in certain places by architects, planners, and administrators, so other types of behaviour are made impossible because of the configuration of the spaces. They become difficult because objects (such as benches) are obstacles to certain types of action. Thus, it is usually very difficult to practice ballet in a subway station, and it is probably foolhardy to skateboard on the grand entrance steps of an old public building. In some cities, such as Atlanta, it is illegal to lie down on a park bench, whether one is sleeping or not. The 'Onlooker' is frustrated by being forbidden to sit on a bench all day at a shopping mall or through the design of benches which are comfortable for only a short while in the 'food court' areas of malls. The 'Flâneur' is deceived by shopping mall corridors or galleria which are deliberately designed to perplex our sense of direction so that more time is spent in the mall and more storefronts are passed by the confused shopper. The 'Drifter' is seduced by colourful banners announcing a sale, or by enticing sights barely glimpsed around a street corner.

Consider several different modes of involvement and comportment and of the manner in which taking pleasure – simply enjoying the city with its built spaces, crowds, and different activities – is linked to the engagement of the body or lack thereof with Others and with the urban environment. In particular, 'consumption spaces' such as market squares, shopping malls, and other such places have increasingly become foci for urban tourism activities. There has been an enormous investment in heritage streetscapes, the revitalization of old market halls, and the creation of elaborately cobbled pedestrian districts. The popularity of these areas is indisputable, however, there has been little comment on the *pleasures* of these spaces or their expensive modifications in terms other than their visual quality. Their privileged status for sociability, crowd-participation, the informal entertainment of buskers and street entertainers (such as various types of mime artists – from clowns and parodists to 'robots' – an important and now widespread activity) and their overall reputation as privileged sites for public leisure is less often discussed (but see Zukin 1991, 1995).

Modes of Participation

Let us explore the different modes of involvement of the body in the urban crowd. Each is a different form of the coordination of the body with others and with the environment. A number might be identified and explored, but for the purpose of giving examples, three will suffice. The Flâneur gives a case of one who participates but always holds back, restraining himself from 'getting into' the pleasures of being with others. The Onlooker sits apart, perhaps on a bench maintaining a distance and blending in with the architecture. The Drifter allows himself to drift so as to fully enjoy the pleasures of urban public life.

Urban Detective Work: Flânerie

What is the participation of the Flâneur in the scene sketched above of a market square? Flâneur is often used loosely in the urban studies literature (Zukin 1991, Shields 1994) for any 'stroller' who is focused on enjoying the crowd of a typical urban environment, rather than on going somewhere in particular. This is closer to Baudelaire's term, 'promeneur' (literally, a 'stroller'). I use this term in Walter Benjamin's strict sense of the ideal-typical prowler, an undercover detective searching for clues about what is going on – not just an onlooker, bystander, or stroller (Benjamin 1973, Shields 1994). In the case of shopping, a store detective is a type of Flâneur who attempts to discern those with criminal intentions from those who are browsing or trying out goods. And a researcher trying to understand the organization of a shopping mall, or a shopper looking for a particular department in a large department store are both involved in flâneurie.

Flâneur is a term derived from the French novels about the new metropolis of Paris in the mid-1800s. The Flâneur is the forerunner of the gumshoe in detective novels – a sort of 'Colombo' type who, while appearing under the guise of nonchalance and the anonymity of the crowd, is as attentive to all clues as the 'Native brave' was thought to be attentive to the clues of the North American forest.[2] Nineteenth-century theorists of urban social interaction such as Tönnies, Taine, Le Bon, and Simmel feared the loss of individual identity and rationality in the emotional, 'faceless' crowd. Crowds were formless and dangerous (for the counter-argument, see Canetti 1962). However, the Flâneur guards his individuality and first-person point of view from the corrosive exuberance of the crowd. While a participant in the crowd, the Flâneur keeps a distance, a knowing consumer – a connoisseur – of street life and (primarily visual) street pleasures. The Flâneur has been traditionally portrayed as a hero (gender intended) who objectifies the world and people around him to pursue his 'researches.' The fascination of the Flâneur is thus discovery: insight and knowledge which allows him to master the urban situation. The pleasure of flânerie, however, lies in being in but not part of a crowd.

The Flâneur was originally a literary figure, more typical of the pages of nineteenth-century French writers such as Honoré de Balzac, Eugène Sue, and Alexandre Dumas than the actual streets of Paris.[3] Even if the Flâneur was more imagined than real, in the early to mid-nineteenth century everyday the readers of these literary works were encouraged to think of themselves as Flâneurs, as (male) armchair detectives, and as amateur gumshoes when they were out in the city. Thus, these readers participated in the invention of an autonomous personal leisure form keyed to the emerging social and spatial relations of the new imperial metropolises of Europe. This was autonomous and personal in the sense that flânerie was based on the postulate of the masculine, monadic, and relatively wealthy but anonymous 'individual.'[4] The Flâneur of the late nineteenth-century French novel has the intentionality and self-directedness that in other narratives is the identifying characteristic of the rational goal-oriented individual and the modernist citizen. The Flâneur imagined himself to be an undissolvable entity within the mass of the crowd – like an undissolved clump of sugar in a cake mix. Flânerie was a sociability of 'Ones' which emphasized and preserved the separateness of men. As such, it was a social practice of a generalized, but patriarchal, democratic individualism which was new to nineteenth-century Europeans. Flânerie embodied a fascination with anonymity and guardedness which also manifested itself in the emphasis placed on public modesty by the middle classes.

Flânerie can be understood as a form of pleasure of the tactile sociability in the new 'contact community' of those rubbing shoulders in nineteenth-century metropolitan crowds. One rubs shoulders with the crowd, but nothing ever 'rubs off,' so to speak. The individual Flâneur's identity and bodily integrity are never eroded by his immersion in the crowd. This is as much a 'real' experience as a way of interpreting the experience of flânerie – thus, returning us to our discussion of the importance of socially defined limits of the body and of hegemonic understandings of the nature of body-to-body 'coordination.' This contact-form of community emerged alongside contract-based social ties (*Gesellschaft*) documented by Ferdinand Tönnies (1957) which supplanted traditional ties based on kinship and growing up together in small villages (*Gemeinschaft*).

But while the Flâneur personifies the ideal-type of the 'Citizen,' he was not fully self-controlled (he is infected with a bit of the detective's intuitive and unpredictable genius), and he indulges in non-rational pleasures as part of his practice. The Flâneur delights in the Street. Like the showgirls of Degas's Impressionist pastels, the Flâneur was a figure of excess: an incarnation of a new, urban form of masculine passion manifest as connoisseurship and couched in scopophilia (a love of looking as a method of understanding the world – of gazing, in the sense of voyeurism). For example, the French authors in Benjamin's notes refer constantly to an '*ivresse*' or 'drunken-ness' on the spectacle of the city. The metropolis is elating, intoxicating. The Flâneur's excessiveness, his pathological '*ivresse*' and resistance to the workaday discipline of bodies by the punch-clock, and his appropriation of the city, is central to Benjamin's fascination with the apparent reverberation between the literary myth of flânerie and everyday living in European cities. A century later in the hands of writers like the Situationist, Guy Debord (1971), or their theoretical mentor, Henri Lefebvre (1996), this activity would become the basis for a more radical rallying cry to repossess the city, its pleasures, *and* its institutions.

The old crowd-practice of the Flâneur prescribed by novelists was part of the embodiment – the fitting to the body – of empire and the new spatialization of social and economic relations. It was one aspect of the practical, tactile fitting of people to empire (that is, to the issues and practices of popular imperialism such as consuming the goods imported from or manufactured from the staples of colonies). Through their personal experience and tactile encounter in urban sites (such as the nineteenth-century arcades) with representative Others from the far-flung colonies and outposts of empire, European populations were tutored in the extent and nature of colonial domination. Mass consumption was a type of popular imperialism. People learned that their country's colonies and the goods produced from the materials brought in from the colonies were 'theirs.'

And what better way to reassure oneself, to re-map the local, than to tour its transformed streets as a Flâneur? Nineteenth-century French engravings show (somewhat fancifully) plumed Natives from the tropics, exotically dressed dragoons, and sumptuously dressed women in the arcades of Paris. What better way to map the diversity and distance of empire than to encounter its characters in cosmopolitan public places? The gaze of the Flâneur is thus part of a tactic to appropriate not only the local, physical spaces of the city as one's own 'turf' (DeCerteau 1984) but also to participate in the popular sense of empire, to master and even revel in the 'emporium.' However, the Flâneur attempts to maintain self-control, not to fully participate in the crowd. This reserve and resistance to full participation inflects the bodily practice of flânerie. Unlike relaxed strolling, the hyper-observant Flâneur is cautious and ultimately cut off from the crowd. Maintaining the fiction of the rational, observing ego is the necessary precondition for flânerie. The Flâneur, thus, presents the ideal-typical example of the modernist monadic individual spatialized as an independent body ultimately free from contamination by his or her environment.

The Onlooker

The Flâneur might be contrasted with the Onlooker who takes the time to sit on a bench in the same market square. Again, what is important to this analysis is not the intentionality of the Onlooker – who might be waiting for someone or simply passing the time away. Rather our interest is in the coordination of the Onlooker's body with others and with the environment. Here one is more clearly not part of a crowd, but rather part of the scene or situation in a given site. This spatial trick of definition, action, and posture allows one the necessary 'distance' to support the belief that one is again in some sense not involved, but merely an Onlooker. Nonetheless, in taking up a position as part of the environmental background, in acceding to the comforts (or lack thereof) of the bench, a more direct coordination of the body and the environment is put into play. The Onlooker becomes almost a part of the environment. Socially separate, but environmentally engaged, the Onlooker is a spectator of urban social interaction. At the same time, the Onlooker is clearly practising a highly distanced form of sociability carried by the gaze (see also Stewart 1996).

Urban Drifting: The situationist Dérive

Dérive or 'drifting' contrasts dramatically with the critical distance of the Flâneur as a self-contained, disciplined detective even within the crowd. Dérive is also quite different from the Onlooker who elects to observe from outside the crowd.

In the late 1950s, the Situationists, a group of avant-garde artists and thinkers associated with the Marxist philosopher of city life, Henri Lefebvre, sought to discover the emotional and non-rational aspects of the urban environment as a way of illustrating how cities could be used and enjoyed according to a completely non-production, non-work-oriented logic. Dérive included drifting with the current of people, floating along, going with the flow, and more importantly, being *diverted* towards the lights and bustle, or being attracted to the activity of one place or another. Dérive, then, is a form of automatist (as one might say, 'going on automatic' without thinking self-consciously) flânerie in which one allows oneself to be diverted by the 'solicitations of architecture and one's desires.' In this case, one enacts – or embodies – one's desires expressing their directional intentionality. Discussing urban representations in film, Perniola refers to this 'movement of desire' as the *transito* in which people in the city are constantly on the move and in transit.[5] Substantively without any objective, the *formal* purpose of Dérive is to find out where one ends up, to know what 'will have happened.'

As a practice of the city, Dérive works against the rational logic of the urban plan and modernist forms of everyday life: that cultural *savoir faire* which directs us to focus single-mindedly on our own 'business' as we move about the city. Although it probably has its origins among the Surrealists, this practice was most elaborated by the Situationists in late 1950s Paris. For the Situationists, Dérive was a 'game played on urban sites' (Home 1988: 13). What is important about both flânerie and Dérive is that they are forms of serious play, of serious pleasures, which destabilize the leisure dualisms of work and play, serious and frivolous, rational and emotional. The precision and seriousness of the 'experiments' parodies the rationality of the planned city where little thought is given to ends or to pleasure, but where all concentration is on means and technique.[6] Attention is directed towards pragmatics and choreographies, reversing the primacy of goal-oriented behaviour and intentions in favour of an emphasis on achieved effects and unanticipated results.

Their creation of *situations* (the connotation is of 'happenings') which disturbed the blasé attitude of urbanites and norms of everyday life was to form the aesthetic medium for the Situationists' plans. Debord describes these 'situations' as 'the concrete construction of momentary ambiences of life and their transformation into a superior quality of passion' (Debord 1957, translated in Knabb 1988: 17). The idea of these original 'happenings' was that people would gather because they were attracted by some intriguing activity, by a bizarre protest, or by the lure of being part of a larger whole or community. Recently, 'raves' and 'house' parties have become important, commodified forms of 'happenings' where people participate for the fun, intrigue, and notoriety of being involved in an indulgent, 'fun' event which is, in essence, a revolt against the social logic of being productive and rational at all times.

Dérive highlights the emotive and pleasurable aspects of the city through the vector of a bodily movement or *transito.* Places are characterized not just by physical data and events (which are mis-labelled as 'attractions') but by powers of 'attraction': who hangs out where and when shapes the identity of sites and spaces. Dérive de-emphasizes the dogma of urban theory and planning: that hidden economic forces shape experiences of the city. Instead, we are confronted by the fractured logic of everyday life which superimposes a less rationalized experience of the city based on appearances, not socioeconomic forces.

For the case of Dérive as Debord explains it, desire and curiosity return in the form of a new concept: 'attraction.' The role of the choosing, selecting rational individual or consumer is side-lined in favour of an idea of the city as a field of attractions in which, once again, the body-simple moves back and forth picking up experiences or engaging in activities and 'passions.' The stress is on the way this hijacks the production-oriented logic of the city. Instead, bodies 'consume' the city without ulterior motives. Pleasure comes from the possibilities for social interaction (or 'sociality') which occur through activities such as Dérive. The pleasure of Dérive is in *being drawn* to something in the city – a window, a person, a view. This is more than a question of fulfilment of desire or the satisfaction of curiosity. 'Being drawn' is, in this sense, allowing one's body to be animated and physically moved by attractions in the urban environment.

Window shopping is a process of exploration and sightseeing akin to tourism which can easily be understood as a form of Dérive. Shopping is also a strong candidate for reconstruction as an opportunity for serious play in the manner of both flânerie and Dérive. As a process, shopping may take the form of an extended period of browsing, perhaps in more than a dozen stores, legitimized by an insignificant purchase, or even that faintly frustrated feeling of unfulfilled desire. Nonetheless, there is the simple pleasure of browsing and even of trying on clothes or trying out tools – looking, feeling, and fitting – which one has even without the fulfilment of desired objectives. Desire in the form of 'being-drawn' to a display or an attention-grabbing commodity reappears in Dérive.

Conclusion

Up to now urban theory has concerned itself primarily with mute objects in the environment, suppressing any consideration of bodies, users, or agents who might find pleasure in achieved projects or who indeed often resist against the directions imposed by planners. People do the unexpected. However, practising architects often think of their plans for public spaces (indoors and out) in terms of what people will be doing – watching from a bench here, meeting a colleague there, cutting across this way, and so on. By thinking of the urban environment as a space in which there are opportunities for different types of comportment and for the coordination of bodies together in different ways allows the possibility of including pleasure directly in the design process, if a bodily conception of pleasure is adopted. For simplicity I have focused only on pleasure. However, one could undertake this study not only for pleasure but for other bodily sensations such as pain or cold (which has been important in the development of Canadian cities – e.g., underground malls connecting buildings – and is central to the issues surrounding homelessness and shelter as well). To focus on pleasure in the urban environment moves towards a momentary suspension of political-economic determinations which structure and legitimate the hierarchy of explanation conventionally appealed to by urban researchers. It also demonstrates the possibility of focusing on the *lack of pleasure* in urban environments and thus of raising questions about our alienation from the cities and towns we live in. Furthermore, questions can be raised concerning *who* experiences pleasure in specific urban environments, and who experiences its opposite, *fear* – an experience of dis-pleasure which is unequally distributed to women (Gardner 1982) and racially stereotyped 'Others' (Phillip 1991) such as visible minorities.

NOTES

1 Is this not the reason why Bosnian muslims play soccer in the middle of a war zone? Let us challenge any geographer or sociologist of leisure to theorize such contingent and fraught moments of pleasure.

2 For a discussion of the way in which the Flâneur was modelled on the natives portrayed in James Fennimore Cooper's early nineteenth-century novels of the American wilderness, see Shields (1994).

3 Above all, the Flâneur is the invention of Dumas (see Shields 1995, Dumas

1863). These works also influenced the formation of the Marxist view of the city and its working populations. Marx spent more time in critiquing Eugène Sue's presentation of French urban society in the mid-1800s than any other literary writer (Sue 1845).

4 The female *flâneuse*, as Janet Wolff (1985) has pointed out, is missing. However,the Flâneur was a primarily literary figure and type of male urban protagonist who allowed writers to maintain a first-person point of view (and thus the fiction of a rational, calculating individual-detective). Concerning the individual, see Shields 1991, Chapter 5.

5 For a fuller discussion see my chapter in King (1995).

6 For example, one Situationist experiment was a 'possible appointment' exercise that involved arranging to meet an unknown person, or attempting to find oneself meeting no one, alone, at a precise time and in a preordained spot. Another was to walk through Germany's Black Forest following a map of London.

REFERENCES

Anderson, B. 1983. *Imagined Communities.* London: Verso.

Bech, H. 1993. Conference paper, presented at 'Spatial differences, sexual preferences' conference, SISWO, Amsterdam, June

Benjamin, W. 1973. 'Paris capital of the 19th century.' In *Reflections: Essays, Aphorisms, Autobiographically Writings.* New York: Harcourt Brace Javonovich

Canetti, E. 1962. *Crowds and Power.* New York: Viking

Debord, G. 1957. 'Report on the construction of situations and on the international situationist tendency's conditions of organisation and action,' translated in Knabb 1988, 17–25

DeCerteau, M. 1984. *The Practice of Everyday Life.* Berkeley: University of California Press

Delaney, J. 1996. 'Civic squares and citizen identity.' PhD Thesis, Department of Art History, State University of New York at Binghamton

Foucault, M. 1973. *The Birth of the Clinic: An Archaeology of Medical Perception* A.M. Sheridan Smith, trans. New York: Vintage/Random House

– 1979. *Discipline and Punish.* New York: Vintage

Gardner, C.B. 1982. 'Analyzing gender in public places.' *American Sociologist* 20: 42–56

Garreau, J. 1991. *Edge City.* New York: Doubleday

Home, S. 1988. *The Assault on Culture. Utopian Currents from Lettrisme to Class War.* London: Aporia Press and Unpopular Books

Jacobs, J. 1984. *The Death and Life of Great American Cities.* Harmondsworth: Penguin, 2nd ed.

King, A. ed. *Representing the Urban.* London and New York: Macmillan 1995.
Knabb, K. 1988. *Situationist International Anthology.* Berkeley: Bureau of Public Secrets
Lefebvre, Henri. 1996. *Writings on Cities.* Oxford: Blackwell
Phillip, N. 1991. *Frontiers.* Toronto: McClelland and Stewart
Riesman, D. 1950. *The Lonely Crowd: A Study of the Changing American Character.* New Haven: Yale University Press
Rybczynski, W. 1988. *Home: A Short History of an Idea.* London: Heinemann
Shields, R. 1991. *Places on the Margin: Alternative Geographies of Modernity.* London: Routledge
– 1994. 'Fancy footwork: Walter Benjamin's notes on Flânerie.' In K. Tester, ed., *The Flâneur.* London: Routledge
Simmel, G. 1950. *The Sociology of Georg Simmel.* K.H. Wolff ed. New York: Free Press
Stewart, K. 1996. A Space by the Side of the Road. Princeton, NJ: Princeton University Press
Tönnies, F. 1957. *Community and Society. Gemeinschaft und Gesellschaft.* London: Harper
Zukin, S. 1991. *Landscapes of Power: From Detroit to Disney World.* Berkeley: University of California Press
– 1995. *Cultures of Cities.* Cambridge, MA: Blackwell

6

Metropolis Unbound: Legislators and Interpreters of Urban Form

ENGIN F. ISIN

Just as we marvel at the rise and fall of the Greek polis or the medieval city, future urban historians will perhaps marvel at the rise and fall of the modern metropolis in the twentieth century. The metropolis was not simply a large city. As Jones (1990) argued, there were large and great cities in history such as Babylon, Rome, and Constantinople – though these were not metropolises. At least since 3000 BC humans have been living in cities. From Ur to Uruk in Mesopotamia, from Mohenjo-daro and Harappa in the Indus Valley to Tikal and Chichén Itzá in Mesoamerica, from Athens in Classical Greece to Lübeck in medieval Germany, the city remained a relatively dense and compact settlement (Mumford 1961: 98; Morris 1994). As Mumford argued, the city remained for millennia a container and a magnet: while it attracted people for security and protection, it focused and gave shape to their energies (Mumford 1961: 543). While the city remained firmly bound by walking distance and early transit technology, it relentlessly expanded in the nineteenth century (Weber 1899). Between the 1851 and 1921 censuses, for example, Canadian industrial cities grew beyond the original boundaries of their settlement and reached an unprecedented size and area (Burke 1990).

As we shall see shortly, the period between 1921 and 1971 was the era of the metropolis: a dominant core city surrounded by several cities, towns and villages economically and socially integrated with it. Yet, since 1971, the continued decentralization of population and employment in the metropolis has been shaping a new urban form that has shattered it. As Gottmann and Harper (1967) state, 'The metropolis was on the move.' By the 1990s most American and Canadian metropolises no longer focus exclusively on the original core cities. New nodes and centres have arisen around the periphery, and these nodes supply most of the daily needs of their adjacent populations. The twentieth-century metropolis has become a polycentric urban region.

This chapter is a review of the arguments put forward by urban policy-makers, practitioners, and planners on the new polycentric urban region since 1971. Rather than focusing on the details of these arguments, however, I review them in broad strokes as mirrored in a few key studies. Borrowing categories from Zygmunt Bauman (1987), I group these arguments into two narratives, 'legislators' and 'interpreters.' Legislators argue against fragmentation and sprawl of the metropolis and urge for regional planning to reverse the trend. Interpreters argue against regional planning and favour current trends. The chapter proceeds as follows. I first describe the concepts metropolis, legislators, and interpreters in more detail. Then I illustrate the transition from metropolis to the polycentric urban form since 1971 with data on Canadian metropolitan growth between 1901 and 1991. I follow these discussions with a critique of the two narratives that evolved since the 1970s against and for the polycentric urban form. I conclude by arguing that both narratives, despite some merits of arguments by 'legislators' against sprawl and fragmentation of the metropolis, are flawed in their neglect of political and economic interests that fuel transformations in urban form. Those legislators who argue against expansion of the new urban regions without analysing the underlying economic and political causes of such changes isolate themselves either into a utopian scheme-building and evangelical advocacy of an 'urban form' they deem satisfactory or into prophets of doom, while those interpreters who celebrate the new, 'postmodern' patterns in urban regions, equally ignorant of underlying economic and political determinants of urban form, serve as apologists for fragmented and formless landscapes of consumption, in which planning urban regions appears redundant.

What *Was* the Metropolis?

As remarkable as its expansion was, the industrial city still remained relatively compact and dense: until the end of the nineteenth century dominant 'commuting' modes in both United States and Canadian cities were walking, carriage, and horse-drawn streetcar. By the 1920s, however, a new urban form was beginning to take shape; it was no longer the compact and dense industrial city but a core city surrounded by a ring of suburbs such as in Montreal and Toronto – the metropolis was in the making. Though the causes of suburban growth were varied and complex, ranging from government policy to practices of utility companies

(Jackson 1985), overall, suburban growth was a reaction to the perceived squalor of the industrial city (Lees 1985). Throughout the twentieth century, the population growth in core Canadian cities levelled off, in core United States cities began declining, and in both the suburbs continually gained in population. This process had begun in the late nineteenth century with the urge to decentralize the city by 'reformers' such as Ebenezer Howard but accelerated in the 1920s with the widespread use of the automobile. With a second wave of suburban expansion, based on a network of urban freeways built during the 1950s and 1960s, the metropolis was crystallized.

The modern metropolis was an urban settlement juxtaposed onto several jurisdictions. It had embodied both annexed and separate municipal jurisdictions and governments within its boundaries. The metropolis was both fragmented and multi-jurisdictional in a way that was distinct to the modern era. It was an economically and socially integrated agglomeration of several municipal corporations, such as townships, towns, villages, and cities, around a core city whose origins reach back to the township system in which American and Canadian territories were settled by European states in the eighteenth and nineteenth centuries (Wood 1982).

Lewis Mumford did not approve of the term 'metropolis' to define this new form of urban settlement that emerged in the 1920s because it meant in classical Greece a mother city that established new cities (Mumford 1961, Blumenfeld 1967). Since the relationship and distance between the Greek mother city and the new polis was very different than that of the modern city, he found this use problematical. Admittedly, the modern relationship between the core city and its peripheries was very different, and it is unnecessary to press the Greek semblance too far. Nevertheless, the term 'metropolis' captured an essential element of this new agglomeration: the modern metropolis as a rule originated in a core city that gradually expanded outward first by the annexation and incorporation of surrounding municipal corporations of varied size and power, and then by entering into formal or informal federal relationships with them. Many United States and Canadian metropolises essentially followed this pattern in the twentieth century (Teaford 1993, Fox 1985).

Who Are the Legislators and Interpreters?

Since the metaphors of 'legislators' and 'interpreters' used here are borrowed from Bauman (1987), a few words of explanation are in order. Bauman attempts to understand the changing role of intellectuals in contemporary economy and society. He defines intellectuals broadly as professionals, writers, academics, and bureaucrats whose positions in society are determined by their relationship with the production, dissemination, and use of knowledge. According to Bauman, therefore, urban policy-makers and planners whose narratives are the object of this chapter can be broadly considered as intellectuals. Bauman identifies two broad roles that intellectuals have fulfilled since the eighteenth century: modern and, more recently, postmodern. Each role assumes a specific view of knowledge and its uses in society. The typically modern view of knowledge is one of mastery over its objects. In this view, knowledge is useful only insofar as it makes prediction and control possible. Modern professions such as policy-making, planning, and design gained legitimacy in this century by virtue of their promise of controlling and predicting their objects – the city. Their 'gaze' is fixed on the city as an object of control and prediction. In the modern view of knowledge, efficacy of control and regulation depends on the adequacy of knowledge. From the modern perspective, the role of the intellectual is characterized as that of the legislator, one who is called on to answer the question: 'What is to be done?' This role consists of making authoritative statements which become binding for policy decisions. The authority to make such statements is legitimized by possession of the knowledge which intellectuals are qualified and certified to produce.

Bauman argued that partly in response to the rigidity of the modern view and partly because of its grand failure in many fields such as in economics and planning, a new, 'postmodern,' view has become dominant among intellectuals. The typically 'postmodern' view of knowledge is one of an unlimited number of statements, each generated by relatively autonomous sets of practices. In this view, knowledge does not aim for authoritative statements but for 'understanding' specific circumstances and contexts in which some statements become true and others false. While the modern view of knowledge always struggles against the relativity of knowledge, the postmodern view sees it as a lasting feature of the world (Bauman 1987: 4). The typically postmodern role of the intellectual is best characterized by the metaphor 'interpreter.' An intellectual, comfortable with relativism, seeks neither engagement with nor intervention in the world. The role of the intellectual is to produce interpretations for the marketplace of ideas. In Zukin's words (1995: 293), 'Many theorists today say that urban spaces can only be interpreted from a variety of different viewpoints, none of which is more authoritative, or more correct, than any others.' Once urban researchers accept and endorse the relativity of viewpoints, however, they lose the grounds on which they can engage with urban spaces. Instead, to merely interpret becomes sufficient in itself. Although such ideal-typical constructs as legislators and interpreters simplify reality, as Sadri (1992) argues, they remain useful by virtue of their assistance in highlighting certain questions. By using these ideal types the question this chapter raises is whether the modern legislator and postmodern interpreter roles and their respective narratives are adequate to understand and regulate the new urban regions that have emerged in the United States and Canada.

The Metropolis Question

The growth of the Canadian metropolis in the twentieth century has been phenomenal. As shown in Table 6.1, Canadian Census Metropolitan Areas (CMAs) have grown continually since 1901. A CMA is defined by Statistics Canada as a core city with a population of at least 100,000, surrounded by cities and towns with a high degree of economic integration. (The United States Bureau of Statistics defines the core city as having a population of at least 50,000.) Although Statistics Canada did not define a CMA until 1951, Table 6.1 attempts to reconstruct metropolitan areas and their core cities between 1901 and 1991, using the definition from the latest census.

In 1901 Montreal was the largest metropolis with a strong core city population of 325,653. But already a sizeable population had surrounded the core city. Toronto was the second largest metropolis with a population of 303,000, of which 218,504 were in the core city. In other Canadian metropolises as well we observe a steady growth, with strong cores and with varying growth patterns in the periphery. As shown in Table 6.2, from 1941 onward, however, the centre of gravity in the metropolis begins to shift from the core cities to the peripheries. This trend is most pronounced in Toronto, Victoria, Quebec, Vancouver, and Montreal metropolitan areas, with these core cities declining to less than a third or a quarter of the metropolitan population between 1941 and 1991. In Toronto, for example, while 73.4 per cent of the metropolitan population lived in the City of Toronto in 1941, it had declined to 16.3 per cent by 1991. As Frisken (1993) argued, the Municipality of Metropolitan Toronto itself became a core city in the sprawling urban region. Similarly, in 1941 the City of Montreal constituted 78.9 per cent of the entire metropolis. In 1991, despite the fact that the City of Montreal is the largest city in Canada with a population of more than a million people, it constitutes a mere 32.5 per cent of the entire metropolis. In metropolises such as Winnipeg, Calgary, and Regina, where core cities still constitute the majority of the metropolitan population, core areas still lost their dominance, and the CMAs grew by annexation.

When we shift from individual metropolises to general statistics, the trend towards first metropolitan concentration and later towards the decentralization of the metropolis becomes clearer. As shown in Table 6.3, while in 1901 only 24.9 per cent of Canadians lived in metropolitan areas (defined retrospectively by using 1991 CMA boundaries), by 1951, 42.5 per cent of Canadians were living in metropolitan areas centred around the core cities founded originally as towns, townships, or cities (Stone 1967). By 1991 Canadians living in metropolitan areas reached 61.0 per cent. With the exception of 1901–11 and 1971–81, in every decade since 1901 the metropolitan growth rate was above that of the national population growth rate as well as the urban growth rate. For the decade 1971–81, a decline in the metropolitan growth rate was briefly seen as a trend towards de-urbanization; Blumenfeld (1986), however, demonstrated that for both the United States and Canada, much of 'metropolitan growth' was occurring in that decade in areas contiguous to metropolitan areas not yet defined as metropolitan. The early twentieth century in Canada was the century of the metropolis. Yet, as the trend towards the *concentration* of population in the metropolis was continuing, another trend, towards *decentralization* in the metropolis, is clearly visible (Blumenfeld 1967). The core city population made up 77.3 per cent of the entire metropolis in 1901, it reached 86.0 per cent in 1911, and hovered around 70.0 per cent until 1941, when it began a steady decline, hitting 43.0 per cent by 1991.

When we break down these trends towards metropolitan concentration and then towards decentralization by province and region, as shown in Tables 6.4 and 6.5, Ontario and Quebec stand out as prominent examples. In Ontario the metropolitan proportion of the population was 29.0 per cent in 1901, and increased to a significant 72.4 per cent by 1991. In other words, almost three-quarters of Ontarians (7,300,386) were living in nine metropolises in 1991. More impressively, by 1991, 61.0 per cent of Quebecois (4,209,217) were living in only four metropolises.

Similar trends were also evident in British Columbia, as shown in Table 6.6. There, the metropolitan population was 55.0 per cent in 1921 and reached 58 per cent by 1991, concentrating in only two metropolises. As well, the metropolitan growth rate was dominant between 1951 and 1981. As in Ontario and Quebec, the core city steadily lost its relative weight in the metropolis. In 1921 the core city population made up 70.0 per cent of

TABLE 6.1
Canadian Census Metropolitan Areas (CMA) and Core Cities, 1901–1991

CMA/Core city	1901	1911	1921	1931	1941	1951	1961	1971	1981	1991
Calgary					**93,021**	**142,316**	**279,062**	**403,319**	**692,743**	**754,033**
City of Calgary	4,392	43,704	63,305	83,761	88,904	133,492	249,641	403,319	592,743	710,677
Chicoutimi – Jonquiere						**76,059**	**105,009**	**133,703**	**135,172**	**160,928**
City of Chicoutimi	3,826	5,880	8,937	11,877	16,040	24,530	31,657	33,893	60,064	62,670
City of Jonquière		2,354	4,851	9,448	13,769	21,618	28,588	28,430	60,354	57,933
Edmonton					**97,842**	**176,782**	**337,568**	**459,702**	**657,057**	**839,924**
City of Edmonton	4,176	31,064	58,821	79,197	93,817	160,691	281,027	438,152	532,246	616,741
Halifax					**98,636**	**133,931**	**183,946**	**222,637**	**277,727**	**320,501**
City of Halifax	40,832	46,619	58,372	59,275	70,488	85,589	92,511	122,035	114,594	253,704
Hamilton					**197,732**	**280,293**	**395,189**	**498,523**	**542,095**	**599,769**
City of Hamilton	52,634	81,969	114,151	155,547	166,337	224,951	273,991	309,173	306,434	318,499
Kitchener					**63,009**	**107,474**	**154,864**	**226,846**	**287,801**	**356,421**
City of Kitchener	9,747	15,196	21,763	30,793	35,657	49,821	74,485	111,804	139,734	168,282
London					**91,024**	**128,977**	**181,283**	**286,011**	**283,668**	**381,522**
City of London	37,976	46,300	60,959	71,148	78,264	120,356	169,569	223,222	254,280	303,165
Montreal					**1,145,282**	**1,471,851**	**2,109,509**	**2,743,208**	**2,828,349**	**3,127,242**
City of Montreal	325,653	490,504	618,506	818,577	903,007	1,021,520	1,191,062	1,214,352	980,354	1,017,666
Oshawa						**51,582**	**80,918**	**120,318**	**154,217**	**240,104**
City of Oshawa	4,394	7,346	11,940	23,439	26,813	41,545	62,415	91,587	117,519	129,344
Ottawa–Hull					**226,290**	**292,476**	**429,650**	**602,510**	**717,978**	**920,857**
City of Ottawa	64,226	87,062	107,843	126,872	154,951	202,045	268,206	302,341	295,163	313,987
City of Hull	13,993	18,222	24,117	29,433	32,947	44,687	82,713	63,580	56,225	60,707
Quebec					**224,756**	**276,242**	**357,568**	**480,502**	**576,075**	**645,550**
Quebec City	68,840	78,118	95,193	130,594	150,757	164,016	171,979	186,088	166,474	167,517
Regina								**140,734**	**164,313**	**191,692**
City of Regina	2,249	30,213	34,432	53,209	58,245	71,319	112,141	139,469	162,613	179,178

Saint John					**70,927**	**78,337**	**95,563**	**106,744**	**114,048**	**124,981**
City of Saint John	40,711	42,511	47,166	47,514	51,741	50,779	55,153	89,039	80,521	74,969
Saskatoon								**126,449**	**154,210**	**210,023**
City of Saskatoon	113	12,004	25,739	43,291	43,027	53,268	95,526	126,449	154,210	186,058
Sherbrooke					**56,128**	**54,511**	**70,253**	**84,570**	**115,983**	**139,194**
City of Sherbrooke	11,765	16,405	23,515	28,933	35,956	51,616	66,554	80,711	74,075	76,429
St Catharines–Niagara						**67,303**	**95,577**	**303,429**	**304,353**	**364,552**
City of St Catharines	9,946	12,484	19,861	24,753	30,275	59,302	84,472	109,722	124,018	129,300
St John's						**68,620**	**90,838**	**131,814**	**154,820**	**171,859**
City of St John's						52,873	63,633	88,102	83,770	95,770
Sudbury					**78,884**	**73,826**	**110,694**	**155,424**	**149,923**	**157,613**
City of Sudbury	2,027	4,150	8,621	18,518	32,203	56,903	80,120	90,535	91,829	92,884
Thunder Bay								**112,093**	**121,379**	**124,427**
City of Thunder Bay								108,411	112,486	113,946
Toronto					**909,928**	**1,210,353**	**1,824,481**	**2,628,043**	**2,998,947**	**3,893,046**
City of Toronto	218,504	381,833	521,893	631,207	667,457	675,754	672,407	712,786	599,217	635,395
Trois-Rivières					**68,306**	**65,946**	**83,659**	**97,930**	**111,453**	**136,303**
City of Trois-Rivières	9,981	13,691	22,367	35,450	42,007	46,074	53,477	55,869	50,466	49,426
Vancouver					**377,477**	**561,960**	**790,165**	**1,082,352**	**1,268,183**	**1,602,502**
City of Vancouver	29,432	120,847	163,220	246,593	275,353	344,833	384,522	426,256	414,281	471,844
Victoria					**75,560**	**113,207**	**154,152**	**195,800**	**233,481**	**287,897**
City of Victoria	20,919	31,660	38,727	39,082	44,068	51,331	54,941	61,761	64,379	71,228
Windsor					**123,973**	**163,618**	**193,365**	**258,643**	**246,110**	**262,075**
City of Windsor	15,198	23,433	55,935	98,179	104,311	120,049	114,367	203,300	192,083	191,435
Winnipeg					**299,937**	**350,813**	**475,989**	**540,262**	**584,842**	**652,354**
City of Winnipeg	42,340	136,035	179,087	218,785	221,960	235,710	265,429	246,246	564,473	616,790

Source: Statistics Canada, Census, 1901–1991. Note that Census Metropolitan Area (CMA) was first defined in 1951. CMA population counts before 1951 are calculated by taking 1991 boundary definitions of core and fringe census subdivisions (CSDs), which are incorporated municipalities.

TABLE 6.2
Percentage Share of Core City in CMA Population, 1901–1991

CMA	1941	1951	1961	1971	1981	1991
Toronto	73.35	55.83	36.85	27.12	19.98	16.32
Victoria	58.32	45.34	35164	31.54	27.57	24.74
Quebec	67.08	59.37	48.10	38.73	28.90	25.95
Vancouver	72.95	61.36	48.66	39.38	32.67	29.44
Montreal	78.85	69.40	56.46	44.27	34.66	32.54
St Catharines–Niagara		88.11	88.38	36.16	40.65	35.47
Trois-Rivières	61.50	59.87	63.92	57.05	45.28	36.26
Ottawa–Hull	83.03	84.36	81.66	60.73	48.94	40.69
Kitchener	56.59	46.36	48.10	49.29	48.55	47.21
Hamilton	84.12	80.26	59.33	62.02	56.53	53.10
Oshawa		80.54	77.13	76.12	76.20	53.87
Sherbrooke	64.08	94.59	94.73	95.44	63.87	54.91
St John's		77.05	70.05	66.84	54.11	55.73
Sudbury	40.82	77.08	72.38	58.25	61.25	59.93
Saint John	72.95	64.82	57.71	83.41	70.50	59.98
Windsor	84.95	73.37	59.15	78.60	78.05	73.05
Edmonton	95.89	90.90	83.25	88.39	81.00	73.43
Chicoutimi–Jonquière		60.67	57.37	46.61	89.09	74.94
Halifax	71.46	63.91	50.29	54.81	41.26	79.16
London	85.98	93.32	93.54	78.05	89.64	79.46
Saskatoon				100.00	100.00	88.59
Thunder Bay				96.72	92.67	91.58
Regina				99.10	98.97	93.47
Calgary	95.57	93.80	89.46	100.00	100.00	94.25
Winnipeg	74.00	67.19	55.76	45.58	96.52	94.55
All CMAs	80.01	70.04	59.08	49.82	46.79	43.00

Source: Calculated from Table 1. Note that CMAs are sorted in ascending order of 1991 core percentage. Significant rises or declines in core city percentages such as in St Catharines between 1961 and 1971, Sherbrooke between 1971 and 1981 and Chicoutimi-Jonquière between 1971 and 1981 are due to boundary changes in Census Subdivisions or Census Metropolitan Areas.

the metropolis, declining to 59.0 per cent in 1951, to 38.0 per cent in 1971, and to 29.0 per cent in 1991.

When we examine the metropolis in the Prairies and Maritimes, in Tables 6.7 and 6.8, we find these trends less pronounced than in other provinces, though the direction is similar. Unlike the three largest provinces, the core city in the Prairies and Maritimes metropolises, seems to have maintained its relative weight, with 87.0 per cent and 69.0 per cent, of the metropolitan population in 1991. However, this is more a reflec-

TABLE 6.3
Urban Growth in Canada, 1901–1991

	1901	1911	1921	1931	1941	1951	1961	1971	1981	1991
Canada	5,371,315	7,206,643	8,787,949	10,376,786	11,506,655	14,009,429	18,238,247	21,568,311	24,343,181	27,296,859
Urban Canada	2,014,222	3,272,947	4,352,122	5,572,058	6,252,416	7,941,222	11,068,848	14,114,970	18,435,927	20,907,135
Metropolitan Canada	1,338,000	2,076,000	3,103,000	4,098,000	4,298,712	5,946,476	8,599,402	12,177,566	13,774,927	16,665,369
Core cities	1,033,874	1,779,604	2,389,321	3,115,475	3,439,363	4,164,673	5,080,586	6,066,632	6,444,605	7,165,544
% Urban	37.50	45.42	49.52	53.70	54.34	56.68	60.69	65.44	75.73	76.59
% Metropolitan	24.91	28.81	35.31	39.49	37.36	42.45	47.15	56.46	56.59	61.05
% Core urban	19.25	24.59	27.19	30.02	29.89	29.73	27.86	28.13	26.47	26.25
% Core city in metropolis	77.27	85.72	77.00	76.02	80.01	70.04	59.08	49.82	46.79	43.00
% Population growth rate		34.17	21.94	18.08	10.89	21.75	30.19	18.26	12.87	12.13
% Urban growth rate		62.49	32.97	28.03	12.21	27.01	39.38	27.52	30.61	13.40
% Metropolitan growth rate		55.16	49.47	32.07	4.90	38.33	44.61	41.61	13.12	20.98

Source: Statistics Canada, Census, 1901–1991. Urban population by provincial breakdown (1901–1961) are from Census of Canada 1961, Catalogue 92-536, Table 12. For census years 1901 to 1961. Statistics Canada defined urban population as the population living in incorporated villages, towns, and cities. For 1971, Catalogue 92-709, Table 10; for 1981, Catalogue 93-901, Table 2; for 1991, Catalogue 93-305, Table 3. For 1971, 1981, and 1991 urban population was defined as the population living in an area with 1,000 people or more and a population density of at least 1,000 persons per square mile. Metropolitan population for 1901 to 1931 (Stone 1967).

TABLE 6.4
Urban Growth in Ontario, 1901–1991

	1901	1911	1921	1931	1941	1951	1961	1971	1981	1991
Ontario	2,182,947	2,527,292	2,933,662	3,431,683	3,787,655	4,597,542	6,236,092	7,703,105	8,625,107	10,084,885
Urban Ontario	935,978	1,328,489	1,706,632	2,095,992	2,338,633	2,753,226	3,620,736	6,343,630	7,047,032	8,253,842
Metropolitan Ontario	629,000	908,000	1,266,000	1,640,000	1,690,840	2,375,902	3,466,121	5,191,840	5,806,471	7,300,386
Core cities	414,652	659,773	922,966	1,180,456	1,297,268	1,550,727	1,800,032	2,262,881	2,232,763	2,396,237
% Urban	42.88	52.57	48,17	61.08	61.74	59.88	58.06	82.35	81.780	81.84
% Metropolitan	28.81	35.93	43.15	27.79	44.64	51.68	55.58	67.40	67.32	72.39
% Core urban	19.00	26.11	31.46	34.40	34.25	33.73	28.86	29.38	25.89	23.76
% Core city in metropolis	65.92	72.66	72.90	71.98	76.72	65.27	51.93	43.59	38.45	32.82
% Population growth rate	—	15.77	16.08	16.98	10.37	21.38	35.64	23.52	11.97	16.92
% Urban growth rate	—	41.94	28.46	22.81	11.58	17.73	31.51	75.20	11.09	17.13
% Metropolitan growth rate	—	44.36	39.43	29.54	3.10	40.52	45.89	49.79	11.84	25.73

Source: Statistics Canada, Census, 1901–1991. Metropolitan population for 1901 to 1931 (Stone 1967).

TABLE 6.5
Urban Growth in Quebec, 1901–1991

	1901	1911	1921	1931	1941	1951	1961	1971	1981	1991
Quebec	1,648,898	2,005,776	2,360,610	2,874,662	3,331,882	4,055,681	5,259,211	6,027,765	6,438,403	6,895,963
Urban Quebec	654,065	966,842	1,322,569	1,813,606	2,109,684	2,728,798	3,900,560	4,861,245	4,993,839	5,351,211
Metropolitan Quebec	532,000	750,000	954,000	1,292,000	1,494,472	1,944,609	2,725,998	3,539,913	3,767,032	4,209,217
Core cities	365,218	547,056	702,293	933,718	1,043,735	1,210,045	1,454,051	1,476,835	1,281,538	1,324,831
% Urban	39.67	48.20	56.03	63.09	63.32	67.38	74.17	80.65	77.56	77.60
% Metropolitan	32.26	37.39	40.41	44.94	44.85	47.95	51.83	58.73	58.51	61.04
% Core urban	22.15	27.27	29.75	32.48	31.33	29.84	27.65	24.50	19.90	19.21
% Core city in metropolis	68.65	72.94	73.62	72.27	69.84	62.23	53.34	41.72	34.02	31.47
% Population growth rate	—	21.64	17.69	21.78	15.91	21.72	29.68	14.51	6.81	7.11
% Urban growth rate	—	47.82	36.79	27.13	16.33	29.35	42.94	24.63	2.73	7.16
% Metropolitan growth rate	—	40.98	27.20	35.43	15.67	30.12	40.18	29.86	6.42	11.74

Source: Statistics Canada, Census, 1901–1991. Metropolitan population for 1901 to 1931 (Stone 1967).

TABLE 6.6
Urban Growth in British Columbia, 1901–1991

	1901	1911	1921	1931	1941	1951	1961	1971	1981	1991
BC	178,657	392,480	524,582	694,263	817,861	1,165,210	1,629,082	2,184,620	2,744,467	3,282,061
Urban BC	90,179	203,684	247,562	394,729	443,394	615,052	781,924	1,654,405	2,139,412	2,640,139
Metropolitan BC	—	—	287,000	408,000	453,037	675,167	944,317	1,278,152	1,501,664	1,890,399
Core cities	50,351	152,507	201,947	286,675	319,421	396,164	439,463	488,017	478,660	543,072
% Urban	50.48	51.90	47.19	56.86	54.21	52.78	48.00	75,73	77.95	80.44
% Metropolitan	—	—	54.71	58.77	55.39	57.94	57.97	58.51	54.72	57.60
% Core urban	28.18	38.86	38.50	41.15	39.06	34.00	26.98	22.34	17.44	16.55
% Core city in metropolis	—	—	70.36	70.02	70.51	58.68	46.54	38.18	31.88	28.73
% Population growth rate	—	119.68	33.66	32.35	17.80	42.47	39.81	34.10	25.63	19.59
% Urban growth rate	—	125.87	21.54	59.45	12.33	38.71	27.13	111.58	29.32	23.40
% Metropolitan growth rate	—	—	—	42.16	11.04	49.03	39.86	35.35	17.49	25.89

Source: Statistics Canada, Census, 1901–1991. Metropolitan population for 1921 and 1931 (Stone 1967).

TABLE 6.7
Urban Growth in Prairies, 1901–1991

	1901	1911	1921	1931	1941	1951	1961	1971	1981	1991
Prairies	419,612	1,328,121	1,956,082	2,353,529	2,421,905	2,547,770	3,178,811	3,542,365	4,232,278	4,626,423
Urban Prairies	103,235	469,422	703,478	885,382	923,605	1,2453,298	1,968,206	2,373,330	3,021,370	3,441,465
Metropolitan Prairies	76,000	307,000	459,000	616,000	657,000	853,000	1,092,619	1,706,466	2,153,165	2,648,026
Core cities	53,270	253,020	361,384	478,243	505,953	654,480	1,003,765	1,353,635	2,006,285	2,309,444
% Urban	24.61	35.34	35.96	27.62	38.14	48.80	61.92	67.00	71.39	74.39
% Metropolitan	18.12	23.12	23.47	26.17	27.13	33.48	34.37	48.17	50.87	57.24
% Core urban	12.70	19.05	18.47	20.32	20.89	25.69	31.58	28.21	47.40	49.92
% Core city in metropolis	70.09	82.42	78.73	77.64	77.01	76.73	91.87	79.32	93.18	87.21
% Population growth rate	—	216.59	47.28	20.32	2.91	5.20	24.77	11.44	19.48	9.31
% Urban growth rate	—	354.71	49.86	25.86	4.32	34.61	58.31	20.58	27.31	13.90
% Metropolitan growth rate	—	303.95	49.51	34.20	6.66	29.83	28.09	56.18	26.18	22.98

Source: Statistics Canada, Census, 1901–1991. Metropolitan population for 1901 to 1951 (Stone 1967).

TABLE 6.8
Urban Growth in Maritimes, 1901–1991

	1901	1911	1921	1931	1941	1951	1961	1971	1981	1991
Maritimes	893,953	937,955	1,000,328	1,009,103	1,130,410	1,618,126	1,897,425	2,057,260	2,234,032	2,322,081
Urban Maritimes	221,623	200,645	270,575	280,979	435,303	597,230	791,158	1,150,130	1,197,475	1,182,986
Metropolitan Maritimes	102,000	111,000	138,000	141,000	169,563	280,888	370,347	461,195	546,595	617,341
Core cities	81,543	89,130	105,538	106,789	122,229	189,241	211,297	299,176	278,885	424,443
% Urban	24.79	32.05	37.05	37.75	38.51	26.91	41.70	55.91	53.60	50.95
% Metropolitan	11.41	11.83	13.80	13.97	15.00	17.36	19.52	22.42	24.47	26.59
% Core urban	9.12	9.50	10.55	10.58	10.81	11.70	11.14	14.54	12.48	18.28
% Core city in metropolis	79.94	80.30	76.48	75.74	72.08	67.37	57.05	64.87	51.02	68.75
% Population growth rate		4.29	6.65	0.88	12.02	43.15	17.26	8.42	8.59	3.94
% Urban growth rate		35.66	23.26	2.81	14.26	27.20	32.47	45.37	4.12	-1.21
% Metropolitan growth rate		8.82	24.32	2.17	20.26	65.65	31.85	24.53	18.52	12.94

Source: Statistics Canada, Census, 1901–1991. Metropolitan population for 1901 to 1931 (Stone 1967).

tion of the scale of our analysis based on Census Subdivisions (CSDs) than of real differences. In the Prairies and Maritimes, the metropolis grew largely through the annexation of surrounding jurisdictions rather than developing a fragmented and fractured form. An analysis based on a finer scale such as the Census Tracts (CTs) would have revealed this fragmentation. In metropolises such as Calgary, Edmonton, and Halifax the political fragmentation is as significant as in other metropolises (Sancton 1992, 1994).

The data confirm the century of the metropolis: Canada has not simply been a highly urbanized country in this century but its urbanization took a metropolitan form. However, although the CMA population statistics presented cannot alone confirm it, another trend particularly since the 1970s is visible. As the decentralization of the metropolis continued, since the 1970s, growth has taken place in several nodes or centres around the periphery of the metropolis. In the Toronto region, for example, such 'edge' cities as Mississauga, Markham, Vaughan, Richmond Hill, and Oakville were among the fastest growing centres across the country. Nor has this growth been limited to population alone. As the core cities continued to lose their employment in industrial and office occupations, the edge cities became significant centres of employment in office and new types of industrial employment (Bourne and Olvet 1995). There has been a clear shift of employment and population from the core city as a centre of gravity in the metropolis towards multiple centres of growth (Bourne 1995). In other words, the Canadian metropolis became unbound from the 1970s. The resulting urban regions with their multiple centres of employment and population growth and multi-directional commuting patterns have become the new urban form. Many Canadians, almost 17 million, whose everyday lives revolve around such urban regions can easily juxtapose onto these statistics everyday experiences of their fragmented, sprawling, and fractured geography. They can relate these statistics to the low-density, commercial, industrial, and residential strip 'developments' that run along highways, regional shopping malls, and superstores dotted across the landscape; expressways dominating visually and spatially the main arteries of the urban region and the ubiquitous automobile.

The 'exploding' metropolis became a concern for policy-makers, practitioners, and planners early in this century. Since the 1920s, 'the metropolis question' preoccupied and evaded various policy initiatives at various governmental levels. The metropolis question has presented urban policy-makers with a bundle of distinct but interrelated problems. Two of these problems can be briefly mentioned. First is the question of governance: how to provide and deliver services traditionally associated with municipal governments in an area marked by several municipal governments, often in competition and conflict with one another. 'Governing the metropolis' became one of the most complex questions in modern democratic societies in this century. Although no model emerged to muster all complexities of metropolitan government, there were nevertheless some attempts, such as Metropolitan Toronto established in 1953, though in the long run it too failed to deal with the complexities of the urban region – the metropolis unbound (Frisken 1993). The question of metropolitan governance is beyond the scope of this chapter (see Rothblatt and Sancton 1993; Sancton 1993, 1994). Second, the problem of planning the metropolis with multiple and conflicting jurisdictions also proved to be elusive. In a way, 'metropolitan planning' became an oxymoron for this century. There are, of course, many aspects of metropolitan planning, but the predominant focus has been on 'urban form.' Just as the metropolitan question had never been adequately addressed or solved, the nature of the question changed dramatically with the metropolis unbound. Since the 1970s there have been many studies and policies declaring 'halting sprawl,' 'sustainability,' 'intensification,' and 'liveability' as their objectives and urging for the reversal of trends towards a dispersed metropolis and the polycentric urban region.

Metropolis and Gaze: Two Narratives

The metropolis unbound became the object of gaze of both legislators and interpreters. Especially since the end of the Second World War the control and regulation of the metropolis has been one of the most debated issues in urban policy. In Europe, North America, and Australia, there has been a discourse – constituted in different terms at different times and milieus – about whether metropolitan sprawl should be avoided or whether containment of urban growth requires far greater planning controls than are available in Western democracies.

Two narratives on the new urban form have evolved. The sources from which these two narratives are compiled for this chapter are varied: they range from print and visual media discussions of the new urban regions, popular magazine and academic articles, legislation, and documents by various levels of government such as federal, state, provincial, and municipal, public and private sector reports, and studies conducted by research institutes and academics (see Isin and Tomalty 1993a). The sources also include the results of a national survey of planning directors and officials in every municipality in all twenty-five Census Metropolitan Areas in Canada (see Isin and Tomalty 1993b).

The first narrative that evolved on urban form was that of the legislators. The legislators urged greater regulation and control of metropolitan form and, over twenty years, they essentially made four arguments diagnosing the ills of the new urban form: the 'sprawling' urban form was (i) socially alienating, (ii) economically unsustainable, (iii) environmentally destructive, and (iv) aesthetically displeasing. Legislators believed that low residential and commercial densities in plazas, shopping malls, neighbourhoods, and workplaces created social alienation and isolation. Research poured forth declaring the suburbs as places of incarceration of women, children, and youth. Research also showed that the poor, the marginal, and the oppressed were excluded from the outer suburbs of the metropolis, creating a segregation based on class, gender, and ethnicity. As a result, legislators argued, the suburbs created segregation that leads to intolerance and racism.

The narrative of legislators also focused on the economics and cost of the new urban form. Legislators argued that, because of low densities, per capita costs of providing sewage, water, waste, education, and social and other services were much higher in the suburbs. 'Costs of sprawl' became one of the factors explaining the higher costs of suburban public services. Legislators argued that in individual terms the suburbs may cost less but in social terms, low-density developments incurred enormous costs, in providing and maintaining municipal services, which were subsidized by governments.

As for the environmental consequences of the new urban form the legislators emphasized the loss of agricultural land and of other natural areas, and the increasing dependency on the automobile as the consequence of low densities. Legislators argued that by losing more agricultural land to urban development every year, the city became more dependent on outside food sources, and hence vulnerable to external market fluctuations. As well, by sprawling into natural areas, the city depleted areas available for leisure and recreation. The sprawling urban form also encouraged automobile use to the extent that the city became one of the major contributors to air pollution, and hence to global warming. Finally, the legislators did not find the bland, repetitive, mass-manufactured, and homogeneous, in short tasteless, appearances of the low-density suburbs aesthetically pleasing either.

As a result of their diagnosis and prognosis on the new urban form, legislators urged local and regional intensification. Regional intensification would mean reversing the decline of the core city and re-establishing its relative population and employment weight in the region. As such it was a radical proposal whose implementation proved elusive. Local or nodal intensification would mean increasing the density of regional centres already developed (Barnett 1995, Calthorpe 1993). The latter has become the emphasis of 'new urbanism' or 'neo-traditional planning' exercises that gained much attention in the 1990s (Katz 1994, Duany and Plater-Zyberk 1992). Yet, despite the widespread attention to new urbanism and intensification initiatives, the outward expansion of the metropolis into a polycentric urban region continued unabated.

The interpreters of urban form disagreed not only with the diagnosis of the legislators but also with their recommendations. They countered legislators with their own myths and metaphors. They argued that social alienation in the suburbs is a myth created by intellectuals and professionals in the core city. The suburbs were, moreover, no longer 'sub'; they were as socially and economically differentiated as the core city. As city intellectuals created their myths, the suburbs, interpreters argued, were transformed into vital, vibrant, edge cities, which were now the next frontier of urbanism. Studies poured forth to illustrate that the suburbs were no longer the bastion of the middle class, but of varied ethnic, economic, and social groups.

As for the economic consequences of sprawl, some interpreters brought forward a body of research that claimed there were no discernible differences in terms of the cost of providing services in the suburbs versus the core cities. Regarding the environmental effects of sprawl, the interpreters argued that the loss of agricultural land is the result of market forces, not urban form. As well, the interpreters argued, automobile use in the United States and Canada was linked to much deeper causes than urban form. The narrative of the interpreters included such metaphors as 'choice' and 'liberty.' According to this narrative, urban form is a result of markets in which consumers and producers enter into exchange relationships. Urban form is an outcome of the entire set of exchange relationships mediated by morals, desires, technology, and law. Altering urban form would mean altering exchange relationships in society for which the legislators have neither the mandate nor the power. Consumers make free choices guided by their desires and morals of a good life. If the resultant urban form does not satisfy the aims of legislators and their public policy objectives, it is not the fault of consumers but of the policies of legislators.

There are serious flaws in each narrative and its metaphors, some of which have been pointed out (Gottdiener 1994). While the arguments about the consequences of the sprawling metropolis revolve around whether higher or lower density environments are more liveable, sustainable, and equitable, there are conflicting attitudes on the existing relationship between planning as a government activity and the market economy. Most legislators and interpreters would recognize a role for each to play, but differ on where to draw the line. For example, legislators favour a more prominent role for government planning agencies as a means of achieving the diverse social goals associated with planning. Interpreters tend to side with a greater role for the market and contend that intervening in the market to produce high density communities clearly violates the wishes of most consumers and will result in market 'distortions.' Each, however, assumes that government urban policy consists of what urban policy-makers and planners do and say. On the contrary, other government authorities engage in investments and other types of decisions that produce significant effects on the urban form. In urban regions such as Toronto, Montreal, and Vancouver, for example, decisions such as building highways, sewage trunks, waste treatment plants, and energy corridors, as well as the location of major government offices are made by and large beyond and outside the control of urban policy-makers and planners as such. While in one provincial ministry planners may be urging for regional and local intensification, in another ministry decisions such as building a major highway would be given on economic and other grounds without regard for planning authorities or their proclaimed policies. As well, 'non-urban' policies such as taxation, economic development, and provision and delivery of social services have major impacts on urban form. Both legislators and interpreters tacitly and wrongly assume that planning powers are concentrated in planning authorities, while the realities of how urban form is produced belie such concentration. Rather, the role of government policy in the production of urban form is much more diffuse, contradictory, unintentional, and staggered than admitted.

Still, both narratives suffer from a deeper flaw that legislators and interpreters so far have not acknowledged. This concerns the issues of causality and power.

The first issue concerns the relationship between cause and effect. Legislators often ascribe causal attributes to urban form such as 'alienation' or 'incarceration.' The question arises as to whether urban form causes social, political, and economic effects. Admittedly, urban form does result in certain consequences such as long commuting times. In the narrative of legislators, however, such consequences as long commuting times become causes of social ills such as family breakdown, social isolation, and alienation. By such questionable logical operations, the legislators attribute causal powers to urban form. They constitute it as a cause of social, economic, and environmental problems. By doing so, they stray away from discussing the complex interplay between urban form and contemporary economy and society.

As for interpreters, they reverse the cause-effect relationships assumed by legislators. They often argue that urban form is either an effect of forces that are beyond the control of individuals and institutions (structuralism) or an effect of individual decisions (voluntarism). Fishman, for example, manages to hold both structuralist and voluntarist positions at the same time. By calling the new suburbs the 'techno-city,' Fishman makes reference to Fernand Braudel and his colleagues 'who have called attention to the remarkable power of "structures" in history: deep patterns of economic and social necessity that operate with little regard for individual plans or government initiatives. Whatever its validity for history as a whole, this view has its value for explaining the emergence of the techno-city' (Fishman 1987: 189). He claims that 'the history of the techno-burb ... is the history of those deeper structural features of modern society ... taking precedence over conscious intentions' (Fishman 1987: 192). Yet, Fishman also thinks that the new city 'was built up piecemeal, as a result of millions of uncoordinated decisions made by housing developers, shopping-mall operators, corporate executives, highway engineers and, not least, the millions of Americans who saved and sacrificed to buy single-family homes in the expanding suburbs' (Fishman 1990: 29–30). Similarly, Garreau argues that 'it was stunning how completely it was the developers who turned out to be our master city builders. The developers were the ones who envisioned the projects, acquired the land, exercised the planning, got the money, hired the architects if there were any, lined up the builders, and managed the project to completion.' (Garreau 1991: 220). By seeing urban form as an effect of either immutable market forces or as a result of free choices of individuals, the interpreters ascribe magical and mystical qualities to the production of urban form.

The second issue is more serious. Both legislators and interpreters are conveniently oblivious to relationships of power at work in producing specific urban forms in different societies – power relations in which both interpreters and legislators are involved but who conceal their own positions in different ways. Legislators assume much more power than they practically possess. By focusing on the negative consequences of sprawl without analysing the underlying causes of such an urban form they urge its radical reversal. Meanwhile, they assume that an entire network of power relationships from the automobile producers to advertising and media agencies, from national retail chains to multinational financiers can be kept intact. The interpreters by and large agree with the tacit assumption of the legislators that power relations in society will not and should not change. They achieve this position by ascribing immutable qualities to such abstract forces as markets and consumers.

By examining both narratives one is struck by the fact that the underlying social, political, and economic causes of the metropolis unbound are rarely, if at all, mentioned. Instead, it is assumed for one reason or another that the metropolis became geographically unbound. While those who find nothing wrong with this 'geographical restructuring' resulting in a new urban form (Garreau 1991, Fishman 1990, Muller 1989) argue that it is the expression of the desire of people, those who do see grave consequences suggest remedies for reversing the trend and intensifying land use in the metropolis (Downs 1994, Calthorpe 1993, Barnett 1995, Kunstler 1993). Both legislators and interpreters fail to consider underlying economic, political, and social interests that create such a pattern, and hence ignore a fundamental assumption of critical urban analysis that urban form is both an expression and embodiment of the economy and society in which it unfolds (Mumford 1938, Morris 1994, Gottdiener 1994).

While urging for intensification, the legislators are burdened by an unbearable thought: despite several decades of advocacy, obviously the interests and practices that unbound the metropolis are far more forceful than the interests and practices that urge intensification (see Teaford 1993). With all their rhetoric, the planning and policy professions are not nearly as powerful as they arrogate themselves to be when they urge grandiose reversals in metropolitan land use patterns. Judging by the criteria that legislators set for themselves, and the relationship of what they urge and what results on the ground, the metropolis unbound is a dismal failure. After nearly fifty years of advocacy for a more dense and compact urban form, legislators find this burden inconvenient as they continue to urge massive reversal in the shape of the metropolis without considering either the consequences of this reversal or the causes of its continuing expansion.

The burden on interpreters is equally heavy. While they continue to argue for the benefits or the inevitability of sprawl, they resort to explanations based on the 'natural' instincts and the desires of people to live in a sprawling metropolis. They become apologists for a shapeless, formless, and vast mess, which Kunstler (1993) calls the 'geography of nowhere.' The new apologist Witold Rybczynski, for example, quotes Canadian architect Moshe Safdie with approval: 'Policy for the coming decades cannot rest on the premise of forcing a reversal of the desire to disperse, but rather, on facilitating and shaping our wanderings: creating new centres of concentration within sprawling districts – in other words, designing the best of both worlds' (Rybczynski 1995: 232). He describes this new world as 'Frank Lloyd Wright's Broadacre City meets Jane Jacobs's Greenwich Village.' And he adds, 'This will please neither the advocates of traditional urbanism [legislators] not the edge city boosters [interpreters], but its chaotic, ideological impurity may be a more truthful accommodation to the way we live today' (1995: 233). Rybczynski's position appears awfully close to the 'edge city boosters' whom he criticizes with his approach towards how we build cities: the new city becomes simply a reflection of a 'desire to disperse' and 'freedom of mobility.'

In an age of powerful 'technologies of the self' such as the print, audio, and visual media, it is doubtful that such desires reflect innate qualities rather than inculcated habits. Just consider the following. If a fraction of the massive spending on advertising by the three big automobile producers in the United States had been put into illustrating the virtues or the 'ethics of high density living,' as Gottmann (1990) put it, would people have the same desire for the automobile or home ownership? To consider such desires as owning an automobile or a home with a large backyard as innate or even legitimate desires is to turn a blind eye to the mechanisms through which such desires become inculcated in our society. One of the richest and most fruitful legacies of the French philosopher Michel Foucault was to question such desires as innate (Martin, et al. 1988). Similarly, French sociologist Pierre Bourdieu (1984) argued rather persuasively that taste is an embodiment of class relations rather than an expression of innate value. As the legislators and interpreters continue to talk about the metropolis, it spreads into nothingness and formlessness, massively privatizing the public sphere (Sorkin 1992). Each house must be equipped with a lawnmower, a circular saw, a basketball hoop, a swimming pool, several automobiles, and the list goes on. The metropolis unbound has become a massive medium of private consumption. It is no wonder then that nothing better symbolizes the new urban region and its sprawling edge cities than the ubiquitous, gaudy, and perfectly controlled, 'postmodern,' shopping mall.

As argued in this chapter, both legislators and interpreters focus on urban form and fail to analyse the underlying economic, political, and social causes of the production of such a form. The new urban region has been both an expression as well as an embodiment of a changing political economy of urbanization in the United States and Canada. It is a fundamental mistake to consider the urban region as though it is isolated from a broader political economy (see, for example, Barnett 1995, Downs 1994, Calthorpe 1993). By using such terms as 'underlying causes' and 'political economy,' however, are we implying another group of 'structural forces' equally immutable as 'market forces'? Are we using a structuralist or a voluntarist approach, for which we criticized the interpreters? Some remarks are in order here to indicate the type of critical analysis of urban form that would go beyond the legislator and interpreter narratives.

Such critical analysis has been associated with Harvey (1989a, 1989b), Soja (1989), Castells (1989), King (1990a, 1990b), Sassen (1991), Featherstone (1993), and Zukin (1988, 1992), who have explored various ways in which urban space is produced. Although the writings of these authors address some of the questions raised in this chapter about the production of urban form, the narratives of legislators and interpreters we have examined in this chapter entirely ignore them. Why do legislators and interpreters ignore critical urban research? Reasons for this are complex and include political, ideological, and literary issues. But two reasons why these authors are ignored by legislators and interpreters are their method and object of analysis. Regarding the method of analysis, critical research on urban form has been based mostly on Marxist or neo-Marxist principles of research. As such, it remains fixated on capital as an explanatory tool. Although there have been attempts to soften this structuralist approach by Castells (1983), Harvey (1993), and Gottdiener (1994), still it remains centred on economic capital and 'its' power to shape the city.

More recent studies by Zukin (1993, 1995), however, highlighting different forms of capital, particularly cultural and symbolic capital, to shape the city are promising attempts of critical urban research, for, while the metropolis started the century as an industrial metropolis, dominated by industrial production, since 1971 it has been the spectacular site of a transformation to a 'postindustrial' economy where service and knowledge industries became dominant. While it started the century as an arena of class conflict between the industrial bourgeoisie and the working class, it became the site of conflict between the new managerial and professional classes employed in knowledge industries with global linkages, accumulating cultural as well as economic capital, and the new working classes employed in service and support industries. As I have argued elsewhere, this shift is not well captured by Marxist analyses that focus on 'flexible accumulation' or a 'post-fordist' regime of accumulation (Isin 1995, 1996). Rather, there is a new class struggle in the United States, Canada, and Europe that is quite different than the industrial capital–labour conflict that characterized the modern era. When critical research focuses on class and its effect on the city, it must take into account this significant class shift and the new role of cultural capital. The transformation of the metropolis from a strong core city surrounded by peripheral suburbs to a polycentric urban region with multiple and conflicting nodes of residential, industrial, and commercial growth must be seen against the background of this class shift.

As for the object of analysis, critical research on urban form has been almost exclusively focused on the core city, unable to broaden it focus to the metropolis, let alone the urban region. As Bloch argues in a recent comprehensive review, rather than dealing with the recent rise of and shift to the metropolitan periphery, 'the efforts of scholars from different perspectives still remain focused on processes within the traditional city' (Bloch 1994: 60). In other words, critical research on urban form has not yet caught up with either the metropolis or the fragmented, spread, polycentric urban region. In part, this is because there is always a lag between emerging realities and their interpretations. Sudjic (1993: 328), for example, argues that 'the equipment we have for making sense of what is happening to our cities has lagged far behind these changes. Both the popular and academic views of what the city is, are coloured more by historical perceptions than by present-day realities.' He says that 'in its new incarnation the diffuse, sprawling, and endlessly mobile world metropolis is fundamentally different from the city as we have known it' (Sudjic 1993: 327). Similarly, Gottdiener (1994: 264) and Knox (1992) argue that our present state of knowledge is inadequate and too flawed to understand the polycentric urban region. Knox writes, 'We face an episode of change that will require not just a realignment of political and economic priorities and an unprecedented degree of sensitivity to social and cultural diversity, but also a retooling of our conceptual and theoretical approaches to urban change, along with a parallel retooling of our approach to urban policy, management, and governance' (Knox 1992: 1217).

After the Metropolis: The Cosmopolis

Since the rapid transformations of the 1970s, the metropolis with its core city and dependent suburban peripheries is no longer the dominant urban form in North America (Gottdiener 1994, Bloch 1994). Rather, the metropolis unbound is characterized by, on the one hand, multiple centres of growth often in conflict with one another and, on the other, the rapidly diminishing political and economic role of the core city. Friedmann (1973: 105) defined the new settlement form as an urban field, which is 'a vast multi-centred region having relatively low density, whose form evolves from a finely articulated network of social and economic linkages. Its many centres are set in large areas of open space of which much is given over to agricultural and recreational use. The core city from which the urban field evolved is beginning to lose its traditional dominance: it is becoming merely one of many specialized centres in a region.' Some interpret this as the end of the monocentric industrial city that characterized the nineteenth century (Soja 1992: 95). But, as has been argued, the monocentric industrial city had already disappeared by the 1920s. The new urban region is not the end of the industrial city but the end of the metropolis that characterized the twentieth century.

Our perceptions of urban forms are inseparable from the words and metaphors we use to describe them and from the practices of legislating and interpreting that make all our conceptions possible. Whatever metaphor we choose to describe the metropolis unbound – the multi-nucleated metropolitan region, the polycentric urban region, the new techno-city, post-suburbia, the galactic metropolis, the city without, the postmodern urban form, the city-state – the new urban form is 'marked by hitherto unimagined fragmentation; by immense distances between its citizens, literal, economic, cultural, social and political; and by novel planning problems, which raise the stakes for, and may very well demand changes in the way we think about urban planning itself' (Bloch 1994: 225). I suggest another metaphor for the metropolis unbound: the cosmopolis. This metaphor marks both the continuity and discontinuity with the metropolis. The cosmopolis marks a departure from the metropolis in the sense that the core city no longer functions as the hub of the metropolis but as one among others. The cosmopolis also signifies the global character of the metropolis unbound (King 1990a, 1990b; Sassen 1991). Yet the cosmopolis is still a polis, albeit a fragmented, sprawling, and global one.

Yet, to propose a new metaphor, a new name is not a substitute for empirical research. Both narratives – legislators and interpreters – have failed in the sense that the contemporary urban form, by the admission of both, has neither heeded the calls of the legislators nor now resembles the language and metaphors of interpreters. Critical urban research failed too in constituting the cosmopolis as an object of analysis and engagement. The retooling Knox is talking about should start at recognizing a new object of analysis – the cosmopolis – and a new representation of the intellectuals shaping it (Said 1994).

Acknowledgments. I am grateful to several colleagues for their help. Jon Caulfield and Linda Peake offered insightful criticisms on several drafts of the chapter. Larry Bourne offered a close reading, made useful suggestions, and pointed out several errors. Frances Frisken made several suggestions to clarify the argument. Evelyn Ruppert caught several errors of judgment and offered remedies. Melissa Troemel was exceptional in her research assistance in compiling statistical data on the Canadian metropolitan areas. Pino Di Mascio and Abby Bushby's comments were most useful in revising the chapter. Fewer errors would have remained if I had the tenacity to respond to every criticism.

REFERENCES

Barnett, J. 1995. *The Fractured Metropolis: Improving the New City, Restoring the Old City, Reshaping the Region.* New York: HarperCollins

Bauman, Z. 1987. *Legislators and Interpreters: On Modernity, Post-Modernity and Intellectuals.* London: Routledge

Bloch, R. 1994. 'Metropolis inverted: The rise of and shift to the periphery and the remaking of the contemporary city.' PhD Dissertation, University of California, Los Angeles

Blumenfeld, H. 1967. 'The modern metropolis.' In P.D. Spreiregen, ed., *The Modern Metropolis.* Cambridge: MIT Press

– 1986. 'Where did all the metropolitanites go?' In E.Y. Galantay, ed., *The Metropolis in Transition.* New York: Paragon House

Bourdieu, P. 1984. *Distinction: A Social Critique of the Judgement of Taste.* Cambridge: Harvard University Press

Bourne, L.S. 1995. *Urban Growth and Population Redistribution in North America: A Diverse and Unequal Landscape.* Major Report 32. Toronto: Centre for Urban and Community Studies, University of Toronto

Bourne, L.S., and A.E. Olvet. 1995. *New Urban and Regional Geographies in Canada:*

1986–91 and Beyond. Major Report 33. Toronto: Centre for Urban and Community Studies, University of Toronto

Burke, M.A. 1990. 'Urban Canada.' In C. McKie and K. Thompson, ed., *Canadian Social Trends.* Ottawa: Statistics Canada

Calthorpe, P. 1993. *The Next American Metropolis: Ecology, Community, and the American Dream.* New York: Princeton Architectural Press

Castells, M. 1983. *The City and the Grassroots.* Berkeley: University of California Press

– 1989. *The Informational City: Information Technology, Economic Restructuring and the Urban Regional Process.* Oxford: Blackwell

Downs, A. 1994. *New Visions for Metropolitan America.* Washington, DC: Brookings Institution

Duany, A,. and E. Plater-Zyberk. 1992. *Towns and Town-Making Principles.* New York: Rizzoli

Featherstone, M. 1993. 'Global and local cultures.' In J. Bird, B. Curtis, T. Putnam, G. Robertson, and L. Tickner, eds., *Mapping the Futures: Local Cultures, Global Change.* London: Routledge

Fishman, R. 1987. *Bourgeois Utopias: The Rise and Fall of Suburbia.* New York: Medieval Academy of America

– 1990. 'America's new city: Megalopolis unbound,' *Wilson Quarterly,* Winter

Fox, K. 1985. *Metropolitan America: Urban Life and Urban Policy in the United States, 1940–1980.* New Brunswick, NJ: Rutgers University Press

Friedmann, J. 1973. *Retracking America: A Theory of Transactive Planning.* New York: Anchor Press

Frisken, F. 1993. 'Planning and servicing the Greater Toronto Area: The interplay of provincial and municipal interests.' In D.N. Rothblatt and A. Sancton, eds., *Metropolitan Governance: American-Canadian Intergovernmental Perspectives.* Berkeley: University of California Press

Garreau, J. 1991. *Edge City: Life on the New Frontier.* New York: Doubleday

Gottdiener, M. 1977. *Planned Sprawl: Private and Public Interests in Suburbia.* London: Sage

– 1994. *The Social Production of Urban Space,* 2nd ed. Austin: University of Texas Press

Gottmann, J. 1990. *Since Megalopolis.* Baltimore: Johns Hopkins University Press

Gottmann, J., and R.A. Harper, eds. 1967. *Metropolis on the Move: Geographers Look at Urban Sprawl.* New York: Wiley

Harvey, D. 1989a. *The Condition of Postmodernity: An Inquiry into the Origins of Cultural Change.* Cambridge: Butterworth

– 1989b. *The Urban Experience.* Baltimore: Johns Hopkins University Press

– 1993. 'From space to place and back again: Reflections on the condition of postmodernity.' In J. Bird, B. Curtis, T. Putnam, G. Robertson, and L. Tickner, eds., *Mapping the Futures: Local Cultures, Global Change.* London: Routledge

Isin, E. 1995. *Who Is the New Citizen? Class, Territory, Identity.* Working Paper No. 16. Urban Studies Programme, York University

– 1996. 'Global city-regions and citizenship.' In R. Keil, G. Wekerle, and D. Bell, eds., *Local Places in the Age of the Global City.* Montreal: Black Rose Books

Isin, E. and R. Tomalty. 1993a. *Resettling Cities.* Main Report. Ottawa: Canada Mortgage and Housing Corporation

– 1993b. *Resettling Cities.* Compendium Report. Ottawa: Canada Mortgage and Housing Corporation

Jackson, K.T. 1985. *Crabgrass Frontier: The Suburbanization of the United States.* Oxford: Oxford University Press

Jones, E. 1990. *Metropolis.* Oxford: Oxford university Press

Katz, P. 1994. *The New Urbanism: Toward an Architecture of Community.* New York: McGraw-Hill

King, A.D. 1990a. *Global Cities: Postimperialism and the Internationalization of London.* London: Routledge

– 1990b. *Urbanism, Colonialism and the World Economy: Cultural and Spatial Foundations of the World Urban System.* London: Routledge

Knox, P. 1992. 'Facing up to urban change.' *Environment and Planning A*, 24: 1217–20

Kunstler, J.H. 1993. *The Geography of Nowhere.* New York: Simon and Schuster

Lees, A. 1985. *Cities Perceived.* New York: Columbia University Press

Martin, L.H., H. Gutman, and P.H. Hutton, eds. 1988. *Technologies of the Self: A Seminar with Michel Foucault.* Amherst: University of Massachusetts Press

Morris, A.E.J. 1994. *History of Urban Form: Before the Industrial Revolutions*, 3rd ed. London: Longman

Muller, P.O. 1989. 'The transformation of bedroom suburbia into the outer city: An overview of metropolitan structural change since 1947.' In B.M. Kelly, ed., *Suburbia Re-examined.* New York: Greenwood Press

Mumford, L. 1938. *The Culture of Cities.* New York: Harcourt, Brace, Jovanovich

– 1961. *The City in History: Its Origins, Its Transformations, and Its Prospects.* New York: Harcourt, Brace, Jovanovich

Rothblatt, D.N., and A. Sancton, eds., 1993. *Metropolitan Governance: American-Canadian Intergovernmental Perspectives.* Berkeley: University of California Press

Rybczynski, W. 1995. *City Life: Urban Expectations in a New World.* Toronto: HarperCollins

Sadri, A. 1992. *Max Weber's Sociology of Intellectuals.* Oxford: Oxford University Press

Said, E.W. 1994. *Representations of the Intellectual.* New York: Pantheon

Sancton, A. 1992. 'Canada as a highly urbanized nation: New implications for government.' *Canadian Public Administration* 35(3): 281–98

– 1993. 'Policymaking for urban development in American and Canadian metropolitan regions.' D. Rothblatt and A. Sancton, eds., *Metropolitan Governance: American-Canadian Intergovernmental Perspectives.* Berkeley: University of California Press

– 1994. *Governing Canada's City-Regions: Adapting Form to Function.* Ottawa: Institute for Research on Public Policy

Sassen, S. 1991. *The Global City: New York, London, Tokyo.* Princeton: Princeton University Press

Soja, E.W. 1989. *Postmodern Geographies: The Reassertion of Space in Critical Social Theory.* London: Verso

– 1992. 'Inside exopolis: Scenes from Orange County.' In M. Sorkin, ed., *Variations on a Theme Park: The New American City and the End of Public Space.* New York: Hill and Wang

Sorkin, M. ed. 1992. *Variations on a Theme Park: The New American City and the End of Public Space.* New York: Hill and Wang

Stone, L.O. 1967. *Urban Development in Canada.* Ottawa: Dominion Bureau of Statistics

Sudjic, D. 1993. *The 100 Mile City.* London: HarperCollins

Teaford, J.C. 1993. *The Twentieth-Century American City.* Baltimore: Johns Hopkins University Press

Weber, A.F. 1899. *The Growth of Cities in the Nineteenth Century: A Study in Statistics.* Ithaca: Cornell University Press

Wood, D. 1982. 'Grand design on the fringes of empire: New towns for British North America.' *Canadian Geographer* 26(3): 243–54

Zukin, S. 1988. 'The postmodern debate over urban form.' In M. Featherstone, ed., *Postmodernism.* London: Sage

– 1992. 'Postmodern urban landscapes: Mapping culture and power.' In S. Lash and J. Friedman, eds., *Modernity and Identity.* Oxford: Basil Blackwell

– 1993. *Landscapes of Power: From Detroit to Disneyworld.* Berkeley: University of California Press

– 1995. *The Cultures of Cities.* New York: Blackwell

PART 2

THE ECONOMY OF CITIES

7

Economic Restructuring and the Diversification of Gentrification in the 1980s: A View from a Marginal Metropolis[1]

DAMARIS ROSE

Over the past three decades economic and social change in Canadian inner cities has been increasingly linked to the fortunes of the 'advanced tertiary' sector (sometimes referred to as the 'quaternary' sector) – an array of private and public sector services needed to coordinate and regulate regionally and globally dispersed economic activities, to control flows of capital and information, to produce and disseminate research, and so on (see, for example, Castells 1989: 126–71). National and regional administrative centres such as Vancouver, Toronto, Montreal, and Halifax saw major downtown investments by private and public branches of the advanced tertiary sector. Provincial and municipal governments have helped maintain or enhance the appeal of a downtown location as a place of employment for the burgeoning professional and managerial workforce of the advanced tertiary sector by making major improvements in physical and cultural infrastructure (Bourne 1992: 71–3; Goldberg and Mercer 1986; Polèse 1988). This growth of advanced services in city centres – and the associated growth of a host of ancillary services – has greatly helped to maintain the tax base of central area municipalities in the face of the de-industrialization of traditional inner city manufacturing and the shift of industries and some office activity to suburban areas (Coffey and Drolet 1994, Filion and Mock 1991).

Moreover, although residential suburbanization remains a dominant tendency (Bourne 1991; Sénécal et al. 1990: 88), substantial numbers of those employed in the upper echelons of the advanced tertiary sector have also opted to *live* in the inner city. This trend is especially prevalent among highly educated 'new urban professionals,' many of whom have gravitated to existing middle-class or elite areas close to downtown, to new residential developments on 'greyfield' sites (former industrial, port, or railway land), and to old working-class neighbourhoods with a 'renovation' potential which may or may not have been exploited by real estate developers (see, for example, Bourne 1992; Bourne 1993a; Dansereau 1988; Dantas 1988; Ley 1988, 1992; Mills 1988). In fact, it is widely accepted in the literature that the growth of a strong advanced tertiary sector in the central city is a necessary (although not sufficient) precondition for the process commonly referred to as 'gentrification,' in which members of the 'new middle class' move into and physically and culturally reshape working-class inner city neighbourhoods (see, for example, Beauregard 1986, Hamnett 1994, Ley 1988, Rose 1989). In this process the producers and consumers of gentrified housing typically either displace existing residents or take over greyfield sites.

Over the past two decades the gentrification issue has generated an enormous amount of discussion from diverse theoretical perspectives (for reviews of various aspects of the debates see, for example, Bondi 1991; Caulfield 1994: 124–47; Filion 1991; Hamnett 1994; Rose 1987; Smith and Williams 1986). One important aspect of this debate concerns the *temporal dynamics* of gentrification, which both neoclassical and structuralist political-economic approaches (Smith and Williams 1986) have typically seen as developing through a series of stages. According to stage models gentrification is typically initiated in inner city neighbourhoods that have become run down but have some architectural merit by a well-educated but economically struggling avant-garde of artists, graduate students, and assorted bohemian and counter-cultural types. The neighbourhoods are then 'discovered' by young singles and couples with a little more money and job security, who purchase inexpensive houses or apartments for owner-occupation, renovate them with their own 'sweat equity,' and are 'oblivious' to the risks involved to their investment – and sometimes even to their personal safety. Subsequent stages increasingly involve real estate developers who capitalize on the 'rent gap' or potential increase in value in these neighbourhoods by buying up dwellings, renovating them, and reselling them to more affluent members of the new middle class, in the process displacing both old-established and new-wave occupants. The social diversity of the neighbourhood thus diminishes. The process is repeated as other working-class neighbourhoods successively encounter gentrification's 'advancing frontier.' The end-state is the creation of a new set of socially homogeneous middle-to-upper-middle class neighbourhoods with an associated economic and cultural transformation of neighbourhood commercial zones (see Caulfield 1994: 125–31 and Kernstein 1990 for succinct presentations of variants on this model).

The purported linearity and inevitability of the transformations of neighbourhoods wrought by gentrification, however, has been criticized as being an unexamined empirical generalization (Sayer 1992: 99–103 and *passim*) derived from research conducted in world cities like New York when they were undergoing prolonged booms involving intense speculative real estate activity. In an article written at the height of the mid-1980s boom, but from the vantage point of a city (Montreal) not fully participating in it, I pointed out that the supply of wealthy 'potential gentrifiers' was likely to be much more bounded in some advanced tertiary cities than in others. The trajectories of gentrification would not necessarily conform to those envisaged by stage models in cities whose position within national or international urban hierarchies was marginal or fragile (Rose 1989), and where the constitution of the new middle class was less bound up with global corporate and financial capital and more bound up with the growth of the public sector and arts and cultural industries (Rose and Villeneuve 1993). In some such cases, economically precarious professionals – associated in stage models only with the early stages of gentrification – might continue to be an important presence in the inner city (Rose 1989). Existing theory had no way of dealing with such cases, except in an ad hoc way as 'exceptions,' perched awkwardly at the margins or relegated to a footnote in the debate on the new middle class and the reshaping of inner cities.

Stage models, moreover, fail to consider that, regardless of the 'stage' their gentrification has reached in terms of average income levels of in-movers, different neighbourhoods may, because of their existing physical and social morphology, attract different kinds of households in terms of, for instance, family structure, gender, sexual orientation, or ethnic identification (Dantas 1988; Kernstein 1990: 623). A related criticism challenges the notion that later-stage gentrifiers are homogeneous in their social and cultural practices; there may, for example, be important differences in orientations to local social movements (Caulfield 1994: 140–7). Another recent article has spoken evocatively of the 'contagious diffusion' of gentrification to more and more inner city neighbourhoods (Ley 1992: 240), but as Dantas (1988: 84) suggests, what may at first appear as a 'spillover' phenomenon from one district to the next may turn out to involve very different kinds of actors and perhaps a different dynamic of residential investment.

Some years ago I made a distinction between wealthy gentrifiers and 'marginal gentrifiers.' The latter notion had both economic and sociocultural dimensions. It referred to certain fractions of the new middle class who were highly educated but only tenuously employed or modestly earning professionals, and who sought out niches in inner city neighbourhoods – as renters in the private or non-profit sectors, or, where local housing market conditions permitted it, as co-owners of modestly priced apartment units. Such inner city residence, it was suggested, could help people deal with precarious employment – by facilitating networking and multiple-job holding, for instance. Moreover, compared with the suburbs, the inner city could accommodate a diversity of cultural practices, including non-traditional gender relations, and, by minimizing space-time constraints, could facilitate the 'dual roles' of groups such as female lone parents. It was argued that to fail to take into account the economic and cultural diversity of social groups practising gentrification was to make it into a 'chaotic concept' (Sayer 1982: 138–9) of dubious explanatory utility (Rose 1984, see also Beauregard 1986).

Proponents of structuralist accounts of gentrification responded to the 'marginal gentrifier' concept and 'chaotic concept' critique by acknowledging the sociological importance of 'marginal gentrification' in some contexts and by recognizing its heuristic utility, especially in pointing out the need to consider the gendering of gentrification (Smith 1987). However, emerging theories of gentrification as a process of 'class constitution' have not seriously attempted a theoretical integration of 'marginal' forms of gentrification into their accounts. Smith (1987: 160) went so far as to argue that marginal gentrifiers should be theoretically 'decoupled' from the 'main dynamic' of the gentrification process, but as Caulfield (1994: 130) points out, such a strategy begs the question as to whether the diverse people and processes involved in gentrification 'may be recoupled as elements of a pattern that is not chaotic but coherent.' Caulfield goes on to sketch out how such a recoupling might be attempted, seeing gentrification (including its marginal forms) in terms of social movements resulting from complex interweavings of class and culture (1994: 131–47).

This chapter takes a tack different from but complementary to that of Caulfield. It makes the case that rather than treating marginal gentrifiers and 'marginal' advanced tertiary cities as supposed 'exceptions' to the main dynamic of gentrification, theories and empirical accounts should consider how the economic fortunes of a city and of its new middle class might affect the process. I shall show how economic and labour market restructuring in Canadian cities bifurcated the new middle class in the 1980s and how in the Montreal case this helped perpetuate the phenomenon of marginal gentrification, as these broader tendencies intersected with particular features of Quebec's political and sociocultural climate and of Montreal's residential morphology. A study of these dimensions of 'marginality' can help enrich our understanding not only of gentrification dynamics in a particular case but also of the processes contributing to the diversity of 'landscapes of gentrification.' This diversity is recognized by a growing number of researchers (Badcock 1993, Beauregard 1990, Bourne 1992, Caulfield 1994, Ley 1992) but remains undertheorized.

In empirical terms, this chapter first provides an overview of changes in locational and employment characteristics of the new middle class in major Canadian advanced tertiary sectors over the 1980s, a period of profound economic restructuring. Trends in earnings within this group are examined, and then the focus is on the particular factors that affected the constitution of Montreal's new middle class in the 1980s and on the implications of economic and urban restructuring for the social composition of the city's gentrifying neighbourhoods.

Labour Market Restructuring in the Advanced Tertiary Sector in the 1980s

During the 1980s and early 1990s the Canadian economy experienced major restructuring. There were two major recessions, separated by a brief but intense boom (Bourne 1991: 29–31) that was fuelled in part by speculative commercial real estate activity in the downtown cores of a few major cities (especially Toronto; see Bourne 1992: 76–80 and Caulfield 1994: 82–7).

The recessions helped pressure the private sector into making longer term adaptations to the competitive pressures of an economy increasingly organized on a global scale. Firms implemented various changes in the organization of their internal labour markets, aiming to cut labour costs, trim their operating budgets, increase productivity, and facilitate quick responses to shifts in market conditions (see, for example, Drache 1991). These changes have included 'downsizing' the permanent workforce and lengthening the working hours of key full-time personnel (Morissette and Sunter 1994), while making increasing use of contractual and part-time staff – usually not entitled to pro-rated benefits (Duffy and Pupo 1992: 153–65) – for short-term assignments, hiring new employees on lower salary scales than those in place for existing workers, and increasing the range of tasks performed by some employees. Such changes have varied between sectors but have affected employment conditions in a wide range of services as well as in manufacturing (Christopherson and Noyelle 1992).

Over the same period, federal, provincial, and even municipal governments began to implement similar types of workforce restructuring in order to reduce expenditures and cope with year-to-year budget uncertainties. Such cuts were initiated in reaction to growing concerns about the deficit and the rising costs of servicing Canada's foreign debt and, in some cases, in response to a rising tide of neoconservative 'anti-statist' ideology. The 1980s thus saw a slowing down – and the 1990s a reversal – of a decades-long growth trend in regular salaried employment in the public administration (government) and parapublic (education, health, and welfare) sectors, as well as in Crown corporations (some of which were privatized or severely rationalized). Moreover, within the regular workforce in these sectors, wage freezes and salary rollbacks began to be regular occurrences.

These restructuring processes have thus led to a rise in the number of workers whose job opportunities are restricted to 'non-standard' or 'precarious' employment. This is occurring not only in low-level service work (the so-called McDonald's economy) but also in a variety of white-collar and professional fields in the advanced services (Economic Council of Canada 1991). For instance, holding multiple part-time jobs in order to make ends meet has become more common, especially among highly educated women working in education, health, and social services (Cohen 1994). The advanced tertiary sectors have also not escaped the general upward trend over the 1980s in the percentage of 'underemployed' workers – those working part-time only because they cannot find full-time work (Moreau 1994).

The incidence of unemployment has also risen considerably. A look at unemployment rates (see Figure 7.1) indicates a secular drift towards much higher levels of structural unemployment, not only in Canada's resource-based periphery but also in its largest metropolitan areas whose economies are largely service-based but also have declining traditional manufacturing activities. Moreover, longitudinal surveys of the labour force show that the percentage of workers experiencing regular bouts of unemployment has also increased, probably reflecting the growth of short-term contractual employment (Ross and Shillington 1992).

Overall, these changes seem to mark a rupture with the decades-long upward trajectory of annual employment incomes among Canadian males. Averaged across all occupations, and measured in inflation-adjusted dollars, male earnings declined slightly between 1980 and 1990

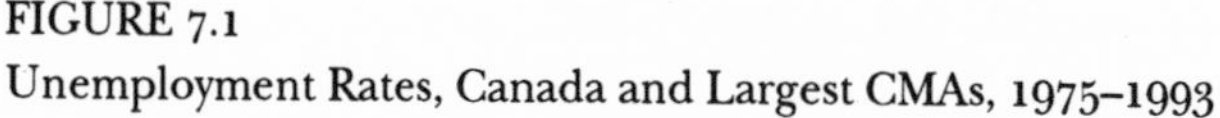

FIGURE 7.1
Unemployment Rates, Canada and Largest CMAs, 1975–1993

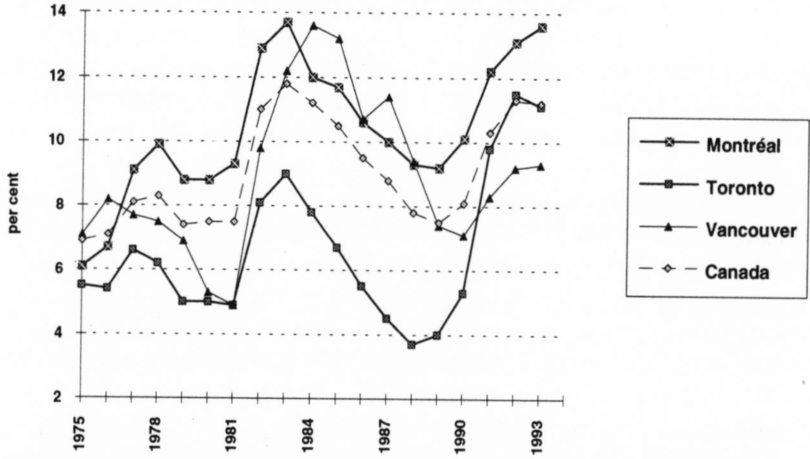

Source: Statistics Canada, *Historical Labour Force Statistics, 1991*, cat. 71-201; Canadian Economic Observer, *Historical Statistical Supplement*, 1992/3, cat. 11-210.

(Rashid 1993: 15), and this decline continued in the early 1990s (Gartley 1994: 44n4). Contributing to this decline was the increase in numbers of those working less than full-time all year round (calculated from Statistics Canada, *Census of 1986*, cat. 93–116, Table 1, *Census of 1991*, cat. 93–332, Table 1). The situation for women was somewhat different. Although the growth of precarious work, wage rollbacks, and the like also affected women, women's annual earnings continued to increase overall because of rising levels of education, growth in the numbers of women in higher-level occupations, pay equity programs, and increases in the number of hours worked for pay (Gartley 1994, Ghalam 1993, Marshall 1987). Indeed, had it not been for the huge increases in the number of married women in the labour force and in the numbers of hours they worked, the average incomes of husband-wife families would have declined as well (Institut Vanier de la famille 1994: 76–7; Rashid 1994: 21).

Moreover, these labour force restructuring processes have affected different fractions of the workforce unevenly. In particular – and not surprisingly since it is newer entrants to the workforce who are most affected by the decline of full-time, stable employment opportunities – there are growing disparities in earnings by age group. The gap between hourly wages and annual earnings of younger workers working full-time all year round and those of the over-35s widened considerably over the 1980s (Gauthier and Mercier 1994: 186–7, Tableau E). This was the case for both men and women within all the major economic sectors and occupational categories (Morissette et al. 1993; Myles et al. 1988). Instability of employment is of course nothing new for young people, but what changed in the 1980s was the length of time that individuals were limited to precarious work – often, until well into their thirties (Gauthier and Mercier 1994: 91; Marcoux, Morin, and Rose 1991).

These recent processes of labour market restructuring should merit the attention of researchers interested in trajectories of social change in inner city neighbourhoods of Canada's major metropolitan centres, particularly those concerned with gentrification. Professionals in the various branches of the advanced tertiary sector have not escaped these restructuring processes. The polarization between professionals in terms of earnings and job security is particularly striking in the public and parapublic sectors (Noël 1994), sectors which have been of particular importance in building the new middle class in many Canadian cities (Rose and Villeneuve 1993). Some subgroups would likely have become wealthier; for considerable numbers of others, the increasingly precarious nature of the employment relation blocked access to the 'career ladders' that characterized earlier boom periods. This leads us to pose the question of what this labour market restructuring might mean for the processes associated with 'social upgrading' and gentrification in major Canadian cities. Is this another part of the explanation for the persistent and increasingly remarked on diversity of 'landscapes of gentrification'?

We will now look more closely at the 'professionalization' of Canadian inner cities in the 1980s. By contextualizing this process within the restructuring trends discussed above, we may develop a more tempered portrait of the links between professionalization and gentrification.

Urban Professionals: Swelling Ranks ...

Statistical indicators continue to tell us that in the *inner cities* of Canada's major advanced tertiary centres, 'urban professionals' have made up an ever-increasing share of the resident labour force over the past two decades (Ley 1988, 1992). Table 7.1a illustrates this point for seven major Canadian cities from 1981 through 1986 to 1991; in all of them, 'professionalization'[2] has been occurring to a greater extent in the inner city than the outer city. Unlike the growth of the 'edge city' phenomenon in

TABLE 7.1
Presence of Professionals in Selected Major Canadian CMAs, 1981, 1986, and 1991

	Inner city			Outer city		
	1981	1986	1991	1981	1986	1991
a) Professionals as a percentage of the total resident labour force, inner city and outer city						
Vancouver	15.5	17.6	19.5	12.5	13.1	13.3
Edmonton	15.2	18.1	18.3	13.8	14.5	14.8
Toronto	16.1	18.8	22.3	14.1	14.3	16.4
Ottawa-Hull	20.1	21.5	22.9	19.3	19.5	20.6
Montreal	15.1	17.7	20.9	13.4	13.8	14.4
Quebec	15.9	19.6	21.0	17.3	18.4	17.9
Halifax	20.0	20.8	24.3	13.2	13.5	13.9

	1981 %	1986 %	1991 %	1991/1981 ratio
b) Inner city share of metropolitan area professionals				
Vancouver	28.1	28.5	28.0	1.00
Edmonton	16.2	13.8	12.8	0.79
Toronto	20.6	20.6	19.3	0.94
Ottawa-Hull	18.8	18.1	15.7	0.84
Montreal	28.7	29.2	27.1	0.94
Quebec	18.3	18.1	16.8	0.92
Halifax	31.2	28.7	29.3	0.94

Source: Statistics Canada, Censuses of 1981 and 1991, special tabulations.

the United States (Garreau 1991), the central cores of these Canadian cities have retained most of their attraction as foci of high-level corporate and government activity, higher education, specialized health care, telecommunications, and arts and culture.

The weight of existing research leaves little room for doubt that the pull of inner city neighbourhoods as places of residence for a sizeable proportion of the metropolitan area's urban professionals – whether existing elite and middle-class areas, older gentrifying neighbourhoods, or 'greyfield' condominium developments – is related to this centrality of advanced tertiary activity (Rose and Villeneuve 1993; see also Ley 1992) as well as to a diverse range of social and cultural attributes contributing to the 'liveability' of the neighbourhoods themselves (see, for example, Caulfield 1994: 134–44, Ley, 1996, *passim*). Indeed, as Table 7.1b indicates, the proportion of metropolitan area professionals who opted for inner city residence remained remarkably stable over the 1980s, considering the continued growth of suburbs and mushrooming of 'exurbs' during the decade.[3]

A recent analysis (Ley 1992) concludes that a major reason why professionals continued to 'gentrify' the inner cities of Canadian advanced tertiary centres in the first half of the 1980s was that they worked in sectors of the economy that were virtually immune to recession (notably the public and parapublic sectors) and therefore could afford to invest in what had by this time become expensive real estate. And data covering the whole decade[4] show that the education, health, social services, and government sectors continued to employ the lion's share of inner city professionals, although in absolute terms employment in this sector grew more slowly than in financial and business services, and in relative terms this sector lost ground, falling from 54 per cent to 49 per cent between 1981 and 1991 in Montreal.

... but Shifting Fortunes

Ley (1992) concluded that gentrification remained a buoyant if increasingly diverse process in the recessionary period of 1981 to 1986. However, he did not have access to data on the employment or household incomes of urban professionals (Bourne 1993a), nor to information about their age structure. Such data can help us develop both a more qualified portrait of the 'buoyancy' of gentrification and a clearer understanding of economic dimensions of the internal differentiation of the 'new middle class' (Butler and Hamnett 1994). This in turn may contribute to a better understanding of the forces producing the diversity of landscapes of physical and social gentrification in the 1980s.

Census data obtained for seven major advanced-tertiary centres show that during the 1980s the average annual employment incomes of urban professionals changed in ways that support the thesis that economic restructuring increased the internal fragmentation of this group. Among males, earnings (measured in constant dollars) fell in four of these metropolitan areas (see Table 7.2). The particularly deep drops in the Montreal and Quebec City regions can be attributed in part to severe cuts in public sector salaries in the early 1980s (Institut de recherche et d'information sur la rémunération 1992) – a foretaste of cutbacks that were to come in the federal public service and in other provincial government services starting in the late 1980s. In contrast, in Toronto, and to a lesser extent Halifax, the boom in financial and business services positively

TABLE 7.2
Changes in Average Annual Employment Incomes of Professionals in Selected Major Canadian CMAs, by Gender, 1980–1990 (in Constant Dollars)

	MALES		FEMALES	
	Inner city %	Outer city %	Inner city %	Outer city %
Vancouver	-1.3	-4.6	9.7	5.7
Edmonton	-2.9	-2.9	6.3	0.5
Toronto	9.4	1.8	15.4	9.4
Ottawa-Hull	1.9	-2.1	-0.9	4.6
Montreal	-4.3	-8.0	0.4	-2.2
Quebec	-6.5	-9.4	0.0	-3.2
Halifax	4.0	10.2	14.8	6.4

Source: Statistics Canada, Censuses of 1981 and 1991, special tabulations.

affected overall employment incomes among professionals. Women professionals' incomes increased in most cases, because – as mentioned earlier – secular trends towards working longer hours as well as aggregate improvements in occupational positions outweighed the effects of public sector retrenchment.

Table 7.2 also shows that, in relative and aggregate terms, professionals living in the inner city weathered the 1980s better than their counterparts living in the outer city in most cases.[5] However, when the statistics are disaggregated by age groups they suggest a more complex portrait. On the one hand, as in the population at large, there has been an aging trend among inner city professionals (especially among males). In both Montreal and Toronto's inner cities, for instance, one-quarter were aged 45 or over by 1991, while the biggest increases occurred in the 35 to 44 age group. This in itself would tend to increase average employment incomes, the overall consumer power of urban professionals relative to other groups (i.e., more older professionals with higher salaries) and thus the *embourgeoisement* of the inner city (Ley 1993). On the other hand, there was a tendency towards increased earnings inequality between younger and older male professionals resident in the inner cities of Toronto and Montreal (see Table 7.3),[6] the divide being between the under-45s and the 45-and-over age groups.

It should be noted that, in general, earnings disparities by age are more pronounced in Canadian inner cities than in the suburbs owing to the importance in the former of older elite areas (such as Montreal's West-

TABLE 7.3
Average Employment Income of Professionals, by Age Group and Gender, Inner Cities of Montreal and Toronto, 1990, Showing Changes Since 1980

	Males		Females	
	Inner-city Montreal	Inner-city Toronto	Inner-city Montreal	Inner-city Toronto
Average employment income, 1990:				
Total (age groups)	$44,114	$54,462	$31,111	$36,428
15 to 24	$13,541	$17,036	$12,176	$17,174
25 to 29	$25,758	$31,449	$23,219	$28,826
30 to 34	$34,848	$43,905	$29,806	$35,978
35 to 44	$48,664	$60,110	$36,759	$43,386
45 and over	$65,657	$78,596	$38,540	$41,569
% change, 1980-1990 (in constant $):				
Total (age groups)	-4.3	9.4	0.4	15.4
15 to 24	-18.1	9.2	-16.1	5.3
25 to 29	-9.9	1.6	-12.9	8.1
30 to 34	-16.6	3.0	-5.6	5.1
35 to 44	-14.7	-3.3	-4.8	15.5
45 and over	2.0	6.3	2.7	12.5

Source: Statistics Canada, Censuses of 1981 and 1991, special tabulations.

mount or Toronto's Rosedale) as well as significant areas of new luxury condominium development on waterfront or other 'greyfield' sites. The weight of these areas on aggregate statistics means that older professionals in the inner city earn *more* than their suburban counterparts. At the same time, younger professionals in the inner city earn *less* than their suburban counterparts. Moreover, although these data pertain only to the employment earnings of *individuals*, we can also infer that income disparities between *households* consisting of at least one professional are greater in the inner city than in the suburbs. Data for professionals disaggregated by family status (not tabulated here) show that the inner city has both a higher concentration of older affluent two-earner couples and a higher concentration of younger one-person households. Furthermore, the income polarization between these two inner city groups is reinforced by the fact that many of the young one-person households – the majority in the Montreal case – are women whose earnings are lower than those of their male counterparts, in spite of the narrowing of the gender gap over the 1980s.

At the scale of the metropolitan area as a whole, the relative importance of the less wealthy and more wealthy fractions of professionals identified above will vary according to the economy of the city concerned. Who actually ends up living where, and when, and their impacts on the social composition of gentrifying neighbourhoods, however, are questions that cannot be reduced solely to the state of the metropolitan economy, to local housing market dynamics, or to cultural factors. Rather, they result from the complex interweaving of all of these on the existing physical and social tapestries of inner city landscapes. We will explore this argument by sketching how this interweaving occurred in the case of Montreal.

Montreal as 'Other'? Economic and Social Restructuring in a Marginal Advanced Tertiary Centre and Its Implications for the New Middle Class in the Inner City

Unlike the case of Toronto (and to a lesser extent Vancouver), Montreal's supply of wealthy 'urban professionals' from whose ranks gentrifiers are drawn was truncated in the 1980s. This was a result of changes in Montreal's position in the Canadian urban hierarchy. As Toronto and Vancouver consolidated their role as international financial and business centres, the 1970s and early 1980s saw the culmination of a decades-long historical process of transfer of corporate headquarters of financial institutions and most other key sectors of the Canadian economy from Montreal to (mainly) Toronto (Levine 1990: 41–3; Polèse 1990). Many anglophone senior managers and professionals left the region – typically because of job transfers as financial institutions and various other major corporations left Quebec or downsized operations in the province in the wake of the first Parti Québécois election victory in 1976 and the subsequent passage of Bill 101 (the language law) (Levine 1990: 120–2, 172–4; Polèse 1990; Rudin 1985: 214–17). Montreal could no longer be classed as a national city for Canada. Its economic hinterland was increasingly limited to the province of Quebec (Coffey and Polèse 1993). Montreal has survived, however, as an advanced tertiary centre. With the growth of the francophone Quebec business class, the city was able to consolidate its hold on the head offices of financial institutions servicing the province (Polèse 1990). It also attracted a panoply of new business services, a key growth area of the advanced tertiary sector. However, in 1991 this sector still accounted for a smaller share of professional jobs in Montreal than it did in the other major Canadian centres. Not surprisingly, Montreal has also maintained its control on the headquarters of print and telecommunications media and cultural industries serving a mainly francophone market (Polèse 1988).

These changes in Montreal's economic position, in the context of cultural and political change in Quebec, had repercussions both for the constitution of the new middle class in the Montreal region and for the formation of 'gentrifier' fractions in the inner city. Although the francophone business elite increased in importance, it was the public and parapublic sector that formed the cornerstone of expansion of Montreal's new middle class from Quebec's 'Quiet Revolution' of the 1960s (Levine 1990: 39–55, 196–8; Sénécal et al. 1990: 18), until recently (Lamonde and Martineau 1992: 100–4). This sector was central to the expansion of high-level employment in or near downtown, including the head offices of many government ministries and provincial corporations, several teaching hospitals, and four universities (Rose and Villeneuve 1993). Although this sector generated many well-paying, stable professional jobs in the 1960s and early 1970s, it also increasingly generated precarious employment. The same can be said of telecommunications, publishing, and arts and cultural industries.

As for the residential choices of new middle-class fractions in Montreal, some inferences can be made from their sector of employment. New high-tech industries employing well-paid professionals and technicians in such areas as pharmaceuticals research, biogenetics, and aerospace engineering have mostly located in the suburbs (Chevalier 1993) and many of their employees have probably followed suit although there also may be some 'reverse commuting' (Collin and Mongeau 1992). Also, the gentrification literature suggests that an important part of the clientele of centrally located condominium markets is the category of the high-paid, geographically mobile professional working for major corporations, since such a residential situation facilitates long working hours and after-hours socializing within the corporate culture (Filion 1991: 557), at least among single men. But the city's downgraded status in the hierarchy of corporate cities has limited the size of this category and the incomes of the people in it. On the other hand, a strong association has been made in the Canadian literature between being a professional working downtown in the public or parapublic sectors and being predisposed to an inner city residence in an old inner city neighbourhood. It has been argued that this segment is likely to have liberal-to-reformist and 'urbane' value systems (Filion 1991, Ley 1994). Other things being equal, this would favour the emergence of gentrification in Montreal.

A number of factors combined to discourage the region's *better-off* professionals (even those in the public and parapublic sectors located downtown) from locating in large numbers in gentrifying areas of Montreal's inner city during the 1980s. Members of the burgeoning new francophone middle class who formed two-parent families opted massively for home ownership in outer suburbs even though their offices remained heavily concentrated downtown (Collin and Mongeau 1992, Turcotte 1980) and in spite of the logistical difficulties a suburban location often poses for dual-earner families (Roy 1990). Among the factors that help explain this situation are a history of pro-automobile planning policies making long car commutes to downtown fairly easy, few regulations restricting 'urban sprawl,' and (until quite recently) the failure of government to pass on infrastructure costs to those purchasing homes in new subdivisions (Bussière 1989; Charbonneau et al. 1994; Divay and Gaudreau 1984; Linteau 1992: 495–9). The lure of the suburbs for families with children has no doubt been reinforced by the lack of green space in the City of Montreal – much less per capita than in Toronto, for example (Comité interministériel 1992: 7). The majority of inner city housing units lack direct ground level access and associated yard space (Dansereau with Lacroix 1988: 84–5); moreover, in some otherwise attractive inner city neighbourhoods there are almost no small local parks where young children could play (Montreal 1992: 77–8). Among both francophone and anglophone Montrealers of working-class origin born in the 1940s or 1950s, who experienced, or whose parents experienced, a lack of privacy living in large families in confined flats (Séguin 1989: 56–60) or in socially gregarious rural milieux, there seems to have been a large-scale rejection of high-density urban living.[7]

By the late 1970s the City of Montreal had become alarmed by this exodus of middle-class professionals and white-collar workers, especially since it was accompanied by the decline of traditional industries and associated mounting long-term unemployment among the traditional working class (Lamonde and Martineau 1992: 80–7; Levine 1990: 149; see Figure 1) and, more recently, by the City of Montreal's rates of family poverty, which are higher than for any other major city in Canada. These developments were taking a severe toll on the municipal tax base. City housing and economic development agencies launched a panoply of efforts[8] to promote middle-class resettlement in inner city areas which had lost population and industry. These measures were and continue to be justified by the City with reference to a discourse of urban decline (see Beauregard 1994) and summed up in a neat spatial metaphor: Montreal is constantly referred to as 'the hole in the doughnut' of the metropolitan area (Aubin 1995).[9]

Consequently, the City has taken a proactive role in trying to repopulate its old core. In the early 1980s it targeted certain sectors of the Plateau Mont-Royal for 'civic beautification' through neighbourhood streetscape improvements and made generous renovation subsidies available in districts of old, deteriorated housing; the largest grants were available in the Plateau Mont-Royal, Mile End, and St-Louis districts. Federal funds were obtained to convert the old industrial Lachine Canal zone into a linear park. Through a series of programs (some of which are ongoing at the time of this writing) the City has also helped private developers and non-profit groups convert industrial buildings into lofts and to build condominiums and townhouses on pockets of formerly non-residential land, on abandoned lots, and on land in working-class areas razed during earlier phases of 'urban renewal' (Charbonneau and Parenteau 1991; *Montreal Gazette* 1995). It has entered into partnership with private sector firms to develop several thousand condominium units in various price ranges on a number of infill sites between downtown and the waterfront (under construction at the time of this writing). Property tax subsidies have usually been available to those purchasing homes under these various programs. In contrast to other major cities, however, very little of this new development in the central city has been of the 'luxury' type;[10] most is aimed at middle-income singles and couples. All the same, it seems reasonable to infer that the City's policies have had an impact on the 'professionalization' of the inner city (Table 7.1).

The mid-1980s saw phenomenal jumps in average housing prices in districts such as the Plateau and St-Louis. Rising demand for home ownership amid a scarcity of owner-occupiable units, renovation and, in some cases, 'flipping' (frequent resale of units) by petty developers all contributed to this trend (Hamel et al. 1988). Moreover, property taxes – assessed on a market-value basis – skyrocketed for duplex and triplex units (Sénécal et al. 1990: 82–5). Concomitantly there were marked increases (in constant dollar terms) in average rents over the 1980s, although these increases were very variable even from one census tract to an adjacent one.

These market trends undoubtedly reflected the significant growth in the comfortably off fractions of middle-class professionals in gentrifying neighbourhoods. Some were drawn to pockets of good-quality single-family housing, or to small duplexes that could be converted to single-family housing, located on attractive sections of streets and close to amenities.

Large and imposing greystone triplexes, originally built for the new middle class of the late-nineteenth to early twentieth centuries (Legault 1989), were favoured targets of conversion to co-ownership or condominium apartments. But prices never reached the dizzying heights seen, for example, in Toronto. For one thing, market demand in gentrifying areas was tempered by the tendency (discussed earlier) of older and more established professionals to locate in existing middle-class or elite areas or in zones of upscale new condominium development. Moreover, for reasons linked to the particular history of city-building in Montreal's older neighbourhoods (Benoît and Gratton 1991: 181–7; Hanna and Olson 1983; Olson and Hanna 1990), 'highly gentrifiable' types of housing are often interspersed at a fine geographic scale with dwellings commanding lower rents and sale prices – smaller and lower-quality triplexes, or four- or five-plex units, as well as newer infill apartments. This, combined with the fact of Montreal's relatively depressed economy, enabled many 'marginal professionals' to continue to live in the inner city, even in the neighbourhoods that were gentrifying the most through renovation.

The ranks of the precarious professionals continued to swell through the 1980s. Many were in the arts and cultural industries. According to 1991 census data (Statistics Canada, *Electronic product C91*, CMAs), these sectors employ a larger share of Montreal's labour force than is the case for any other Canadian CMA, and this labour force is extremely concentrated in the central city – no doubt largely because of the cultural ambience of certain inner city neighbourhoods, but perhaps also because access to contracts by freelance workers in the arts and media could also be facilitated by living centrally (Chicoine and Rose 1995). During the 1980s cutbacks in government grants and subsidies increased the precariousness of large numbers of workers in this sector (at the CBC, for example, one can repeatedly be hired for contracts of a few weeks' to a couple of months' duration). As already discussed, the rise of precarious work in the public and parapublic sectors also generated numbers of marginal professionals, especially in government agencies and the higher education sector. The ranks of the low-to-modestly earning professionals also included many young francophones in such overstocked professions as architecture, urban planning, and law.[11] Marginal francophone professionals – many originally from Montreal, others migrants from smaller Quebec communities – have tended not to move elsewhere in Canada in search of better career prospects. A major reason is that language and associated cultural factors inhibit mobility to other Canadian cities. In this sense Montreal is 'the end of the road.' Yet anecdotal evidence suggests that even substantial numbers of younger anglophone professionals (in fields other than business) opted for marginal employment and residence in multicultural neighbourhoods of inner city Montreal rather than for higher earnings but a perceived lower quality of life at the other end of Highway 401.

The relative affordability of housing in Montreal undoubtedly enters into the calculus for both francophone and anglophone professionals with little prospect of regular full-time employment in Montreal. 'Marginal professionals' have been able to slot themselves into the inner city landscape with relative ease. It is very convenient for those who worked at more than one job or pursued self-employment, working out of their home (Chicoine and Rose 1995). The large linear-plan flats in the triplex units which predominate in much of Montreal's inner city are ideally suited for home offices, and municipal zoning laws are permissive in this respect. In the Plateau Mont-Royal and Mile End districts, neighbourhood photocopy and fax centres, computer supplies, and cafés have proliferated to service these groups' needs.

The nature of the housing stock and the relations of housing tenure provided exceptional opportunities in spite of the rising prices noted above. Some economically marginal professionals lived in non-profit housing cooperatives funded under federal and provincial programs. A sizeable minority could afford to buy triplex apartments in 'undivided co-ownership' tenure (in which each resident owns a share of the building but does not have legal title to her or his unit). Co-ownership units are cheaper than condominiums and usually subject to much lower municipal taxes. Co-owners would often work out informal and cooperative arrangements for doing renovations and exchanging services. Economic insecurity may actually have encouraged many of these professionals to purchase such modestly priced housing in order to control future housing costs and obtain a measure of ontological security (Chicoine and Rose 1995; see also Beauregard 1986: 45). As late as 1986 almost half of the owner-occupied dwellings in the Plateau Mont-Royal/Centre Sud *arrondissement* (planning district) owned by non-immigrant households were valued at less than $60,000;[12] a few years later prices were still reasonable, in the $70,000–80,000 range. In addition, census data for 1991 suggest that the central Plateau is still a favoured area for female lone-parent professionals, identified in earlier research as a significant section of the 'marginal gentrifiers' and condominium purchasers (Rose 1984, Choko and Dansereau 1986). As for renters – still the vast majority among professionals living in 'gentrifying' inner city districts (Table 7.4) – living alone

TABLE 7.4
Professionals in the Three Montreal Districts That 'Professionalized' the Most in the 1980s: Selected Characteristics

	Montreal Census Metropolitan Area	St-Louis/ Mile End	Plateau Mont-Royal (central part)	Little Burgundy/ Ste-Anne/ Griffintown
Total employed labour force 1991	1,531,850	19,085	13,695	4,505
Professionals, 1991	229,555	4,135	3,635	1,145
as % of employed labour force, 1991	15.0	21.7	26.5	25.8
as % of employed labour force, 1981	12.8	11.4	13.5	9.2
Professionals by economic sector, % distribution 1991:				
education, health, social services	39	39	38	29
business services	19	16	18	27
communications, personal, misc. services	9	24	21	11
public administration	7	6	9	10
finance, insurance, real estate	6	2	4	5
manufacturing, utilities, transportation, trade	21	12	11	13
Professionals' mean annual employment income:				
Males, 1990	$46,024	$29,343	$32,491	$44,104
as % of CMA average for 1990	100	64	71	96
% change since 1980 (in constant $)	–4	4	7	29
Females, 1990	$30,965	$24,220	$29,066	$36,586
as % of CMA average for 1990	100	78	94	118
% change since 1980 (in constant $)	2	21	17	n.a.
Professionals, women as % of total, 1991	45.4	51.6	49.8	32.5

Source: Statistics Canada, Censuses of 1981 and 1991, special tabulations.

in a good-sized apartment remained much more affordable than in other large Canadian cities. Sharing by couples or non-family households brought rents down to very reasonable levels.

Centring the Margins: The Tenacity of Economically Marginal Gentrifiers in Montreal Neighbourhoods 'Professionalized' in the 1980s

Ley (1992) argues that the landscapes of gentrification diversified in the 1980s as older, wealthier professionals invested in luxury condominium developments while younger professionals, unable to buy into already gentrified older neighbourhoods where prices had skyrocketed, began moving into more affordable, still working-class and sometimes multi-ethnic districts. He concludes, in concurrence with stage models, that the gentrification of the latter will continue to proceed apace, eventually creating housing affordability problems for lower-income people throughout most of the inner city. Bourne, on the other hand, believes that while displacement could be a major problem in inner cities with overheated real estate markets, such as in Toronto in the late-1980s boom (Bourne 1992), the scale and impact of gentrification on older working-class districts may have been exaggerated (Bourne 1993a). He points out that, at least in the Toronto case, much of the growth in the ranks of wealthier urban professionals was absorbed not only by new developments on formerly non-residential land but also by *existing* elite and stable middle-class neighbourhoods, and he remains agnostic as to the intensity and spatial extent of pressures on inner city areas that are still mainly working class.

In the case of Montreal, the bifurcation of the fortunes of urban professionals in the 1980s discussed above, as well as factors specific to Montreal's economic, social, and cultural development and residential morphology, lead us to believe that the truth may lie somewhere between the Ley and Bourne versions of the trajectories of gentrification over the decade. The severe declines in professionals' employment earnings, even among women, and Montreal's changing position in the urban hierarchy, certainly give cause to question the notion of a widespread *embourgeoisement* of its inner city. But one must look at trends at a finer geographic scale to get a clearer feeling for what happened during the 1980s.

A preliminary examination of spatially disaggregated census data (in which the Montreal CMA is divided into ninety-three zones) about the numbers and employment incomes of professionals leads to the conclusion that, between 1981 and 1991, about 60 per cent of the increase in *numbers* of urban professionals took place in low-to-modest income districts where 'social upgrading' mainly took the form of renovation (Sénécal et al. 1990: 73–86 give details of renovation activity). However, most of the increase in aggregate *earnings* of inner city professionals took place in existing elite and middle-class areas, such as the 'enclave' municipalities of Outremont and Westmount, and the inner suburb of Notre-Dame de Grâce,[13] or in areas where there has been considerable new condominium development (most notably at Île-des-Soeurs just southwest of downtown Montreal).[14]

Both in the older elite and middle-class areas of the inner city and in areas of new condominium development, employment earnings were – not surprisingly – much higher than the CMA average. However, in those lower-to-modest income areas of the inner city which saw marked relative increases in the numbers and proportions of professionals (that is, greater than the increases seen for the metropolitan area as a whole), the trends in professionals' employment incomes over the decade varied considerably – up in some areas, down in others. One outcome of these income trends is that the 1990 earnings of male professionals remained much lower than the metropolitan average in districts at the periphery of the inner city which are still predominantly working class and where there is little visual evidence of gentrification activity. It could be, as Ley (1992) suggests, that young professionals of modest means have increasingly moved into more peripheral areas as housing prices have increased in central neighbourhoods. One might also infer that the pattern of change in these peripheral districts is consistent with the predictions of the stage models discussed earlier.

Yet, if we consider the inner city districts where change in housing stock mainly took the form of renovation rather than new construction, some of the *lowest* average 1990 employment incomes of professionals in the entire Montreal metropolitan area could be found not only in more peripheral zones but also in the two districts that underwent a marked process of gentrification in the 1980s as identified by two indicators: a very high percentage of professionals in 1991 *and* the greatest relative increases in professionals during the 1980s.[15] These districts are the central part of the Plateau Mont-Royal and the contiguous St-Louis and Mile End neighbourhoods (Map 7.1).[16] A similar pattern emerges even when the family incomes of couples consisting of two professionals (the Yuppie archetype) are compared between different types of inner city neighbourhoods and the CMA.

These findings on employment incomes are suggestive of a persistence throughout the 1980s and early 1990s of the phenomenon of 'marginal

MAP 7.1
Inner-City Montreal and Environs, Showing Location of Study Areas

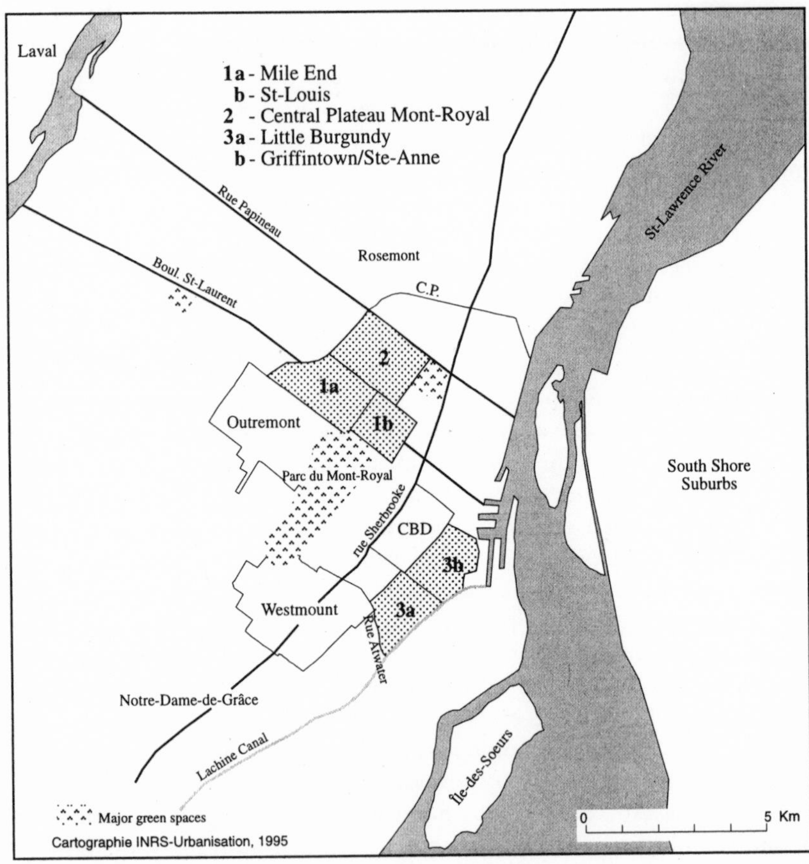

gentrification.' The census data show that those professionals who live in neighbourhoods at the periphery of the inner city that are still mainly working-class – districts that stage models would see as experiencing the beginnings of gentrification – have low average incomes compared with professionals in general. But, contrary to the predictions of stage models, many low-to-modest income professionals also continue to live in the central neighbourhoods *most* touched by renovation activity. This is the case in spite of considerable increases in house prices, property evaluations, and rent levels.

Moreover, professionals living in the Central Plateau and St-Louis/Mile

End neighbourhoods have a distinct profile in terms of the economic sector they work in. In 1991, as in 1981 (Dansereau and Beaudry 1986, Rose 1989), these professionals were still much more likely to work in the communications and artistic fields – where contractual and freelance work is endemic – than are professionals in the CMA as a whole (see Table 7.4). This profile is also consistent with the notion of marginal gentrification.

In addition, given that the gender gap in earnings persists among professionals in spite of the progress women have made, zones where women count for a high proportion of the professional 'principal household maintainers' may also be considered areas where economically marginal gentrification is prevalent – although to explore this question more fully one would need data on *household* incomes. On this indicator, the central Plateau and St-Louis/Mile End once again score the highest ranking (48–49 per cent; see Table 7.5). Interestingly, they are followed closely by some of the adjacent but less central neighbourhoods that have seen significant increases in professionals – in particular, parts of the Villeray, Rosemont, and Hochelaga-Maisonneuve districts (beyond the CPR tracks; see Map 7.1) originally developed as suburbs for the skilled working class (see Linteau 1992: *passim*).

There is no trace of marginal gentrification, however, in the third of the three zones that experienced the most 'professionalization' in the 1980s. In Little Burgundy, Ste-Anne, and Griffintown, where new condominium and townhouse complexes were developed during this period, average incomes of professionals for 1990 were noticeably higher than the CMA average, and these professionals were not concentrated in economic sectors characterized by economically marginal conditions (Table 7.4).

Beyond the Epiphenomenal: The Persistence of Social Mix in Montreal's Gentrifying Neighbourhoods – Diversity or Polarization?

Contrary to the predictions of 'rent gap' and 'stage' theories of gentrification, it is not inevitable, even in advanced tertiary cities, that all neighbourhoods where a 'beachhead' of 'first wave gentrifiers' is established will ultimately be caught up in an irreversible dynamic largely driven by major real estate interests and leading to their transformation into homogeneous Yuppie preserves (Rose 1989). In this chapter I have argued that Montreal has not conformed – at least, not as yet – to this vision of an ineluctable advance of gentrification. The truncation of the wealthier fractions of the Montreal region's urban professionals and their tendency

TABLE 7.5
Households Whose Principal Maintainer Is a Professional in the Three Montreal Districts that 'Professionalized' the Most in the 1980s: Selected Characteristics

	Montreal Census Metropolitan Area	St-Louis/ Mile End	Plateau Mont-Royal (central part)	Little Burgundy/ Ste-Anne/ Griffintown
Total Households 1991	1,220,520	15,835	13,140	4,590
Change, 1981–1991	18.9	3.1	–0.5	87.0
% distribution of all households by occupation of principal maintainer, 1991:				
Managers	6.8	4.5	4.5	7.5
Professionals	12.1	17.8	20.2	17.8
Technical, supervisory, specialized white- and blue-collar and service occupations	29.1	26.5	26.9	22.1
Non-specialized white- and blue-collar and service occupations	22.8	25.4	20.1	13.6
Not in labour force, or occupation not stated	29.2	25.9	28.5	39.0
% of all households having a professional as principal maintainer, 1991	12.1	17.8	20.2	17.8
Type of 'professional' household:				
Family household	8.4	7.3	8.1	9.9
One-person household	3.0	7.6	9.4	5.6
Non-family household, 2 or more persons	0.7	2.9	2.7	2.3
% of family households having a professional as principal maintainer	12.5	15.5	22.0	19.5
% of one-person households having a professional as principal maintainer	11.1	19.6	19.0	14.5
% of non-family households of 2 or more persons having a professional as principal maintainer	12.1	20.4	19.6	20.8
Home-ownership rates among households having a professional as principal maintainer, 1991 (%)	57.8	24.1	30.4	64.8
% of households whose principal maintainer is female, among households having a professional as principal maintainer, 1991	32	49	48	27

to congregate in elite and existing middle-income parts of the inner city and in certain suburban areas, combined with a fine-grained residential morphology which predisposes districts like the Plateau Mont-Royal to the maintenance of a considerable degree of socioeconomic diversity, have meant that marginal and middle-income professionals widely continue to 'share' the neighbourhoods that underwent the most gentrification through renovation in the 1980s. Moreover, since the economic slump of the late 1980s to early 1990s, rents and house prices have stopped rising (and have fallen back in some areas), and the supply of potential wealthy gentrifiers seems not to be increasing. Significantly, market values of condominiums previously priced above $150,000 have slumped since the late 1980s.

While urban professionals in gentrifying neighbourhoods remain an internally diverse group, it is also important to consider to what extent the process of gentrification in the 1980s transformed the broader social composition of the neighbourhoods affected. Stage-based theories of gentrification have tended to dismiss 'social diversity,' like marginal gentrification, as an epiphenomenon, a transient stage a neighbourhood goes through en route to *embourgeoisement.* For some neo-Marxist scholars, the consideration of social mix is an irrelevant diversion for critical urban research agendas (Smith 1987). But findings for Montreal in the 1980s give cause to question such assumptions. Might not social diversity turn out to be an enduring feature of many inner city neighbourhoods – depending on, among other things, variations in residential morphology at a micro-scale and the nature of state intervention in local housing markets?

In the Montreal case, as the 1991 data indicate (in Table 7.5), low-skilled workers and people not in the labour force still comprised about half of all 'principal household maintainers' in the central Plateau Mont-Royal and St-Louis/Mile End districts, although their numbers did drop in absolute and relative terms.[17] The diversity of residential form referred to above reduced (although certainly did not eliminate; see Lessard 1983) the extent of direct and indirect displacement of lower-income households out of the neighbourhoods, since better-quality housing and more gentrifiable units are interspersed with plexes and apartment buildings remaining affordable to low-income households. In addition, especially in the predominantly francophone Plateau Mont-Royal, the presence of lower-income households is partly sustained by the interspersal of small pockets of 'infill' public housing (Office municipal d'habitation de Montréal 1990) and by a substantial number of non-profit housing cooperatives, often in converted school buildings (Klodawsky et al. 1985: ch. 9, p. 35).

Moreover, in the St-Louis/Mile End district – Montreal's traditional immigrant 'corridor' astride St Lawrence Boulevard ('The Main'), and a socioeconomically heterogeneous area since the late nineteenth century – substantial numbers of triplex units were bought by southern European immigrants in the 1960s and 1970s and renovated mainly with their own 'sweat equity' (Krohn et al. 1977, Lavigne 1987). While many better-off members of these ethnic communities have moved to the suburbs – bringing their extended families with them and retaining their linguistic community (Linteau 1992: 588n9) – many working-class immigrant homeowners remain in the inner city. This type of 'incumbent upgrading' by working-class European immigrants has helped to maintain social diversity and reduce housing turnover even on street segments with quite extensive gentrification. Moreover, particularly among the Azorean Portuguese, it is common practice to rent out units at below-market rents to other members of the same ethnic community (Lavigne and Texeira 1990). Furthermore, substantial segments of several streets in the Mile End district saw a major expansion in the early 1980s of an ultra-orthodox Hasidic Jewish community of generally modest financial means. Buildings that might otherwise have been gentrified were bought up by members of the community for residential use or conversion to neighbourhood religious and social institutions. In addition, the part of Mile End east of the Main remains mainly industrial; its garment and textile industry employed several thousand women and men from within and beyond the neighbourhood in the early 1980s (Chicoine and Rose 1989) and remains important in spite of a decline over the decade. The residential blocks interspersed with industrial uses have only interested a small number of gentrifiers; this zone, as well as the large number of apartments on two of the busiest thoroughfares in the district, remains a low-rent area still accessible to low-income new immigrants. Moreover, Mile End is trisected by two very busy and noisy thoroughfares which still have many low-rental apartments.

In Little Burgundy/Griffintown/Ste-Anne, the third of the three districts identified as having 'professionalized' the most during the 1980s, 'social mix' is no less persistent but takes on a very different form and connotation (Tables 7.4 and 7.5). This historic area is located southwest of downtown, sandwiched between an expressway and the Lachine Canal (Map 7.1). The canal zone, once the centre of old industrial Montreal, is now being redeveloped as a recreational corridor. While Griffintown was the historical centre of the working-class Irish community (Benoît and

Gratton 1991), Little Burgundy was a focal point for Montreal's oldest-established black communities (Williams 1989). Large tracts of the area were razed by urban renewal operations in the 1970s (Filion 1988: 103), and much residential space was lost to expressways. The City then built hundreds of public housing units in Little Burgundy, which increasingly came to be occupied by low-income black families from other parts of the city. New condominiums and townhouses were (and are still being) erected in Little Burgundy and in the other sectors, on formerly residential and former railway land, and a number of industrial buildings have been converted to 'lofts.' These developments have attracted many young professionals, of whom a higher proportion work in business services than is the case for those in the central Plateau or St-Louis/Mile End. Moreover, far more men than women have been drawn to this area (Table 7.4). Most are white francophones or anglophones, but some middle-income Southeast Asian immigrant families have also bought townhouses in this area (Germain 1995). The City overcame opposition by local community organizations to the latest condos by invoking the 'doughnut hole' metaphor referred to above: money for improved services could only be found if more middle-class people could be brought in (*Montreal Mirror* 1992). In addition, there is a small amount of gentrification (by white and black professionals) on the few remaining sections of streets with Victorian architecture of merit.

In contrast to the Plateau and St-Louis/Mile End districts, the urban fabric of this area is highly fragmented. Streetscapes lack a sense of 'intimacy,' and basic commercial services and public amenities are lacking. Although the gentrifiers are still not, on average, wealthy, their average employment incomes are considerably higher than in the central Plateau or St-Louis/Mile End. Unlike the other two zones, the majority of the new urban professionals are homeowners (Table 7.5). At the same time, in two out of five households the principal maintainer is not in the labour force (Table 7.5), and in Little Burgundy some 40 per cent of households live in public housing (Germain 1995). The social contrasts between them and longer-established residents thus seem even greater than those in the central Plateau or in St-Louis/Mile End.

The co-residence of urban professionals of varying levels of income and job security, of traditional residents, and of other groups has proven to date to be an enduring phenomenon in the three Montreal neighbourhoods that underwent the most 'professionalization' in the 1980s. Even at the scale of a city block, rare are the instances where a new social homogeneity has taken hold.

This question of social diversity at a micro-scale has taken on a renewed importance because, in the past few years, we have been entering a period when decentralization or the 'return to the local' is *à la mode* in terms of the administration of local politics, community services, community economic development corporations, and so on (Lemelin and Morin 1991). This tendency has arisen out of an uneasy coalescence of, on the one hand, neoconservative policies in which governments attempt to reduce costs by passing the responsibility for services onto low-cost or volunteer labour in the community sector and, on the other hand, calls for democratization at the local scale stemming from the legacy of the urban social movements of the 1970s and early 1980s (Morin and Parazelli 1994, Shragge 1993). In gentrifying areas, who represents the interests of a 'neighbourhood' or a 'community' on local advisory boards and umbrella organizations of various kinds? In the process of establishing agendas for local social action through these organizations, what advantages accrue to the various fractions of the new middle class whose education and socialization have equiped them with more 'cultural capital' than traditional residents? What factors determine whether issue-oriented coalitions or conflicts develop between gentrifiers and other groups of local citizens around, for example, the provision of urban services? When various types of 'neighbourhood improvements' are obtained, how widely shared are the benefits? These questions are not new ones in the gentrification literature (see especially Filion 1991), but they are not treated seriously by theories which see 'social diversity' in gentrifying neighbourhoods as only a transient stage.[18]

Some recent writing – for example, Germain et al. (1995), Harris (1993), and van Weesep (1994), the latter specifically in regards to gentrification – underlines the continuing importance of the social mix question for housing and social services policies in inner cities, while cautioning against a priori assumptions that social mix (at various scales) is unequivocally beneficial to lower-income residents. Yet little theoretical or empirical work (apart from the occasional isolated but interesting case study, for example, Buchan 1985, Dineen 1974) exists to date as to how the meanings of 'social mix' and the compatibility of different kinds of 'urban lifestyles' are negotiated on the terrain of different kinds of partially gentrified neighbourhoods – whether we are referring to the everyday relations of neighbouring or to who participates and who represents whom in locally anchored political and administrative structures.

Caulfield's research on the life-worlds of Toronto gentrifiers indicates that their attraction towards neighbourhoods of social and ethnic diversity goes way beyond 'a kind of flâneurism or an interest in a simulacrum of cosmopolitanism' (1994: 185). However, little research exists as to how gentrifiers are perceived by various kinds of 'existing residents.' At what point, and how, for example, does a neighbourhood become 'culturally appropriated' by one group so that another no longer feels at home there even if they can still afford to live there? Moreover, one must be very circumspect about the generalizability of Caulfield's finding across different types of revitalizing neighbourhoods or between cities (Germain and Rose 1993).

We know particularly little about what happens in the case of multi-ethnic neighbourhoods where differential access to cultural capital by professionals from the dominant culture and immigrants and ethnic minorities may result in the former 'making over' services to meet their own needs while (perhaps inadvertently) excluding others (see Rose 1990 for the case of childcare). Or, to reiterate one of the long-standing arguments in favour of 'engineering' social mix, groups possessed of this cultural capital may help to obtain needed services that will benefit all residents as well as improving the social reproduction conditions of the new middle class (Filion 1991: 564n9). In Montreal's Mile End district a local residents' association whose key members are a group of urban professionals mostly of European origin has been in the forefront of successful lobbies to reduce traffic hazards, expand a multi-ethnic library, and get a badly-needed community and sports centre, catering to the diverse ethnic groups of the area, built through a unique joint initiative of the YMCA and the City of Montreal (Rose 1995). Yet in Little Burgundy – rebaptized, significantly, by real estate agents as 'Downtown Adjacent' – urban professionals have taken little interest in the problem of urban services in spite of local community organizations' attempts to get them involved. Many identify themselves more as downtown commuters than as residents of the neighbourhood (Germain 1995). Even the recent granting (under a federal-provincial infrastructure project) of a new sports complex has led to 'mutterings' from some segments of the community as to whether the location chosen for this complex will lead to it benefiting 'gentrifiers' or existing residents (*Montreal Gazette* 1994).

It might also be argued that one of the clearest indexes of a neighbourhood's cultural appropriation by the new middle class might lie in the transformation of commercial services and particularly that of a neighbourhood's retail infrastructure (J. Caulfield, personal communication, 8 September 1994). It is perhaps unfortunate that the gentrification literature has tended to see 'commercial gentrification' as a separate sub-issue rather than integrating it into the overall conceptual framework (but see Beauregard 1986). In this respect, the extent to which 'old' and 'new' residents frequent the same local shops becomes an interesting empirical question (Rose 1995).

Where, one might ask, does 'social diversity,' with its usually positive connotations, end, and where does the more ominous-sounding 'social polarization' begin (cf. Dansereau 1988: 105)? And what is the appropriate scale at which to explore this question?[19] This is an issue that theoretical and empirical work, taking a critical perspective on Canadian urbanism in the recent past and the 1990s, surely needs to address in a more systematic way.

Conclusion

This chapter has questioned the utility of two interrelated presuppositions prevalent in theorizing about gentrification in helping us to understand the nature of the process in Canadian cities during the 1980s. First, by means of a theoretically informed empirical account of how restructuring of the advanced tertiary workforce in the 1980s affected the constitution of the 'new middle class,' I have tried to show that the 'production' of both well-off and economically marginal gentrifiers was related to this economic restructuring process. Therefore, it seems unproductive to theoretically 'decouple' economically marginal gentrification from the body of theory that strongly relates gentrification to the formation of the new middle class in the course of wider processes of economic restructuring. At the same time I have suggested that the empirical importance of marginal gentrification might be greater in Montreal than in other Canadian cities for reasons linked to particularities of urban form and cultural process that are not reducible to economic restructuring but affect the impacts of this restructuring.

Second, by focusing in on the three inner city districts of Montreal which underwent the most marked 'professionalization' in the 1980s, I have questioned one of the key assumptions of stage models of gentrification, namely, the ineluctability of the transformation of a working-class neighbourhood to a fully 'bourgeoisified' one, once gentrification processes had started. The debate over the applicability of this model to Canadian cities has suffered from confusion over the question of scale and a lack of attention to the spatial specialization of housing markets for different fractions of the new middle class. The Montreal data presented here lend support to Bourne's (1993b) argument that the undeniable overall *embourgeoisement* (in terms of income) which has been observed in the inner cities of advanced tertiary centres, taken as a whole, is largely the result of highly localized new upscale condominium developments and the settlement of wealthy households in existing elite and middle-class areas. Gentrification in the narrow sense of movement by new middle-class groups into existing housing (or infill pockets of new housing) in old working-class neighbourhoods, is a cultural and social phenomenon of considerable portent, as Caulfield (1994) and others have argued. But in Montreal in the 1980s there was insufficient economic 'muscle' behind this facet of inner city 'professionalization' – that is, there were not enough wealthy potential gentrifiers and the city's economy was too weak – to unleash a dynamic of wholesale transformation of the most 'professionalized' neighbourhoods, particularly given their diverse residential morphology and the existing strength of other social groups in these neighbourhoods. Hence social diversity becomes an issue to be reckoned with rather than dismissed in gentrification theory.

These elements of critique do not invalidate the notion that working-class neighbourhoods can be transformed into bourgeois enclaves in a series of somewhat predictable stages. What they do question is the universality of this model across space and time and the assumption that this is the dominant process through which the 'professionalization' of inner cities of advanced tertiary centres occurs. Stage models are woefully inadequate in helping us to understand the rich diversity of landscapes of consumption and reproduction of new middle-class fractions that now characterize Canadian inner cities from Vancover to Halifax via Montreal, and in helping us to think about the kinds of social practices this diversity can engender.

While Caulfield's (1994) project seems to be to use 'culture' in the broad sense as a unifying concept to recreate coherence in the wake of the critique of gentrification as a chaotic concept, I am inclined to believe that Sayer's observation that 'it is not always possible or desirable to reduce the object so that it is less chaotic, because it may nevertheless be of interest as a whole, perhaps because, chaotic or not, it is to such objects that people respond' (1992: 250) may apply in the case of the gentrification debate in Canadian cities. I would suggest, then, that future research on gentrification be grounded in the historical specificities of particular cities and particular neighbourhoods but never lose sight of how locally experienced change relates to broader processes of economic and social restructuring. This would seem a more fruitful strategy than that of footnoting or constituting as 'other' those cases which fail to fit into our generalized models, and it is a strategy capable of generating 'intermediate-level' concepts that can help us move between the 'global' and the 'local.' Moreover, future progress in understanding how class, ethnic, gender and sexual identities in the inner city are constituted and negotiated, and how they intersect, will necessitate, among other things, a greater emphasis on the relations between gentrifiers and the internally diverse groups who make up what Beauregard (1986: 49–51) has called the 'gentrified.' And even if future economic booms do create pressures to greatly accelerate the gentrification process in neighbourhoods such as those discussed in this chapter, it will be no less important to study how strategies and struggles around questions of neighbourhood diversity are constructed and resolved.

NOTES

1 Parts of the material covered in this chapter were initially presented at conferences of the Canadian Association of Geographers (Vancouver, 1992), the International Geographical Union (Washington DC, 1992) and the Association of American Geographers (San Francisco, 1994). My thanks to all who provided comments at various stages, and to Nathalie Chicoine for research assistance on the question of precarious employment. The research was funded by grants from the Social Sciences and Humanities Research Council of Canada and the Fonds FCAR (Quebec Ministry of Education).
2 Ley uses a broader operational definition of urban professionals than that employed in this chapter and in previous and ongoing research by Paul Villeneuve and myself. Our definition excludes managers and specialized technicians and zeroes in on a subset of the middle class: those in occupations in which power is conferred through control over knowledge and information (i.e., over 'cultural capital,' to use Bourdieu's (1984) term), rather than control over people. Higher education (often including a professional degree) is a prerequisite for access to these occupations. For a set of reasons, linked to complex and still-incompletely understood interactions of class, culture, and gender dynamics, this subset of the middle class is much more likely to live in the inner city than are the managerial or technical fractions (see, e.g., Butler and Hamnett 1994). For a fuller explanation of our classification see Villeneuve and Rose (1988). It may be noted from Table 5 that unlike professionals, managers are under-represented in the two Montreal districts which 'professionalized' the most through renovation, compared with the CMA as a whole. Nonetheless, our empirical findings do not diverge substantially from Ley's.
3 Edmonton, where planning policies have failed to make the inner city attrac-

tive to substantial numbers of professionals (Ley 1992), and, to a lesser extent Ottawa-Hull, form exceptions to this trend.

4 These and all other unattributed census data used in this chapter are drawn from special tabulations of the 1981, 1986, and 1991 censuses obtained by Damaris Rose and Paul Villeneuve.

5 Women professionals in Ottawa-Hull appear to be a notable exception. In fact, however, data disaggregated by sector (not presented in the table) show that among public sector professionals in the inner city, employment incomes fell for both men and women, in absolute terms and relative to their suburban counterparts. This may be an effect of the growth of the 'pool' of non-permanent civil servants and workers on short-term contracts to federal government agencies. Many of these people probably live in inner city rental apartments. A second exception is the drop in earnings of inner city Toronto males aged 35–44, but not in those of their suburban counterparts; most of the drop actually took place among the public sector category (it did not affect the financial and business services sector, for example). Halifax experienced a major boom through most of the 1980s as its regional service sector function consolidated (Ley 1992); suburban male professionals were, in the aggregate, greater beneficiaries than those in the inner city.

6 The trends for the 15–24 group are difficult to interpret as their numbers are small and many of them are students.

7 Little, if anything, has been written on this dimension of Quebecers' 'love affair' with the suburbs. I base my impressions on conversations with a number of colleagues, students, researchers, and friends over the past few years.

8 First initiated in the late 1970s under the autocratic Drapeau administration, but continued by the reformist Montreal Citizens' Movement in power from 1986 to 1994.

9 Ironically, City efforts were often at cross-purposes with provincial programs designed to stimulate the construction industry; these measures mainly favoured new residential developments in the suburbs.

10 Many affluent professional households have opted to locate in luxury condominiums on Ile-des-Soeurs in the City of Verdun, easily accessible to downtown Montreal (Map 7.1).

11 Overstocked as a result of the rapid growth of specialized undergraduate programs in these and related fields. These programs (rare elsewhere in Canada) were part of Quebec government policy to quickly create a supply of francophone professionals during the Quiet Revolution of the 1960s. With economic slowdowns and cutbacks supply has greatly exceeded demand for many years.

12 Data from a special compilation of census data for INRS-Urbanisation and the Ville de Montréal, obtained by Jaël Mongeau and Anne-Marie Séguin.

13 For accounts of the historical development of these districts see Linteau 1992: *passim*); see also Benoît and Gratton (1991: 242) for the case of Notre-Dame de Grâce.

14 This assessment is based on a zone-by-zone examination of changes in numbers of professionals, in employment incomes of female and male professionals, and in the numbers and incomes of two-earner families in which one or both spouses is a professional.

15 Areas defined as having experienced the most gentrification were identified as those zones in which the proportion of professionals to total residents in 1991 was much higher than the CMA average, and where the rate of increase from 1981 to 1991 was much greater than for the CMA as a whole. These proportions were calculated in two ways: by using the variable 'occupation of individuals in the labour force;' and by using the variable 'occupation of "principal household maintainer"' (the latter category is used by the Census to identify the person who makes the largest contribution to a household's housing-related expenses, which are usually the biggest item in household budgets). The calculations were done using location quotients and relative change quotients (see Filion 1987 for an example of the use of these simple statistical techniques). Of the three areas which scored the highest, in two (central part of Plateau Mont-Royal and St-Louis / Mile End) the influx of professionals was associated mainly with renovation and in the third (Little Burgundy / Ste-Anne / Griffintown) mainly with new condominium development on 'greyfield' sites (Choko and Dansereau 1986, Sénécal et al. 1990). The measure of gentrification used here does not take into account changes in the proportion of residents with a university degree, a measure which has been found to be one of the key indicators of a neighbourhood's social and cultural transformation (see, e.g., Ley 1988). My primary interest in the relationships between economic restructuring and gentrification leads me to focus more narrowly here on those employed in professional occupations. However, separate calculations of census-tract level changes in the proportions of residents aged 15 and over with a university degree yield a virtually identical spatial patterning of change within the inner city to that outlined here.

16 The general pattern differs little by gender except that in one of the most gentrified areas (the central part of Plateau Mont-Royal) women's 1990 earnings came close (94 per cent) to the CMA average.

17 Dual-professional couples, whose consumer spending power is very high, are a very important component of the new middle class in elite, middle-class, and gentrifying inner city neighbourhoods (Butler and Hamnett 1994, Rose and Villeneuve 1995, Villeneuve and Morency 1990). Therefore, measuring a

neighbourhood's social status using the occupation of the principal *household* maintainer will underestimate the presence and economic weight of the new middle class, because only one household member's occupation is taken into account. Such a measure will also underestimate occupational diversity within a neighbourhood in the sense that there is often considerable 'asymmetry' between the occupations of wives and husbands. However, it may still be preferable to use *household*-based measures in research on gentrification's impacts at a neighbourhood scale, because with such measures the proportions of 'professional households' can be related to total numbers of households. Needless to say – and especially in areas with a high proportion of retired or unemployed principal household maintainers – this may yield a different perspective on the quantitative importance of the new middle class than a measure of the proportion of individuals in the labour force who are professionals.

18 Bourne (1993a) is a rare exception among gentrification researchers in pointing to the persistence of strongly bipolar household income distributions in a Toronto neighbourhood typical of those gentrified through renovation, and to the presence of high proportions of low-income households (30% or more) in all such neighbourhoods.

19 Hanna and Olson (1983: 259) make the perceptive observation that microscale census data analysis tends to overestimate social mix because enumeration areas (the basic building blocks of areally reported census data) are constructed using the city block, that is, each street section is divided and then recombined with half of the adjacent street. In reality, however, the city-building process usually results in the two facing sides of a street section – i.e., the 'block faces' – closely resembling each other while the adjacent street may be of a different socioeconomic status.

REFERENCES

Aubin, H. 1995. 'Montreal's 'doughnut effect' remains a pressing problem.' *Montreal Gazette*, 17 January, B3.

Badcock, B. 1993. 'Notwithstanding the exaggerated claims, residential revitalisation really is changing the form of some Western cities: A response to Bourne.' *Urban Studies* 30(1): 191–5

Beauregard, R.A. 1986. 'The chaos and complexity of gentrification.' In N. Smith and P. Williams, eds., *Gentrification of the City*, 35–55. Boston: Allen and Unwin

– 1990. 'Trajectories of neighborhood change.' *Environment and Planning A* 22(6): 855–74

Benoît, M., and R. Gratton. 1991. *Pignon sur rue: les quartiers de Montréal.* Montreal: Guérin

Bondi, L. 1991. 'Gender divisions and gentrification: A critique.' *Transactions of the Institute of British Geographers – New Series* 16(2): 190–8

Bourdieu, P. 1984. *Distinction: A Social Critique of the Judgement of Taste.* Andover, UK: Routledge and Kegan Paul

Bourne, L.S. 1991. 'Addressing the Canadian city: Contemporary perspectives, trends and issues.' In T.E. Bunting and P. Filion, eds., *Canadian Cities in Transition,* 25–44. Toronto: Oxford University Press

– 1992. 'Population turnaround in the Canadian inner city: Contextual factors and social consequences.' *Canadian Journal of Urban Research* 1(1): 66–89

– 1993a. 'Close together and worlds apart: An analysis of changes in the ecology of income in Canadian cities.' *Urban Studies* 30(8): 1293–1317

– 1993b. 'The demise of gentrification? A commentary and prospective view.' *Urban Geography* 14 (1): 95–107

Buchan, R. 1985. 'Gentrification's impact on neighbourhood public service usage.' M.A. thesis. University of British Columbia, School of Community and Regional Planning.

Bussière, Y. 1989. 'L'automobile et l'expansion des banlieues: le cas de Montréal, 1901–2001.' *Revue d'histoire urbaine/Urban History Review* 18(2): 159–65

Butler, T. and C. Hamnett. 1994. 'Gentrification, class and gender: Some comments on Warde's 'Gentrification as consumption.' *Environment and Planning D: Society and Space* 12(4): 477–93

Castells, M. 1989. *The Informational City: Information Technology, Economic Restructuring and the Urban-Regional Process.* Oxford, UK, and Cambridge, MA: Basil Blackwell

Caulfield, J. 1994. *City Form and Everyday Life: Toronto's Gentrification and Critical Social Practice.* Toronto: University of Toronto Press

Charbonneau, F., and R. Parenteau. 1991. 'Opération 20 000 logements et l'espace social de Montréal.' *Recherches sociographiques* 32(2): 237–54

Charbonneau, F., P. Hamel, and M. Barcelo. 1994. 'Urban sprawl in the Montreal area – policies and trends.' In F. Frisken, ed., *The Changing Canadian Metropolis: A Policy Perspective,* 459–96. Berkeley: University of California, Institute of Governmental Studies Press, and Toronto: Canadian Urban Institute

Chevalier, J. 1993. 'Toronto-Ottawa-Montréal: Concentrations majeures canadiennes de l'innovation par la recherche-dévéloppement.' *Canadian Geographer/Le géographe canadien* 37(3): 242–57

Chicoine, N., and D. Rose. 1989. 'Restructuration économique, division sexuelle du travail et repartition spatiale de l'emploi dans la région métropolitaine de Montréal.' *Espaces, populations, sociétés* no. 1: 53–64

Chicoine, N., and D. Rose with N. Guénette. 1995. 'Vivre et travailler au centre de Montréal: stratégies de jeunes professionnels face à la précarité d'emploi.'

Paper presented at the Second Conference on Urban Research, Montreal, 7–9 June

Choko, M., and F. Dansereau. 1986. *Restauration résidentielle et copropriété au centre-ville de Montréal.* Montreal: INRS-Urbanisation, *Études et documents* no. 53

Christopherson, S., and T. Noyelle. 1992. 'The U.S. path toward flexibility and productivity: The re-making of the U.S. labour market in the 1980s.' In H. Ernste and V. Meier, eds., *Regional Development and Contemporary Industrial Response: Extending Flexible Specialisation,* 163–78. London: Belhaven Press

Coffey, W., and R. Drolet. 1994. 'La décentralisation des services supérieurs dans la région métropolitaine de Montréal.' *Canadian Geographer/Le Géographe canadien* 38(3) 215–28

Coffey, W., and M. Polèse. 1993. 'Le déclin de l'empire montréalais: regard sur l'économie d'une métropole en mutation.' *Recherches sociographiques* 34(3): 417–38

Cohen, G. 1994. 'Le cumul d'emplois à la hausse.' *L'emploi et le revenu en perspective* (Statistique Canada, cat. 75–001F) 6(3): 38–46

Collin, J.-P., and J. Mongeau. 1992. 'Quelques aspects démographiques de l'étalement urbain à Montréal de 1971 à 1991 et leurs implications pour la gestion de l'agglomération.' *Cahiers québécois de démographie,* 21(2): 5–30

Comité interministériel des espaces verts et bleus du Grand Montréal. 1992. *Les espaces verts et bleus du Grand Montréal. Les besoins. Les moyens.* Montréal: Gouvernement du Québec, Secrétariat du Grand Montréal

Dansereau, F., with B. Lacroix. 1988. *Habiter au centre: tendances et perspectives socio-économiques de l'habitation dans l'arrondissement Centre.* Montréal: Ville de Montréal and INRS-Urbanisation, *Dossier Montréal* 3

Dansereau, F., and M. Beaudry. 1986. 'Les mutations de l'espace habité montréalais: 1971–1981.' In *La morphologie sociale en mutation au Québec,* 283–308. Montreal: Association canadienne-française pour l'avancement de science. *Cahiers de l'ACFAS* 41

Dantas, A. 1988. 'Overspill as an alternative form of gentrification: The case of Riverdale, Toronto.' In T.E. Bunting and P. Filion, eds., *The Changing Canadian Inner City,* 73–86. Waterloo: University of Waterloo, Department of Geography

Dineen, J. 1974. *The Trouble with Coops.* Toronto: Green Tree

Divay, G., and M. Gaudreau. 1984. *La formation des espaces résidentiels: le système de production de l'habitat dans les années soixante-dix au Québec.* Sainte-Foy: Presses de l'Université du Québec

Drache, D. 1991. 'The systemic search for flexibility: National competitiveness and new work relations.' In D. Drache and M. Gertler, eds., *The New Era of Global Competition,* 251–69. Montreal and Kingston: McGill-Queen's University Press

Duffy, A., and N. Pupo. 1992. *Part-Time Paradox: Connecting Gender, Work and Family.* Toronto: McClelland and Stewart

Economic Council of Canada. 1991. *Employment in the Service Economy.* Ottawa: Supply and Services Canada

Filion, P. 1987. 'Concepts of the inner city and recent trends in Canada.' *Canadian Geographer/Le Géographe canadien* 31(3): 223–32

– 1988. 'The Neighbourhood Improvement Program in Montreal and Toronto: Two approaches to publicly sponsored upgrading.' In In T.E. Bunting and P. Filion, eds., *The Changing Canadian Inner City,* 87–106. Waterloo: University of Waterloo, Department of Geography

– 1991. 'The gentrification-social structure dialectic: A Toronto case study.' *International Journal of Urban and Regional Research* 15(4): 553–74

Filion, P. and Mock, D. 1991. 'Manufacturing in Canadian cities.' In T.E. Bunting and P. Filion, eds., *Canadian Cities in Transition,* 401–31. Toronto: Oxford University Press

Garreau, J. 1991. *Edge City: Life on the New Frontier.* New York: Doubleday

Gartley, J. 1994. *Les gains des Canadiens.* Cat. 96–317F. Ottawa: Statistics Canada and Scarborough: Prentice-Hall Canada

Gauthier, M., and L. Mercier. 1994. *La pauvreté chez les jeunes: précarité économique et fragilité sociale: un bilan.* Québec: Institut québécois de recherche sur la culture [name since changed to INRS-Culture et Société]

Germain, A. 1995. 'La Petite-Bourgogne: un quartier tourmenté à la reconquête de son image.' In A. Germain, J. Archambault, B. Blanc, J. Charbonneau, F. Dansereau, and D. Rose, *Cohabitation interethnique et vie de quartier,* 169–200. Final report to the ministère des Affaires internationales, de l'Immigration et des Communautés culturelles and to the Ville de Montréal. Québec: Les Publications du Québec, MAIICC, Direction des communications, *Études et recherches* no 12

Germain, A., C. Éveillard, and F. Dansereau. 1995. 'Le Quartier Angus: une réussite en matière de mixité sociale programmée?' INRS-Urbanisation, Montreal.

Germain, A., and D. Rose, with N. Chicoine, A.-M. Séguin and with the collaboration of F. Dansereau and R. Morin. 1993. *Vie de quartier et immigration.* Montreal: ministère des Communautés culturelles et d'Immigration, Direction des communications, *Collection Notes et Documents* no. 2

Ghalam, N.Z. 1993. *Women in the Workplace,* 2nd ed. Cat. 71–534E. Ottawa: Statistics Canada

Goldberg, M., and J. Mercer. 1986. *The Myth of the North American City: Continentalism Revisited.* Vancouver: University of British Columbia Press

Hamel, P., M. Choko, and F. Dansereau. 1988. *La spéculation foncière.* Montreal: INRS-Urbanisation

Hamnett, C. 1994. 'Social polarisation in global cities: theory and evidence.' *Urban Studies* 31: 401–24

Hanna, D., and S. Olson. 1983. 'Métiers, loyers et bouts de rue: l'armature de la société montréalaise, 1881 à 1901.' *Cahiers de géographie du Québec* 27(71): 255–75

Harris, R. 1993. 'Social mix, housing tenure and community development.' In J. Miron, ed., *House, Home and Community: Progress in Housing Canadians, 1945–1986*, 308–19. Montreal and Kingston: McGill-Queen's University Press and Canada Mortgage and Housing Corporation

Institut de recherche et d'information sur la rémunération. 1992. *La décennie 80: qu'en est-il du pouvoir d'achat des salariés du secteur public québécois?* Montréal

Institut Vanier de la famille. 1994. *Profil des familles canadiennes.* Ottawa

Kernstein, R. 1990. 'Stage models of gentrification: An examination.' *Urban Affairs Quarterly* 35(4): 620–39

Klodawsky, F., A. Spector, and D. Rose. 1985. *Single Parent Families and Canadian Housing Policies: How Mothers Lose.* Report prepared for Canada Mortgage and Housing Corporation, External Research Program

Krohn, R., B. Fleming, and M. Manzer. 1977. *The Other Economy: The Internal Logic of Local Rental Housing.* Toronto: Peter Martin Associates

Lamonde, P., and Y. Martineau. 1992. *Désindustrialisation et restructuration économique. Montréal et les autres grandes métropoles nord-américaines, 1971–1991.* Montreal: INRS-Urbanisation, *Rapports de recherche* no. 14

Lavigne, G. 1987. *Les ethniques et la ville. L'aventure urbaine des immigrants portugais à Montréal.* Montreal: La Préambule

Lavigne, G., and C. Teixeira. 1990. 'Mobilité et ethnicité.' *Revue européenne des migrations internationales* 6(2): 123–32

Legault, R. 1989. 'Architecture et forme urbaine: l'exemple du triplex à Montréal de 1870 à 1914.' *Urban History Review / Revue d'histoire urbaine* 18(1): 1–11

Lemelin, A., and R. Morin. 1991. 'L'approche locale et communautaire au développement économique des zones défavorisées: le cas de Montréal.' *Cahiers de géographie du Québec* 35(95): 285–306

Lessard, M.-J. 1983. 'La copropriété indivise dans les petits immeubles: le cas des locataires évincés.' MSc. A. thesis, Faculté de l'Aménagement, Université de Montréal

Levine, M. 1990. *The Reconquest of Montreal: Language Policy and Social Change in a Bilingual City.* Philadelphia: Temple University Press

Ley, D. 1988. 'Social upgrading in six Canadian inner cities.' *Canadian Geographer Le géographe canadien* 32(1): 31–45

– 1992. 'Gentrification in recession: Social change in six Canadian inner cities, 1981–1986.' *Urban Geography* 13(3): 230–56

– 1993. 'Past elites and present gentry: Neighbourhoods of privilege in the inner city.' In L.S. Bourne and D. Ley, eds., *The Changing Social Geography of Canadian Cities,* 214–33. Montreal and Kingston: McGill-Queen's University Press (Canadian Association of Geographers Series in Canadian Geography)

– 1994. 'Gentrification and the politics of the new middle class.' *Environment and Planning D: Society and Space* 12(1): 53–74

– 1996. *The New Middle Class and the Remaking of the Central City.* Toronto: Oxford University Press

Linteau, P.-A. 1992. *Histoire de Montréal depuis la Confédération.* Montréal: Boréal

Marcoux, R., R. Morin, and D. Rose. 1990. 'Jeunes et précarisation économique: analyse de la situation des couples.' *Cahiers québécois de démographie* 19(2): 273–307

Marshall, K. 1987. *Who are the Professional Women?/Qui sont les femmes des professions liberales?* Cat. 99–951. Ottawa: Statistics Canada

Mills, C. 1988. 'Life on the upslope: The postmodern landscape of gentrification.' *Environment and Planning D: Society and Space* 6(2): 169–89

Montreal Gazette. 1994. 'Black community wants control of sports complex,' by C. Clark. 27 June, A3

– 1995. 'Prime building lots at bargain prices; City bids to lure lost residents back,' by C. Clark. 4 July, C1

Montreal Mirror. 1992. 'Condos 1800, people 0. How John Gardiner put down a revolt in Little Burgundy,' by A. Roslin. 24 September–1 October, 7

Montréal, Ville de. 1992. *Orientations and Strategies of the Montreal City Plan: Project.* Montréal: Ville de Montréal, Service de l'habitation et du développement urbain, Plan d'urbanisme

Moreau, N. 1994. 'Le travail à temps partiel "non choisi."' *L'emploi et le revenu en perspective* (Statistique Canada, cat. 75–001F) 6(3): 30–7

Morin, R., and M. Parazelli. 1994. 'Développement local communautaire.' *Territoires* (June): 2–17

Morissette, R., J. Myles, and G. Picot. 1993. *What Is Happening to Earnings Inequality in Canada?* Ottawa: Statistics Canada, Analytical Studies Branch, *Research Paper* no. 60

Morissette, R., and D. Sunter. 1994. *What Is Happening to Weekly Hours Worked in Canada? Analytical Studies Branch Research Paper 17.* Ottawa: Statistics Canada

Myles, J., G. Picot, and T. Wannell. 'The changing wage distribution of jobs, 1981–1986.' *The Labour Force / La population active.* Statistics Canada, cat. 71-001 (Oct.): 85–138

Noël, A. 1994. 'Les politiques sociales et la polarisation des revenus.' *Nouvelles pratiques sociales* 7(1): 217–27

Office municipal d'habitation de Montréal. 1990. *Descriptive List of Low Rental Dwellings as of December 31, 1989.* Montreal: Ville de Montréal, OMHM

Olson, S., and D. Hanna. 1990. 'The social landscape of Montreal, 1901.' In D. Kerr and D.W. Holdsworth, eds., *Historical Atlas of Canada.* vol. 3, *Addressing the Twentieth Century, 1891–1961,* Plate 30. Toronto: University of Toronto Press

Polèse, M. 1988. *L'emploi dans le centre-ville de Montréal: structure, évolution et perspectives d'avenir.* Montreal: Ville de Montréal and INRS-Urbanisation, *Dossier Montréal* 2

– 1990. 'La thèse du déclin économique de Montréal, revue et corrigée.' *L'Actualité économique* 66(2): 133–46

Rashid, A. 1993. 'L'évolution des salaires durant sept décennies.' *L'Emploi et le revenu en perspective* (Statistics Canada, cat. 75–001F) 5(2): 10–23

– 1994. *Revenu de la famille au Canada.* Cat. CS96–318F. Ottawa: Statistics Canada and Scarborough: Prentice-Hall Canada

Rose, D. 1984. 'Rethinking gentrification: beyond the uneven development of marxist urban theory.' *Environment and Planning D: Society and Space* 2(1): 47–74

– 1987. 'Book review: N. Smith and P. Williams, eds., *Gentrification of the City.* New York: Allen & Unwin, 1986.' *Economic Geography* 63(4): 361–3

– 1989. 'A feminist perspective of employment restructuring and gentrification: The case of Montreal.' In J. Wolch and M. Dear, eds., *The Power of Geography: How Territory Shapes Social Life,* 118–38. Boston: Unwin Hyman. [Originally published in 1987 in *Cahiers de geographie du Quebec,* 31 (83)]

– 1990. '"Collective consumption" revisited: Analysing modes of provision and access to childcare services in Montreal.' *Political Geography Quarterly* 9 (4): 353–80

– 1995. 'Le Mile-End: un quartier cosmopolite?' In A. Germain, J. Archambault, B. Blanc, J. Charbonneau, F. Dansereau, and D. Rose, *Cohabitation interethnique et vie de quartier.* Final report to the ministère des Affaires internationales, de l'Immigration et des Communautés culturelles and to the Ville de Montréal. Quebec: Les Publications du Québec, MAIICC, Direction des Communications, *Études et recherches,* no. 12

Ross, D., and R. Shillington. 1992. *Mobilité de la main-d'oeuvre. Deux années dans la vie du marché du travail canadien.* Cat. 71–538F. Ottawa: Statistics Canada

Roy, D. 1990. 'L'aménagement des banlieues et le quotidien des femmes actives.' *Canadian Woman Studies/Les cahiers de la femme* 11(2): 71–5

Rudin, R. 1985. *The Forgotten Quebecers: A History of English-Speaking Quebec.* Quebec: Institut québécois de recherche sur la culture

Sayer, A. 1992. *Method in Social Science: A Realist Approach,* 2nd ed. London and New York: Routledge

Séguin, A.-M. 1989. 'Madame Ford et l'espace: lecture féministe de la suburbanisation.' *Recherches féministes* 2(1): 51–68

Sénécal, P., Tremblay, C., and Teufel, D. 1990. *Gentrification or Urban Sprawl? Cen-*

tral Montreal and Surrounding Area. Montreal: Société d'habitation du Québec, Direction générale de la planification et de la recherche

Shragge, E. 1993. 'The politics of community economic development.' In E. Shragge, ed., *Community Economic Development in Search of Empowerment,* 1–17. Montreal: Black Rose Books

Smith, N. 1987. 'Of yuppies and housing: Gentrification, social restructuring and the urban dream.' *Environment and Planning D: Society and Space* 5(2): 151–72

Smith, N., and P. Williams. 1986. 'Alternatives to orthodoxy: Invitation to a debate.' In N. Smith and P. Williams, eds., *Gentrification of the City,* 1–12. Boston: Allen and Unwin

Turcotte, G. 1980. *Différenciation sociale et accessibilité à l'espace neuf.* INRS-Urbanisation, Montreal, *Études et documents* no. 18

van Weesep, J. 1994. 'Gentrification as a research frontier.' *Progress in Human Geography* 18(1): 74–83

Villeneuve, P., and R. Morency. 1990. 'Couples à double emploi et hétérogénéité sociale dans les quartiers de Montréal.' *Le géographe canadien/The Canadian Geographer* 34(3): 239–50

Villeneuve, P., and D. Rose. 1988. Gender and the separation of employment from home in Metropolitan Montreal, 1971–1981. *Urban Geography* 9(2): 155–79

Williams, D. 1989. *Blacks in Montreal, 1628–1986: An Urban Demography.* Montreal: Éditions Y. Blais

8

Restructuring the Local State: Economic Development and Local Public Enterprise in Toronto

GRAHAM TODD

By 1990 the culmination of long-term economic crisis and the trough of a cyclical recession had left 283,800 people relying on some type of social assistance payment in Metropolitan Toronto (*Toronto Star*, 14 November 1991). In Canada the latest North American recession was geographically concentrated in southern Ontario and it had a severe impact on employment levels in the urban region of Toronto. Under such conditions there was considerable pressure for local governments to act to redress problems that had resulted from the actions of markets. The pressure to act gave rise to several local government initiatives in Toronto and reinforced the expanding role of the Toronto Economic Development Corporation (TEDCO), a paramunicipal corporation wholly owned by the City of Toronto. The creation of these kinds of entrepreneurial fragments of the local state marks a departure from previous institutional structures and approaches to local economic development. Since its inception in 1986, TEDCO has had to balance entrepreneurialism with a longer term developmental approach that focuses less on visible market success.

Governments play a crucial role in the economies of all the older industrialized countries whether through spending, providing services, or merely establishing the rules of the game for the private market. The institutions through which governments exercise this role, and the ideas which shape the way government involvement in the economy is viewed, change over time, especially as the social organization of the economy shifts in response to technological and political developments. However, the 'translation' of economic change through the grid of predominant ideas and into policy frameworks and institutions is never straightforward but is fraught with conflict between competing interests in the existing political and economic structures. Economic development policy becomes particularly relevant in periods of restructuring and economic downturn because it is seen as a preventative means of dealing with market-induced social costs by stimulating new growth and employment. This chapter examines how changes in the economy have materialized in the policies of the local state by focusing on examples of local government economic development activities in Toronto.

A critical perspective raises questions regarding the conventional account of political economic developments over the past decade. While the ideology and rhetoric of neo-liberalism have championed a reduced role for government in the economy, the reality is quite different. Less government and freer markets have been the neo-liberal rallying cries, but in fact new kinds of state institutions have appeared as a result of the rapid pace of change that characterizes the contemporary economy. The restructuring of capitalism has not only produced a more internationally integrated economy, but it has also led to the restructuring of public sector institutions and the formation of new ones.

These institutional changes reflect the predominant ideological commitments of the actors involved and the relative power of competing groups to influence the process. For example, the ideologically predominant view of government is that it must reduce spending and encourage growth. Thus, in a period of economic crisis, a rise in the welfare case load in Metropolitan Toronto has led to cutbacks in benefits, and the partial 'privatization' of social services through the proliferation of a volunteer-based system of food banks and related charities (Laws 1988). At the same time, however, the commitment of local government to economic renewal has led to new forms of public joint ventures with the private sector (Leo and Fenton 1990). The point is not that these two policies are incompatible, only that more powerful groups are better able to have their interests recognized than those disadvantaged in the economy. Thus, while neo-liberal approaches emphasize the need to reduce government-run programs, there has also been a corresponding trend in the opposite direction. At the international and national levels the establishment of the legal framework of freer trade has required the expansion of certain kinds of institutions. Examples are the creation of the World Trade Organization to settle disputes under the General Agreement on Tariffs and Trade and the expansion of various ministries and departments of trade in countries around the world.

At the local level, economic restructuring has had an impact on patterns of land use, labour markets, and the delivery of services, and it has influenced the policies of local governments in these areas. Government initiatives including large real estate development projects, the establishment of local labour market training schemes and public promotional offices in the film and tourism sectors, and the de facto privatization of social services mentioned above can all be seen as attempts to deal with the changing political economy. It is important then not only to look at *how much* government intervention there is but *what kind* of state activities are taking place. The example that I will discuss in this chapter concerns the effort to create more competitive and market-oriented institutions of local government in the field of economic development. This is a relatively new role, one which forms part of what David Harvey (1989) calls a shift from 'managerialism to entrepreneurialism' in local governance. In Canada's larger cities local governments have responded to the forces of economic change by creating economic development offices and expanding their promotional activities and by creating public sector economic development corporations (EDCs) such as TEDCO and la Commission d'initiatives et de développement économique de Montréal (CIDEM). Encouraging economic growth by promoting the particular advantages of one's own urban location has long been the purview of local government, but by participating in the economy more directly and focusing on new sectors of activity, local government has changed its role. A critical perspective is important here because, if we persist in thinking of changing government involvement in the economy simply in terms of 'more' or 'less,' we risk obscuring important changes of *kind* in the contemporary political economy. Throughout the chapter I refer to the growth of the organizational structures of the local state as instances of *state formation*. This concept refers to the political process whereby new agencies and apparatuses of the state are formed in response to changing political and economic conditions.[1]

In the section that follows I set out some conceptual categories relating to processes of economic change and their impact on state formation. In the second section, I outline the recent history of EDCs and the economic development activities of the local state in Toronto during the 1970s and 1980s. In the third and concluding section, the entrepreneurial turn of the local state is analysed in light of general trends towards the marketization of state activities in the context of fiscal crisis.

A New State for the New Economy

There has been considerable discussion of the emergence of new forms of economic activity and work organization (Mahon 1991; Goodwin, Duncan, and Halford 1993). Boosters of the 'new economy' (Beck 1992), for example, emphasize the growing demand for more highly skilled and knowledgeable workers. Work organization is also changing in response to new information technologies and flexible specialization in production. But economic change is sensitive to place as well. The geography of innovative and competitive firms in the new high-technology and knowledge-intensive sectors of the economy reveals a concentrated locational pattern of 'new industrial spaces' (Scott 1988). In Canada these districts tend to be located in or on the edges of large cities (Britton 1993). The importance of place creates at least the opportunity for local governments in these cities, whose role is the management of urban space, to influence economic development in important ways. The shift towards a more locationally sensitive economic geography encourages all levels of the state to be more 'local' in their economic policy. Internationally, a number of observers have remarked on the more active role of local governments in the planning and promotion of economic development and their potentially greater influence in the context of these locational patterns (Clavel and Kleniewski 1990, Preteceille 1990). Although in Canada the process has been mediated by the particularities of federalism and the limited autonomy accorded to local governments by provincial statutes, local governments in Canadian cities have participated in this trend (Leo and Fenton 1990, Gertler 1990). The place of municipal governments as constitutional 'creatures of the provinces' and the existence of provincial statutes that limit the ability of local governments to engage in 'bonussing' (Gertler 1990: 42–3) have led to a particular kind of local institutional adaptation in Canada.

Since the 1970s, both in the private market and at the level of state planning, economic growth has been premised on restructuring the economic regime of accumulation and the political mode of regulation that were typical of the era of postwar mass manufacturing.[2] As indicated this restructuring process has spatial dimensions as well, meaning that economic change will implicate local government planning and land use decisions. While in the immediate post–Second World War or 'Fordist' period the state's activities were focused on mass or standardized forms of service delivery, the 'post-Fordist' state is more flexible, entrepreneurial, and institutionally dispersed (Goodwin, Duncan, and Halford 1993; Jessop 1993). Public sector economic initiatives are now more likely to be tailored for specific localities and communities. The new competitive environment has also created conditions for bidding wars between local governments for their share of investment and economic development dollars from other levels of the state, international capital, and large Canadian firms. The current 'prizes' in these wars are likely to be large-scale sports facilities such as arenas and stadiums, convention facilities, world trade centres and office/shopping complexes (Magnusson 1990).

The process recalls practices typical of an earlier period of boosterism in Canadian urban history (Baskerville 1986). But while there are important historical continuities in the contemporary actions of local governments, the current neo-boosterist policies of municipal governments take place in a changed political economic setting for the local state. The new context is one of a radically altered set of relations between the federal and provincial governments and the global economy. In terms of legitimating local state activities as a response to the new economic reality, public sector economic development corporations and local state agencies fit well with both the 'public enterprise culture' typical of Canadian capitalism and with the rhetoric of the new global competitiveness (Laux and Molot 1988).

A critical perspective suggests that we should not consider these new activities of local government merely as the outcome of bureaucratic growth and expansion. The creation of public enterprises in the form of economic development corporations does represent an expanded role for municipal and city governments. But the formation of these kind of quasi-public bodies devoted to promoting economic growth cannot be seen as a simple expansion of state intervention in the economy of the 'more' or 'less' variety – it is a different kind of intervention. As Preteceille notes, the political and economic restructuring of the 1970s and 1980s has produced a 'paradoxical' political conjuncture: 'Economic change is characterized by a growing interdependence among local enterprises and increasingly international markets, financial institutions and flows, processes of technological innovation and diffusions. At the same time, most countries experience a revaluation of local politics. Local governments are promoted as major actors of urban, social and economic change, often with responsibilities and resources increased by policies of state decentralization' (1990: 27).

In Canada, because many important local public sector actors are actually institutions of the provincial and federal governments, *representative local government* does not overlap as neatly with the local state agencies through which such decentralization might be implemented. Many local agencies, boards, and commissions are outside of the political control of local elected representatives (Magnusson 1985). But this lack of representativeness and diffusion of political accountability does not diminish the importance of actors such as Harbourfront Corporation in Toronto, Vieux Port in Montreal, the Core Area Initiative in Winnipeg (all with federal and some provincial government involvement), or municipally owned EDCs such as TEDCO or CIDEM in Toronto and Montreal. This seeming devolution, however fragmented, reflects the fact that restructuring and capitalist development must take *place* – i.e., must proceed in specific sites, where the articulation of diverse social, economic, and political institutions and forces requires some form of local mediation. Even if the economic forces that lead to institutional change are international in character, their impact varies locally. As global and interdependent as the contemporary economy is, the resurgence of institutions at the local level is consistent with these developments however 'paradoxical' – to use Preteceille's terms – it may be at the practical level of policy initiatives.

The Entrepreneurial State

Various explanations have been put forward to explain the rise of state-run corporations in the 1970s. Laux and Molot (1988) argue that the centrality of the state in economic development is a continuous feature of Canadian economic history, as the early example of public railways demonstrates. Since the early 1970s, capitalist crisis, the growth of state enterprises, and the subsequent privatizations of these institutions have gone hand in hand. The fiscal crisis of the state and the incapacity of policy-makers to effect growth or productivity led the state in Canada and Europe to increase direct investment in productive activities. Subsequently, rather than wholesale privatization, streamlining and partial divestment have created conditions for more entrepreneurially oriented public corporations. The growth of this sort of state capitalism was predicated upon the 'use of state ownership to ensure national participation in internationally competitive industries' and thus reflected the commitment of the central state to some form of economic development policy (Laux and Molot 1988: 24). Industrial policy is now being displaced by trade policy at the level of the national state. In their study of public enterprises such as the Canada Development Corporation, Petrocan, and CN, Laux and Molot chronicle the related entrepreneurial turn of Crown corporations away from their original policy objectives towards goals in which success is defined in market terms.

In similar fashion, with a slight historical lag, local government EDCs have followed a pattern of more direct participation in the economy. The extent of this has been nowhere near as significant as in the case of public corporations owned by senior levels of the state, but it represents the same motivation to ensure continuing participation in the changing economy. In the Canadian case, the fragmentation of the local state has at least partly muted the movement towards policy coordination at the local level, but EDCs do serve as boosters in attracting outside investment, and increasingly, as in the case of TEDCO, they have come to play an important role in land assembly and the planning of growth strategies.

Since their inception in the late 1970s and early 1980s, local EDCs have evolved in response to changes in the national and global economy. As mentioned, the emergence in the 1980s of a neo-liberal consensus on the need to reduce the role of the state in the economy produced a significant drive for the restructuring and privatization of public enterprise in Canada. As comparative analysis reveals (Keating 1991), it was during this period that local EDCs and the economic development offices of municipal governments began to take a different approach to urban economic development and engage more directly in development activities. Some of these planning innovations have taken the form of 'entrepreneurial' paramunicipal corporations (Herland 1992: 67; Judd and Ready 1986). As Mayer observes, economic development is now cast in larger terms: 'Instead of luring investors into the city with tax cuts, reduced government regulations, or 'reasonable' wage levels, the new municipal economic development programs include job creation measures, retraining programs, and city initiatives to create short term municipal jobs for the unemployed; these programs also encompass strategies to enhance the city's overall ambiance. The strategies tend to cut across conventional lines, combining social with labour-market policies, including cultural activities as part of economic development agendas, or subsidizing community initiatives as part of employment programs' (1991: 115).

One result has been more 'flexible' and innovative forms of state intervention that have become increasingly local and focused in their orientation. Christopher Leo and Robert Fenton (1990) document one widely used strategy in which arm's-length public corporations involving multiple levels of government, such as Toronto's Harbourfront or Winnipeg's Core Area Initiative, act to 'mediate' the political and financial requirements of specific development projects. Supposedly, this creates projects more tailored to local conditions; but as Leo and Fenton argue, a fairly secretive, private, and 'depoliticized' planning and development process results. Deploying the vehicle of a special-purpose public corporation for redevelopment purposes allows the state to intervene in what Leo and Fenton call a 'mediated' way: using the institutional form of the development corporation to avoid the possible criticism that a costly project may entail in a fragile economy. The state intervenes, but indirectly, and thus in a manner consistent with predominant views regarding a more limited role for the state in the economy. This kind of state formation process can be seen as responding to a new context of legitimation and to the pressure to maintain and enhance favourable local conditions for accumulation. The result is a more entrepreneurial and more 'flexible' state structure at the local level. However, from a critical perspective the question remains whether the adoption of a strategy of shadowing the private sector is merely a more roundabout way of providing public subsidies to private property.

While these sorts of initiatives operate as joint ventures, other examples of innovations in state intervention in response to economic restructuring have involved creating more directly entrepreneurial public sector corporations at the local level. In Metropolitan Toronto, long-term shifts in economic activity beginning in the 1970s had continuously reduced manufacturing employment, and by the late 1980s large tracts of former industrial land in the central downtown area lay idle. The Port Lands, under the management of the Toronto Harbour Commission – a local agency created by federal legislation in 1911 – was one example of disused space in the downtown area: an extensive infrastructure of past capital investments no longer appropriate to Toronto's present economy. With so much space under the administration of the Harbour Commission – a fragment of the local state whose own orientation to economic development policy was decidedly *ancien régime* – a variety of actors came to conclude that a more flexible and activist state corporation was needed to develop the lands in accord with the priorities of the 'new economy' by shifting control over the lands to the Toronto Economic Development Corporation (TEDCO).

The Example of TEDCO

The history of the City of Toronto Economic Development Office and its related public enterprise, the Toronto Economic Development Corporation (TEDCO), reflects the connections between global economic restructuring, the local political economy, and the process of state formation discussed above. The Economic Development Office (EDO), a department in the City of Toronto bureaucracy, dates from the 1960s. Originally the EDO was known as the Economic Development Department (EDD) until 1978 when, for all intents and purposes, it was shut down by Toronto's city council. As a political response to widespread redevelopment during the 1960s and early 1970s, subsequent 'reform' era city councils under Mayors David Crombie and John Sewell had advocated a slow growth approach to development. The EDD became a target of the urban reformers because of its implication in traditional growth machine politics and its focus on promoting the sort of large-scale urban renewal which was anathema to reform activists. The EDD had advocated large-scale projects such as the redevelopment of the central downtown rail and subway hub in Union Station and the assembly of land for high-rise office and residential developments. The suspension of EDD activities in 1978 lasted for four years, during which a specific department for municipal government economic development activities did not exist in the City of Toronto bureaucracy. Harbourfront, a public development corporation formed in 1978 by the federal government to develop approximately 100 acres along Lake Ontario, remained the main institution of the sort of mediated state involvement in local economic development referred to previously.

During the four-year hiatus from active economic development policy, in order to try to staunch job losses in the manufacturing sector, the reform council enacted protective industrial zoning by-laws to prevent commercial use conversions and the bidding up of industrial land prices. But continued losses of industrial jobs in the City of Toronto and suburbanization of manufacturing heightened the demand for new land uses in the city. The 1976 *Central Plan*, a slow growth official plan for the city drafted by the reform council, had fallen from favour by 1982 when cyclical recession began threatening the tentative re-industrialization of the city in emerging sectors like film production and fashion design; growth was back in style. With the potential for an important coordinating role for local government in mind, the economic development function of the city of Toronto was re-established in 1982 as an Office of the Planning Department. Its terms of reference were established in a 1980 report entitled *A Selective Economic Development Strategy for Toronto.* The report focused attention on strategies for encouraging 'selective' development in key new growth sectors in the local economy as well as in the areas of traditional manufacturing and industrial employment. Similar offices have now also been established by Metropolitan Toronto's five other city governments and by the Municipality of Metropolitan Toronto itself. In their most recent promotional activities, the focus of many of these offices has been targeted at competitive and innovative sectors such as high technology and 'green industry.'

During and after the office construction boom of the 1980s most local government economic development policy concentrated on retaining industrial land uses, with mixed success. The Industrial Liaison program in Toronto – a 'round table' designed to seek solutions necessary to retain existing industry in the city – has become a forum through which city councilors' offices have become involved in the politics of economic restructuring mainly by channeling the concerns of local manufacturers to city council. Essentially, many of the activities of the City of Toronto EDO came down to playing a coordinating role in the provision of local state services to business. But traditional approaches to economic development, while they had taken on a new sheen with fashion and film and video production, proved limited. In Toronto what remained to be done after the re-establishment of the EDO was to create the institutional space for a more direct and activist approach to development in the form of a local public corporation. As such, TEDCO constituted a new direction for economic development activities in Toronto.[3]

Incorporated in 1986, TEDCO is a wholly owned subsidiary corporation of the City of Toronto, a legacy of the concern of the administration of pro-business Mayor Art Eggleton for the industrial manufacturing sector. Because it was felt to be necessary to gradually expand TEDCO's role, much like a growing business, the corporation was first 'nurtured' within the organizational structure of the Parking Authority of Toronto – itself a tax-and dividend-generating city-owned public corporation with assets in 1993 of over $1 billion. TEDCO was then subsequently spun off into an independent arm's-length corporation. The board of directors of TEDCO now includes fourteen representatives from business, labour, and city government, all chosen by city council. Established after a period of decline in the manufacturing sector, TEDCO's original strategic focus was on preserving traditional blue-collar industry. However, competitive pressure from greenfield sites outside Toronto and elsewhere was too intense, so the focus of the organization has shifted to sectors like telecommunications, industrial design, new business 'incubators,' and business services. Described as the 'entrepreneurial, bricks and mortar side of the economic development office,' TEDCO has now moved into property management and development. At present, the corporation's real estate projects total one million square feet of office/commercial and light industrial space. TEDCO's activities also include providing financial services in the form of loan guarantees for small film production companies. The largest project planned includes industrial site development on the

Port Area lands – approximately 300 acres of which TEDCO will acquire from the Harbour Commission for a nominal cost.

The entrepreneurial character of TEDCO has been reinforced by the general acceptance of the need for Toronto to be a more competitive location, a view articulated by key city officials. In 1992, in a report presented to the Economic Development Committee of City Council, Toronto's Commissioner of Planning and Development, Robert Millward, recommended changing the focus of the city's economic development strategy to take a 'competitive' rather than 'selective' approach to economic development. The new growth strategy articulated by the local state must recognize and respond to the fact that 'unlike manufacturing firms, commercial companies do not have large fixed capital investments making them captive over time' (Commissioner of Planning and Economic Development 1992: 4). In this view rather than an exclusive focus on manufacturing jobs, an economic strategy promoting competitiveness over a broad range of taxes and services is the best way to ensure that these companies stay. While these sorts of policy proposals conflict with the industrial and small business sector orientation of the EDO's initiatives and certainly are in contrast with the original thrust of TEDCO's operations, it is not surprising that they would arise at this conjuncture when the most recent cyclical recession has hit hard in the service sector. Toronto's economy is now heavily dependent on medium- and large-sized commercial and business services firms and on headquarters office location; job loss from a decline in the competitive position of this sector would be more extensive than in manufacturing. If broader competitiveness strategies are adopted and TEDCO shifts from an emphasis on manufacturing to providing business services, then its independent position outside of the state will allow it to benefit, just as any private sector corporation, from lower taxes and land costs. In discussion with TEDCO officials it is clear that the assumption is that the entrepreneurial character of TEDCO's operations will insulate it from development politics because decisions will be more objective and market-based. But this perspective itself is a political one. Indeed it is difficult to conceive of a situation in which TEDCO's corporate decisions regarding the possible disposition of public lands would *not* be political.

The corporatist structure of TEDCO's board does little to promote access or ongoing accountability to city council (even though TEDCO is ultimately responsible to the city as sole shareholder), which is supposed to promote the arm's-length independence of the corporation. The present board consists of six private sector appointments, three labour appointments, and four political representatives from city council which, if it were to function as an effective corporatist organizational structure, would provide a fairly narrow institutional bias. As a means of ensuring public sector participation in the planning of economic development strategies, TEDCO serves more to privatize practices formerly managed directly by the state than it does to generate public involvement. What I am suggesting is that TEDCO stands as an example of state formation in an era of post-Fordist accumulation – the state too, it seems, can be flexible when it comes to economic development policy in the present political and economic context. Given the corporation's market orientation, the goals of retention of industrial land and the promotion of the environmental and high technology sectors may eventually take a back seat to more fiscally responsible commercial development.

In its 1990 *Watershed* report the federal Royal Commission on the Future of the Toronto Waterfront – another fragment of the local state – recommended that TEDCO take control of the Port Area lands from the Toronto Harbour Commission. In August 1994 TEDCO became one of the largest property holders in the city assuming ownership of approximately 400 acres of land in the Port Area. The Port Area lands is a large, contiguous site near the downtown core covering almost as much area as Toronto's present downtown and readily accessible from the present street grid. The present plan for the area focuses on an industrial park which would emphasize environmentally responsible industries and green technologies. TEDCO's income stream, derived from the initial development of part of the parcel, would go towards improving the visual appearance of the area and operating a Centre for Green Enterprise and Industry and a Technology Transfer Centre in conjunction with a consortium of universities and private sector firms. The Technology Transfer Centre would focus on bringing telecommunications applications and 'green technology' to the market and bringing technical design knowledge to the private sector. A report designed to familiarize the public with the corporation's activities underscores the strategic value of the Port Area proposals: 'TEDCO recognizes the great potential existing in these lands. An environmentally responsible industrial park located in the Port Area would give the City of Toronto the ability to be a world leader in supporting and developing 'green' industries. Companies with new leading edge technologies would be attracted to the area. The Industrial Park would create thousands of jobs and contribute to the revitalization of the Port Area. It would be a positive step towards achieving environmentally responsible development in the City of Toronto' (Toronto Economic Development Corporation, n.d.).

The report virtually describes the role of the state in establishing a new economic accumulation strategy and the beginnings of a new approach to local economic development. Sounding a progressive note with respect to the environmental politics of any future post-Fordist mode of regulation, the Waterfront Commission further recommends that a Centre for Green Enterprise and Industry be set up and managed by TEDCO, with a mandate to develop products and manufacturing processes that are environmentally friendly.

Setting aside so large a space for this sort of local development cannot help but effect the pattern of economic development in the city. But as an entrepreneurially oriented public corporation there is no guarantee that the policy objectives of TEDCO will not be subverted by pursuit of market success. In most comparable cases, such as London's Docklands and the London Docklands Development Corporation, the structural 'paradox of public enterprise' has largely been resolved through a 'shift in the basis of legitimation of state enterprise toward the application of business logic' (Laux and Molot 1988: 78). TEDCO's own promotional literature emphasizes the fact that it operates in a fiscally prudent manner, a required image for any legitimate public corporation in an era of deficits and government cutbacks. But it is precisely this orientation that may undermine its chances of achieving environmental regeneration goals. At the very least, these goals may work at cross purposes with the kind of development that eventually does take place on TEDCO land and the kind of projects TEDCO is called upon to finance.

For the time being, though, the overbuilt commercial real estate market and TEDCO's relative autonomy from city council may actually help preserve its focus on innovative industry and manufacturing. More direct control by council may only result in TEDCO being *politically* reoriented towards more lucrative or 'fiscally responsible' projects such as providing infrastructure and land assembly for commercial development or actually developing medium-sized office buildings for the finance, insurance, and real estate industry and other 'global city' sectors of the economy. Behind the overtly entrepreneurial flourish, TEDCO does serve notice that new, locally constituted forms of bargaining and negotiation between the state and capital are beginning to emerge in the global economy. Besides their role in state formation these kinds of political forces may seek to redefine the authority of city and municipal governments within the range of organizations that comprise the local state, pushing for economic interventions that serve their competitive interests. But I do not wish to sound a strictly pessimistic note here. As I have implied throughout this discussion, the decisions which bear on the governance of the local economy and which give rise to state formations and institutions are political ones. While there is much political work to be done by groups that wish to advocate alternative approaches to economic development, the new institutions do present opportunities for more democratic and accountable forms of economic management that have the added bonus of being more local and community-based.[4]

Conclusion: Political Economic Space and the Form of the State

Internationally, the changing political economic environment and the continuous crisis of Keynesian economic policies of the post–Second World War era have provoked retrenchment and rolling back of the state at the national level. The process of rolling back or 'hollowing out' the functions of the state corresponds with a 'triple displacement of [state] powers upward, downward and to some extent outward' (Jessop 1993: 10). The political organization and formation of the state undergirding the regulation of this postwar or Fordist economic regime is being restructured in the transition to a post-Fordist political economy. The relative success of the resulting new state forms will lie in their capacity to coordinate the crisis-induced search for a new economic accumulation strategy with specific political projects. In this context, local entrepreneurial partnerships between the state, private sector actors, and social organizations now have a special role to play in the global economy. As Magrit Mayer notes, 'Since the specific conditions of production and reproduction can be orchestrated only by local political systems, their skills in negotiating with supraregional and multinational capital, and the effectiveness with which they tailor the particular set of local conditions of production, have become decisive factors in shaping a city's profile as well as its place in the international urban hierarchy' (1993: 2).

The adoption of sectorally focused interventionist strategies and a more direct entrepreneurial role by the local state is a symptom of structural changes in the regulation of capitalist economies as well as a symptom of the resurgence of a certain ideological perspective regarding the 'proper role' for local government. In the process of struggling and strategizing that takes place between capital, labour, and community interests around their place in the global economy, local social formations come to adopt particular solutions and organizational variations, all within the general framework of a capitalist economic system. In this way, ideological notions regarding the role of the state in the economy materialize in specific local political institutions and projects, such as bolstering local competitiveness, encouraging industrial restructuring, or seeking changes in labour legislation. Historically, Canadian policy-makers have favoured an important public sector role in the economy while the new matrix of ideas regarding the state advocates efficiency and flexibility. Entrepreneurial paramunicipal corporations offer a compromise between these two principles. The willingness of local political actors to undertake these projects underscores the belief that the rolling back of state programs at the federal and provincial levels is a problem that needs to be addressed, and that it is possible to tailor local programs to capitalize on unused urban land and resources in ways that other levels of government are unable to do.

In theoretical terms, one observer, Bob Jessop, sees three main approaches or 'hegemonic political projects' being pursued as part of the restructuring necessary for regulating the new flexible post-Fordist economy. The most well known of these is the *neo-liberal* project, concerned with a market-led transition to a new regime of accumulation – the familiar economic ideology of Thatcherism and Reaganism. But depending on the setting, there are also several variations on statist (i.e., direct state intervention) and corporatist (institutionalized forms of state, capital, and labour cooperation) approaches to economic restructuring which can be viewed as instances of *neo-statism* or *neo-corporatism.* Although these latter institutional forms are more likely to be found in Europe than in North America, Laux and Molot (1988) have pointed out the similarities between Canada and Europe in terms of public enterprise culture. Neo-liberal rhetoric regarding the limited state may be the most familiar mode of thought for the new mode of regulation, but the free marketeers are not the only advocates of a new form of state to deal with the exigencies of the post-Fordist economy. As Jessop points out neo-corporatist approaches to regulating the new economy are giving rise to different forms of state institutions.

With competitiveness, innovation, and entrepreneurialism as the watchwords, a variety of corporatist state formations for managing economic change are possible. During the present period of intensive economic restructuring TEDCO and institutions like it – that lie in the grey area between state and private capital – may actually be more characteristic of the new economy than they are dinosaurs from the past. Post-Fordist neo-corporatism may take different forms but it will still be concerned with balancing competition and concertation in the economy and, according to Jessop, its institutions are bound to become more localized: 'Corporatist arrangements may also become more selective (e.g., excluding some previously entrenched industrial interests and peripheral or marginal workers, integrating some sunrise sectors and giving more weight to core workers); and reflecting the greater flexibility and decentralization of key features of the post-Fordist economy, the centres of neo-corporatist gravity will move toward the micro-level of firms and localities at the expense of centralized economic concertation ... Whether at the local, national, or supranational level, the state is just as involved in such neo-corporatist strategies as it is in the neo-liberal and neo-statist approaches' (Jessop 1993: 31).

The strategy adopted by TEDCO bridges the neo-corporatist and neo-liberal approaches. The board is nominally structured for concertation but the corporation acts in its own market-determined interest as part of an overall entrepreneurial and developmental strategy rather than at the behest of the local state.

A critical perspective on the formation and growth of these kinds of mediating state organizations poses the question of democracy and community control. While potentially placing control over the development of the Port Lands in the hands of a more *politically* accountable public corporation, a decidedly *private* approach to development focusing on financial accountability has actually been reconstituted in the guise of promoting a new, environmentally sensitive path for the local economy. While offering the potential for greater democracy in planning and local economic development policy, there is still little that is disturbing about TEDCO for business or the status quo. For organizations like TEDCO local economic development refers to capitalist economic growth and accumulation within the usual configuration of state, market, firm, and capital-labour relations. Whether in the 'real' private sector or as part of a public sector 'shadow strategy,' capitalist development harbours the same social or political implications – it is never value-free. If a fragment of the local state like TEDCO adopts an approach that reinforces the power of private interests and the socioeconomic inequities introduced by the market, then in what sense are public sector corporations pursuing alternative policy objectives? Bringing a critical perspective to bear on the activities of parapublic agencies such as TEDCO raises this question in regard to the role of the local state. Will economic development be any different if it is managed according to the same rudimentary practices as the private sector, and is the kind of strategy being pursued an appropriate form of public policy? The political issues these questions raise can perhaps be clarified in my concluding remarks by contrasting development patterns that are based in market principles and in what I will call community economic development (CED).

Community economic development implies the involvement of state organizations, but with a generally much broader outlook towards the well-being of the community and towards what constitutes a well-functioning economy. The focus is on development for the community rather than simply for the sake of accumulation. For Kuyek (1990) CED includes enabling local communities to gain more control of the economy and promoting ecologically sustainable and socially just forms of economic development in the non-profit and cooperative sectors – something EDCs seldom consider. A viable local economy must also establish a means of retaining wealth in the community ('Where does the money go?' is as important a question as 'Where does the money come from'?). In Kuyek's alternative economic paradigm the means of achieving these ends include loan circles, community-managed investment funds, land trusts, and other cooperative organizations focusing production on the provision of basic goods such as housing and food. The explicit political aim of CED is to promote small-scale local solutions to the economic displacements brought about by the operation of the market. These sorts of strategies thus serve to democratize and institutionalize a new form of economics – something which the more market-oriented approach and the organizational structure of TEDCO proscribes.

In a similar vein Marguerite Mendell argues for a more democratic community-controlled form of economic development outside the traditional pale of state-led initiatives. In an account of the activities of the Centre de développement économique communautaire Grand Plateau, created under the auspices of a Quebec government programe, she highlights the importance of the Montreal Community Loan Association in helping to establish an alternative local economic strategy based on principles of self-help and independence from state or private sector control (Mendell 1993, Mendell and Evoy 1993). Christopher and Harriet Gunn (1991) outline possibilities for creating alternative institutions of accumulation and investment based on public ownership of land and the development of local public assets that explicitly run counter to the market logic of profit maximization. Examples include development of publicly held lands in ways that create assets for communities including daycare facilities, workers' cooperatives, and community land trusts that prevent speculation and land use conversion. A key contribution of this literature has been to point out the extent to which a more progressive agenda for economic development depends on the socialization and democratization of capital and investment.

Community economic development thus differs substantially from state-led initiatives of local economic development which respond mainly to the hegemonic view of the 'new economic reality.' These latter initiatives are usually collaborative with business and capital and are not always successful in extracting social benefits.[5] TEDCO, for example, operates film studio facilities and business 'incubators,' while CIDEM in Montreal manages an industrial park. Rather than seeking to concretize a form of economic development emphasizing a diversity of institutions existing in the alternative sector, state initiatives at local economic development have attempted to participate in a new economy which is defined as one based on flexible specialization and market-oriented trade competitiveness. Thus, the goals of state actors differ little from those of private business. However, except for its commitment to neo-liberal ideas of fiscally prudent business practices and the decidedly business-oriented make-up of the board, there is nothing preventing TEDCO from advocating and helping to establish self-sustaining cooperative and non-profit enterprise in addition to its present role as landlord/incubator and financial services provider.

The most useful role to be played by the state is in establishing and maintaining the cooperative links in the economy – between firms, producer groups, labour, and capital – that markets often undermine. As a response to economic restructuring, what is needed is an institutionalization of new social partnerships between labour, the public and private sectors, and social, cultural, and community organizations. It is here that the state could play an important enabling role in encouraging a different and local strategy of economic development rather than merely adjusting to the competitive workings of globalization. The market will work its developmental logic whether or not the state participates as an entrepreneurial player or acts to promote more democratic and public alternatives. Despite the novel institutional formations that economic crisis has given rise to at the local level, public sector EDCs like TEDCO have merely reconstituted the social relationships of the larger political economy in the form of flexible and responsive (to the market) state-owned corporations. Paralleling the state form of political response to economic crisis there has been an emergence of smaller scale community initiatives that Mendell and others working in a comparative and international context have identified (see Mayer 1993). The existence of both the alternative model and more mainstream local state initiatives reflect ongoing attempts to respond to long-term economic crisis and change. The predominance of the state model over the community-led initiatives reflects the relative balance of political forces shaping the emergence of post-Fordism, and the important role of the state in applying the 'combination of force and persuasion' necessary for structural political economic change.[6]

Just as with the national economy, the 'tone' of the local political economy is set by the configuration of public institutions by which it is regulated and defined. Advocates of more community-centred economic development then need to pursue political strategies that pressure local and senior-level governments to address local priorities and to enable community institutions to play a role in the establishment and stabilization of new forms of economic activity that are resilient in the face of global markets. In patterning state initiatives on the market, the present mix of institutions does not provide the space for these alternative approaches. The political viability of the community-based option will depend partly on the dissemination of a critical account of contemporary urban economic development practices – a counterpoint to the dominant 'mode of thought' – and on winning political support for a more decentralized and less glamorous form of economic development policy.

In this chapter I have examined how the formation of certain kinds of local state institutions is consistent with the emergence of a new post-Fordist mode of economic development. To be aware of the formative institutional changes taking place at the level of the local state and of their potential for transformation alerts us to engage in shaping their development. If there is one important capacity of progressive local politics it is that it is able to bring together diverse community-based groups seeking a more democratic, socially just, and environmentally sound kind of development. If this leads to demands for a greater correspondence between the institutions of local government and the apparatuses of the local state, then it can serve as an impetus for the formation of a different set of local state institutions than what has been discussed here. As Warren Magnusson puts it, progressive urban politics in Canada requires a 'language or politics that obviously challenge the rightward course of the senior governments' (1990: 191).

This language might also be seen as an implicit source of further demands for the democratization of the local state and the creation of more responsible and less jurisdictionally fragmented local government in the long term. For the present, at least some part of local economic development policy needs to be linked to the smaller scale initiatives typical of the CED approach where there is greater community involvement in the process. The examples of TEDCO and other local public EDCs suggest that a different kind of local state and more fiscally innovative approaches to economic development do not necessarily imply substantial policy changes or increased accountability. In fact entrepreneurial approaches and democratic deficiency seem to go hand in hand. As one among many potential focal points for political conflict in the restructured economy, local public sector corporations merit the attention and scrutiny of their citizen-owners. More participatory and inclusive decision-making structures could go a long way towards addressing this democratic deficit and at the same time serve to increase the relevance and legitimacy of local government with respect to economic questions.

NOTES

1 My use of this term is quite distinct from the accepted usage in political anthropology where reference is to the origins and mythical legitimation of state structures in a comparative and long-term historical context (Cohen and Toland 1988).

2 The concepts 'regime of accumulation' and 'mode of regulation' are drawn from the regulation school approach to political economy. The term 'regime of accumulation' refers to the manner in which dominant economic actors organize the social relations of a given mode of production (capitalism). Examples include mass production, flexible accumulation, and international trade regimes. The 'mode of regulation' refers to the institutions within a given state (or, more rarely and less effectively, at the international level) which serve to 'regularize' a given regime such as unions, labour codes, and established techniques of work organization. Examples include the Keynesian welfare state and what some consider to be its successors: the competitive state, or the Schumpeterian workfare state (Jessop 1993).

3 For much of the history which follows I am indebted to Peter Tomlinson, Director, City of Toronto Economic Development Department, and Vivian Lear, Special Projects Director of TEDCO.

4 Despite its eventual elimination by the Thatcher government, the accomplishments of the Greater London Council serve as a positive example of the potential for alternative approaches (MacKintosh and Wainwright 1987).

5 Linkage policies which contractually stipulate the social benefits that must be provided by developers are one attempt to institutionalize this practice.

6 'Force and persuasion' comes from Gramsci's essay on the emergence of Fordism, 'Americanism and Fordism' (1971: 285).

REFERENCES

Baskerville, P. 1986. 'Financial capital and the municipal state: The case of Victoria, British Columbia, 1910–1936.' *Studies in Political Economy* 21: 83–106

Beck, N. 1992. *Shifting gears: Thriving in the new economy* Toronto: Harper Collins

Britton, J. 1993. 'A regional industrial perspective on Canada under free trade.' *International Journal of Urban and Regional Research* 17(4): 559–77

Clavel, P., and N. Kleniewski. 1990. 'Space for progressive local policy: Examples from the United States and the United Kingdom.' In J. Logan and T. Swanstrom, eds., *Beyond the City Limits: Urban Policy and Economic Restructuring in Comparative Perspective*, 199–234. Philadelphia: Temple University Press

Cohen, R., and J. Toland, eds., 1988. *State Formation and Political Legitimacy*. New Brunswick, NJ: Transaction Press

Commissioner of Planning and Economic Development. 1992. Report to Economic Development Committee of Council, City of Toronto, 16 June

Gertler, M. 1990. 'Economic development.' In R. Loreto and T. Price, eds., *Urban Policy Issues: Canadian Perspectives*, 35–57. Toronto: McClelland and Stewart

Goodwin, M., S. Duncan, and S. Halford. 1993. 'Regulation theory, the local state, and the transition of urban politics.' *Environment and Planning D: Society and Space* 11: 67–88

Gramsci, A. 1971. *Selections from the Prison Notebooks*. London: Lawrence and Wishart

Gunn, C., and H. Gunn. 1991. *Reclaiming Capital: Democratic Initiatives and Community Development*. Ithaca: Cornell University Press

Harvey, D. 1989. 'From managerialism to entrepreneurialism: The transformation of urban governance in late capitalism.' *Geografiska Annaler* 1: 3–17

Herland, K. 1992. *People, Potholes, and City Politics*. Montreal: Black Rose Books

Jessop, B. 1993. 'The Schumpeterian workfare state?: Preliminary remarks on post-Fordist political economy.' *Studies in Political Economy* 40: 7–39

Judd, D., and R. Ready. 1986. 'Entrepreneurial cities and the new politics of urban development.' In G. Peterson and C. Lewis, eds., *Reagan and the Cities*. Washington, DC: Urban Institute

Keating, M. 1991. *Comparative Urban Politics: Power and the City in the United States, Canada, Britain and France*. Brookfield, VT: Edward Elgar

Kuyek, J. 1990. *Fighting for Hope: Organizing to Realize Our Dreams*. Montreal: Black Rose Books

Laux, J., and M. Molot. 1988. *State Capitalism: Public Enterprise in Canada*. Ithaca: Cornell University Press

Laws, G. 1988. 'Privatisation and the local welfare state: The case of Toronto's social services.' *Transactions of the British Institute of Geographers* 13: 433–48

Leo, C., and R. Fenton. 1990. ''Mediated enforcement' and the evolution of the state: Development corporations in Canadian city centres.' *International Journal of Urban and Regional Research* 14(2): 185–206

MacKintosh, M., and H. Wainwright. 1987. *A Taste of Power: The Politics of Local Government.* London: Verso

Magnusson, W. 1985. 'The local state in Canada: Theoretical perspectives.' *Canadian Public Administration* 28(4): 575–99

– 1990. 'Progressive politics and Canadian cities.' In D. King and J. Pierre, eds., *Challenges to Local Government,* 73–194. London: Sage

Mahon, R. 1991. 'The 'new' Canadian political economy revisited: Production, space, identity.' Occasional Papers. Ottawa: Carleton University, School of Public Administration

Mayer, M. 1991. 'Politics in the post-fordist city.' *Socialist Review* Jan.-Mar.: 105–24

– 1993. 'Urban governance in the post-Fordist city.' Paper presented at the conference on 'Challenges to Urban Management,' Newcastle, 25–7 March

Mendell, M. 1993. 'New social partnerships: Crisis management or a new social contract.' Paper presented to the Annual Meeting of the Association for Evolutionary Economics, Anaheim, California, Jan.

Mendell, M., and L. Evoy. 1993. 'Democratizing capital: Alternative investment strategies.' In E. Shragge, ed., *Community Economic Development: In Search of Empowerment and Alternatives.* Montreal: Black Rose Books

Preteceille, E. 1990. 'Political paradoxes of urban restructuring: Globalization of the economy and localization of politics?' In J. Logan and T. Swanstrom, eds., *Beyond the City Limits: Urban Policy and Economic Restructuring in Comparative Perspective,* 27–59. Philadelphia: Temple University Press

Royal Commission on the Future of the Toronto Waterfront. 1990. *Watershed: The Second Interim Report of the Royal Commission on the Future of the Toronto Waterfront.* Toronto: Royal Commission on the Future of the Toronto Waterfront

Scott, A.J. 1988. 'Flexible production systems and regional development: The rise of new industrial spaces in Europe and North America.' *International Journal of Urban and Regional Research* 12(1): 171–86

Toronto Economic Development Corporation. n.d. *A Brief History – The Founding of TEDCO.* Toronto

9

The Impact of Global Finance in Urban Structural Change: The International Banking Centre Controversy

MICHAEL GOLDRICK

This chapter is based on the proposition that a comprehensive analysis of urban change must be grounded in an understanding of the global nature of political economy. In addition, such analysis requires an understanding of the relationship between global processes and more locally proximate determinants of urban social change. Global, regional or national, and local are inherently interactive.

Cities change not only as a result of the requirements of global or local capital but also as a result of power relations at these levels. There are, in effect, two world-wide logics: an economic (capitalist) logic and a socio/political logic. These are interrelated and interdependent. Accordingly, this chapter contends that urban development patterns are best understood as the long-term outcomes of action taken by economic and political actors operating within a context of global and national forces.

A considerable number of researchers have investigated this connection. Most work in this respect probably has been done in the areas of technology, production systems, and spatial distributions of labour. Michael Timberlake, among others, calls for more specification of the ways in which local modes of regulation mediate the impact of the evolving regime of accumulation on the global system of cities (Timberlake 1987: 59). But one area in particular has not received enough attention. John Short observes that 'much of urban research in the last two decades has been concerned with the relationship between the mode of production and urban structure. Too little attention has been paid to the importance of the mode of investment. Yet finance capital has had an enormous impact on the landscape and life of cities ... it has had an impact not only on the motives and institutions that propel investment by finance capital ... but on finance capital itself as an industry with all the spatial and social consequences its expansion or contraction might involve' (Short 1989: 74). More specifically, Desmond King points to one mediating institution that has been neglected in urban political economy literature. That is the key role played by the state in guiding investment and shaping capital flows (King 1987: 215 *passim*).

This chapter addresses that deficiency. It focuses on international financial services and the impact of their growth and restructuring on the urban structure of Canada as it was mediated by a variety of political institutions. Specifically, it shows how the government of Canada and two of the country's subnational or regional states, the governments of British Columbia and Quebec, by and large unsuccessfully attempted to divert the trajectory of the global marketplace away from the city of Toronto, the national financial centre and principal link with global finance, to their own principal cites of Vancouver and Montreal. This process was to be accomplished by a combination of regulatory adjustment and the application of tax concessions.

The project was taken up by the federal government in 1984, led by a recently elected Conservative party whose agenda, like that of any political party, included the enhancement of its popular base. Support of regional development goals in British Columbia and Quebec was one means to achieve that goal. The government's initial political judgment was that benefits to be derived from increasing financial activity in Montreal and Vancouver would exceed the political costs it might incur by ignoring the profit-making needs of the most powerful fraction of the finance industry, known as 'core capital,' which was based in Toronto.[1] Risks of such a strategy were increased by two circumstances: one was that the industry at that moment was engaged in an extraordinary restructuring process that was sweeping through international finance, and another was that the finance industry represented the major financial support base of the governing party.

This chapter seeks to link the global and the local, to show how emergent trends in the global economy are etched in the political consciousness and urban places of contemporary society.

Montreal

In 1981 the Montreal Board of Trade and la Chambre de Commerce requested the government of Canada to designate Montreal an international banking centre (IBC). They were supported in this proposal by thirty members of the Parliament of Canada and an influential minister of that government from Quebec. The initiative also carried the strong support of the provincial government.

The proposal was made in an attempt to shore-up the economy of Montreal that had been gravely weakened through the wave of economic restructuring that swept North America during the 1970s. The aim was to capture so-called high-end jobs in the financial and business services sectors. But lying behind this motive was a complex mixture of factors. One of these was that Montreal had suffered severe losses of manufacturing over the previous decade. As well, the city had lost its pre-eminence as the dominant financial centre of Canada to its historic rival, Toronto (Linteau et al. 1991: ch. 33). This shift occurred for reasons that went well beyond simple commercial considerations. Many of the financial firms that had transferred their operations to Toronto had done so in a manner that implied or explicitly identified rising Quebec nationalism as their motive for leaving. This fact added a considerable cultural edge to the reaction of Quebecois to their leaving (Fraser 1987: ch. 4).

The IBC proposal also owed a lot to the emergence over the previous decade and a half of a strong, self-confident, and aggressive cadre of francophone entrepreneurs. The abrupt and rancorous departure of anglophone businesses had created 'space,' 'an opening' for this to occur. But more than anything else it was a product of radical changes that had occurred in Quebec society. From the Quiet Revolution of the early 1960s onwards, the provincial state became identified as the key instrument responsible for preserving Quebec's unique culture and the promotion of its economic development. A highly interventionist provincial state, which became the engine of reform, created the material and psychological conditions which produced a group of highly skilled business leaders, large pools of capital accessible to francophone business, and an attitude of creativity and partnership between business and the provincial state (McRoberts 1988: ch. 5; Coleman 1991: 175).

Given this 'critical mass,' leaders of Quebec sought a role for the province and the City of Montreal to replace activities lost to Toronto. The project became one of reorienting the city from the regional centre of eastern Canada that it had become to an internationally focused, 'second-tier' global city (Reed 1982: 227; Ruddick 1991: 286). Though proponents of this 'internationalism' invoked images of Europe as a major trading partner with Quebec, it was the U.S. market that in reality was their principal target (Chodos and Hamovitch 1991: 198; Canada, House of Commons, Standing Committee on Finance and Economic Affairs, 21 January 1987: 22:5).

The notion of becoming an international financial centre flowed easily from these aspirations and from the new business culture of Quebec. Moreover, as acknowledged by business leaders in Canada, the financial industry in Quebec was in the vanguard of innovation (MacIntosh 1991: 273). Whereas the highly protected and conservative anglophone-dominated banking industry made marginal accommodations to the sweeping changes occurring in international finance during the 1980s, perceptive leaders in Quebec not only foresaw the dramatic opportunities that would emerge but were inclined to pursue them. Financial leaders in Quebec tested the limits of the intractable 'four pillars' of finance – banking, insurance, securities, and trust or fiduciary functions – with new corporate structure and financial relationships.[2]

Thus, the proposal for an international banking centre was the product of the intersection of several factors: some originating from the domestic realm of Quebec, others from the relationship of Quebec and Canada, and still others from the rapidly changing context of international financial restructuring.

Vancouver

The City of Vancouver also became a principal player, though the circumstances surrounding its aspirations to be designated an IBC were somewhat different from those of Montreal. Economic conditions in British Columbia were no less dire than those in Quebec. Vancouver was dependent on a highly volatile resource-based, export-led economy that faltered badly in the early 1980s (Resnick 1987). And whereas Montreal had developed an indigenous financial sector, in Vancouver that sector either was locally based and largely parochial in outlook or it was composed of branch offices of national organizations, representing cosmopolitan capital, which were headquartered in Toronto.

IBC designation for Vancouver was sought in a fairly casual way, certainly without the vision or energy of the proponents in Montreal. The local growth coalition, organized under the umbrella of the Board of Trade, was essentially composed of consumers of financial services, not producers of financial products (D. Rezac, interview 13 November 1991). Consequently, interest and commitment were weak and the city's application for designation may well have been stillborn had its participation not become an important *political tactic* for proponents of the IBC in Montreal. The inclusion of Vancouver was seized on by them as a response to the objection of the government of Canada that it could not be seen to be giving special treatment to Montreal to the exclusion of other cities in the nation, several of which, in addition to Vancouver, had sought designation. The promotion of Vancouver, ostensibly to offer international financial services to the Pacific Rim, provided a rationale for Montreal to serve a European market and, most importantly, gave the scheme a pan-Canadian image (La Chambre de Commerce du Montréal 1984, 7 February).

Two Governments – Two Proposals

The first proposal for IBC designation, made in 1981, was addressed to the powerful Department of Finance of the government of Canada. The department was custodian of the regulations governing banking and taxation which would be affected by designation. The Liberal Party was the government of the day in 1981, and it had little reason to accede to the proposal. In the first place, it recently had successfully fought a pitched battle with the incumbent government of Quebec, the Parti Québecois, over the highly emotional issue of that province's separation from the Canadian federation. On this count alone, the Liberals had no inclination to give Quebec a 'special deal' as IBC designation would have been interpreted throughout the rest of Canada.

Moreover, there had been a struggle during the previous decade over national development policy. The Liberal Party, architect of the Keynesian era of activist government in the postwar period, was identified with a strong central government involved in regional equalization and economic development. But as its philosophical inclination and financial ability to perform this function faltered in the 1970s, provinces throughout the country attempted to go their own way and to make whatever plans and deals they could to the advantage of their citizens (Atkinson and Coleman 1989: 69). The emergence of what is known as 'provincialism' or provincial self-reliance was judged by the government of Canada to be vexatious and an obstacle to the realization of its own attempts to adjust to the emerging conditions of the 1980s (Brodie 1990: 202). As a result, any ceding of special powers to Montreal and Vancouver was seen as an intensification of the problem, not a solution.

Finally, the position of the federal Department of Finance influenced the reaction of the Liberals. Over the years, the department had gained substantial power in the federal bureaucracy, and it had developed a close, symbiotic relationship with the interest group that represented the banking community, the Canadian Bankers Association (CBA). Coleman refers to it as a co-optive, clientelist relationship (Coleman 1988: 184–92). The department commissioned in-house studies of the IBC proposal it had received from proponents in Montreal and, after consulting with the CBA, concluded that the idea was neither technically practical nor economically desirable (Canada, Department of Finance 1983: 3). In this instance, the department provided abundant technical advice that supported the government's predisposition. Later, when the government changed and the Conservative party elected to proceed with the IBC designation, the department did not produce comparable, supportive technical evidence (*Globe and Mail*, 6 October 1986). This greatly complicated the new government's job of justifying its support of the proposal.

There matters stood until the Conservative party trounced the Liberals in the 1984 election, winning a landslide victory both in Quebec and the West. Not only had the Liberals run out of ideas about national development but the deep recession of 1981–2 was the *coup de grâce* to their tenure in office. The Liberals' traditional, overwhelming support in Quebec eroded drastically over the sovereignty issue. Moreover, the steep decline in world prices for resources, particularly those for energy, which were the economic foundation of provinces in Western Canada, left the Liberals with little support there as well. This situation paved the way for their stunning defeat.

The victorious Conservatives ran on a classic neo-liberal platform. Their rhetoric rejected state intervention, supported market-driven growth, and encouraged the concept of 'provincialism.' Yet despite this *laissez-faire* philosophy, their leader, Brian Mulroney, a businessman from Quebec and very much a part of the emerging Quebec bourgeoisie, pledged support for Montreal's international banking objectives (*Montreal Gazette*, 24 January 1987; Canada, House of Commons, Standing Committee 20 January 1987: 21:24). Not only were there electoral debts to repay and future support to be secured in Quebec and the West, but the new prime minister shared many of the aspirations of Quebec business leaders. This translated into favourable consideration of the IBC proposal and, ironically, a ringing triumph of pragmatic state intervention over the Conservative party's neo-liberal philosophy of deregulation. Thus encouraged, the growth coalition in Quebec resolved to expand on the international banking concept previously rejected by the Liberals and to urge its adoption on the new government in Ottawa.

The original 1981 IBC proposal had been fairly limited in scope. It was concerned only with international banking activities conducted in foreign currencies and across national boundaries on a world-wide basis. Its essential aim was to induce Canadian banks that made loans and accepted deposits through their branches abroad to bring that business back to offices in a Canadian city that was designated as an IBC. Business repatriated in that manner would attract advantageous tax treatment, and it was claimed that the public interest would be served by an expansion of employment and related activities. The limited objective of the proposal reflected two issues. One was that the class of foreign transaction targeted by the proposal, known as sovereign loans, had declined substantially in relative importance. Throughout the 1970s such loans represented a very high proportion of foreign currency assets and liabilities booked abroad by Canadian banks. But by the 1980s they were only about 40 per cent of the approximately $80 billion in foreign business conducted by the banks. The balance of 60 per cent comprised commercial loans which were not included in the proposal[3] (Canada, Department of Finance 1983: 1). A second issue was tactical; IBC proponents in Quebec argued that it was possible to distinguish between national and international banking with the former performed by core finance in the metropole of Toronto leaving the putative IBCs of Montreal and Vancouver to repatriate business that otherwise was conducted offshore. It was claimed that this would ensure that such transactions would not impinge on the interests of financial institutions in Toronto and thereby avoid probable conflict with them.

But in the span of four to five years the shape of international finance changed enormously. By 1985 securitization of risk and assets (the conversion of financial assets and debts into tradable securities) had led to massive expansion of financial instruments and markets[4] (Kalymon 1989: 4). For example, the value of securities traded in the United States increased from $22 billion in 1980 to $269 billion in 1985 (Sassen 1991: 71). As well, a dramatic world-wide trend was under way to deregulate the finance industry. The traditional separation of its sectors between insurance, banking, trusts, and securities was breaking down in the face of growth in money markets, the proliferation of conglomerates with interests across sectors, and the intensification of a highly charged and competitive global environment.

It was in this context that business leaders in Quebec replaced their 1981 IBC proposal with one that called on the new Conservative government to establish an international *financial* centre (IFC). This was far more than a mere change in name. The new proposal envisaged favourable tax treatment for a much wider range of financial services than its predecessor. As well, it proposed a regime of deregulation that would essentially eliminate divisions between sectors of the industry. Individual firms would be permitted to perform virtually any and all transactions that came their way, thereby collapsing the compartmentalized structure of the 'four pillars' of the industry.

The IFC proposal represented a quantum leap in the scale and scope of financial activity that its proponents now sought. The anodyne distinction that previously had been made between national and international financial business could no longer be sustained; if the IFCs were established, institutions – banks in particular – which were located outside Montreal or Vancouver and thus unable to enter the burgeoning securities business, would miss out on enormous opportunities. Furthermore, the international business in sovereign loans that would be left to banks located in Toronto represented a rapidly diminishing share of international financial activity. Sovereign loans had amounted to 60 to 70 per cent of international financial transactions in the early 1980s, but by 1986 they accounted for only 16 per cent of the total (United Nations 1989: 112). Clearly, the new proposal struck at the immediate interests of core finance in Toronto whose business leaders had expressed little concern with the initial IBC proposal. Now, the government in Ottawa could expect to be challenged if it fulfilled its commitment to Montreal and Vancouver.

Government Adopts IFCs

In rejecting previous overtures from Quebec when in office, the Liberals had accepted technical counsel provided by the influential Department of Finance and by the Canadian Bankers Association (Coleman 1990: 104). The Conservatives, on the other hand, took a partisan route and vested responsibility for the achievement of IFCs directly in the Prime Minister's Office (PMO) (*Globe and Mail*, 11 February 1987). This arrangement effectively by-passed the custodians of orthodoxy in the Department of Finance and also reduced the influence of banks that customarily had enjoyed preferred access to decision-making through their close association with the Department of Finance (Canada, House of Commons Standing Committee 4 February 1987: 31). This fairly dramatic change in the fortunes of the department and CBA was revealed when a report, commissioned by the new minister of finance and written by two respected former officers of the Bank of Canada, whose findings strongly opposed the establishment of either IBCs or IFCs, was buried for a year (Canada, House of Commons Standing Committee 4 February 1987: 31: 10).[5]

While retaining carriage of the issue in his own office, the prime minister also moved to 'politicize' the leadership of the Department of Finance by replacing a career 'finance-man' and Liberal of long-standing with a trusted colleague as deputy minister (CCH 6 August 1985; Hoy 1987: 82).

With these changes in place, the government turned to the IFC proposal. Its commitment to strengthening the economy of Montreal was very clear. For example, an unprecedented committee of the federal Cabinet was struck to plan for the development of the Montreal region (*Macleans*, 26 January 1987: 34; Canada, House of Commons Standing Committee, 20 January 1984: 21: 31). As well, the new deputy minister of finance quickly opened discussions with IFC proponents in Montreal and Vancouver.

Considerable contrast between the two cities arose from the composition of their business communities and the relation of these to their respective provincial governments. As previously noted, the finance community in Vancouver focused primarily on the exploitation of natural resources. Risk taking was a forte, and its proclivity in this regard was characterized by the wide-open reputation of its stock exchange and investment markets. Despite occasional attempts to create regional banks and other financial institutions, Vancouver took its financial services primarily through branch offices of the big five national banks based in eastern Canada.[6] As a consequence, the financial community was small, dependent, and not particularly inclined to be entrepreneurial in the sense of creating value by exploiting opportunities for wealth creation that were occurring globally through the development and exploitation of new financial products and markets.

Two consequences flowed from this situation. In the case of Vancouver, there were few finance people to support the IFC concept. The way was made by a coalition of general business, under the auspices of the Board of Trade and the city government together with some local financial people (D. Rezac, interview 13 November 1991). As might be expected, the intensity of promotion that a self-interested producer lobby could generate was not present. A second consequence was that in the absence of a strong business presence, the provincial government was obliged to assume much of the initiative for promoting the IFC proposal. In its view, there were substantial benefits to be derived by the province as a whole which the limited Vancouver-based business community was not capable of addressing (M. Goldberg, interview 17 July 1990).

Ironically, this diffuse support base in Vancouver was not unattractive to the emissaries from the federal government. Potentially embarrassing opposition from the banking community was avoided as the resident representatives of Toronto-based national banks essentially stayed on the sidelines while consultation with general business widely publicized the government's message that it intended to enhance economic opportunities in Vancouver and throughout the West.

The situation in Quebec stood in sharp contrast to this relatively low key approach. A cohesive, indigenous financial community in Montreal, acting in close liaison with the provincial government, civic officials, and the federal Cabinet aggressively pushed for IFC designation. The total support of the provincial government was clear. At the end of 1985 it tabled legislation which fully exploited the province's limited constitutional powers to offer incentives and facilities to international financial institutions wishing to locate in Montreal (Quebec, National Assembly, Bill 2). With this demonstration of commitment, financial leaders pressed Ottawa to enact federal legislation needed to operationalize fully the IFC program. Months later it appeared that the project had taken an important step forward when the federal government officially announced in its 1986 budget address that it would work towards the designation of financial centres in Montreal and Vancouver (Canada, House of Commons Debates, 26 February 1986).

When the government's declaration is placed in context, it is understandable that the banks and other elements of Canadian core capital, most of which were headquartered in Toronto, now took the issue very seriously indeed. The legislation tabled in the Quebec National Assembly contemplated a full roster of activities for an IFC including securitization, currency swaps, loans, deposits, and note issuance facilities. It opened these to common ownership structures, which essentially eliminated the traditional distinctions within the industry, and proposed favourable tax regimes to support them. The province also had pioneered by deregulating the insurance industry in the previous year, and in the view of financial observers in Toronto, Quebec intended to treat Canadian finance in the same manner as that of any other (foreign) country (MacIntosh 1991: 274).

From the perspective of a staid and protected banking industry, such aggressive liberalization would seriously erode the business of financial institutions, particularly banks, located outside the proposed IFCs. By the summer of 1986, the financial community in Toronto, general business associations, civic authorities, and the government of Ontario were moved to fight back vigorously. Immediately following the adoption of IFC legislation in Quebec, the Ontario government reciprocated by announcing that it too would permit securities firms to be owned by banks and that it also would permit foreign investment dealers to do business in Ontario. Moreover, the government promised to match Quebec's IFC legislation (Ontario 1986: 583). In practical terms, this did little more than put Quebec and Ottawa on notice since the move, like the provisions of the Quebec legislation, required federal supporting legislation to become operational.

The Impact of International Restructuring

Taken together, these events comprised a virtual paradigm shift for the finance industry. The banks in particular found themselves in uncomfortable and unaccustomed turbulence, both at home and abroad. They had been confronted with two major issues that influenced their response to these government initiatives. The first was that with the decline in the volume of sovereign loans, along with the prohibition against their participation in the securities business, the banks stood to lose out badly in terms of foreign business since a rapidly growing proportion of financial transactions, as noted above, were taking the form of securitized assets and liabilities (MacIntosh 1991: 276).

The second issue, which was shared with the federal government, was that the aggressive activity at the provincial level in financial deregulation challenged federal leadership in the field. Observers have remarked on the isolation of banks and the CBA from provincial regulatory agencies, resulting from exclusive federal authority over banking (Coleman 1988: 181). For banks, any erosion of the authority of the government of Canada seriously compromised their access to the principal public decision-making system of their industry. So it was important for both the banks and Ottawa to neutralize the provinces and regain the initiative.

Despite the extensive restructuring that was occurring in international finance, there had been no concentrated thought in Canada at least until 1986 of allowing banks to own securities dealers (MacIntosh 1991: 271). But by then, the momentum for change was inexorable. Internationally, securitization predominated while domestically the governments of both Quebec and Ontario had signalled that they would deregulate the securities sector giving it advantages relative to the rest of the financial industry. The government of Canada and the banks recognized that change was inevitable. In late June 1987, Bill C-64 authorized banks, insurance companies, and trust and loan companies to acquire securities dealers (Canada, House of Commons, Debates 30 June 1987).

This important milestone in the evolution of the Canadian finance industry led banks to acquire investment firms at a rapid pace and to position themselves to participate fully in the burgeoning securities markets at home and aboard (Kalymon 1989: 14).

The effect on the IFC proposal was equally significant. By giving banks access to the same powers that it had been proposed would be given exclusively to financial institutions located in IFCs, much of their attraction as deregulated, tax-advantaged havens in a segregated and highly regulated national financial system was lost. For the Conservatives, this seriously emasculated the IFC policy with which they had hoped to win popular support in Quebec and the West. Thus, an important political strategy of the government, having significant implications for urban structure, became a victim of its own dramatic liberalization measures, whose adoption was forced on the government by the extraordinary changes occurring during the early 1980s in the world's financial systems.

In practical terms, the government had few other options. Coleman suggests the concept of 'distance from the accumulation process' to explain some forms of political behaviour. He proposes that 'the closer ... [a policy advocated by a party] ... is to the central factors in capital accumulation, the less freedom it will have to manoeuvre as a government and the more it will respond to the dominant fractions of the capitalist class' (Coleman 1991: 173). In this case, the government's declared support for the IFC proposal threatened the existing structure of wealth creation controlled by the Toronto-based capitalist class. The response of the state to this situation was twofold. On the one hand, resistance by core capital made it clear that, if the IFC proposals went ahead at all, they would have to be substantially modified. On the other, the state was obliged to adopt extensive liberalization policies which essentially rendered IFCs redundant. It was forced to do so in order to provide the finance industry in Canada with a regulatory environment compatible with that of its competitors abroad (Canada, Department of Finance 1987: 4). As well, liberalization re-established federal dominance in the regulation of the industry.

The Political Fallout

While the reconciliation of the banks' concerns may have solved one problem for the federal government, it was left with others that in terms of the electorate were very severe. The evisceration of the IFC concept, along with other problems of a mid-term mandate, drove the government's popular support to record lows throughout the country (*Globe and Mail* 5 September 1986). To make matters worse, the government's own members from Toronto joined the Opposition and the influential Chair of the Standing Committee of Finance and Economic Affairs of the House of Commons to condemn unanimously the components of the IFC proposal that still were on the table (Canada, Standing Committee 28 April 1987). Proponents of the scheme in Vancouver and Montreal felt betrayed by the government, which they judged to have caved in once again to the interests of Toronto's Bay Street. Criticism of the government reached what the *Montreal Gazette* described as 'hysteria' when the premier of Ontario warned that the IFC proposal could put national unity at risk and when a full-page advertisement placed in the Toronto *Globe and Mail*, by the City of Toronto, was headlined 'The Great Toronto Bank Robbery' (*Gazette*, 6 July 1987, B-2; *Globe and Mail*, 29 January 1987; 29 June 1987).

The IFC package that remained was severely diminished from the ambitious 'wish-list' urged on Ottawa in 1986 by the Quebec National Assembly. But the depleted package still was deplored by the finance industry outside Quebec and by Toronto partisans because it was judged to be nothing more than, as it was characterized by its opponents, 'the thin edge of the wedge'; that is, though the benefits conferred immediately were of a minor nature, they would be used by IFC proponents as precedents for future expansion of the concept (Canada, Standing Committee 20 January 1987: 21:6). And there was justification for this view as proponents from Quebec made it plain that the new proposal was no more than a downpayment which had to be improved upon in the future (Canada, Standing Committee 21 January 1987: 22:7).

The government had effectively manoeuvred itself into a virtual 'no-win' situation, and its immediate task was to salvage some political benefits from the mess it had created. For Ontario, much was made of the benefits, direct and indirect, that Toronto would derive from the deregulation of the securities and banking industries (Canada, Department of Finance 21 August 1987). For British Columbia and Quebec, placation came swiftly on the heels of the government's decision to drastically pareback the IFC package. This took two forms. The first was material. The governments of Canada and British Columbia signed an accord which pledged federal assistance for regional development; while no money was attached to the pledge, it had the appearance of concrete action (*Vancouver Sun* 17 December 1986). For Quebec, the government of Canada awarded Montreal a $1.2 billion contract for servicing military aircraft, a highly contentious decision since the government pointedly ignored a lower cost bid submitted by a firm in Winnipeg (*Gazette* 6 July 1987: C-11).

The second form of placation was largely illusory. The government agreed to establish international banking centres in Montreal and Vancouver, reverting to the title and much more modest concept proposed in 1981 (Canada, Department of Finance 1987: 03). The centres were permitted to accept deposits from abroad and loan the funds on deposit to foreign borrowers; domestic transactions were excluded. The government pledged modest tax concessions which, when matched by similar provincial concessions, might attract business to financial institutions locating in the designated IBCs.

The benefits of this arrangement were deceptive. First, the tax benefits relative to competing centres abroad were not particularly attractive. As well, employment opportunities had been vastly exaggerated with no more than a dozen jobs likely to materialize in either Vancouver or Montreal (Canada, Standing Committee 4 February 1987: 31:18). Most important, however, was the fact that the kind of financial transactions permitted by the government's proposal constituted a rapidly shrinking share of business conducted in international financial markets. As noted above, sovereign loans were rapidly declining in importance and commercial bank loans too were being superseded by trade in securities issued by major corporations to raise funds. By 1986 about 85 per cent of cross-border transactions in international finance were in the form of securities (MacIntosh 1991: 276). In practical terms, the government had bequeathed upon Montreal and Vancouver opportunities that few would care to exercise. Not only had they been tossed some dry bones, but worse, bones that had been ravaged by osteomalacia.

Ironically, the illusion worked for the Conservatives on a popular, political level. One Vancouver newspaper cynically (or naively) claimed: 'Ottawa kept a promise to Vancouver' (*Vancouver Province* 29 January 1987). The reaction in Montreal was more realistic and pragmatic as the 'settlement was received favourably ... but only as a downpayment. On an industry and governmental level, the reality was well understood' (*Vancouver Sun* 14 February 1987).

Conclusion

The first conclusion to be drawn from this case study is that it gives an insight into the intense competition between cities to attract command

and control functions associated with high finance and government regulation. It is not that these functions comprise a zero-sum game in which gains by one city must cause losses for another. On the contrary, the variety, volume, and value of international financial transactions has grown at a tremendous rate. But this does not necessarily expand opportunities for cities to share the benefits attributed to them. Harvey, for instance, has pointed out that command and control functions by their nature tend to be highly centralized in spatial terms. This tendency increases as financial services, as a form of production, are subject to intense diversification, expansion, and specialization. As well, command and control functions are 'characterized by monopoly power that is hard to break' (Harvey 1989: 49). Moreover, as the evolving regime of accumulation impels the further intensification of an unusually concentrated structure of capital in Canada and abroad, it is likely that economic 'control points' will tend to be concentrated in fewer urban centres (Semple and Green 1983: 395; Logan and Molotch 1987: 265).

So in the case under review, the inertia of present location tended towards maintenance of the status quo; Toronto had the financial base, the people, the established relationships, the infrastructure. But consequences of the restructuring of global finance imparted a strong tendency towards concentration as well.

The second conclusion concerns the composition of capital and the ability of cities to capture financial services. In Canada, as elsewhere, profound changes in the nature of economic activity have encouraged the growth of financial capital relative to industrial capital (Niggle 1988: 581). This has had the obvious effect of reducing the bargaining power of a peripheral centre, like Vancouver, which has a weak base of indigenous financial capital, though a well-developed structure of resource-based venture capital. This combination meant that proponents of the IFC were too few, too diffuse, and too weak to mount a credible campaign. As well, the ability of Vancouver to compete was affected by the institutional structure of finance in Canada. The banking system is a national one which is centralized in Toronto. When the banks, representing cosmopolitan capital, opposed IFC designation, and their regional representatives in Vancouver took a neutral position, there was no strong base of parochial capital to take up the cause (D. Rezac, interview 13 November 1991).

The structure in Quebec was quite different. There an indigenous financial base relatively independent of the anglo-dominated national banking system, together with a supportive regional state and a vigorous francophone business community, comprised a cohesive force that could challenge cosmopolitan capital on the IFC issue. The challenge failed primarily because liberalization policies that were adopted by the national state and core capital in response to global restructuring essentially negated the advantages of the proposed IFC. Had global restructuring not triggered this response, the result for Montreal at least could have been different.

A third conclusion has to do with regional corporatism. One does not have to move into a determinist camp to acknowledge that the trajectory of international capital is not easily diverted. And in Canada, the omnipotence of core capital reinforces the momentum. It appears from this issue that if the preferred path of capital is to be refracted, local, parochial capital cannot do the job on its own.

In the case of both Montreal and Vancouver, the regional state played a crucial role in the promotion of the IFC concept. In part, this can be explained by the division of powers between the federal and provincial levels of government. But the tradition of an activist state and corporatist structures is strong in Quebec specifically because of the need for the concertation of resources to achieve cultural goals. The case of British Columbia is different inasmuch as the regional state there normally has been much more reactive than interventionist and proactive. For the IFC campaign, however, the government of British Columbia was obliged to act as a surrogate for a weak or disinterested business community in order to promote the general interests of the regional economy.

The final conclusion refers to the limits of state action. In the book, *Contradictions of the Welfare State*, Claus Offe specifies the dilemma of democratic government in a capitalist state (Offe 1984: 120). While the state's institutional form is determined by the conventions of democratic and representative government, the material content of state power is conditioned by the requirements of the accumulation process. This is the case because powerholders are in fact powerless unless the accumulation process is strong enough to produce the material resources (that is, public revenues) needed to achieve political objectives. Yet at the same time groups which seek political power must win sufficient electoral support in general elections to achieve it. Thus, powerholders who are dependent on wealth creators for material resources are also dependent on popular electoral support for legitimate institutional control.

Initially, the IFC issue was about electoral support; the Conservative Party saw it as one which would contribute to its popular base. But as the antipathy of core finance to the issue grew, it became apparent that persistence with it would damage the government's support from core finance. To reiterate Coleman, as the 'distance' diminished between the policy and the vital interests of finance, tension between the two imperatives grew. The issue was resolved when both the government and core finance, pressured by global forces, agreed on a deregulation scheme which coincidentally rendered the IFC concept largely redundant.

In conclusion, it might be proposed that the market in international financial services can be refracted towards the achievement of national, social goals, like the redistribution of urban economic activity through IFCs, only insofar as the material interests of a dominant fraction of capital are not compromised. In this respect, perhaps the case of financial services is a precursor for urban centres. As the sovereignty of nations erodes through globalization, and is constrained by trade agreements like the FTA and WTO, it is likely that commercial considerations increasingly will take precedence over homemade, democratically determined social and economic policies affecting urban life. Like other commodities, civic life and social opportunities for ordinary citizens more than ever will come to reflect priorities determined by the market.

NOTES

1 The term 'core capital' refers to the principal financial institutions of the industry: banks, trust and insurance companies, investment dealers, and such financial services as merchant banking venture capital and money management. These are predominately located in Toronto.
2 Historically these sectors of the financial industry had been virtually isolated from one another. This occurred through practice and government regulation. Banks, for example, did not trade in securities nor did insurance companies engage in the administration of estates which was the preserve of trust companies, and so on.
3 Sovereign loans, also known as syndicated bank loans, are loans to governments or loans that carry a government guarantee.
4 Securitization of risk and assets refers to the development in the 1980s of new financial instruments which permitted lenders and borrowers to hedge against extremely volatile shifts in foreign exchange rates and interest rates. Accordingly, financial futures markets and foreign exchange markets developed to provide increased flexibility in the management of fixed rate obligations. As well, financial institutions converted fixed assets, like mortgages or receivables,

into new financial products known as asset-backed securities through the purchase of which, for instance, an investor acquires a direct interest in a portfolio of mortgages or notes.

5 Though the document was neither made public for approximately a year, nor revealed to the CBA, which traditionally would have been invited by the Finance Department to vet the report, it is significant that representatives of the general business communities in Vancouver and Montreal were given access to it. See the testimony of the Assistant Deputy Minister of Finance before the Standing Committee of Finance and Economic Affairs, 4 February 1987: 31:9.

6 The banks are: the Canadian Imperial Bank of Commerce, the Royal Bank of Canada, the Bank of Montreal, the Bank of Nova Scotia, and the Toronto-Dominion Bank.

REFERENCES

Atkinson, M.M., and W.D. Coleman. 1989. *The State, Business, and Industrial Change in Canada.* Toronto: University of Toronto Press

Brodie, J. 1990. *The Political Economy of Canadian Regionalism.* Toronto: Harcourt, Brace, Jovanovich

CCH, *Ottawa Newsletter*, 6.8.85, Ottawa

Canada, House of Commons, Proceedings of the Standing Committee of Finance and Economic Affairs: 20.1.87; 21.1.87; 27.1.87; 4.2.87; 28.4.87

– 1986. House of Commons, *Debates*: 26.2.86

– 1987. House of Commons, *Debates*: 30.6.87

– 1983. Department of Finance, 'The International Banking Centre Issue,' mimeo

– 1987. Department of Finance, Press Release, 28.1.87

Chambre de Commerce du Montréal, Montreal Board of Trade, letter to the Minister of Finance of Canada, 7.2.84

Chodos, R., and E. Hamovitch. 1991. *Quebec and the American Dream.* Toronto: Between the Lines Press

Coleman, W.D. 1988. *Business and Politics.* Kingston: McGill-Queen's University Press

– 1990. 'The banking policy community.' In W.D. Coleman and G. Skogstad, eds. *Policy Communities and Public Policy.* Toronto: Copp Clark Pitman

– 1991. 'The political economy of Quebec.' In W. Clement, and G. Williams, eds., *The New Canadian Political Economy.* Kingston: McGill-Queen's University Press

Fraser, M. 1987. *Quebec Inc.* Toronto: Key Porter Books

Gazette, Montreal, 24.1.87: 'Feds banking on Montreal,' B-3

– Montreal, 6.7.87: 'Hysteria doesn't help,' B-2

Globe and Mail, Toronto, 5.9.86: 'Montreal "action plan" promised'

– Toronto, 6.10.86: 'International banking centre not for Toronto, Wilson says'

– Toronto, 29.1.87: 'Banking plan stirs up regional tensions, Peterson says'

– Toronto, 11.2.87: 'PMO gets more laughs than kudos for banking scheme'

– Toronto, 29.6.87: 'The Great Toronto Bank Robbery' (advertisement)

Harvey D. 1989. *The Urban Experience.* Baltimore: Johns Hopkins University Press

Hoy, C. 1987. *Friends in High Places.* Toronto: Key Porter Books

Kalymon, B.A. 1989. *Global Innovation and the Impact on Canada's Financial Markets.* Toronto: Wiley

King, D.S. 1987. 'The State, Capital and Urban Change in Britain.' In P.M. Smith, J.R. Feagin, eds., *The Capitalist City.* Cambridge, MA: Basil Blackwell

Linteau, P-A., R. Durocher, J.-C. Robert, and F. Ricard. 1991. *Quebec since 1930.* Toronto: Lorimer

Logan, J.R., and H.L. Molotch. 1987. *Urban Fortunes.* Berkeley: University of California Press

MacIntosh, R. 1991. *Different Drummers.* Toronto: Macmillan

Maclean's Magazine 26.1.87, Toronto: 'Stakes in metropolitan power'

McRoberts, K. 1988. *Quebec: Social Change and Political Crisis.* Toronto: McClelland and Stewart

Niggle, C.J. 1988. 'The increasing importance of financial capital in the U.S. economy.' *Journal of Economic Issues*, 22(2): 581–8

Offe, C. 1984. *Contradictions of the Welfare State.* London: Hutchinson

Ontario 1986 Proceedings of the Legislative Assembly, 13.5.86

Reed, H.C. 1982. 'Appraising corporate investment policy: A financial centre theory of foreign direct investment.' In C.P. Kindleberger and D.B. Audretsch, eds., *The Multinational Corporation in the 1980s.* Cambridge, MA: MIT Press

Resnick, P. 1987. 'Neoconservatism on the periphery: The lessons from B.C.' *B.C. Studies* 75: 3–23

Ruddick, S. 1991. 'The Montreal Citizens' Movement: The Realpolitik of the 1990's?' In M. Davis, S. Hiat, and M. Sprinkler, eds., *Fire in the Hearth.* London: Verso

Sassen, S. 1991. *The Global City.* Princeton: Princeton University Press

Semple, R., and M. Green. 1983. 'Inter-urban corporate headquarters relocation in Canada.' *Cahiers de Géographie de Québec* 27: 389–406

Short, J.R. 1989. 'Yuppies, yuffies and the new urban order.' *Transactions of the Institute of British Geographers* 14: 173–88

Timberlake, M. 1987. 'World-system theory and the study of comparative urbanization. In M.P. Smith and J.R. Feagin, eds., *The Capitalist City*, Cambridge MA: Basil Blackwell

United Nations. 1989. *Transnational Corporations in World Development.* New York: United Nations

Vancouver Province, 29.1.87: 'City buoyed up at Bank-Centre move'

Vancouver Sun, 17.12.86: 'Banking centre bill pledged'

– 14.2.87: 'Minister launches banking "mission"'

10

Women and Work in a Canadian Community[1]

BETH MOORE MILROY

The research reported here was stimulated by the widely observed fact that increasing proportions of women of all classes are employed full-time in the labour market.[2] Primary interest lay in the effect this change would have on community life. It therefore took the point of view of a community as a whole, looking back in time at the work women contributed to its development; the aim was to understand better what was in the process of changing.

The perspective for what follows is urban planning. It is appropriate for planners to investigate social issues of this kind because their professional statement of values calls for them to plan for all-around, good-quality communities.[3] To date, the principal planning response to the trend towards increasing numbers of women in paid employment has been to try to improve women's *access* to the labour market, which is clearly essential so that women and men are comparably placed to compete for jobs. That is, planners have directed their actions to employment, where women intend to put more time and effort, not to community and domestic work where they expect to put less.

Women's increased participation in paid labour is not being generated from a vacuum. Women were not idle because they were not employed. They were working in homes and communities. The argument made in this chapter is that community, domestic, and traded work are all inter-related.[4] Therefore, the shift to employment needs understanding and accommodating within the context of domestic and community work. The reason for making this argument is to stimulate societal debate about non-traded work – how it is valued, how it should be accomplished, and by whom. It is emphatically not made to encourage returning to past eras or working arrangements. The normative position taken in this research is that all three kinds of work – community, domestic, and traded – are equally important, each making unique and essential contributions to the overall well-being of individuals, households, and communities.

For the most part, planning initiatives directed towards access to paid employment have not been instigated by planners themselves.[5] Rather, they have been urged to re-think and revise their usual methods by women doing community work, that is, by women who were organizing to assist, resist, devise alternatives, and urge change. This political action is part of the conceptualization of community work used in this research, and it will be discussed more below.

This study fits the definition of critical social research in the following ways. First, it questions the legitimacy of the existing order of things, in this case why women's community work is largely discounted. Second, it proceeds from an explicit concern with social justice pursued via democratic social change. Third, this research was done not only for the sake of informing ourselves and others about women and work in the study area, but also in order to change how they were valued. We want to profile that work as part of the puzzle of understanding urban development and have it incorporated in models of urban development that planners use when making recommendations to elected officials.

The aims of this essay are (1) to illustrate how women's work in one community compares with work as it is conventionally characterized; (2) to raise some questions about theories of urban development that rely on conceptualizations of work as solely paid employment; and, in the process, (3) to illustrate critical social research in practice.

The next section describes how work and urban development are ordinarily defined and characterized in the literature. This is followed by an overview of the study, the description and analysis of two findings emerging from the research, and discussion of their significance.

Theories of Work and Urban Development

Common Characterizations of Work

Work is generally conceptualized in one of two main ways, either as employment in the formal labour market or as activity in dual (formal and informal) sectors. The first assumes that work is essentially co-extensive with formal paid employment. Here it will be referred to as the 'work-as-employment' approach. Work is understood this way in conventional economics. The second approach assumes that work is made up of various types of activities over and above formal paid labour including barter, exchange, volunteer, and domestic work. This is work as individuals and households experience it in the course of developing strategies for managing their livelihoods in the face of shifting economic conditions. Here it is called the 'continuum-of-work' approach.

Work as Employment

Far and away the vast majority of literature assumes that work and employment are virtually synonymous. This is the case whether it is being described in disciplines such as economics or political science, in fields of practice such as architecture or community economic development, or in the popular media. Work is routinely thought of as activities having to do with producing and distributing goods, resources, and services.

When work is envisaged this way – as a formal economic labour market made up of jobs to be filled by largely unencumbered individuals – then the solutions to women's disadvantaged position *vis-à-vis* the labour force that seem most logical are those that compensate for their encumbrances (such as responsibility for young, ill, or elderly people) or for past injustices (such as inadequate opportunities and training, or lack of role models). This logic corresponds with the principal focus of work-related public policy, which is jobs – creating jobs, designing training programs, and regulating working conditions related to jobs.

Broadly speaking, proposed solutions include programs to ensure equal pay for work of equal value (see, for example, Lamarche 1990); facilities for care of children and the elderly (Canadian Aging Research Network 1993, McKinnon and Odynak 1991, Lero et al. 1993, Tindale 1991); greater spatial integration of jobs with housing, retail, and commercial services; better public transportation; programs for flexible working hours (Lero et al. 1993); more training opportunities (Canadian Labour Market and Productivity Centre 1994); and strategies for managing stress (Long and Kahn 1993). Governments, industries, and community organizations are making some efforts to advance these solutions, but this work is occurring slowly and unevenly (Beach, Friendly, and Schmidt 1993; Canadian Labour Market and Productivity Centre 1994; Modlich 1988; Paris 1989). For example, skilled and unskilled workers' concerns and needs are not met equally, according to a study by Lero et al. (1993). They found that managers and professionals have superior access to such arrangements as family-responsibility leaves and flexible working hours compared with less skilled employees. From other studies it appears that most employers think it is mainly up to employees to find solutions to their work-family dilemmas (Paris 1989) and that women have less access to alternative scheduling than do men (Duxbury et al. 1991). There are still enormous discrepancies between what people want and what is being provided. A survey of 11,000 Canadian workers in 1990 reported that what employees want most are childcare support in on-site centres and subsidies for childcare, while a 1989 survey of 385 employers reported that only 4.8 per cent offer these benefits (Canadian Labour Market and Productivity Centre 1994: 13).

A Continuum of Work

The inappropriateness of reducing work to employment has been questioned continuously, and especially since the 1970s, yet a discussion of alternatives is never prominent in national debates. The main alternative, a continuum-of-work, takes various forms but the common thread is that work is described as occurring in both the market/state sector and in the private social sector. In the former it is called 'formal' because it is incorporated into the annual compilation of a nation's accounts, whereas work done in the latter is called 'informal' and is characterized negatively by the absence of calculated value. The components of informal work include a hidden economy, in which work is monetarized but neither regulated nor captured by the state in its accounting or taxation; barter and exchange of services which may or may not be valued monetarily; domestic work in households; and such service to others as community volunteering done both inside and outside organizations.[6]

Some researchers describe the full continuum-of-work as 'productive' (Herzog et al. 1992: 211), noting that formal and informal work are integral to one other (Gershuny 1985: 129). Further, Henry (1987) has argued in more detail that work in the informal end of the continuum is sometimes in opposition to capitalist institutions (e.g., self-help which is activity that deprives capitalists of profit because it is done by oneself for oneself) and sometimes in support of them (e.g., domestic work, which mainly reproduces workers, it is argued). Similarly, capitalist institutions might oppose informal work (e.g., illegal work, which cuts into legal trade or production) or support it (e.g., community care, which frees more workers from home-based care). Still others have examined how work is divided up in a specific community (Pahl 1984, Mingione 1991) or is allocated among unevenly developed regions (Sharpe 1988).

Those approaches to defining work in relation to the formal capitalist economy and as occurring in dual sectors have been challenged by an important departure which looks at work from the point of view of household coping strategies. A major contributor to research on work in geographic space, Pahl notes his own evolution in thinking from his work with Gershuny (Gershuny and Pahl 1979) when they were intent on describing the ways in which services are provided, to his own 1984 study in which the focus is on ways of getting work done. In the models described by Pahl (1984) and later by Mingione (1991), the household is the basic unit for 'getting by' in the face of specific, but unstable, conditions in the formal economy. 'Getting by,' as Pahl aptly calls it, refers to ways of managing economically and socially. Note that while Pahl recognizes that households may aggregate in order to improve on 'getting by,' he does not incorporate political action within his model of work. Still later in 1989 Pahl proposed that the focus be on work, as such, rather than on the economy, and that forms of work be defined 'by the social relations they are embedded in' (1989: 106).[7]

Morris, another scholar studying work, also focuses on household strategies but in her theoretical exposition explicitly recognizes that the household is not an unproblematic unit in that the power distribution among household members may be very unequal, and in addition each may have a different relationship to traded labour (1990). The interpersonal negotiating and decision-making that go into developing 'getting by' strategies will, in all likelihood, be partly shaped by the conventional gender relations of the era and location.

This brings us close to the conceptualization of work used in this research in which the types of work people do and how it is valued are political questions. Feminists assume it is not by accident that women, as a whole, across nations, are paid less than men in formal employment, work longer hours in combinations of formal and informal work, and control few of the world's resources. They are searching for the causes of such a gross imbalance in the sociocultural practices which created and maintain this situation. This entails examining work and, at the same time, the relations between genders, to see how one influences the other, that is, how doing particular kinds of work constrains the way that one is regarded in the society and, conversely, the way that one is regarded circumscribes the work one does.[8]

Conventional Models of Urban Development

Before moving to the case study, it is important to explain how conceptualizations of work, such as the two found above, are related to urban development models and planning. My argument is that the conceptualization of work that is dominant in national debates is the one that will appear in the most influential models of urban development. That conceptualization will also be the one planners use most to justify one plan of action over another.

Planning as a field of public practice is largely conducted within the confines of public opinion and political will. It is virtually never avant-garde in its proposals although it may at times operate near the margin of conventional wisdom, be it the progressive or the conservative margin. As a public practice it is definitely not radical. It therefore turns to non-radical theorists for its models of urban development. Indeed, planners are more likely to borrow from capitalist economics than from any other discipline for modelling spatial development.[9]

Such economic-based models of urban development involve the standard assumption that work is co-extensive with employment. In addition, or perhaps as a consequence, employment in producing and distributing goods and services is at the core of the principal models of how urban development occurs.[10] The motor for development is the competition among economic actors. Stated in an over-simplified manner, people wanting retail, commercial, or industrial real estate compete with those who want residential real estate. Fractions of these groups also compete with one another – banks against legal firms, Eaton's against The Bay, seekers of single-family dwellings against seekers of apartments, and so on. The outcome of such competition is said to be that people's needs, wants, and capacities to pay for space are realized in concrete, visible urban development. In that raw model competition brings urban form into reality. However, it can be observed that this process is modified by sociospatial management practices, of which planning is one. These practices clarify relations among actors by setting rules (e.g., zoning and development standards) and moderating excesses that may arise (e.g., developing parks in strategic locations; revising the development controls) in the process of competition-driven urban development.

In order to formulate recommendations, planners gather information about what is currently occurring in a region and then relate this to the model described above, or a variant of it, to explain how urban development occurs. By putting the specific information and the model together, they hope to deduce what should be done to steer development in ways that will achieve good-quality standards and meet the aspirations of the people served by their plans.

That, then, is the trajectory from generalized acceptance of an idea in good currency (that is, that work is co-extensive with employment) to its expression in urban land use. The model assumes the urban forms we find on the ground emerge independently of the work done outside employment. It also assumes that who exactly is doing the paid employment (men, women, which racial or ethnic group or class, and so on) is inconsequential. The model is even oblivious to the fact that the percentage of people in developed countries for whom work-as-employment is the standard is in a long and continual decline.[11]

If we want to value a range of work wider than just employment, and to have this change represented in land use arrangements, then we need to change the models of urban development. A major part of doing that is changing the model of work dominating national debates.

Let us now turn from the theoretical backdrop against which this research was done to the study itself.

The Study

The Study Area

Kitchener and Waterloo, in southwestern Ontario, are separate cities. They have their own city councils and administrations, and long-time residents view them as qualitatively different communities. Nonetheless, they are often treated together as Kitchener-Waterloo, and this is done here for several reasons: they are spatially contiguous; they were settled by people with broadly similar Germanic cultural backgrounds which, until the last few decades, distinguished the region from predominantly Anglo-Saxon southern Ontario; they share civic organizations and many such institutions as schools and hospitals; they are mainly served by the same media; and they fall within the same regional municipality for purposes of planning and delivering many civic services. In 1995 the population of Kitchener-Waterloo was approximately 250,000.

Extensive descriptions exist of community building in Kitchener-Waterloo. They capture in detail the pioneering spirit of the German Mennonite settlers who first came to the area in 1805 (Tiessen 1979; Uttley 1937; English and McLaughlin 1983; McLaughlin 1990; Bloomfield 1980, 1983, 1987a, 1987b). Among other things, they describe the industries started by the settlers; the industrial policy of the area dating from the 1870s; the influence the area's economy had on the rest of Canada; the effort to secure the rail line through the cities; Kitchener-Waterloo's enterprising model for financing utilities, which was copied by other Ontario communities; the tax and other incentives given to 'good' companies to encourage them to settle in the region; the low wage rates and rates of unionization; the invitation to Thomas Adams, a celebrated city planner, to prepare the first town plan for a Canadian community; the work of the German clubs and the churches to maintain some of the German heritage; and the tearing of the social fabric of the communities when conscription was called for during the First World War.

The reason for listing those topics is to illustrate the type of stories told in published works about how Kitchener-Waterloo developed over time. The emphasis is on industry, trade, employment, economic cycles, institutions, and war. The literature describing Kitchener-Waterloo's history is very much in keeping with the conventional models of work and urban development described above.[12] The shared emphasis on economic processes as the motor of urban development in the popular, academic, and professional literatures is a clue that this presumed causal relationship is widely established in people's minds. It therefore appears *in the writing* that the most important things happening in Kitchener-Waterloo have had to do with stimulating the economy and strengthening structures that support it.

Conceptualizing the Study

The primary interest of this study is the work done by women in the community sphere, including how they described it, valued it, and fitted it around domestic and traded work.[13] It was assumed that it would indicate some of the aspects of urban development women considered important, and that these findings could challenge aspects of the theories of work and urban development in current use by showing what women's community work contributed to building and maintaining a community over time.[14]

It was further assumed that where a particular type of work was done, by whom, and under what conditions, were explicitly or implicitly ratified by the decision-makers of the community acting as citizens, as members of households, and where applicable, as workers and employers. Thus, gender relations whether occurring in households, places of employment, or public community spaces were to be opened up to scrutiny in this research.

We were particularly anxious that the identification and assessment of women's contributions to community-building emerged from women themselves. There already was an image of work in the context of community building in Kitchener-Waterloo, the one found in the stories told about the study area. We did not want that existing image, which perfectly fit nationally recognized, economically based images of 'good' urban development, to unduly shape the new one. Consequently, we began the research by documenting women's activities as described by them. After seeing the work as much as possible from the perspective of the women who engaged in it, we would subsequently try to define what it contributed. Via traditional research its value had already been assigned: it was not altogether absent from the histories; it was conveyed as laudable, but ultimately of lesser importance than economic activity.

Method

An historical-comparative research method was used in which the preponderance of data were qualitative – that is, word-based rather than number-based. It was also a case study. This method was chosen in order to look closely at several relationships at once and compare them over the period 1900 to 1980. In this approach one immerses oneself in the details of the case and then looks for patterns in the data, rather than beginning with fully formed hypotheses which are then tested by searching for evidence that supports or refutes them. It is also a form of 'grounded' research: instead of starting with a conventional understanding of work as either paid employment or as a continuum, it began with asking what purposeful activity women were engaged in in Kitchener-Waterloo, letting a conceptualization of work emerge from the data.

Data Sources

Primary sources controlled by women were sought and used first. Major sources were open-ended interviews, oral history tapes, family papers, and the records of women's organizations.[15] These were then supplemented by standard library research sources such as books, monographs, city council minutes, censuses, and newspapers. This 'first-second' strategy was used in order to define the scope and significance of community work according to women's, rather than dominant, interpretations. However, the data for a study such as this are dispersed, meagre, and constantly threaten to be male-biased. In addition they reflect a class bias, because wealthier women were better able to preserve and publicly record their activities than poorer women, and a cultural bias, because the voices of women of minority backgrounds are rarely heard. So, despite our best efforts, the findings are partial.

Findings

Two of the study's findings are described next and analysed in the following section.

Work to Be Done Changes Categories but Does not Disappear

This finding became evident from comparing the work women were doing in the early part of the research period with that in the latter. The biggest shift was from the domestic and community categories to traded work.

Before 1900, most community work done by women was carried out informally or through religious organizations. Although religious organizations continued to be very important in Kitchener-Waterloo,[16] an increasing number of secular organizations soon sprang up to take on the various tasks of an industrializing community.

One task was to look after young women. Because industry was burgeoning hundreds of young women were recruited by local manufacturing firms and businesses from the surrounding countryside and towns. Their care was handled extensively by the Young Women's Christian Association (Montonen, Milroy, and Wismer 1990) which built a residence and offered lodgings where the young women could be protected and guided in their development, meet other employed young women, and learn social and domestic skills. Besides the housing services, the volunteer women who ran the YWCA also toured the local factories, entertaining 'the girls' in a different one every month in the hope of finding new converts to the YWCA movement. Interested in the overall development of all young women, the YWCA offered a wide range of educational, social, domestic, and physical exercise opportunities.

Other organizations were launched to look after children on a continuing basis (orphanages and, subsequently, the Children's Aid Society), and to offer special events such as picnics and camping. The House of Industry and Refuge looked after some of the indigent and elderly; many visiting committees looked in on the elderly, handicapped, and sick. Newcomers to the community were greeted by representatives of several organizations and, in addition, immigrants had the support of the Kitchener-Waterloo Council of Friendship. The Local Council of Women, a branch of the National Council of Women, was active in the community between 1921 and 1951. The organization took the long view, identifying areas where action was needed. For example, it launched numerous campaigns to get women elected to various community boards (libraries, schools, hospitals) and to promote public health, citizenship, education, legal reforms, child welfare, housing, and town planning. It set its own agenda, with help from the national office, but extended its reach by also working through seventeen to twenty women's organizations affiliated with it. The YWCA and later the Local Council of Women encouraged the formation of various 'professions of improvement,' as Boyer called a number of these fields (1983: 7). One example was the Organized Social Workers which was formed in 1912 within the YWCA and eventually moved out on its own in 1915. Women learned practical home nursing via the Organized Social Workers and used the new knowledge in their approaches to the social problems they were encountering in their volunteer community work.

Looking in on the community in about 1970 it is evident that essentially the same work still needed to be done. Children were still orphaned or neglected; women were still abused; people were still sick, indigent, elderly, and handicapped. However, in the later time period the work was handled differently within the community.

First, many tasks had been professionalized and transferred into the paid work category. For example, work with youngsters had been incorporated into the Children's Aid Society, and the job of overall social planning for the community was in the hands of the Social Planning Council and the Social Resources Board. These agencies were either wholly or partly funded by governments. Assistance to immigrants, which had been provided by the Kitchener-Waterloo Council of Friendship from 1943, now had several sources. Part of the council's work was absorbed by government-sponsored training organizations; part was taken up by a proliferation of uni-ethnic clubs[17]; and pan-ethnic matters fell to one modest organization and to municipal cultural awareness programs.

Second, along with professionalization came specialization. By the 1970s organizations tended to be single-purpose. Whereas the YWCA and LCW had had committees covering everything from town planning to athletics to public health, they had also had active, overarching boards and annual meetings where the full range of the organization's concerns could be discussed. The contemporary organizations had narrow specialities. Even the YWCA had reduced its focus to housing and daycare, and the LCW had disbanded. Major organizations such as home and school associations fragmented into divergent interest groups and, in the process, lost an overall vision of the community.[18] No non-governmental organization that scanned the whole community or took the whole community as its interest seems to have survived.

Third, secular organizations were more numerous than religious ones in community work, which had not been the case at the turn of the century. The absolute number of religious organizations dropped substantially in the early 1960s when two large religious denominations each consolidated its women's organizations into single umbrella organizations. At the same time, church attendance was declining in Kitchener-Waterloo, as it was elsewhere in Canada. In 1978 formal, secular women's organizations numbered about forty-five,[19] compared with about eighteen in 1922.

Activities in the Community Work Category Tend to Be Multifaceted Rather than Discrete

One example illustrating this finding is that much of the loosely organized and unorganized activity in which women were engaged across the whole time period was *both* task-focused *and* 'keeping an eye out for one another.' That is, the work is as much a form of *interaction* as task *achievement.* The actual tasks that are done do matter, but they do not define all of the effort or results achieved. What matters as well as the task done is the interaction it entails.

For instance, the information gathered for this study shows that while women were making a quilt to raise money, sorting clothes to be sent to a community in need, or visiting a sick neighbour, they were simultaneously finding out if Mrs G needed an extra hand because her husband was ill, if young B was shaping up, or if some food should be taken in to Mr Y. In addition to this, they were learning skills and getting information within non-threatening, non-commercialized environments – how to raise money and keep accounts, how to make bandages and perform first aid, what problems were emerging in the local schools, and so on. The knowledge could subsequently be useful in any of the categories of work.

One woman in her late thirties who was interviewed, a mother of three young children, indirectly expressed a felt need for 'keeping an eye out.' She regretted that people in the community 'are becoming more independent'; 'it is just "not done" to ask for help – we are supposed to be so independent'; and 'families are independent – everyone is to do their own living' (Interview G.2.A, 17 May 1989). One of the values of 'keeping an eye out for one another' as a function in a community is that needs are seen or heard directly. Small needs can be met before they become large, and before the needy have to apply for formal help. Formal channels continue to be necessary and effective but are not a substitute, only an alternative, for informal channels.

There is a second example of this finding that the task is not just the task. Community work was often *both* service *and* politics. Some of the organizations engaging in both service and politics to varying degrees across their organizational histories were the Local Council of Women, the YWCA, and Mothers and Others Making Change.[20] One form that the service/politics combination took was gender solidarity:

> Part of any organization you were involved in was feeling women should have more say in what was going on. [We had the] feeling that being women we were on the top crust. You cheered for women when there was the opportunity. (Interview S.1, 2 June 1989)

> No person has to face a crisis alone. X [the name of the organization] will be there to support them through that, through anything, whatever it is. (Interview O.3.B, 19 April 1991)[21]

Analysis of Findings

How could the Kitchener-Waterloo community interpret these findings? First, the finding that work changes categories but, for all intents and purposes, does not disappear suggests that a community-based analysis of work is plausible and useful. A community can assess which tasks involved in maintaining itself have changed categories, whether or not the tasks have shifted from certain citizens to others, and, very importantly, ask why this has happened and if the changes are in the community's interests. It focuses the discussion about work on the well-being of the community as a whole instead of only on citizens' relationships to employment.

Second, there is evidence that although changing sectors alters the conditions within which a task is done, it does not necessarily alter the relative value society places on a task or its agent. In the example given, care of children, elderly people, and immigrants shifted during the study period from predominantly unpaid domestic and community work to paid work. Current statistics show that the work continues to be done mainly by women and, while now remunerated, the level of pay in those jobs is low. Women must necessarily ask themselves whether the pay is poor because it is they, as women, who are doing the work, whether it is because caring work is not valued enough to be paid well, or both

(Baines, Evans, and Neysmith 1991). Why, and what can be done to change the Kitchener-Waterloo situation?

Third, when work moves from the community to the traded sector much more than salary conditions alter. Judith Trolander contrasts the approaches of the new professionals working in settlement houses and neighbourhood centres in the United States around 1939 to those who had worked in them nearer their inception around the turn of the century: 'They usually declined to live in the settlement house. They tended to think of the house's neighbors as clients, in effect telling them, "We're helping you because we have MSWs, not because we are your neighbors." In place of spontaneity and being available around the clock, they made appointments and "treatment plans." Instead of seeking to do *with* the neighborhood, they sought to do *for* the neighborhood. Their "professional" detachment from the neighbourhood was not only physical, it was psychological' (1987: 39).

The work became 'only one rung on a career ladder' (1987: 41). On the other hand, there was some levelling of power because, now that the settlement house workers had credentials, the board members stopped 'regarding the staff as servants' (ibid.) In Kitchener-Waterloo, gradual professionalization of some organizations is evident in their minutes, especially from the early 1960s; examples include the Children's Aid Society and the YWCA.

Who in the community is served well, and who badly by the changes? Trying to return to the past would clearly be retrograde. Rather, there are lessons to learn from the mid-twentieth century restructuring as a new shift approaches. By the late 1980s studies were showing that some traded work was being de-monetarized and shifted to the domestic and community spheres. The types of work currently changing categories are the same ones women were doing in the domestic and community sectors earlier in the century (Coyle 1985, Ungerson 1987). The market/state sectors of the economy use communities and households to fill in and do the work that is unprofitable and politically vulnerable.[22] *Plus ça change, plus c'est la même chose.*

Fourth, with respect to specialization, somebody said of the Council of Friendship that it was disbanded in the early 1970s because it was not needed anymore – every ethnic minority had its own group. Parallel observations could be made about a wide spectrum of overarching organizations in health, education, youth, and social services. The Consumers' Association collapsed in the 1970s and home and school associations declined nearly to extinction.[23] New and continuing organizations were tightly focused on specific interests. As this happened, attention to the wide sweep of public ground seems to have substantially diminished. Indeed, even the scope of the public ground and the responsibility citizens share not only for its pieces but for its totality seemed hazier. The enthusiasm and belief in the capacity to 'do good' that marked the records of organizations early in the century seemed rather naive and idealistic when read in the 1980s. Special interest associations had advantages such as efficiency, but they were no substitute for broad purpose ones. There no longer seemed to be a language or a forum in which to discuss a wide range of long-term and ethical interests, a vehicle for Kitchener-Waterloo citizens beyond the spheres of influence of the media and elected politicians and their respective preoccupations with the dramatic and the short term.

Fifth, secularization reduced the potency of the invocation to 'do good deeds' which God-fearing adherents had absorbed in the many Christian churches in Kitchener-Waterloo. Over the study period community work was less obviously based on a religious code ('We were put here for a definite purpose and it is to help one another'[24]), and more on a personal moral stance (looking out for her elderly neighbour, X says this is 'not really community work but human being to human being; if I can't do that, what am I doing in this world?'[25]), or on recognizing self-other complementarity ('It's amazing how helping other people actually helps you to help yourself'[26]). In organization documents, ethical positions tended to be increasingly described using rational terminology and arguments.

Sixth, the significance of finding that community work activities are multifaceted is that tasks transferred from the community sector to the traded work sector lose something in the transition. Every woman interviewed, every set of organization records, and most of the other documents examined to learn about community work in Kitchener-Waterloo, revealed a powerful commitment to others and to the community generally. The women wanted to help;[27] and they recognized the mutuality and interdependence upon which a community builds. However, mutuality and interdependence weaken when work transfers to the traded sector virtually by definition because people become bound to one another contractually; these are what are lost in the transition.

Finally, and again on the multifaceted aspect of community work, women organizing around issues such as safety, child care, or social services, were also pushing open spaces for women in their community. This changed the political scene within Kitchener-Waterloo, if very gradually.

Women in our study enthusiastically declared their involvement in 'service.' But few would say they were engaged in 'politics' because they were only infrequently involved in the formal electoral process or making representations to elected bodies. This observation accords with recent findings concerning women's politics. Feminists have been describing politics to include actions which have usually been considered private helping, not public politics. For example, West and Blumberg point out that the service and political dimensions of voluntarism are 'deeply interwoven and often related pragmatically in the home, in the church, in the schools, and in places of work' (1990: 29). To 'attempt to expand the definition of the public and political, to have one's interests and actions interpreted as significant to the political community' is itself a crucial political act, as Sapiro notes (1989: 4).

Those, then, are aspects to consider in a community-based analysis of work.

Models of Work and Urban Development Revisited

To conclude, let us consider how the findings relate to the theories of work and urban development with which this chapter is concerned. With respect to theories of work, the two findings described here do not fit into the work-as-employment model by definition, because the Kitchener-Waterloo research included non-monetarized work on the grounds that this is essential in order to grasp women's experiences of work and explain its differences from those of men. Very generally, however, the findings lend support to the view that employment studies are most useful when they show how work is embedded in specific social relations which are formed within the employment sphere but also in the domestic and community spheres. Many recent studies, such as those noted in the work-as-employment section above, focus on paid work but also demonstrate its connection to domestic work, making them more relevant to women's experiences than studies which assume women relate to the labour market in the same way men do.

This study shows that work does not disappear but instead is shifted to another sphere, a finding which is more in keeping with the continuum-of-work approach. From a planning perspective an adequate model of work must capture the full range of work being done in a community because planners will not plan for that which is not recognized as significant.

However, just as important as modelling the full range of work and its distribution in the different categories will be incorporating in the model the processes through which values are shaped. In the work of Pahl, Mingione, and Morris, the basic unit for managing is the household. In the research reported here, strategies for 'getting by' are also community-based, formed by *parts* of households acting outside of households and employment – by women banding together to do community work. Much of the work is service-oriented, yet some is reform-seeking, and some takes the form of gender solidarity to act against oppression. The findings suggest a need for a more activist conceptualization of work than coping strategies imply. The message to take from this is that a model of work should incorporate a community sphere in order to recognize that community work is often political, and that people group themselves differently in it than in the traded and domestic spheres.

To conceptualize work to include community work transcends both the structuralist theorists' duality in which individuals and households compete against capital-based enterprises, and that of functionalists in which opposing public and private spheres serve well-modulated, complementary purposes. One can also make the normative argument for incorporating the community sphere on the grounds that it is essential in order to challenge politically the work which falls into that sphere and the repartition of all work into the three categories. For example, the community sphere is where neighbouring and volunteer work occur, but it is also where struggles take place over the oppression that results from the less-than-benign aspects of volunteering, over identity as citizens, and over decision-making about resource use. These struggles can transform community work and its relationship to domestic and traded work. It is how the value of 'women's work' will be changed, if it ever is.

Turning now to models of urban development, it is evident that those which focus on the uses of capital and land miss the work described in this research. The conventional models of urban development focus on employment in production and distribution which is associated with a narrow range of human beings in limited age and ability ranges. Because women have not had access to as much money as men or to careers in most sectors, they have rarely been the physical builders of communities but instead have focused on building social relations. It is therefore consequential if women and the work they have been doing are increasingly drawn into the state and market category where task performance entails entirely different social relations (especially replacing commitments to mutuality and interdependence with contractual relationships), and where there is less capacity to organize around social issues. It is also of consequence to social well-being if the work of caring for children and vulnerable adults is cynically shifted like a yo-yo to suit market conditions instead of what is best for those involved and the community.

The findings from this research challenge the absence of community work from dominant urban development models, and propose its inclusion in models of how urban development actually happens.

NOTES

1 I wish to acknowledge Dr Susan Wismer's contributions to the research project and thank her especially for the many long and stimulating discussions when we mused about the findings. We no longer know which ideas began with whom. We were fortunate to have very able research assistance from Susan Montonen over an extended period, and acknowledge the brief but fine help of Sabine Behnk Furino. Also, thanks to Sarah Rix for conversations about 'work' and for some readings. Jon Caulfield and Linda Peake's editorial comments were much appreciated. Funding for the research came from the Social Sciences and Humanities Research Council of Canada.

2 In 1991, 58 per cent of all women 15 and over were in the paid labour force. The comparable figure for 1976 was 45 per cent. By 1991 they constituted 45 per cent of the total paid labour force compared with 38 per cent in 1976 (Statistics Canada 1992). By 2005 the participation rate is expected to be 63 per cent (Employment and Immigration Canada 1992).

3 See, for example, the 'Statement of Values' of the Canadian Institute of Planners, adopted April 1994.

4 As will be seen later, the incorporation of domestic work into discussions of traded work are increasingly common. This is not the case for community work.

5 Where access-oriented initiatives have been taken they include improved transportation for women with children, zoning that accommodates daycare, measures to improve street safety, and more mixing of land uses.

6 An idea of the size of the voluntary work sector alone is gleaned from the 1987 National Survey of Voluntary Activity in Canada. About 5.3 million Canadians volunteered in formal organizations in a 1986–7 twelve-month period, each giving an average of 191 hours over the year. This is equivalent to over 1 billion hours or over half a million full-year jobs. The work had an imputed value in 1987 of $12 billion (Ross 1990). In addition another 13.2 million Canadians – about two-thirds of the population – volunteered informally outside any organizations. They mainly helped friends, neighbours, co-workers, and kin living outside their own households. If a similar calculation was made for the

informal as for the formal volunteering it would be valued at over $158 billion in 1987 dollars.

7 The social relations in which work is embedded are extremely complex. See Pahl's (1984) wonderful illustration of this where he speculates for five pages about the social relations that might embed an image of a woman ironing a garment.

8 Extensive studies in which the complex relationship between work and gender in specific communities is pursued include, among others, Hanson and Pratt 1995, Parr 1990, Mackenzie 1989, and Luxton 1980. Others report smaller studies such as those in Kobayashi's (1994) collection by Bradbury, Kobayashi, Rose and Villeneuve, and Christopherson.

9 See Stevens 1990 for an empirical study of the influence of economics in planning; for a planning-specific contextual explanation of this, see Milroy 1993: 489–90; and for a more general argument about the power of conventional economics on practices, see Granovetter 1985, and Mingione 1991: ch. 1.

10 For a description and critique of these models, see Milroy 1991.

11 For a full description of this argument, see Aronowitz and DiFazio 1994: esp. ch. 3, 'The End of Skill,' and ch. 10 'Quantum Measure: Capital Investment and Job Reduction.'

12 Other stories are conveyed in less widely read and circulated sources, for example, Dunham's (1941) history of Trinity United Church from 1841 to 1941 and Staebler's *Sauerkraut and Enterprise* (1966).

13 A three-part categorization of work accords with the data from this case study. Here are definitions of the three broad types of work we found. *Community work* is not monetarized and refers to work done in or for spatial or social communities. While there may be personal or family benefits from this work, it is always also intended to provide benefits to a wider group of people than only one's family or household. *Domestic work* is done in households. It too is unmonetarized, and is work done mainly for oneself and members of the household or family. *Traded work* may or may not be monetarized, but if it is not, it will always involve some form of barter or exchange (Milroy and Wismer 1994: 72–3). Each type of work has a primary, yet not mutually exclusive, spatial location – homes, communities, and places of employment; and each is distinguished from the others by how people's relationships in the work are structured.

14 Both men and women do community work. In terms of the contemporary situation in contrast to the historical, the 1987 National Survey on Volunteer Activity found that women were more likely to volunteer than men (30 per cent versus 24 per cent). In Kitchener-Waterloo 30 per cent of the population participated in formal volunteering, which placed it seventh among 26 census metropolitan areas in Canada after Saskatoon, Edmonton, Calgary, Winnipeg,

Halifax, and Victoria. It ranked tenth in informal volunteering with 74 per cent of the population involved. Overall, the survey's findings show more similarities than differences in the types of activities men and women volunteer to do, and that the differences which are evident reflect 'an almost stereotypical sex role differentiation.' This is true for both formal and informal voluntary work (Catano and Christiansen-Ruffman 1989: 3).

15 Interviews were conducted and holdings researched at the following locations: Doris Lewis Rare Book Room, University of Waterloo; Grace Schmidt Room of Local History, Kitchener Public Library; Wilfrid Laurier University Archives; Mennonite Historical Archives, Conrad Grebel College, University of Waterloo; Kitchener Family and Children's Services Archives; Mutual Life of Canada Archives, Head Office, Waterloo; Doon Heritage Crossroads; Joseph Schneider Haus; Waterloo Public Library; and Stratford Public Library. Interviews were conducted with others who have studied the area including Dr T.E. Bunting, Dr E. Bloomfield, and K. Lamb. Five sets of personal and family papers were consulted: Mr and Mrs Charles Everett Hoffman Collection; Ella Cook Collection; Breithaupt Family Papers; Dorothea Palmer Collection; Breithaupt Hewetson Clark Collection. Clipping files and the records of women's (and some mixed women's and men's) organizations in Kitchener and Waterloo were systematically reviewed. The organizations most fully studied were the Young Women's Christian Association (annual reports, Executive Committee minutes, Board of Directors minutes; The Day Book of Roomers, 1918 to 1923; and minutes of various committees 1906 to 1977); the Organized Social Workers, minutes, 1913 to 1917; the Local Council of Women (yearbooks 1921 to 1924 and 1933 to 1951); the Children's Aid Society from 1912; and women's organizations based in the largest churches, 1900 to 1980. References to a great many other organizations, either women-based or in which women figured centrally, were noted during the research and investigated to a lesser extent. These included musical organizations which were especially important in the lives of Kitchener-Waterloo residents. The findings are also based on fifteen open-ended interviews and twenty-seven oral histories reflecting the daily lives of women ranging in age from twenty-eight to ninety-two.

16 In their history of Kitchener, English and McLaughlin say that the main focus of social life was the churches at least until the late 1930s: 'Kitchener stood outside the religious patterns of the nation, and perhaps for that reason the churches' hold upon the community was more tenacious' (1983: 161). An example of the differences was that 'churches, such as the Swedenborgian and the Evangelical, were insignificant in numbers nationally; but in Kitchener there were important congregations whose membership included such leading families as the Schneiders (Swedenborgian) and the Breithaupts (Evangel-

ical)' (1983: 162). Both families were prominent from the mid-nineteenth century. The Schneider family developed a very successful meat processing and packing corporation; Louis O. Breithaupt (1890–1960) was appointed Lieutenant-Governor of Ontario in 1952.

17 In 1989 the Community Information Centre of Waterloo Region listed thirty-six such organizations in Kitchener-Waterloo, another seventeen in the adjoining city of Cambridge, and three in smaller towns in the immediate vicinity of Kitchener-Waterloo.

18 Interview S.3, 16 June 1989.

19 Doon Heritage Crossroads, 'Waterloo Regional Women's Organizations,' no date, and various other sources.

20 For the case of the YWCA, see the description in Milroy and Wismer (1994).

21 Whether solidarity, as distinct from service, crossed class lines is not clear from the data. It is unlikely that it did. Note that in her study of Rochester, New York, Hewitt found that class strongly predicted the types of organizations a woman would belong to and the degree of social change she would espouse (1984).

22 By comparison to community work, the use of domestic work as a buffer has been widely researched. See, for example, the review in Hamilton and Barrett 1986.

23 *Kitchener-Waterloo Record*, 30 May 1970, 26 September 1979, and 21 November 1981. The exception to the trend towards smaller, more specialized organizations was the consolidation of women's church groups into umbrella organizations in two of the main denominations, as already mentioned. An explanation for this is proposed in Milroy and Wismer 1994.

24 Interview S.1, 2 June 1989.

25 Interview G.1.A., 16 May 1989.

26 Interview O.2.A, 10 April 1991. Doing voluntary 'work that benefits your children, family or self' is seen as very important or somewhat important to 69 per cent of respondents to the 1987 national survey. See Duchesne 1989, Table 10: 33.

27 Wanting to help others was considered an important reason for doing informal and formal community work by over 90 per cent of respondents in the 1987 survey on voluntary activity. Indeed, it was the most important reason overall. See Duchesne 1989, Table 10: 33.

REFERENCES

Aronowitz, S., and W. DiFazio. 1994. *The Jobless Future: Sci-Tech and the Dogma of Work.* Minneapolis: University of Minnesota Press

Baines, C.T., P.M. Evans, and S.M. Neysmith, eds., 1991. *Women's Caring: Feminist Perspectives on Social Welfare.* Toronto: McClelland and Stewart

Beach, J., M. Friendly, and L. Schmidt. 1993. *Work-Related Child Care in Context: A Study of Work-Related Child Care Centres in Canada.* Toronto: The Child Care Resource and Research Unit, Centre for Urban and Community Studies, University of Toronto. Occasional Papers, no. 3

Bloomfield, E. 1980. 'Economy, necessity, political reality: Town planning efforts in Kitchener-Waterloo, 1912–1925.' *Urban History Review* 11(1): 3–48

- 1983. 'Building the city on a foundation of factories: The "industrial policy" in Berlin, Ontario, 1870–1914.' *Ontario History* 75(3): 206–43

- 1987a. 'Building industrial communities: Berlin and Waterloo to 1915.' In D. Walker, ed., *Manufacturing in Kitchener-Waterloo: A Long-Term Perspective,* 5–33. Waterloo: Geography Department, University of Waterloo

- 1987b. 'The maturing industrial economy: Kitchener-Waterloo 1915–1945.' In D. Walker, ed., *Manufacturing in Kitchener-Waterloo: A Long-Term Perspective,* 35–59. Waterloo: Geography Department, University of Waterloo

Boyer, M.C. 1983. *Dreaming the Rational City: The Myth of American City Planning.* Cambridge: MIT Press

Canadian Aging Research Network. 1993. *Work and Family: The Survey.* Guelph: Gerontology Research Centre, University of Guelph

Canadian Labour Market and Productivity Centre. 1994. *Women and Economic Restructuring.* Ottawa: Canadian Labour Market and Productivity Centre

Catano, J.W., and L. Christiansen-Ruffman. 1989. *Women as Volunteers.* Profile No. 3 based on the 1987 National Survey on Volunteer Activity. Ottawa: Secretary of State

Coyle, A. 1985. 'Going private: The implications of privatization for women's work.' *Feminist Review,* 21

Duchesne, D. 1989. *Giving Freely: Volunteers in Canada.* Ottawa: Statistics Canada, Cat. 71-535

Dunham, B.M. 1941. *So Great a Heritage: Historical Narrative of Trinity United Church, 1841–1941.* Kitchener: Cober Printing Service

Duxbury, L., C. Higgins, and C. Lee. 1991. *Balancing Work and Family: A Study of the Canadian Federal Public Sector.* London: Western Business School, University of Western Ontario

Employment and Immigration Canada. 1992. *Canadian Occupational Projection System Reference, 1992 Projections.* Ottawa: Employment and Immigration Canada

English, J., and K. McLaughlin. 1983. *Kitchener: An Illustrated History.* Waterloo: Wilfrid Laurier University Press

Gershuny, J.I. 1985. 'Economic development and change in the mode of provision of services.' In N. Redclift and E. Mingione, eds., *Beyond Employment: Household, Gender and Subsistence.* Oxford: Basil Blackwell

Gershuny, J.I., and R.E. Pahl. 1979. 'Work outside employment: Some preliminary speculations.' *New Universities Quarterly* 34(1): 12–135

Granovetter, M. 1985. 'Economic action and social structure: The problem of embeddedness.' *American Journal of Sociology* 91(3): 481–510

Hamilton, R., and M. Barrett, eds., 1986. *The Politics of Diversity: Feminism, Marxism and Nationalism.* Montreal: Book Center

Hanson, S., and G. Pratt. 1995. *Gender, Work and Space.* London: Routledge

Henry, S. 1987. 'The political economy of informal economies.' *Annals of the American Academy of Political and Social Science* 493 (Sept.): 137–53

Herzog, A.R., R.L. Kahn, J.N. Morgan, J.S. Jackson, and T.C. Antonucci. 1992. 'Age differences in productive activities.' In L.A. Ferman, L.E. Berndt, and S. Henry, eds., *Work Beyond Employment in Advanced Capitalist Countries: Classic and Contemporary Perspectives on the Informal Economy,* 211–34. Lewiston: Edwin Mellen Press

Hewitt, N. 1984. *Women's Activism and Social Change: Rochester, New York, 1822–1872.* Ithaca, NY: Cornell University Press

Kobayashi, A., ed., 1994. *Women, Work, and Place.* Montreal: McGill-Queen's University Press

Lamarche, L. 1990. *Les programmes d'accès à l'égalité en emploi.* Montreal: Louise Courteau

Lero, D.S., L.M. Brockman, A.R. Pence, H. Goelman, and K.L. Johnson. 1993. *Workplace Benefits and Flexibility: A Perspective on Parents' Experiences.* Ottawa: Statistics Canada

Long, B.C., and S.E. Kahn, eds., 1993. *Women, Work, and Coping: A Multi-disciplinary Approach to Workplace Stress.* Montreal: McGill-Queen's University Press

Luxton, M. 1980. *More Than a Labour of Love: Three Generations of Women's Work in the Home.* Toronto: Women's Press

Mackenzie, S. 1989. *Visible Histories: Women and Environments in a Post-War British City.* Montreal: McGill-Queen's University Press

McKinnon, A., and D. Odynak. 1991. *Elder Care, Employees, and Employers: Some Canadian Evidence.* (Discussion paper presented for the Demographic Review Secretariat.) Ottawa: Health and Welfare Canada

McLaughlin, K. 1990. *Waterloo: An Illustrated History.* Windsor: Windsor Publications

Milroy, B.M. 1993. 'Planning, the humanities, and the circulation of ideas.' *University of Toronto Quarterly* 62(4): 488–503

- 1991. 'Taking stock of planning, space, and gender.' *Journal of Planning Literature* 6(1): 3–15

Milroy, B.M., and S. Wismer. 1994. 'Communities, work and public/private sphere models.' *Gender, Place and Culture* 1(1): 71–90

Mingione, E. 1991. *Fragmented Societies: A Sociology of Economic Life beyond the Market Paradigm.* Oxford: Basil Blackwell

Modlich, R. 1988. 'Planning Implications of "Women Plan Toronto."' *Plan Canada* 28(4): 120–31

Montonen, S., B.M. Milroy, and S. Wismer. 1990. 'Siting the Berlin YWCA.' *Waterloo Historical Society* 78: 39–53

Morris, L. 1990. *The Workings of the Household: A US-UK Comparison.* Oxford: Polity Press

Pahl, R.E. 1984. *Divisions of Labour.* Oxford: Basil Blackwell

- 1989. 'From "informal economy" to "forms of work": Cross-national patterns and trends.' In R. Scase, ed., *Industrial Societies: Crisis and Division in Western Capitalism and State Socialism,* 90–119. London: Unwin Hyman

Paris, H. 1989. *The Corporate Response to Workers and Family Responsibilities.* Ottawa: Conference Board of Canada

Parr, J. 1990. *The Gender of Breadwinners.* Toronto: University of Toronto Press

Ross, D.P. 1990. *Economic Dimensions of Volunteer Work in Canada.* Ottawa: Secretary of State

Sapiro, V. 1989. 'Political connections: Gender and the meanings of politics.' Paper presented to the 1989 meeting of the Société Québecoise de Science politique. Mimeo

Sharpe, B. 1988. 'Informal work and development in the West.' *Progress in Human Geography* 12(3): 315–36

Staebler, E. 1966. *Sauerkraut and Enterprise.* Kitchener-Waterloo: University Women's Club of Kitchener-Waterloo

Statistics Canada. 1992. *Labour Force Annual Averages, 1991.* Ottawa: Statistics Canada cat. no. 711–220

Stevens, G. 1990. 'An alliance confirmed: Planning literature and the social sciences.' *Journal of the American Planning Association* 56(3): 341–9

Tiessen, P., ed., 1979. *Berlin, Canada: A Self-Portrait of Kitchener, Ontario before World War One.* St Jacob's, Ont: Sand Hills Books. Reprint of *Berlin: Celebration of Cityhood* (1912), with new introduction and street and business directories for 1912

Tindale, J.A. 1991. *Older Workers in an Aging Work Force.* Ottawa: National Advisory Council on Aging

Trolander, J.A. 1987. *Professionalism and Social Change: From the Settlement House Movement to Neighborhood Centers 1886 to the Present.* New York: Columbia University Press

Ungerson, C. 1987. *Policy Is Personal: Sex, Gender and Informal Care.* London: Tavistock

Uttley, W.V. 1937. *A History of Kitchener, Ontario.* Waterloo: Chronicle Press

West, G., and R.L. Blumberg, eds. 1990. *Women and Social Protest.* New York: Oxford University Press

11

Unemployment and Labour Markets in Hamilton during the Great Depression

ROBERT LEWIS

> The past year has been an unusual one, but you should avoid talking about hard times and depression. Don't talk blue ruin. Don't talk about the depression. Be cheerful and optimistic ... This period of unemployment is not going to stay, because the economic laws are going to cure it.
>
> J.D. Monteith, Ontario Minister of Public Works and Labour, May 1931

To the thousands of Hamilton workers who faced the prospect of long periods of extended unemployment, mortgage foreclosures, and homelessness, Monteith's comments to the Annual Conference of Ontario Employment Office Superintendents, at Toronto's King Edward Hotel, would have been not only personally offensive, but also indicative of the low priority given by the state to solving the worst economic depression Canada had ever faced. The economic laws Monteith identified did not solve the problems of Hamilton's unemployed women like Elizabeth McCrae who wrote to Prime Minister R.B. Bennett in the spring of 1934 that 'this day I am faced with starvation and I see no possible means of counteracting or even averting it temporarily,' nor the employed men working at the Steel Company of Canada's sheet mill 'who have been in a bad way for so long and have been so patiently hoping things would better themselves without resort to force or violence' (Grayson and Bliss 1971: 82; Ontario Ministry of Labour 1935).

As these examples suggest, the 1930s were difficult times for Canadian workers. The combination of Canada's most severe depression, a humiliating relief system, an unsympathetic state, hostile employers, and internal political infighting ensured that the working class in communities such as Hamilton would find it difficult to construct cohesive and viable policies with which to combat economic recession. Indeed, several writers have stressed that the 1930s in Hamilton was a period of political passivity, despite the activism of a small segment of the city's working class (Archibald 1992, Heron 1981, Storey 1981). A factor that had a critical bearing on the shape of Hamilton's political economy during the 1930s was the labour market. The question of the changing character of the Canadian labour market during the Depression has been examined from a number of angles: the impact of technological change in the railway industry (Rountree 1936), the growth of new working conditions in the garment trades (Scott and Cassidy 1935), the rise of organized labour in the steel industry (Storey 1981), and the changing ideological climate towards the role of women and immigrants in the paid labour force (Avery 1979, Hobbs 1993, Strong-Boag 1988). For the most part the literature on unemployment has emphasized the impact at the workplace or the experience of particular groups. There has been, however, little research on the differentiated character of unemployment in urban labour markets.

This chapter examines how the development of Hamilton's labour market contributed to political passivity during the 1930s. It is argued that Hamilton's workers experienced a more difficult labour market during the 1930s than the 1920s as a result of conditions in the workplace, the reluctance of the state to initiate policies that could relieve their plight, and contradictions in the domestic sphere. The essay begins with a brief review of some of the primary features of labour markets. This is followed by an analysis of the different rates of unemployment among four segments of the city's labour market, a discussion of the state's role in managing the labour market, and an examination of the reproduction of the labour market within the context of the home. A concluding statement considers the impact of the labour market for working-class political activism.

Urban Labour Markets

It is widely recognized that labour markets are a critical element shaping contemporary (Haughton et al. 1993; Offe 1985; Peck 1989a, 1989b; Wilkinson 1981) and historical (Edwards 1979; Gordon, Edwards, and Reich 1982) employment opportunities. It has been stressed that a set of historically constructed practices and structures has created a segmented labour market – the ascription of individuals to particular segments of the labour market along the lines of skill, gender, ethnicity, and age. These practices and structures include the control strategies of employers, the exclusionary practices of trade unions, cultural conditioning – especially the dynamics of patriarchy and race – and the role of state policies and programs. The result is that people have differential access to working opportunities in terms of wages, job security, opportunities for career advancement, and working conditions. By the Depression, Hamilton's labour market was distinguished by a variety of labour market segments: home work (textiles and clothing); permanent low-paid, semiskilled, and unskilled jobs (immigrant labourers, textile and metal-working operators, female sales clerks); seasonal factory work (canning); and skilled craft work and supervisory work (in a variety of industries).

Labour markets reflect the highly asymmetrical power relations between capital and labour. Although employers' control over the labour market is restricted by their competition for labour and their need for different types of labour power, their disadvantage is minimal compared with the structural obstacles faced by labour: the relative inelasticity of the supply of labour power over the long term, workers' dependence on jobs for survival, and the limited adaptability of individuals to the changing needs of industry (Offe 1985). During the first decades of the twentieth century, despite short periods of successful activism and protest – for example, the immediate period following the First World War – Hamilton's workers encountered a hostile and powerful group of employers who, in conjunction with the state, imposed severe constraints on autonomous working-class activity (Heron 1981, Storey 1981).

Labour markets are a principal institution – in the sense of a formalized set of practices and structures – mediating the structural trends of national economic changes with local ones. During the 1930s broad structural pressures associated with industrial recession were channelled to cities such as Hamilton through local labour markets. Disinvestment, technological change, and shifting markets at a national scale had a twofold impact at the local level. First, they forced management, especially in industries severely effected by the Depression, to rework local work practices, turn to different sources of labour, find new strategies for survival, and place strong pressure on local government. Second, the resulting shifts in the dynamics of local labour markets played a decisive role in determining the ability of workers to find alternative strategies to such problems as unemployment and falling living conditions.

The systematic analysis of the segmented character of urban unemployment during the 1930s poses some methodological difficulties. The appropriate data to reconstruct even basic points such as who was unemployed are not available. For example, the publications of the federal government – an annual index of unemployment by city and a major monograph on unemployment by industry and occupation for cities based on the 1931 census – provide little information useful for an examination of the internal structure of the urban labour market. It is possible, however, to construct a profile of the segmented character of the urban labour market by linking the city directory with the property assessment rolls. Vernon's *Hamilton City Directory*, provides annually for the 1920s and 1930s, the name, occupation, workplace, address, and, in the case of men, the name of their wives of every working person over the age of eighteen. Linking these data with information on tenure, housing value, household size, and citizenship taken from the property assessments – collected for local taxation purposes – it is possible to build up a multi-variable profile of individuals and households.

To reconstruct the employment history of Hamilton's workers I have taken a sample from the 1929 directory of 1,426 Hamilton metal, or textile workers and followed them through to 1938.[1] The sample consists of men and women who stated that they worked in one of the city's textile, metal, or electrical appliance firms, and whose surname began with A, B, C, or D.[2] The 1,426 were then followed through the directory and linked with assessment roll data for 1928, 1931, 1934, and 1937. If a person from the sample did not specify a workplace in the latter three sample years they were considered to be unemployed in that year.[3] As not all individuals could be traced from 1928 through the three latter years, the numbers in the sample decreased: there were 1,086 in 1931, and 991 and 912 in 1934 and 1937 respectively. Together these two data sets supply a wealth of information about the unemployment history of Hamilton's workers.

Unemployment and Labour Markets in Hamilton, 1929–1938

The growth of Hamilton as one of the most important industrial centres in Canada in the first half of the twentieth century was built on the development of a highly segmented labour market (Heron 1981, Storey 1981). Although robust growth after 1900 propelled Hamilton to a prominent position in Canada's hierarchy of cities, the Depression showed just how fragile this growth was. Hamilton, along with a few other cities such as Winnipeg, had the highest unemployment rates in Canada (Archibald 1992: 6). Its dependence on a small range of industries – especially iron and steel and agricultural implements, which were hit hard by the

TABLE 11.1
Hamilton Unemployment Rates, 1931–37

	1931		1934		1937	
	(n)	(%)	(n)	(%)	(n)	(%)
Number in sample	1086	100.0	991	100.0	912	100.0
Unemployed	274	25.2	245	24.7	212	23.2

Source: Hamilton sample of 1,426.

Depression and recovered very slowly – ensured that unemployment in the city would be high. This is borne out by the federal employment index, which measures the variation of people at work at any one time. Using 1926 = 100 as the base point, employment in Hamilton had fallen from 128.4 in 1929 to a low of 69.4 in May 1933. During the rest of the decade there was slow improvement, and by 1939 the index stood at only 103.7 (Canada 1933–9). A similar trend in unemployment is evident in the sample data (Table 11.1). What the data show are that in the three sample years after 1929, the proportion of the sample unemployed hovered around 25 per cent, although it decreased as the decade progressed.

During the 1920s the segmented character of the labour market posed a serious constraint on the ability of workers to mount a wide-ranging challenge to the power of employers. With high unemployment after 1929, the problems faced by workers in the highly divided labour market were intensified as labour supply outstripped demand, and economic insecurity promoted the intensification of exclusionary and discriminatory strategies by employers and different groups – especially men of British origin – within the labour force. Hamilton's employers took advantage of labour's weak position and, along with laying off large numbers of the workforce, implemented changes to the workplace, such as the reduction of wages, introduction of new machinery, and implementation of new working practices (Archibald 1992, Lewis 1994, Storey 1981). This meant that working opportunities for Hamilton's workers were severely constrained. As one industrial commentator stated, 'Many workers, male and female, have been forced to accept low wages rather than be counted among the unemployed ... It is a case of accepting what is offered or getting no job,' while another pointed to the prevalence of replacing better paid employees by cheaper ones (Ontario, Department of Labour [ODL] 1933: 54, 21). One important result of the obstacles to employment and the intensification of the structured inequality of

TABLE 11.2
Characteristics of Unemployment in Hamilton, 1931–37

	1931 Unemployed		1934 Unemployed		1937 Unemployed	
	(n)	(%)	(n)	(%)	(n)	(%)
Firms						
Steel Co. of Canada	233	18.9	216	22.2	201	20.9
International Harvester	150	36.0	142	29.6	126	29.4
Westinghouse	243	20.2	219	24.7	201	24.9
Otis-Fensom	70	25.7	63	31.7	59	25.4
Greening Wire	40	15.0	37	16.2	34	14.7
Cotton firms	85	32.9	83	33.7	75	25.3
Hosiery firms	265	24.5	231	20.3	216	20.4
Ethnicity						
British origins	997	23.0	902	22.5	834	21.7
Non-British origins	89	50.6	89	47.2	78	39.7
Gender						
Male	959	23.0	894	23.9	830	21.1
Female	127	41.7	97	32.0	82	45.1
Age (years)						
<30	62	21.0	58	22.4	29	6.9
30–44	296	21.3	280	18.9	254	11.8
45–54	232	21.1	231	23.4	222	23.4
55–64	85	22.4	122	21.3	146	21.9
>65	48	35.4	50	44.0	59	49.2

Source: Hamilton sample of 1,426.

Hamilton's labour market was that unemployment was differentiated along four major fault lines: industry, ethnicity, gender, and age.

According to the 1931 census, the city's construction and manufacturing industries had higher rates of unemployment than the trade, finance, service, and transportation sectors (Canada 1934). There were also differences within the manufacturing sector: iron and steel workers, for example, had much higher rates of unemployment than those in the chemical and textile industries. The firms represented in the sample also indicate a great diversity of unemployment rates (Table 11.2). Unemployment in the cotton and hosiery sectors remained significant throughout the 1930s, with cotton workers much more likely to be without a job than hosiery workers. This reflects the general state of the two branches. The cotton industry faced intense competition from newly established synthetic silk firms and foreign cotton companies, rapid changes in materials and styles, and a cumbersome distribution network. In contrast, demand for hosiery products and the relatively disintegrated character of this industry cushioned the impact of the Depression. Indeed, during the 1930s, while the gross value of cotton production fell by more than a third, there was a rapid recovery in hosiery (Lewis 1994). The firm with the highest unemployment rates throughout the 1930s was the agricultural implements maker, International Harvester. Agricultural implements was one of the severely hit industries of the decade, with a decline in gross value of production greater than the iron and steel and auto industries, and with employment falling from its 1929 high by 75 per cent. International Harvester's sales fell from $12 million in 1929 to only $4 million in 1933 (Phillips 1956: 70–2). During the early 1930s the implement makers spent large amounts of money on research and made extensive changes to existing lines and the development of new lines (such as tractors), which then 'appeared on the market in the early years of recovery' (Phillips 1956: 98; Neufeld 1969: 32). In the steel industry, during the worst years of the Depression, the Steel Company of Canada only worked at 25 per cent capacity, resulting in the lay-off of many workers and in wage reductions. For example, the wages of the company's sheet-metal workers fell by 33 per cent between 1929 and July 1932. Furthermore, and accounting for the company's relatively low unemployment figures, most employees did not work their full weekly set of hours (Storey 1981: 152–3).

Of all the social groups in Hamilton, non-British immigrants suffered the highest rate of unemployment during the 1930s. In 1932 more than half of the non-British workers in the sample indicated that they had no workplace, compared with less than a quarter of those of British extraction (Table 11.2).[4] By the end of the decade more than a third of non-British immigrants were still unemployed. Their high level of unemployment was partly the effect of the position of ethnic workers in the industrial division of labour. New immigrants from continental Europe formed an ethnic layer at the bottom of Hamilton's occupational hierarchy: they replaced native workers in factories because they worked for lower wages, were willing to do dirtier work, and were more amenable to replacing existing routines for new ones (Heron 1981: 74–87). As a result, most immigrants were concentrated in certain companies and jobs: Armenians worked at International Harvester; Italians worked in the open hearth, blast furnace, coke ovens, and labouring gangs at the Steel Company; and Ukrainians, Poles, and Rumanians laboured on the ingot floor and finishing department at Dominion Foundry (Cumbo 1985; Shahrodi 1989; Storey 1981: 124–30). Historically, the ethnic division of labour functioned as a labour queue in which workers with particular origins were the worst paid and the first to be laid off. This was accentuated during the 1930s. Another reason for high unemployment among immigrants was discrimination. Immigrants were viewed by the state, business, and other workers as being a major reason for rising unemployment, deteriorating working conditions, and falling wages (Avery 1979). As one local person wrote Prime Minister Bennett, 'Why not put some of these foreigners and Indians in their own country & give a white man some show, as they are taking work from the Canadian men' (Grayson and Bliss 1971: 58). In Hamilton the city council took an active role in dealing with demands such as this. In the summer of 1932, for example, the city deported twenty non-Canadian residents back to Europe, because 'there is no immediate possibility of these men obtaining employment and the majority of them will probably remain a charge during the period of the present depression' (Hamilton, *Minutes 1932*: 419). In other words, the high rate of unemployment among immigrants was related to their inferior position within the local labour market and to the discriminatory activities of a significant proportion of the city's population.

Like immigrant workers, Hamilton's paid working women functioned in specific segments of the city's labour market and were hard hit by the Depression. As was common throughout Canada, female and male work in Hamilton was distinguished by at least two features. First, women were predominantly young and single and were involved in the workplace at specific times during their life. Second, women worked at jobs specifically designated as women's work – food, clothing, textiles, nursing, and teaching – at low wages (Bird 1983; Heron 1981: 391–6; Strong-Boag 1988). Although working opportunities for women increased during the 1920s, it was to prove a fragile experience in the 1930s. Even though female unemployment rates were not as high as those of immigrants, they were still significantly higher than those of men from all ethnic backgrounds (Table 11.2). From the early stages of the Depression, jobs for women were scarce. In Hamilton one commentator stated, 'The demand from the manufacturing plants was almost nil' (ODL 1931: 26). In July 1932 city council adopted the policy that all male city employees who had working wives were to be fired if their wives did not give up their jobs (Hamilton *Minutes 1932*: 461). Although women were being called back to their old positions by the end of 1933, the unavailability of other types of work forced many other women – especially clerical workers and high-paid factory workers – to take the most dreaded of 'female' jobs, domestic work (ODL 1931, 1934). Even by the end of the decade the number of female applicants to the Employment Offices for work was much higher than the number of available jobs, and they were given short-term jobs over permanent jobs at a rate of two to one (ODL 1939). In the hosiery industry, for example, the number of working male and female workers dropped at the same rate between 1929 and 1933, but during the recovery the increase among males was much greater than among females.

Age was also a sorting factor in who found work. Although in the early stages of the Depression workers of all ages felt the hardship of unemployment, the chances of unemployment were much higher among older workers than younger ones as the decade progressed (Table 11.2). The growth of long-term unemployment for those over sixty-five increased, while the fairly stable unemployment rates among other age groups in 1931 became more polarized. By the end of the decade, paralleling national trends (Saunders 1939: 40), workers older than forty-five were much more likely to be unemployed than were younger workers (ODL 1933: 7; Saunders 1939: 40). As recovery took place, opportunities for older workers did not materialize. A 1934 survey indicated that many of the unemployed were older men who had 'little chance of securing factory employment' (ODL 1934: 20). One reason was that older workers tended to command higher wages and were replaced by younger workers who were paid lower wages. This process was partly made possible by the introduction of new machinery which reduced the need for skills accumulated through long workplace experience. Older workers were also viewed as being unable to keep up with the torrid pace and heavy character of work. The lack of training among young workers, and the decision 'adhered to by many industrial concerns' not to hire workers older than forty-five, were obvious assets in a strategy seeking low wages and a malleable workforce (Weir 1939).

During the 1930s Hamilton's labour market was reshaped as firms reorganized the workplace, redefined the content of labour queues, reduced wages, and laid off thousands of workers. When we delve behind the general unemployment figures, it is possible to identify a highly segmented labour market where women, immigrants, older workers, and employees from certain firms were subject to higher rates of unemployment than young males of British origins. Workers were restricted in their ability to construct a viable alternative strategy to the economic conditions of the 1930s by their failure to promote significant workplace solidarity. The divisions of age, gender, ethnicity, and occupation, along with the dwindling resources of union coffers only reinforced existing forms of inequality and discrimination among Hamilton's working class. Furthermore, the attempts that were made by workers to deal with the problems of the Depression were sporadic and unorganized, while left-wing parties such as the Communist party remained marginalized (Archibald 1992, Heron 1981, Storey 1981). Although the dynamics of the workplace were critical to changes to the city's labour market during the Depression, the new contours of labour demand and supply cannot be assessed without considering how the local state responded to the economic problems of the 1930s.

The State and Unemployment in Hamilton

The state played an important role in shaping Hamilton's labour markets during the 1930s. Historically, business interests had been deeply imbricated in all levels of state economic and social policy. Even though there were competing pressures on the form that state intervention would take – capitalist in-fighting and demands from workers – the ideological and practical influence of capital over government was the most powerful (Clark 1939, Cuneo 1980, Reynolds 1940, Storey 1981, Traves 1979). The 1930s were no different. In response to the Depression, the federal government introduced measures, such as an archaic relief system and a tariff policy designed to protect industry, that were to prove ineffective in combating unemployment. Governments not only created inadequate relief machinery but one in which the 'difficulties in the way of securing aid ... were responsible for cases of acute suffering and the breakdown of morale' (King 1939: 106). Furthermore, both the federal and the provincial governments enacted little new legislation regarding such issues as labour conditions, terms of employment, and wage rates (Cuneo 1980; Russell 1984; Struthers 1983; Thompson 1985: 193–221). As a consequence, employers were left with an unregulated labour market in which they had decisive control over issues such as wages and job security and in which they benefited from the inadequacies of the relief system. Although relief functioned to the extent that it 'provided a bare livelihood for the destitute,' the growth of poverty and the inability to solve problems arising from unemployment – such as housing need and self blame – only exacerbated labour's subordinate position within the labour market (Cassidy 1934: 132).

With few resources, local governments were left to deal with the day-to-day crises. Throughout the 1930s Hamilton was controlled by conservative political and business leaders who were uninterested in dealing with wider questions of unemployment. At the same time there were severe financial restraints which ensured that the city's economic viability was a constant struggle (Archibald 1992). The major step that the city took to deal with the contradiction between rising relief expenditures and falling revenues was the establishment of the Public Welfare Board. A quasi-public institution made up of city councillors and private citizens, its purpose was to control relief expenditures by determining who could receive money. Its administration of public welfare was characterized by 'harsh investigation procedures [which] tended to destroy self-respect and initiative' (Paterson 1957: 3). Not only did investigators pay fortnightly visits to the homes of people on relief, but the very act of receiving relief was tied to strict control over material conditions and moral behaviour. The board possessed a number of important controls: it checked bank accounts, cut off relief for those who refused work, cooperated with firms 'to keep a close check on all those who obtain work in the factories,' and provided relief only when an individual's 'conduct [was] exemplary' (Hamilton *Minutes 1934*: 312; *Minutes 1933*: 236). Furthermore, the board played a role in the employment opportunities of women. For example, it subsidized a YWCA course which trained 'unemployed girls' to become domestics (Hamilton *Minutes 1935*: 350). The end result was the creation of a relief system which shaped the local market through its control over a poverty-stricken labour force and the types of work available to it.

Also playing an important role in the shaping of Hamilton's labour market were local organizations and charities, such as the Hamilton Recreation Committee (HRC), Family Service Bureau, and the Lions Club. The HRC was organized in December 1932 to provide clubs for unemployed men and women. Although the organizers may have been moved by the plight of workers, the HRC and the many other similar organizations in Hamilton were more concerned with keeping the workforce from more dangerous pursuits – such as joining unions and demanding employment – and with ensuring the maintenance of a viable labour force. The committee's secretary told members in 1934, 'One of the major problems associated with unemployment is the challenge whether the unemployed are to be saved to a life of usefulness or graduate into confirmed liabilities.' In this context the committee's task was to provide 'wholesome organization of leisure time ... This is where recreation steps in, and that is why in Hamilton a group of citizens have organized to promote the movement for providing wholesome recreation for the unemployed of our city' (HRC 1934).

Business was also instrumental in shaping the evolution of state control over the local labour market. During the 1930s business leaders had a number of important concerns, such as keeping taxes low, maintaining social order, and ensuring an accessible workforce. In order to achieve these goals, business leaders became heavily involved in local affairs after 1929. A major organizer of the establishment of the Unemployment Committee in September 1930, the Hamilton Chamber of Commerce (HCC) made recommendations to the city regarding such concerns as the need for sleeping quarters, rest rooms, and food for the unemployed. The labour force was to be kept intact at a minimal level of sustenance. But it also demanded 'that a system of registration be provided to prevent advantage being taken of the accommodation by those not deserving.' There was a need for a central organization to oversee relief payments because 'a danger existed of many being neglected while others might receive more help than was necessary' (HCC 1931: 19). This pressure continued. In January 1932 a committee made up of members from the Chamber of Commerce, the Canadian Manufacturers' Association, the Hamilton Construction Association, and the Real Estate Board presented a brief to the mayor and city council 'calling for a period of retrenchment and economy.' More specifically, the committee called for a survey to determine the most appropriate places to undertake 'economies' such as lay-offs and wage reductions; an administrative officer to oversee city expenditures; greater coordination between the city government and the various organizations involved in the running of the city so that 'the latter may postpone any expenditures they can get along without and modify any program they have to meet the situation and comply with the public's demand for economy'; and a policy of services being paid for by users. In other words, the aim of the brief was to ensure 'that every endeavour be made to reduce capital expenditure and operating expenses and to reduce, or at least not increase the taxes' (HCC 1932: 25). Most of these demands were complied with as the city agreed that the costs of unemployment were not to be pressed onto those with jobs. As well as orchestrating the reconstitution of local government's response to the Depression, industrial managers were unwilling themselves to take responsibility for unemployment. At the beginning of the Depression, the city's Manufacturers' Association made it clear 'that it is not their duty or right to do anything more' for the city's jobless, other than 'employ all the men consistent with their [employers'] demands and requirements' (Hamilton *Minutes 1930*: 89).

During the 1930s Hamilton's unemployed faced a local government that was both unwilling and unable to promote policies other than the provision of resources which kept workers at a level of existence barely above starvation. As in other cities, workers in Hamilton had to contend with a hostile city hall which received few resources from other levels of government and which was ideologically opposed to structural changes to local labour markets (Copp 1988, Riendeau 1977, Taylor 1979). Local manufacturers were also unwilling to take responsibility for the deteriorating conditions of the period. Obviously, workers had to find other strategies that would enable them to find some way to cope with the overwhelming pressures of economic recession. As in the past, they turned to the family and the home.

Home and Unemployment in Hamilton

The relationship between the domestic economy and work was a third important component of the labour market during the 1930s. Historically, although there was a formal separation of home and work, the two were inextricably intertwined; there was a clear and decisive relationship between labour markets and domestic life. Paid work, except for the short period between school and marriage for women, had been the prerogative of men (Strong-Boag 1988). While men were expected to participate in paid work for their entire life after leaving school and to be the family breadwinners, the role of women was predicated on providing valuable assistance to the domestic wage before marriage and emotional and practical support within the home. During the interwar period, female labour force participation rates increased; still, by 1941 fewer than one in five paid workers were women (Strong-Boag 1988: 43).

The contradictory nature of domestic life and labour markets came into full glare during the 1930s. The economic problems associated with the Depression placed families and especially women in a particularly difficult position. On the one hand, women's wages became a critical contribution to many households. This had always been the case, but there were several factors pushing women into the paid workforce after 1929: general economic insecurity, unemployment among male family members, the lower wages of women compared with those of men, and the more rapid recovery of sectors with a large female workforce. On the other hand, there was mounting, and often fierce, criticism of women entering the paid labour force. The idea that the home, not the factory or the office, was the 'natural' place for women gained a large number of adherents during the Depression (Hobbs 1993, Strong-Boag 1988). Even

Nora-Frances Henderson, a leading local feminist and a Hamilton city councillor, argued that it is 'wrong' for 'married women holding positions of all kinds ... whose husbands are earning good salaries and ... girls who are living in well-to-do homes holding down jobs for the sake of pin money' to work and thus take jobs from men. She went on further, 'When a woman marries she should become a homemaker, which, so far as we can see, is in organized society one of the prime reasons for marriage as a social contract' (Ontario Ministry of Labour 1931). The clash between the demands for women to work and not to work played itself out in a number of ways. Marriage and birth rates dropped dramatically after 1929, allowing women to stay in the workforce longer, and only rose with economic recovery in the second half of the decade. The pre-Depression pattern of children leaving the house at marriage changed: women stayed at home longer, and married couples moved in with parents (Archibald 1992: 13–14).

A decisive factor contributing to the pressure on women to enter the paid labour force during the 1930s was the cost of decent housing. Deteriorating housing conditions and the lack of cheap housing forced families to concentrate their energies on finding cheap housing, paying land taxes, and maintaining mortgage payments. As early as 1931 a survey undertaken by the Hamilton Council of Social Agencies found that up to a quarter of all houses were either 'thoroughly and completely bad [or] ... all-round unsatisfactory' (Taylor 1936). Surveys taken in the second half of the decade found that the housing problem had 'deep roots in low and uncertain income' (Haak 1937: 6; Clarey and O'Hanley 1938). Even though rents fell – but only slightly – between the onset of the Depression and the fall of 1935, and then increased, the ability to pay rents was problematic. While average manufacturing wages fell 25 per cent between 1929 and 1933, the decline in rent for a six-room house with modern conveniences in the same period was just 14 per cent (*Labour Gazette* 1930–40; Heron and Storey 1986: 223). In 1933 the city council was told that 'the rent problem continues to be a very serious one,' and that the rent allowance paid to reliefers by the Public Welfare Board was inadequate (Hamilton, *Minutes 1933*: 383). The problem was compounded by the fact that as late as the winter of 1934, the city was paying out rent relief to almost 5,000 Hamilton families (Hamilton, *Minutes 1934*: 83). Furthermore, the chances of mortgage default increased during the 1930s: while the proportion of Hamilton home owners defaulting was between 1 and 2 per cent in the first three decades of the century, the rate increased to 15 per cent in the 1930s (Ragonetti 1994: 97). Even by the mid-1930s, when there were signs of a resurgence in new housing construction, conditions in the housing market remained difficult. As housing prices increased, so did rents, and by 1937 a severe housing shortage existed. Furthermore, the rate of mortgage defaults was much higher after 1935 (Anon. 1937: 26–7; Ragonetti 1994: 105–7).

Poor housing conditions and high rents were directly related to unemployment. To deal with this problem, Hamilton families could choose from a number of strategies. One way was to fall back on intensifying female labour within the home by taking in lodgers. Lodging, which involved extra work for a household's females, was a means by which extra money could be made to supplement the family's meagre income (Harris 1992, 1994). All of the housing surveys of the 1930s reported that the number of people per room was high and that substandard housing was occupied by those on relief or in a near-relief situation. As A.E. Grauer (1939: 49), in his overview of housing prepared for the Royal Commission on Dominion-Provincial Relations explained, the 'shortage presses hardest on low-income groups and leads to overcrowding.' This was associated with families moving into smaller houses and taking in lodgers, sometimes in combination. This is highlighted in the sample. In 1929 only 8.6 per cent of the sample households had lodgers. This increased over the next six years, peaking at 21.4 per cent in 1935, then falling to 13.2 per cent three years later. While taking in lodgers was not new, it played a critical role in the array of strategies that families devised to cope with the depressed conditions of the 1930s. In this context, female labour was utilized not in the paid labour force but in the informal, and socially acceptable, provision of domestic services to a rent-paying clientele.

Another strategy was for female family members to find paid work. As one woman worker stated, during the 1930s 'her wage were essential to the family's survival' (Bird 1983: 127). There were, however, a number of difficulties associated with finding work and providing decent wages for the family. First, as has already been mentioned, paid work by women during the 1930s encountered strong opposition. High unemployment among men – the traditional breadwinners – engendered a great deal of hostility to working women. Second, female work was ghettoized in a few poorly paid segments of the city's labour market, which meant that the wage they brought home was almost always lower than that of a man. Third, the supply of labour power greatly outweighed demand. This posed two major problems: great difficulty in finding work in the first place and, once a job had been found, low wages. Nonetheless, many families had little choice but to depend on female paid labour. Linda Murray, who worked in the city's canning and tobacco factories during the 1930s, gave most of her $12 a week pay to her mother, because 'men just couldn't get work' (Bird 1983: 130). Ann Mackness, a mother of seven, was forced to work on an assembly line at a radio factory because her husband could not find steady work (Bird 1983: 131–2).

Conclusion

The development of a weak and divided working class in Hamilton in the 1930s was strongly associated with changes to the city's labour market. During the 1920s a political climate was created in which local elites masked 'the material interests of the dominant industrialists in a political appeal that emphasized community of interest across class lines' (Heron 1981: 524). This was achieved through a segmented, ethnic- and gender-based, hierarchical labour market. During the 1930s as workers attempted to cope with the confusion of industrial change and the severity of depression, these divisive elements of the labour market were deepened. There were three major contributing elements to the worsening condition of Hamilton's working class. First, employment became much more scarce and insecure, and labour markets more stratified, flexible, and under the control of employers, compared with the case in the 1920s. Second, the state, in conjunction with business, created a ramshackle structure of welfare provision, open labour markets and rigid tariff barriers, and strong social control, which – while maintaining most people above starvation – reproduced a labour force desperate for work at almost any cost. Third, the home was the site not only of the intensification of the contradictions with respect to traditional male/female roles within home and workplace but also of pressing everyday concerns about rents, mortgages, and housing conditions. As a result, immigrants and women were forced on the defensive, men and women turned to the known gender relationships of previous decades, and families struggled to make ends meet.

This had important implications for working-class political activity. As a number of writers have noted, only a small number of people in Hamilton actively resisted and attempted to find alternative measures to the policy of state and employers of squeezing labour (Archibald 1992, Storey 1981). The working class was unable to devise alternative political strategies for a number of reasons: intra-class fighting which functioned along the lines of ideology and politics; the development of a labour market fragmented by ethnicity, gender, age, and sector; and the struggle to maintain home life – in terms of both the ideological manifestation of the domestic economy and in the material context of falling living standards. Working-class politics during the 1930s functioned within a context where acceptable answers to the prevailing material and ideological problems were difficult to formulate. The national government through its economic and fiscal policies left Hamilton's politicians with little choice in terms of local policy; the maintenance of social order and the administration of meagre resources reinforced continued internal dissension among the city's working class. Firms faced remaking their economic competitiveness at a national level while imposing discipline and control over a local workforce in the face of unprecedented rates of unemployment. Families attempted to maintain a semblance of a household controlled by a male breadwinner, while the economic imperatives of family survival forced many women into the workplace. The labour market was an essential structure which uneasily mediated the wider context of national economic and ideological trends with the day-to-day pressures of home, work, and local institutions. After 1935 some workers were able to gain some control over the labour market through industrial unionism. For most workers, however, the Depression of the 1930s meant that the wider structures of industry organization and state policy together with the demands of family life ensured that there would be a general deterioration of their power in the labour market. It also meant that the chances of establishing viable alternatives to unemployment, insecurity, and the power of industrial and political elites were, for all practical purposes, non-existent. Despite the important differences between the Depressions of the 1930s and 1990s, the similarities in the dynamics underlying the weakened position of the working class in the Canadian labour market are extremely obvious.

Acknowledgments The author would like to thank Richard Harris, Jon Caulfield, Linda Peake, and two anonymous reviewers for their valuable comments. The essay was written with the support of a postdoctoral fellowship from the Social Sciences and Humanities Research Council of Canada, and a grant from Labour Studies, McMaster University.

NOTES

1 The directory for any year consists of data from the preceding year. Thus, the 1929 directory contains information gathered in the fall of 1928.

2 Although the choice of surnames beginning with these letters was an arbitrary one, this method does provide an unbiased sample of Hamilton's working population and facilitates the search through the various primary sources.

3 Although there may be some question of the reliability of using the directories for assessing unemployment, analysis of the data leaves me with little doubt, for a number of reasons, that the directories reflect unemployment rates throughout the period in a meaningful way. The rise and fall of directory unemployment rates parallel what is already known about the general course of unemployment in Hamilton and elsewhere in Canada. The data also reflect the generally accepted (un)employment history of specific social groups in the country during the 1930s. It would be a mistake to state that they definitively provide a complete register of unemployment. However, they do furnish, especially when used in conjunction with other sources, such as the assessment rolls, an important glimpse into the employment history of Hamilton. For a discussion of the usefulness of the directories see Harris and Bloomfield (1994).

4 The property assessments defined Canadians and those from the British Isles as 'British subjects,' while other individuals were labelled 'Aliens.' People from Britain were, of course, immigrants and 'ethnics.' Because of the definitions provided by the assessment, however, 'immigrant' or 'ethnic' refer, throughout this chapter, only to people from continental Europe.

REFERENCES

Anon. 1937 'Hamilton real estate activity.' *Building in Canada* 17 (Summer): 26–7

Archibald, P. 1992. 'Distress, dissent and alienation: Hamilton workers in the Great Depression.' *Urban History Review* 21: 3–32

Avery, D. 1979. *'Dangerous Foreigners': European Immigrant Workers and Labour Radicalism in Canada, 1896–1932*. Toronto: McClelland and Stewart

Bird, P. 1983. 'Hamilton working women in the period of the Great Depression.' *Atlantis* 3: 126–36.

Canada. 1933–9. *Annual Review of Employment in Canada.* Ottawa: King's Printer

– 1934. *Seventh Census of Canada, 1931*, vol. 6. Ottawa: Patenaude

Cassidy, H.M. 1934. 'Is unemployment relief enough?' *Canadian Forum.* 14: 131–3.

Clarey, A., and J. O'Hanley. 1938. 'Report on some housing conditions.' Typescript presented to Hamilton's Medical Officer of Health, located at Hamilton Public Library

Clark, S.D. 1939. *The Canadian Manufacturers' Association: A Study in Collective Bargaining and Political Pressure.* Toronto: University of Toronto Press

Copp, T. 1988. 'Montreal's municipal government and the crisis of the 1930s.' In M. Horn, ed., *The Depression in Canada: Responses to Economic Crisis,* 145–61. Toronto: Copp Clark Pitman

Cumbo, E. 1985. 'Italians in Hamilton, 1900–1940.' *Polyphony* 7: 28–36

Cuneo, C.J. 1980. 'State mediation of class contradictions in Canadian unemployment insurance, 1930–1935.' *Studies in Political Economy* 3: 37–65

Edwards, R. 1979. *Contested Terrain: The Transformation of the Workplace in the Twentieth Century.* New York: Basic Books

Gordon, D., R. Edwards, and M. Reich. 1982. *Segmented Work, Divided Workers.* New York: Cambridge University Press

Grauer, A.E. 1939. *Housing.* Ottawa: King's Printer

Grayson, L.M., and M. Bliss, eds. 1971. *The Wretched of Canada: Letters to R.B. Bennett 1930–1935.* Toronto: University of Toronto Press

Haak, L. 1937. 'A housing survey in Hamilton.' *Social Welfare* 17: 4, 6

Hamilton Chamber of Commerce. 1929–1940. 'Annual Report.' Typescript located at the Hamilton Public Library

Hamilton, City of. 1929–39. *Minutes.* Hamilton: Hamilton Typesetting

Hamilton Recreation Committee. 1934. 'Report of Secretary.' Typescript located at the Hamilton Public Library

Harris, R. 1992. 'The end justified the means: Boarding and rooming in a city of homes, 1890–1951.' *Journal of Social History* 26: 331–58

– 1994. 'The flexible house: The housing backlog and the persistence of lodging, 1891–1951.' *Social Science History* 18: 31–53

Harris, R., and A. Bloomfield. 1997. 'The impact of industrial decentralization on the gendered journey to work.' *Economic Geography,* in press

Haughton, G., S. Johnson, L. Murphy, and K. Thomas. 1993. *Local Geographies of Unemployment.* Aldershot: Avebury

Heron, C. 1981. 'Working-class Hamilton, 1895–1930.' PhD dissertation, Department of History, Dalhousie University

Heron, C., and R. Storey. 1986. 'Work and struggle in the Canadian steel industry, 1900–1950.' In C. Heron and R. Storey, eds., *On the Job: Confronting the Labour Process in Canada,* 210–44. Montreal: McGill-Queen's University Press

Hobbs, M. 1993. 'Equality and difference: Feminism and the defence of women workers during the Great Depression.' *Labour/Le Travail* 32: 201–23

King, D. 1939. 'Unemployment aid (direct relief).' In L. Richter, ed., *Canada's Unemployment Problem,* 59–110. Toronto: Macmillan

Labour Gazette. Various years

Lewis, R.D. 1994. 'The restructuring of the Canadian textile industry: The workplace and the state, 1929–1933.' Unpublished ms

Neufeld, E.P. 1969. *A Global Corporation: A History of the International Development of Massey-Ferguson Ltd.* Toronto: University of Toronto Press

Offe, C. 1985. *Disorganized Capitalism: Contemporary Transformations of Work and Politics.* Cambridge: MIT Press

Ontario, Department of Labour. 1930–40. *Annual Report*, Sessional Papers. Toronto: King's Printer

Ontario, Ministry of Labour. 1931. 'Feminine Focus.' In Deputy Minister – Correspondence files at the Public Archives of Ontario, RG 7–12

– 1935. 'Letter from Alexandra to Mitchell Hepburn.' In Low Wages and Industrial Standards Act, files at the Public Archives of Ontario, RG 7–15

Paterson, W.N. 1957. 'Report of the president.' In Hamilton Community Chest, *Thirty Years of Service: The Hamilton Community Chest and the Council of Community Services*, 3–4. Hamilton

Peck, J.A. 1989a. 'Labour market segmentation theory.' *Labour and Industry* 2: 119–44

– 1989b. 'Reconceptualizing the local labour market: Space, segmentation and the state.' *Progress in Human Geography* 13: 42–61

Phillips, W.G. 1956. *The Agricultural Implement Industry in Canada: A Study of Competition.* Toronto: University of Toronto Press

Ragonetti, D. 1994. 'The impact of the Depression on domestic home ownership: A case study of Hamilton, 1901–1951.' MA thesis, Department of Geography, McMaster University

Reynolds, L.G. 1940. *The Control of Competition in Canada.* Cambridge: Harvard University Press

Riendeau, R. 1977. 'A clash of interests: Dependency and the municipal problem in the Great Depression.' *Journal of Canadian Studies* 14: 50–8

Rountree, G. M. 1936. *The Railway Workers: A Study of the Employment and Unemployment Problems of the Canadian Railways.* Toronto: Oxford University Press

Russell, B. 1984. 'The politics of labour-force reproduction: Funding Canada's social wage, 1917–1946.' *Studies in Political Economy* 13: 43–73

Saunders, S.A. 1939. 'Nature and extent of unemployment in Canada.' In L. Richter ed., *Canada's Unemployment Problem*, 1–58. Toronto: Macmillan

Scott, F.R., and H.M. Cassidy. 1935. *Labour Conditions in the Men's Clothing Industry.* Toronto: Nelson

Shahrodi, Z. 1989. 'From sojourners to settlers: The formation of Polonia in Toronto and Hamilton, 1896–1929.' PhD dissertation, Department of History, University of Toronto

Storey, R.H. 1981. 'Workers, unions and steel: The shaping of the Hamilton working class, 1935–1948.' PhD dissertation, Department of History, University of Toronto

Strong-Boag, V. 1988. *The New Day Recalled: Lives of Girls and Women in English Canada, 1919–1939*. Markham: Penguin

Struthers, J. 1983. *No Fault of Their Own: Unemployment and the Canadian Welfare State, 1914–1941*. Toronto: University of Toronto Press

Taylor, J. 1979. '"Relief from relief": The cities' answer to Depression dependency.' *Journal of Canadian Studies* 14: 16–23

Taylor, K.W. 1936. 'The Council of Social Agencies housing study: Summary of preliminary tabulations.' In M.A. Nixon, 'The Urban Housing Problem in Canada,' BA thesis, McMaster University

Thompson, J.H., with A. Seager. 1985. *Canada 1922–1939: Decades of Discord*. Toronto: McClelland and Stewart

Traves, T. 1979. *The State and Enterprise: Canadian Manufacturers and the Federal Government, 1917–1931*. Toronto: University of Toronto Press

Weir, H.A. 1939. 'Unemployed youth.' In L. Richter, ed., *Canada's Unemployment Problem*, 111–71. Toronto: Macmillan

Wilkinson, F. 1981. *The Dynamics of Labour Market Segmentation*. London: Academic Press

PART 3

URBAN SOCIAL MOVEMENTS

12

New Social Movements and Women's Urban Activism

GERDA WEKERLE AND LINDA PEAKE

Women are at the forefront of urban protest movements and urban activism. In Toronto, in recent years, women have been active in tenant movements directed at gaining access to affordable housing. Single-parent mothers, including many immigrants and visible minority women, have organized to improve the security of the public housing projects where they live. Neighbourhood women have set up action groups to address crime and fear of crime in their neighbourhoods. At a city-wide level, women have been instrumental in establishing a Safe City Committee at City Hall to focus on preventing crime and violence against women, and women have taken to the streets in annual 'Take Back the Night' marches to assert their rights as citizens to urban safety.

Women in Toronto have also led protests against cutbacks to the social safety net, as first federal, then provincial, and finally municipal governments have tried to save money by restructuring and cutting back essential services. They have organized demonstrations demanding access to daycare spaces. Nurses have protested proposed cutbacks to long-term care facilities. Women's organizations like INTERCEDE have organized to improve the working conditions of domestic workers – many of them women of colour – and the negative impacts of proposed changes to immigration policies.[1] Lesbians were prominent in organizing for the passage of Bill 167 in Ontario which would have entitled same-sex couples to social benefits similar to those of heterosexual couples. Despite the failure of the bill in the Ontario legislature, lesbian and gay organizations are pursuing other avenues to keep the issue alive. Women in Toronto have also been leaders in anti-poverty movements and environmental movements, often forming caucuses to establish the visibility and legitimacy of women's issues, and they have been particularly active in the union movement (Johnston 1994, McDermott and Briskin 1993).

These myriad examples of women's activism are repeated in cities across Canada. Yet when we think of urban activists – either in relation to activities with an integral relationship to the form or structure of the city or in groups that have a geographical location in the city – women do not immediately spring to mind. If we turn to the literature on new social movements, women's urban activism has not been taken seriously. Here, women are depicted primarily as mothers, consumers, or reformers who stop short of being 'real' social transformers (Castells 1983, Scott 1990). Meanwhile, the extensive literature on the women's movement tends to focus on actions and campaigns that are national and global in scale (Adamson et. al. 1988, Backhouse and Flaherty 1992). The local, whether based in neighbourhood, city, or region, receives scant attention. The location and place of women's movement activities is often taken for granted and not taken into consideration as being a constitutive element of these activities (Bookman and Morgen 1988, Garland 1988, Wine and Ristock 1991). Yet women's activism is often contextual, initiated by particular women in specific circumstances who work collectively for change. And women's organizing to effect social change has most frequently begun in urban areas and then moved out to smaller communities and rural areas.

We argue that women's activism and protest movements in urban areas comprise both urban social movements *and* women's movements, part of the pattern of new social movements that has emerged in a variety of postindustrial societies. In this chapter, we briefly review the goals and meanings of new social movements and urban social movements. We then attempt to disentangle some current suppositions about the range of women's activities that constitute urban activism, without initially prejudging whether these are women's movements activities, feminist movement initiatives, or urban social movements. In so doing, we develop a typology of activities which seeks to illuminate the diverse forms these take. By addressing the new meanings that women's urban-based activities are creating, we hope to advance the study of new social movements by better understanding how women's urban activism shapes and transforms urban areas.

New Social Movements

New social movements have gained prominence in response to the current crises of political cultures, economic restructuring, structural adjustment policies, and ecological disasters (Boggs 1986). According to Scott (1990:6), 'A social movement is a collective actor constituted by individuals who understand themselves to have common interests and, for at least some significant part of their social existence, a common identity. Social movements are distinguished from other collective actors, such as political parties and pressure groups, in that they have mass mobilization, or the threat of mobilization, as their prime source of social sanction, and hence of power.'

Within postindustrial countries since the mid-1960s, new social movements have become important political actors. Such movements as the student, environmental, and women's movements initially developed outside the state apparatus, political parties, and electoral systems.[2] They defined themselves as creating a new politics based on cultural transformation and participatory styles of decision-making, with a grounding in everyday life that defined the personal as political. New social movements have been characterized by their focus on civil society[3] as opposed to the state and by their operation in the realm of culture, engaging in struggles for 'control over the production of meaning and the constitution of new collective identities' (Canel 1992: 22).

Hence, new social movements pose new issues, shape consciousness, and open new arenas of political discourse. They politicize civil society by contesting the traditional definitions of private and public spheres and by seeking to transform private concerns into public agendas that challenge the boundaries of institutional politics (Laclau and Mouffe 1985). Carroll (1992: 8) argues that the leitmotif of new social movements are '*discursive practices* that construct new political subjects, create new political spaces in which to act, and may ultimately lead people to rethink the meaning of community [and] power.' In so doing new social movements are engaged in developing 'forms of praxis with a potential to transform both everyday life and larger institutional practices' (Carroll 1992: 6). This means more attention is given to outcomes, implementation, and processes by which social movement initiatives are incorporated into state policies.

In constituting both cultural and political practices that form new identities through the transformation of existing institutions and the social relations of everyday life, new social movements raise issues that go beyond a concern with the economics of class as the central element of social change. In the literature on new social movements, there is attention to both agency and strategy, contrasted with the earlier political economy focus (dominant in analyses of social change) on class structure and events. New social movements address the implications of such matters as gender, environmental crises, ethnicity, age, sexual orientation, and race as these affect both people's life chances and their experience of cities. By expanding grievances and feelings of deprivation beyond only class identity and the world of work, which have been the traditional basis of much oppositional social practices, new social movements address the concerns of people in their roles as consumers, clients, and citizens.

Critiques of this literature have begun to emerge. In their zeal to differentiate new social movements, which focus primarily on discursive practices and on culture, from older social movements based on class interests, new social movement theorists often tend to underplay the extent to which these movements are also directed to changing economic conditions. For example, the U.S. civil rights movement was not only directed to demanding rights to vote for African Americans but also to fundamentally improving the material conditions of their daily lives, including access to education, employment, and services. Similarly, women's movements have focused specifically on changing the material conditions for women and their families not just in the workplace but also in the domestic economy of the home, in the neighbourhood, and in the city as a whole. A primary goal has been the improvement of women's material conditions in concert with fundamental change in societal structures of domination and subordination. For example, lower-income women's leadership of welfare rights movements has been specifically directed to improving women's entitlements within the structure of the welfare state (West 1981).

Furthermore, although they start from a position outside formal politics and the state apparatus, new social movements also make essentially political demands expressed in terms of the expansion of citizenship and the inclusion of excluded groups into the polity (Scott 1990). There are also new claims for resources and legal and legislative changes. Contradicting the view that new social movements lie essentially outside the formal structures of the state, Scott (1990) argues that the integration of social movement agendas into the mainstream is an indicator of movement success insofar as it marks a fundamental shift in the character of conventional politics.

Some new social movements are actively engaged with the state in attempting to institutionalize their agendas. For example, the European Green parties have become part of the formal political process both at the national level and in cities like Frankfurt, Germany, where the Greens hold the balance of power. The establishment of women's bureaus within federal, provincial, and municipal state agencies in Canada is another example of institutionalization of social movement agendas. The active engagement of women's organizations like the National Action Committee on the Status of Women (NAC) in contesting government policies like the North American Free Trade Agreement (NAFTA) and changes to immigration policy are further indications that Canadian women's movements do not stand outside the formal political system but seek to be active agents of social transformation. Within women's movements, the objective of affecting change through transforming the state, even if this means only piecemeal reform, has been a key element. However, despite the presence of women activists within state structures and civil society, their presence and the urban context in which they operate have received little attention in the new social movements literature. The following sections address these omissions.

Urban Social Movements

Despite the location of a number of new social movements in the urban arena, the urban nature and focus of such movements has often not been considered an integral aspect of their analysis. Many environmental groups, for example, are based in particular cities and have a territorial focus such as preservation of a bioregion, through sustainable development or recycling. However, it is also the case that many new social movements, although urban-based, are not urban-oriented insofar as they are rights-based groups with no locality or territorial base. Many women's movements issues such as equal pay, abortion rights, or reproduction rights are of this nature. Magnusson (1992) points out that movements may be simultaneously local, national, and global: membership, goals, and strategies may flow among these three levels. This describes contemporary women's movements but it also begs the question where does the 'urban' begin and end? Does it include the global as well as the local when multinational companies located in Toronto or New York make decisions that affect urban dwellers in Guyana, or when global restructuring decimates the unionized garment industry in cities like Toronto, Montreal, New York, and San Francisco resulting in an increase in homeworkers? Are these issues for urban movements, for worker movements, or for global movements? More exactly, under what conditions do specific locality-based issues serve a wider purpose of raising political consciousness that challenges identities and broader institutional frameworks?

Only a few authors have addressed this question by examining the urban character of social movements, Castells (1983) being the most notable example. In his initial accounts urban social movements had the aim of securing collective consumption, that is, the provision of goods and services by the state, but he expanded his attention to include the goals of political self-management and cultural identity. For example, Castells recognizes that it is gendered human agents who create, maintain, and transform structures in their struggles to create new urban meanings (Peake 1994). This would imply that urban social movements share the characteristics of new social movements generally; they are engaged primarily in the production of new meanings through the creation of new discourses, paradigms, and ways of seeing and knowing.

Over the past decades, however, the critical social science literature on cities has focused less on urban social movements and more on the impacts of the globalization of the economy and the internationalization of capital on urban restructuring (Fainstein et al. 1983, Logan and Molotch 1987, Sassen 1991). The focus has been on the decisions of global actors, multinational companies, and supra-national organizations such as the European Community and NAFTA in shifting capital and jobs from one city, region, and country to another. Recent research on urban social movements has emerged more through a concern with issues of citizenship than with this literature.

Susan Smith (1989) argues that globalization is always experienced through a locality. This is manifested, for example, through the spatial reorganization of citizens' entitlements to collective consumption benefits, that is, citizenship is framed in terms of 'entitlements bound to the social institutions through which they are exercised' (Smith 1989). The way a given locality responds to globalization pressures, and who wins and who loses in this process, become critical. At the same time as globalization may undermine the identity and autonomy of place, Smith (1989) also points out that there is a focus on the uniqueness of places and the creation of the meaning of place. This is experienced, for example, in the efforts of historic preservation groups and in the creation of place identities through the promotion of ethnically distinct neighbourhoods, carnival arenas, and sites for consumption and spectacles. It is also manifest in the 'mobilization of locality' (Smith 1989) through local economic development projects and through new forms of collective action at the local level, often focused on the environment, sustainability, and the creation of community. Localities may also become the focus of new experiments in citizenship that are directed to more open and participatory forms of decision-making.

As we continue further into the 1990s we can expect the goals of urban social movements to receive further attention. As the population in general has become more and more alienated from federal and provincial politics and at the same time has experienced a declining quality of life, there has been more awareness of and concern with city-level issues such as waste management, urban safety, and transportation.

Municipalities, according to Magnusson (1992), are particularly susceptible to disruptions by social movements. Municipalities operate at the juncture of the local and global and at intersections of capital, individuals, and social movements. This creates new opportunities for both municipalities and urban social movements depending on the extent to which the former will operate 'as an organizational node in the flow of critical and creative social movements' (Magnusson 1992: 84). But despite the very active, and often catalytic, role played by women in these urban social movements, and their pivotal role both as the largest group of employees of municipalities as well as the largest group of recipients of services provided by the municipality, little attention has been paid to them. What light does feminist literature on the range of urban-based activities in which women are involved throw on this omission? What role have women been playing in the creation of new urban meanings?

Women's Urban Activism

Like other new social movement groups, contemporary women's movements have been actively engaged in the creation of discursive practices that challenge traditional politics, raise new issues, operate in new terrains, and employ new modes of action and organizational forms. It is in the context of the creation of new meanings and alternative ways of seeing and knowing that we will examine the impact of women's urban-based activities.

Several feminist theorists divide the history of women's activism into initiatives that reveal 'female consciousness' (Kaplan 1982) and 'feminist consciousness' (Taylor and Rupp 1993).[4] For example, in the eighteenth and nineteenth centuries European women were involved in food riots and market disturbances (Stacey and Price 1981). Cott (1989) characterizes such activities – organizing working-class food protests and strikes – as examples of female consciousness, that is, arising out of women's common roles as mothers and caregivers. The efforts of working-class and minority women to improve living conditions, services, and working conditions in cities might be described as based on 'female consciousness,' when the objective is advocacy on behalf of families or communities. This contrasts with activism which reveals a feminist consciousness based on a critique of male supremacy. This is characterized, for examples, by struggles to end male violence against women, to create separate women-only spaces, and to end economic, political, and legal discrimination against women. In urban areas we find examples both of female consciousness, with a maternalist base, and of feminist consciousness, based in opposition to prevailing patterns of gender relations. In the urban and feminist literature, several authors focus on one or the other form of women's activism and draw different conclusions about their meaning and impact. However, if we contextualize women's activities in the light of new social movement frameworks, different dimensions of these activities, that could not be revealed when using only the binary categories of female and feminist consciousness, come to light.

The remainder of this essay outlines the diverse forms of women's urban activism in recent years. Women have been leaders of urban protest movements to improve the quality of life for themselves and their families. They have organized demonstrations and alternative services to fill gaps in the human service system. Increasingly, they have used the city as a site for the mobilization around identity politics, for example, in lesbian organizing. And, finally, the municipality itself has become the focus of feminist-oriented struggles to change the planning system of cities. Each of these four areas of activities will be examined in turn with an emphasis on highlighting the connection of these activities to new social movements and their role in the creation of new urban meanings.

Quality-of-Life Urban Protests

Women living in cities have frequently engaged in strategies for empowerment, but these strategies have often remained undocumented and unnoticed. In part this may be because they are strategies in which women have come together in their gendered roles as mothers; these are women's empowerment-directed activities centred on family, kinship, and local neighbourhood networks (Bystydzienski 1992). According to Fincher and McQuillen (1989), low-income women, demonstrating concern for their families, frequently turn to the local state for solutions to problems of housing, poor educational quality in the schools, or social welfare. In these instances, similar to the rent strikes of the nineteenth century, women's activism is an extension of the domestic sphere, expressing concerns about the deterioration of urban services and the decline in the quality of family life.

One current example of such activities are the collective cooking projects that are being established in Canadian cities. Starting in Montreal in the 1980s, these projects, under the rubric of the Regroupement des cuisines collectives du Québec, bring low-income women together not only to provide cheap and nourishing food for their communities but also to promote the creation of solidarity through mutual support networks (Norman 1991). In the long term they also aim to create jobs for women in the field of food provision. These multiple objectives are expressed through a desire not only to combat physical hunger but also to combat the emotional and psychological hunger in the communities in which these women live. They are combining material and social criteria in their efforts to place a higher value on one of women's primary caregiving roles and at the same time are politicizing their attempts by reasserting their rights to 'provide nourishment to the community' (Norman 1991: 7). Moreover, a number of collective cooking projects are utilizing food from food banks, thereby extending their networks into broader communities and strengthening their resource base. Collective kitchens today are organized in low-income neighbourhoods as a survival strategy for families who have been hard hit by urban restructuring and are dependent on food banks. They are collaborative activities either organized by local state agencies or by community organizations akin to the earlier food-protest groups. Such projects show that women can redefine their traditional activities as caregivers of the family and meld them with community-based political activism.

Although an example of 'female consciousness' activity, these community kitchen projects' potential for change emerges when they are viewed as new social movement activities, most obviously in the role they play in the creation of new collective identities for women, as carers and as producers. These projects are rarely addressed, however, by the literature on either urban activism or women's movement activities. Similarly, when women's empowerment strategies have been directed through economic development projects which are not explicitly women-defined, women's contributions to urban change have also tended to be hidden. For example, women have been at the centre of conflicts around the urban environment, often on behalf of protecting their families: a group of mothers in East Los Angeles organized to prevent the area from becoming a dumping ground for hazardous waste treatment plants (Pardo 1990); the mothers of Love Canal also led the fight against chemical pollutants (Gibbs 1982); and single mothers living on New York City's Lower East Side have organized to create community gardens that would provide a place for children to plant flowers in place of the empty lots that attracted drug trafficking. These forms of women's urban activism, based on a shared female consciousness and the experiences of day-to-day life, have expanded the arenas considered political and have provided women with the opportunities to shape the urban environment.

Creating Alternative Services

Throughout urban neighbourhoods, women undertake community-based political activities to protect their communities and to improve local services such as hospitals, housing, or education. Yet national political struggles or civil rights movements have often ignored these forms of social activism, defining them as 'merely local.' Peake (1986: 75–6) has argued that women tend to be more involved in struggles around collective consumption and issues that directly affect their daily lives, including the provision of school crossings, play space for children, or bus services and has labelled these as the 'informal sphere of urban politics.' This informal and daily community involvement of women in women's associations and protest groups creates community-based networks for women's influence, but these tend to be dismissed by the formal power structure of cities unless they become part of a formal pressure group.[5]

In a number of Canadian cities including Toronto, Vancouver, Montreal, Halifax, and some smaller cities, women, in the early 1980s, began to develop permanent housing for women, including single parents, older women, and visible minority and ethnic women (Wekerle 1993, 1988; Wekerle and Muirhead 1991). Although these projects were locality-based and collective consumption oriented, the creation of a national network of almost 100 women-developed housing projects managed and controlled by women also operated at the level of image and symbol creation. In each community, and cumulatively across the country, the message changed from a predominant image of women as victims of the housing system, to an alternative narrative of women taking charge and successfully creating housing that met their needs.

Women have also been responsible for the development of parallel social service networks that are gendered and also respond to diversity. These are grassroots organizations that often have a decentralized, flat organizational structure based on participatory decision-making. The national network of more than 300 battered women's shelters in Canada fits this model. The women's services found in every major Canadian city grew out of localized struggles and organizing efforts. They have contributed immeasurably to the quality of life in cities, addressing needs that the formal state sector did not meet. At the same time the provision of women's services in cities has contributed to the growth of women's urban activism by providing opportunities for networking and the learning of political skills.

In these ways women's urban activism has also had a substantial impact on other new social movements in the past decade. According to Taylor and Whittier (1993) the gay and lesbian movements, AIDS movement, environmental movements, and animal rights movement have all been influenced by trained feminist activists who through their participation in other new social movements have integrated feminist concerns into those movements. By establishing roots in other social movements, women's urban activism may be less visible today than in the past as its concerns become subsumed or dispersed. At the same time, feminist issues have also become more pervasive and more established (Taylor and Whittier 1993), and there are more examples of women working together in coalitions to provide services for women, both within and outside state structures.

The City as a Site for the Mobilization of Identity Politics

New social movements, including the feminist movement, have introduced the politics of identity as a new theme in civil society (Mooers and Sears 1992). Within the feminist movement it has been marginalized women who have pushed to the forefront their concerns around their identities, thereby highlighting women's differences and linking the oppression of women to other systems of domination. The women's movement of the early 1970s was characterized more by theoretical differences among socialist, radical, and liberal feminists than by any concern for issues of difference associated with race, life stage, disability, or religion (Gabriel and Scott 1993). By the end of the decade, however, numerous groups had emerged over single issues, including violence against women, abortion, pay equity, and so on. Moreover, even within seemingly homogeneous communities a differentiation of identities proliferated, as Ross (1990: 88) pointed out in her analysis of lesbian organizing in Toronto: 'In large urban centres across Canada and other Western countries, the 1980s have heralded the subdivision of activist lesbians into specialized groupings: lesbians of colour, Jewish lesbians, working class lesbians, leather dykes, lesbians against sado-masochism, older lesbians, lesbian youth, disabled lesbians and so on.' Within the women's movement(s) debate and discussion emphasized that women cannot be thought of as one social collective as this standpoint treats all women as equally powerless and oppressed (Young 1994).

Taylor and Rupp (1993) assert, 'In some ways, as an ideology, feminism has come full circle; by focusing on women's differences based on race, class, and sexuality, it is renewing its alliance with other movements for human rights from which it has emerged in this country and around the world.' Within the urban milieu this has had various consequences. Women's organizations interested in representing women's interests on a city-wide basis, such as Women Plan Toronto, find it increasingly difficult to secure a diverse representation and are often subject to the criticism that they represent only white, middle-class, professional women. At the same time, new city-based organizations serving specific minority and immigrant women's populations have proliferated. Lesbian organizations, including lesbian groups serving specific ethnocultural populations have become established, as have organizations like the Older Women's Network and the Disabled Women's Network (DAWN). Agnew (1996) argues that in the mid-1970s middle-class immigrant women's groups of Asian, African, and Caribbean women began to organize to gain access to social services for women from their ethnic and racial groups. In the 1980s many more groups emerged to address the needs of working-class immigrant women. A number of broad-based, national-level umbrella groups also exist, such as the Congress of Black Women, but it is at the community level that there has been a proliferation of groups, some organizing services to women in their own communities, for example, in Toronto the Filipino Community Center, the Somalian Women's Group, and some based on advocacy, for example, Women Working with Immigrant Women and INTERCEDE (the Toronto Organization for Domestic Workers' Rights).

With all the emphasis, however, on the emergence of identity politics within the women's movement, the way that cities become the site for such struggles has tended to be ignored (with the exception of Castells' (1983) work on the gay community of San Francisco). Yet cities provide the critical mass of lesbian women, or lesbian women of a particular ethnic group, or women from specific ethnocultural communities, that make it possible to define an identity politics and to develop cultural practices that influence the nature of urban change.

Struggles Around and in the Municipality

Traditionally, the activities and priorities of municipal government in Canada have not been linked to women's movements policy priorities. Canadian cities have defined their mandate narrowly to encompass economic development and growth politics, planning, and building infrastructure (Andrew 1992). Recently, however, women have been turning to the local state as policies at the national or provincial levels have been increasingly viewed as conservative or right-wing or anti-woman. The local state has come under new scrutiny as a rights-providing or rights-denying social institution. Invoking their social rights as citizens (Marshall 1949), and their entitlement to the principle of 'equality in distribution' (O'Connor 1993), women are demanding that local governments respond to their needs and policy agendas.

In the 1980s, and increasingly into the 1990s, female municipal councillors and women's community organizations have attempted to expand the municipal agenda into areas more closely linked with women's interests, primarily social policy areas such as childcare, welfare policies, or poverty issues. At the same time, women's movement groups have begun to define the traditional jurisdictions of municipal governments as gendered: policing and public safety, public health, access to housing and transportation, and zoning and land use planning (to reduce the segregation of land use) (Wekerle 1991, 1994a; Weisman 1992). The conjuncture of these activities is resulting in a destabilizing of the relation between politics and the state; matters outside the realm of state regulation have become politicized. In the context of women's movement groups and the local state, this includes making previously private issues public, such as violence against women, or they make previously unregulated activities a matter of state policy, for example, by-laws to improve security in parking garages. Such 'challenging of the boundaries of institutional politics' is a direct contribution to the development of new social movements by women's urban activism.

Women's organizations in cities have also focused on issues of equitable political process (reminiscent of the participation of nineteenth-century women's organizations in the reform of machine politics in municipal governments). This turning to the state by women and feminist movement organizations is not new. Women have turned to the state for progressive policies on abortion, domestic violence, and equal opportunities (Kofman and Peake 1990). Women have also increasingly become employees in the state sector. This has increased the potential for alliances between female employees and clients of state agencies (Piven 1984). In contrast to women's earlier urban activism which focused on redistribution and issues of equality and was often oppositional to the local state, women's urban social movement activity in the 1990s often demands that differences be recognized, as part of the rights of citizenship, in order for all women to become full participants in political processes. This often involves transforming participatory processes and organizational forms so that different groups of women can be involved. For example, the Safe City Committee of the City of Toronto has developed a new organizational structure that involves women's community groups and city councillors as committee members, with the active involvement of staff from major city departments. Such a structure lends legitimacy and organizational support to citizen activities which also benefit from being able to use the resources of municipal government to engage in local action and networking.

Indeed, much innovative activity of municipal governments in recent years has resulted from the formal and informal networks that exist between municipalities. Often these innovations come from formal and informal links with new social movement organizations (Magnusson 1992). For example, the Safe City concept in Canadian cities rapidly disseminated from the City of Toronto to Ottawa, Montreal, Winnipeg, Vancouver, and Dartmouth both through the networks of municipalities, but most importantly, through the informal networks of city staff and feminist movement group members (Wekerle and Whitzman 1995). In this way municipal councils connected 'movements with one another, legitimizing their concerns, exploring the possibilities for local initiatives, and establishing links between movements in one locality and another. In this process, the municipal council constitutes itself as a site for global politics' (Magnusson 1992: 89). While Magnusson comes to this conclusion about social movements in general, it increasingly applies to the innovations introduced by women's movements organizations in municipalities.

A positive outcome of the institutionalization of social movement goals is their implementation through local state funding and staffing. A negative outcome is the dilution and accommodation of social movement goals through negotiation with the political process. Successful projects like the Safe City initiative become disassociated from women's movements and their success is attributed to local governments. Through this process of institutionalization the success of social movement initiatives is usually hidden. However, as individual women and women's organizations have gained experience and some successes in dealing with state structures, they have extended this experience in organizing to their localities. For example, in 1991, women fought against poverty by organizing protests against social service cutbacks in Metropolitan Toronto. Fightback Metro was a joint protest effort of women organized against poverty and welfare advocates. They protested local social service cutbacks in the context of national and global restructuring and its impact on low-income women (Carty 1993).

Within the context of the local state, however, women have been relatively slow to recognize that the special committees of local councils that cross-cut city departments (e.g., committees on aging, on AIDS, on race relations, or on safe cities) could be taken over or shaped to fit feminist agendas. Similarly, organized women's community groups have only recently grasped the importance of claiming resources to participate in cities' public participation or public consultation activities. For example, Women Plan Toronto recently obtained a contract from Metropolitan Toronto to conduct focus groups with women for input to the Draft Metropolitan Official Plan, *The Liveable Metropolis.*

Magnusson (1992: 88) also notes that 'movements reposition the locality in relation to the state, disrupting the hierarchy that subordinates local politics to national politics.' This is very much the case with Canadian municipalities that have initiated Safe City committees. By following feminist movement initiatives to reduce violence against women, cities like Toronto, Montreal, Vancouver, and Ottawa have provided leadership on a public policy issue that the federal government only picked up on several years later with a recent federal initiative on community crime prevention (Wekerle 1994b).

As struggles around and in the municipality have shown women's involvement has generated political resources by creating new political issues, new solidarities, and new agencies that could be used by women to organize. Such contributions to the development of new social movements and the creation of new urban meanings are manifold across Canadian urban centres.

Conclusion

Women's activism in cities has taken diverse forms, from maternalist initiatives where women advocate on behalf of children, their families, 'the poor,' or welfare mothers, to expressly feminist initiatives where women focus on the links between patriarchal domination and women's disadvantage. Increasingly, however, this dual categorization fails to capture the full range of women's urban protest movements and urban activism; it renders invisible dimensions of women's engagement which do not fall neatly into these categories. This essay has revealed that the extent of women's urban activism overlaps this binary divide. It is more inclusive to analyse women's activities in terms of ways in which they have redefined traditional domains and terrains.

Women have created community gardens, kitchens, and food co-ops, established a network of childcare options including parent-run co-operatives, initiated programs to reclaim public housing to make it more responsive to resident needs, and developed women-controlled housing options. They have established an extensive network of alternative urban service structures including battered women's shelters, women's hostels, rape crisis centers, feminist counselling and referral centres, childcare centres, and ethno-cultural agencies for aboriginal women and women of colour, and employment and job-skill retraining centres. Moreover, these activities have resulted in a proliferation of modes of organizing, from informal women's groups focused on single issues, through local state commissions and coalitions of community and municipal groups.

Increasingly, women's activism and social movement activities have been differentiated into ethnocultural, or other, organizations based on identity politics. As a result women's politics are more targeted and not as diffuse. As women's social movement activities become more widespread within cities, they may, paradoxically, also become more hidden. Women's organizing may be subsumed under housing movements, or environmental movements, or movements of visible minorities. Women's organizing within unions may be rendered invisible during strikes even though union membership is predominantly female. This is not to say that women's impact on the shape, form, and transformation of cities is waning. On the contrary, the influence of women has spread into areas not traditionally viewed as 'women's issues,' and women's activism is changing the culture of city life and the nature of urban change.

NOTES

1 The Live-in Caregiver Program, for example, is an anomaly within the current liberalization of Canada's immigration policy, resulting in a loss of rights to citizenship by immigrant domestic workers.

2 These movements grew out of, and built on, the civil rights movements. Another impetus for the emergence of women's movements was as a reaction to the male sexism of the leadership of the new Left.

3 Civil society can be defined as a set of interests and social struggles including independent organizational bases outside the political structures of the state that advance alternative visions of the way society can be organized (Carroll 1992).
4 Iris Young (1994) points out that women often group self-consciously on the basis of their gendered condition, but this grouping is not necessarily feminist.
5 In a recent book by Logan and Molotch (1987) *The City as a Growth Machine*, women are mentioned only once as engaged in activism in the neighbourhood sphere.

REFERENCES

Agnew, V. 1996. *Resisting Discrimination: Women from Asia, Africa and the Caribbean and the Women's Movement in Canada*. Toronto: University of Toronto Press

Adamson, N., L. Briskin, and M. McPhail. 1988. *Organising for Change: The Contemporary Women's Movement.* Toronto: Oxford University Press

Andrew, C. 1992 'The feminist city.' In H. Lustiger-Thaler, ed., *Political Arrangements: Power and the City*, 109–22. Montreal: Black Rose Books

Backhouse, C., and D.H. Flaherty, eds. 1992. *Challenging Times: The Women's Movement in Canada and the United States.* Montreal: McGill-Queen's University Press

Boggs, C. 1986. *Social Movements and Political Power.* Philadelphia: Temple University Press

Bookman, A., and S. Morgen, eds. 1988. *Women and the Politics of Empowerment.* Philadelphia: Temple University Press

Bystydzienski, J.M. 1992. 'Introduction.' In *Women Transforming Politics: Worldwide Strategies for Empowerment*, 1–11. Bloomington: Indiana University Press

Canel, E. 1992. 'New social movement theory and resource mobilization: The need for integration,' In W. Carroll, ed., *Organizing Dissent: Contemporary Social Movements in Theory and Practice*, 22–51. Toronto: Garamond Press

Carroll, W.K., ed. 1992. *Organizing Dissent: Contemporary Social Movements in Theory and Practice.* Toronto: Garamond Press

Carty, L., ed. 1993. *And Still We Rise: Feminist Political Mobilizing in Contemporary Canada.* Toronto: Women's Press

Castells, M. 1983. *The City and the Grassroots.* Berkeley: University of California Press

Cott, N. 1989. 'What's in a name? The limits of 'social feminism,' or, Expanding the vocabulary of women's history.' *Journal of American History* 76(3): 809–29

Fainstein, S., N. Fainstein, R. Child Hill, D. Judd, and M. Smith 1983. *Restructuring the City: The Political Economy of Urban Redevelopment.* New York: Longman

Fincher, R., and J. McQuillen. 1989. 'Women in urban social movements.' *Urban Geography* 10(6): 604–14

Gabriel, C., and K. Scott. 1993. 'Women's Press at twenty: The politics of feminist publishing.' In L. Carty, ed., *And Still We Rise: Feminist Political Mobilizing in Contemporary Canada*, 25–52. Toronto: Women's Press

Garland, A.W. 1988. *Women Activists: Challenging the Abuse of Power.* New York: Feminist Press

Gibbs, Lois. 1981. *Love Canal: My Story.* Albany: State University of New York Press

Johnston, P. 1994. *Success While Others Fail: Social Movement Unionism and the Public Workplace.* Ithaca: ILR Press

Kaplan, T. 1982. 'Female consciousness and collective action: The case of Barcelona, 1910–1918.' *Signs* 7(3): 545–66

Kofman, E., and L. Peake. 1990. 'Into the 1990s: A gendered agenda for political geography.' *Political Geography Quarterly* 9(4): 313–36

Laclau, E., and C. Mouffe. 1985. *Hegemony and Socialist Strategy: Towards a Radical Democratic Politics.* London: Verso

Logan, J.R., and H. Molotch. 1987. *Urban Fortunes: The Political Economy of Place.* Berkeley: University of California Press

Magnusson, W. 1992. 'The constitution of movements versus the constitution of the state: Rediscovering the local as a site for global politics.' In H. Lustiger-Thaler, ed., *Political Arrangements: Power and the City*, 69–193. Montreal: Black Rose Books

Marshall, T.H. 1949. 'Citizenship and social class.' In *Class, Citizenship and Social Development*, 71–134. New York: Doubleday (republished in 1964)

McDermott, P., and L. Briskin, eds. 1993. *Women Challenging Unions: Feminism, Democracy, and Militancy* Toronto: University of Toronto Press

Mooers, C., and A. Sears. 1992. 'The new social movements and the withering away of state theory.' In W. Carroll, ed., *Organizing Dissent: Contemporary Social Movements in Theory and Practice*, 52–68. Toronto: Garamond Press

Norman, D. 1991. 'Collective kitchens.' In *Women and Poverty. Report on the Regional Symposium*, 7. Montreal: Canadian Advisory Council on the Status of Women

O'Connor, J. 1993. 'Citizenship, class, gender and labour market participation in Canada and Australia.' In *Gender, Citizenship and the Labour Market: The Australian and Canadian Welfare States.* Reports and Proceedings, Social Policy Research Centre, No. 109, University of New South Wales, New South Wales, Australia

Pardo, M. 1990. 'Mexican American women grassroots community activists: Mothers of east Los Angeles.' *Frontiers* 11(1): 1–7

Peake, L. 1986. 'A conceptual inquiry into urban politics and gender.' In K. Hoggart and E. Kofman, eds., *Politics, Geography and Social Stratification*, 62–85. London: Croom-Helm

–1994. 'Engendering change: The place of women's work in urban social theory.'

In A. Kobayashi, ed., *Women, Work and Place.* Montreal: McGill Queen's University Press

Piven, F.F. 1984. 'Women and the state: Ideology, power and the welfare state.' *Socialist Review* 14(2): 11–19

Ross, B. 1990. 'The house that Jill built: Lesbian feminist organizing in Toronto, 1976–1980.' *Feminist Review* 35: 75–91

Sassen, S. 1991. *Global City: New York, London, Tokyo.* Princeton, NJ: Princeton University Press

Scott, A. 1990. *Ideology and the New Social Movements.* London: Unwin Hyman

Smith, S. 1989. 'Society, space and citizenship: A human geography for the new times?' *Transactions of the Institute of British Geographers,* n.s. 14: 144–56

Stacey, M., and M. Price. 1981. *Women, Power and Politics.* London: Tavistock

Taylor, V., and N. Whittier. 1993. 'The new feminist movement.' In L. Richardson and V. Taylor, eds., *Feminist Frontiers III,* 533–48. New York: McGraw-Hill

Taylor, V., and L.J. Rupp. 1993. 'Women's culture and lesbian feminist activism: A reconsideration of cultural feminism.' *Signs* 19(1): 32–61

Weisman, L.K. 1992. *Discrimination by design: A feminist critique of the man-made environment.* Chicago: University of Illinois Press

Wekerle, G.R. 1988. *Women's Housing Projects in Eight Canadian Cities.* Ottawa: CMHC

– 1991. 'Gender politics in local politics: The case of Toronto.' Paper given at the Association of Collegiate Schools of Planning-AESOP Congress, Oxford

– 1993. 'Responding to diversity: Housing developed by and for women.' *Canadian Journal of Urban Research* 12(2): 95–113

– 1994a. 'Women's urban social movement groups as agents of change in cities.' Paper given at XIII World Congress of Sociology, International Sociological Association, Bielefeld, Germany

– 1994b. 'Violence against women/safer cities: Canadian federal and municipal initiatives.' Paper given at OECD Conference, Paris

Wekerle, G.R. and B. Muirhead. 1991. *Canadian Women's Housing Projects.* Ottawa: CMHC

Wekerle, G.R. and C. Whitzman. 1995. *Safe Cities: Guidelines for Planning, Design, and Management.* New York: Van Nostrand Reinhold

West, G. 1981. *The National Welfare Rights Movement.* New York: Praeger

Wine, J.D., and J.L. Ristock. 1991. *Women and Social Change: Feminist Activism in Canada.* Toronto: Lorimer

Young, I.M. 1994. 'Gender as seriality: Thinking about women as a social collective.' *Signs* 19(3): 713–38

13

Anti-Racism Organizing and Resistance: Blacks in Urban Canada, 1940s–1970s[1]

AGNES CALLISTE

Following the Halifax 'mini-riot' in July 1991, the African-Nova Scotian community pressured the province to initiate and develop an anti-racism plan in order to avoid a repeat of the incident. It argued that the 'mini-riot' focused attention on black youths' frustrations regarding the impact of racism which, in addition to immediate concerns regarding admission to night clubs and bars, included longstanding grievances in such areas as education, employment, housing, and police-community relations (Lee 1991, Nicoll 1991, NSAG 1991). An Advisory Group on Race Relations, comprising representatives from the three levels of government and the African-Nova Scotian community, was appointed to recommend a plan that governments and the community should take towards eliminating racism and racial discrimination as it affects black people in Halifax and across Nova Scotia (NSAG 1991: 2). Its ninety-four recommendations dealt with seven areas: education, employment, and economic development; black community participation and access to services; policing; justice and human rights; black community development; the media; and tourism and culture.

The Halifax community's struggle against racism is not unique to Nova Scotia nor to Canada. Blacks in Canada had been resisting racism for over 200 years (Walker 1976), particularly in the period since the Second World War, when they became more political with the influence of the Black Power Movement in the United States and the decolonization of African and Caribbean states. Some researchers (Davis and Krauter 1971, Winks 1971) argue that, before 1971, because of the lack of national black leadership, the most effective aid to the black struggle for racial equality in Canada came from non-blacks, such as the Canadian Labour Congress (CLC) and its National Committee on Human Rights. Although it is true that black organizations in the period from 1940 to 1970 collaborated with other organizations in the struggle for racial equality because they did not have the economic and political power resources to do it alone, blacks themselves also took initiatives in resisting racism and other forms of oppression. Their contribution to the anti-racist struggle, however, has been largely ignored in social science research (Bruner 1979).

The porters' struggle for employment equity on the railways[2] serves as an illustration. The Toronto Labour Committee on Human Rights did assist a few Canadian Pacific Railway (CPR) porters in Toronto to obtain promotion to junior sleeping car conductor positions in the 1950s. But the Canadian National Railways (CNR) porters themselves took the initiative in resisting both management and the Canadian Brotherhood of Railway Transport (CBRT) in the period from the 1940s to 1964 until they eliminated segregated porters' and dining car employees' locals and the submerged split labour market (Bonacich 1972, 1976) which restricted blacks to portering (Calliste 1988, 1995). (A submerged split labour market demarcates a colour line beyond which only white workers can advance.) In contrast to the CPR porters who used test cases to pressure management and the state to enforce the 1953 Fair Employment Practices Act,[3] the CNR porters took class action to remedy systemic racism. (Systemic racism is defined as the collective body of institutional values, traditions, regulations, policies, and practices that have an adverse effect on minority access to equality in a society which may appear non-discriminatory.) The CNR porters felt that the CLC Human Rights Committee could not be impartial given its funding from trade unions, including the CBRT; for example, a CLC report blamed the railways for racial discrimination but exonerated the CBRT (Blum 1961). Lee Williams, who led the CNR porters' struggle, labelled the CLC report 'a whitewash' to suit the trade union hierarchy (Magnus 1961).

Blacks also resisted systemic/institutionalized racism in other institutions, such as education and housing as well as in immigration policy. (Institutionalized racism appears when discriminatory practices against certain racial or ethnic groups are legally sanctioned by the state and formalized within its institutional framework.) In the 1940s the Halifax Colored Citizens Improvement League put pressure on nursing schools to accept black students, a battle later taken up by Pearleen Oliver, founding member of the Nova Scotia Association for the Advancement of Colored People. As a result, the Children's Hospital in Halifax accepted two black students who graduated in 1948 (Congress of Black Women of Canada 1991, Pachai 1990).

Similarly, the Toronto Negro Veterans' Association, led by Wilson Brooks, presented a brief to the Ontario Minister of Health in 1947 asking for the cancellation of government grants to provincial hospitals which discriminated on the basis of colour. The brief resulted from the Owen Sound Hospital's refusal to admit Marisse Scott to its nurses' training school and 'the general policy of discrimination against Blacks in hospitals' (*Campus*, 10 October 1947). This challenge also was supported by the trade union congresses of Canada and by the Catholic church. Ms. Scott was finally admitted to the St Joseph's Hospital school of nursing in Guelph (Canada, House of Commons 1953).

But despite their anti-racist struggles, blacks in Canada (particularly in Nova Scotia), continue to occupy a subordinate position in economic, political, and ideological relations.[4] The status quo has resisted blacks' demand for societal transformation and power-sharing; and following the politicization of racial consciousness and increased black militancy in the late 1960s, the state sought to contain the movement for black equality through its policies towards funding black organizations and towards the appointment of commissions and through Royal Canadian Mounted Police surveillance of the black community.

This chapter discusses African-Canadian organizing and resistance in Halifax-Dartmouth, Montreal, and Toronto in the period from the 1940s to the early 1970s from a social movement perspective. These cities were chosen because they were the main urban centres of black settlement. Before the liberalization of Canada's immigration policy in 1967, which resulted in an influx of Africans and Caribbeans to Canada, particularly Montreal and Toronto, Nova Scotia had the largest black population in Canada; most of them were Canadian-born. For example, in 1961, the black population in Canada was 32,127. Of these, 37 per cent lived in Nova Scotia, 34.4 per cent lived in Ontario, and 13.3 per cent in Quebec (*Census of Canada* 1961). The following section draws on new social movement theory to explain the black social movement in the post–Second World War period.

Race and Social Movements

Social movements are a heterogeneous array of sociopolitical forms of activism against different oppressions such as racism, sexism, and militarism (Cohen 1983, Epstein 1990, Laclau and Mouffe 1985, Urry 1981). In contrast to orthodox Marxian theory, some writers on new social movements (Laclau and Mouffe 1985, Melucci 1989) argue that the transformation of advanced capitalist societies in more democratic and egalitarian directions is likely to emerge from a plurality of social struggles, with no central role relegated to the working class. They see movements as networks composed of fragmented groups based less on material interests and more on cultural transformation. Their focus on identity politics (for example, the positive re-articulation of social difference and collective subjectivity), distinguishes new social movements from pre–Second World War movements. New social movements theory also shifts the focus of struggle towards civil society. It argues that social power is not centrally located in the state or the economy but is exercised and resisted at every level of society.

Some new social movements writers (Mooers and Sears 1992, Omi and Winant 1983, Wood 1986) disagree with the view that the working class is not central to the struggles. They argue that new social movements theory ignores the relation between political economy and political praxis or between structure and culture. As Barbara Epstein (1990: 47–8) points out, although new social movements have been based mainly in middle-class constituencies, and it is unlikely that significant progressive social change could occur without substantial working-class involvement. Moreover, movements of people of colour consist largely of working-class people. Similarly, in emphasizing the particularistic, fragmentary character of many contemporary movements and their wariness to unify or to even construct a shared agenda, many new social movements theorists have tended to underestimate the extent to which these movements might share a universal vision organized around such themes as social justice and human rights (Offe 1985: 841–2). Kauffman (1990: 78) argues that the emphasis on identity politics with its attention to lifestyle and lack of collective organization could lead to an anti-politics of identity mirroring the ideology of the market place. She advocates an approach that balances 'concerns with identity with an emphasis on solidarity' and 'other key categories like interests and needs' (1990: 79).

Blacks' activities have not been solely an expression of working class struggle in the sense of labour's resistance to capital. But racism does interact with class exploitation. In respect to railway porters, for example, their struggle against the split labour market was directed against both capital and higher-paid white labour – a case in which race fragmented the working class. Other African-Canadian struggles were carried out by community-development organizations led mainly by the professional middle class, stable blue-collar workers, and students. In addition, some organizations – such as the National Black Coalition of Canada – in the

1970s comprehended the issues of struggle mainly in terms of race rather than class. More militant organizations in the early 1970s, on the other hand, such as students' organizations, the Afro-Canadian Liberation Movement, and the Toronto Chapter of the Afro-American Progressive Association, which were influenced by the Black Power Movement, analysed the problem of racial oppression in the context of capital, imperialism, and the international political economy (Douglas in Tullock 1975, O'Malley 1972).

In Canada, the black movement from the 1940s to 1970s aimed at eradicating barriers to full economic, political, and social equality (for example, in education, employment, and housing) to blacks. The Black Power Movement in the 1960s to 1970s also focused on identity politics emphasizing black identity and enhancing self-conception, for example, through black history and culture. The phrase 'Black Power' called for black economic and political power as well as a redefinition and reaffirmation of the black self at the centre of its politics (*Contrast*, 16 October 1970; Khan 1972; Ture and Hamilton 1992). Since racism was as much an issue of identity and culture as it was an issue of access to state institutions, or of discrimination in employment and social relations, the Black Power Movement questioned the legitimacy of the entire social order.

African-Canadians have always occupied a subordinate position in economic, political, and ideological relations. Historically, they migrated to Canada as enslaved people, refugees, fugitives, or as cheap labour to do mostly unskilled work (for example, as domestics, porters, and steelworkers). They provided a reserve army of labour employed in segregated and split labour markets where they were paid less than white workers for doing the same work (Calliste 1991, 1994; Winks 1971).

Moreover, such racism interacted with gender and class inequality. Racially constructed gender images portrayed black women as 'naturally' suited for jobs in the lowest stratum of a labour market segmented along gender lines. Before the late 1950s the only jobs available to most black women in Canada were in domestic work; for example, Harold Potter estimates that, in 1941, 80 per cent of black women in Montreal's labour force worked as domestics (Potter 1949: 29).

The educational system perpetuated and reproduced this inequality through segregated schools and a curriculum that bred negative stereotypes and low expectations for blacks. This resulted in a low self-concept of ability, negative racial identity, and low achievement. There was a low retention rate in high school, over-representation in general and vocational courses, and severe under-representation in higher education. Sea-ley estimated that in 1969, for example, only 3 per cent of black students in Nova Scotia graduated from high school and only 1 per cent of the graduates would attend university (Pratt 1972: 80). However, as blacks have resisted inequality, particularly since the late 1960s, there has been a growing dialectic between oppression and resistance.

Black Organizing and Resistance, 1940s to early 1960s

The national and international climate during the Second World War and in the postwar period was favourable to promoting racial equality. After a war to defend freedom and democracy against fascism and Nazism, blatant racism increasingly became untenable in the context of democracy. The emergence of new African nations made racial discrimination a diplomatic embarrassment, and the United Nations Charter firmly endorsed the rights of racial, ethnic, and religious minorities as a guiding principle of international society. Social change in Canada, including increased employment opportunities for blacks (because of the postwar industrial boom), gave them some political leverage. In addition, there was a heightened sense of racial pride which grew out of the war service of black Canadians, the movements for African independence, and the civil rights movement in the United States – factors which provided an important impetus for the struggle for racial equality in Canada. Most of the initiatives in this struggle came from blacks and their white allies, particularly in the Jewish community, which was experiencing anti-Semitism (Calliste 1991, 1995).

Changes in labour legislation protecting workers' right to organize (Woolmer 1951) gave black Canadian workers some further freedoms. For example, the Brotherhood of Sleeping Car Porters (BSCP) was certified to represent CPR porters in 1942 (Randolph 1942). In that same year, Velmer Coward (King), secretary-treasurer of the Montreal Division of the Ladies Auxiliary of the BSCP, asked A. Phillip Randolph, international president of the BSCP and a vice-president of the National Association for the Advancement of Colored People (NAACP), to assist blacks in Montreal to organize a chapter of the NAACP, particularly to combat racism in employment (Coward 1942, 1943). In 1944–5, Randolph assisted each CPR division of the BSCP in Montreal, Toronto, Winnipeg, Calgary, and Vancouver organize chapters of the Canadian League for the Advancement of Coloured People (CLACP) 'to fight for a civil rights bill, and provincial and federal Fair Employment Practices laws' (*Black Worker* 1945, Coward 1944). League members included blacks, other people of colour, and 'liberal' whites who were dedicated to the struggle for racial liberation.

The CLACP achieved some success. Individual blacks began to break the colour bar in employment. For example, in January 1947 the Vancouver division reported that through its efforts, a black chemical engineer, Mr D. Cromwell, became a member of the Junior Board of Trade. Similarly, a black woman obtained employment as a sales clerk in 'one of Vancouver's smartest and most fashionable dress shops' (*Black Worker* 1947).

Though the Montreal, Toronto, and Winnipeg chapters became defunct, the BSCP, particularly the CPR Toronto division, collaborated with other organizations (such as the Negro Citizenship Association) in the struggle for racial equality – for example, pressuring the federal government to liberalize its racialized, gendered, and class-biased immigration policy (*Black Worker* 1952, BSCP 1956). The Calgary and Vancouver chapters of the league were revitalized and renamed the Alberta and British Columbia Associations for the Advancement of Coloured People (AAACP and BCAACP), and similar organizations were formed in Nova Scotia and New Brunswick (NSAACP and NBAACP) in 1945 and 1959 respectively. With the support of such other black organizations as the African United Baptist Association (AUBA) and the Canadian Labour Committee for Human Rights, the NSAACP and NBAACP were at 'the forefront of the struggle to bring about comprehensive anti-discrimination legislation' in these provinces (NBAACP 1970: 4; see Wedderburn 1969). For example, the NSAACP played a prominent role in Viola Desmond's challenge to segregated sitting at the Roseland Theatre in New Glasgow, Nova Scotia. Desmond, a Halifax beautician, was arrested in 1946 for sitting on a downstairs seat instead of in the balcony seats to which blacks were relegated. Though the manager had rejected her offer to pay the difference in price because a downstairs seat was slightly more expensive, she was convicted for attempting to defraud the state of one cent in entertainment tax and sentenced to a fine of $20 plus costs or thirty days in prison. She paid the fine. The NSAACP organized public meetings and raised funds for an appeal which they lost on a legal technicality – failure to file notice within the required ten days. The judge did acknowledge, however, that a public statute had been misused to enforce a Jim Crow rule (Milner 1947, Pachai 1990).

In the 1950s and 1960s, through speeches, conferences, press statements, and representations to the state, the NSAACP sought to get more black history and literature included in the school curriculum. In 1965 it worked with the Nova Scotia Department of Education to establish both adult education classes in black communities and an Education Incentive Fund to encourage black students to continue their education beyond elementary school. The association sought to get more blacks employed and, through the collection of data on racism, made a strong case for such anti-discriminatory laws as a Fair Employment Practices Act and a Fair Accommodation Practices Act and for the creation of a Human Rights Commission (Hinds 1969, Wedderburn 1969, Pachai 1990). But despite these moderate successes, African–Nova Scotians remained marginalized in the economy, with high unemployment rates and severe under-representation in skilled and professional jobs (Oliver 1968, Walker 1981). This indicated the need for the community to be better organized and empowered to pressure the state for change.

In Toronto the Negro Citizenship Association (NCA), with the support of existing black organizations and the Toronto Labour Committee for Human Rights, challenged Canada's discriminatory immigration policy. They argued that a racialized immigration policy demonstrated the second-class status of blacks and was a structural barrier to integration. They held public meetings, invited Caribbean politicians visiting Canada to give public lectures, and demonstrated and sent petitions to Ottawa. A delegation presented a brief to Prime Minister Louis St Laurent in 1954 with explicit proposals for such policy reforms as equal treatment of applicants from the British Caribbean with other British subjects and opening an immigration office in the Caribbean (Moore 1985, NCA 1954). The NCA also assisted Caribbean immigrants in trouble, particularly those threatened with deportation, and facilitated the immigration of Caribbean blacks (for example, nurses and domestics) to Canada.[5]

In the 1950s and early 1960s blacks did not have the power to pressure the Canadian state to liberalize its immigration policy. The 'exceptional merit' clause[6] under which Caribbean female domestics and nurses were admitted to Canada indicated the racial, patriarchal, and class biases underlying Canadian policy. For example, immigration regulations stipulated that one of the conditions for admitting black nurses into the country was that the hospital administration which offered them employment had to be 'aware of their racial origin' (Acting Chief, Admissions 1956). Unlike white nurses, who were admitted to Canada as landed immigrants on the basis of their general admissibility, black nurses were admitted solely on the basis of their nursing qualifications, with only those who were eligible for registration with the provincial Registered Nurses Association given landed immigrant status; others were admitted as temporary migrant workers (Calliste 1993a, 1993b). Instead of liberalizing the immigration policy, the state admitted a small number of domestics and skilled workers such as nurses and stenographers to help fill the urgent labour demand. This minor concession in immigration policy was also intended to appease Caribbean people in Canada and the Caribbean in order to foster continued Canadian trade and investment in the region.

Blacks in Toronto and Montreal also were actively involved in the struggle for the enactment and enforcement of Fair Employment Practices and Fair Accommodation Practices acts in the 1950s. For example, as chairperson of Local 439 of the United Auto Workers–Congress of Industrial Organizations Fair Practices Committee and representative on the Toronto and District Labour Council, Bromley Armstrong visited restaurants to test for racial discrimination and collected hard evidence that led to the passage of Ontario's Fair Accommodation Practices (FAP) Act in 1954. Armstrong and Hugh Burnette, secretary of the National Unity Association – a black civil rights organization in Dresden, Ontario – were instrumental in desegregating restaurants in Dresden. After Ontario passed its FAP Act, they tested Dresden's restaurants, found that two refused to serve them, and filed complaints with the Department of Labour under the act. The Ontario Minister of Labour, Charles Daley, was reluctant to press charges against the restaurants' operators, claiming that 'communist-sponsored Negroes were behind the trouble in Dresden' (Toronto Labour Committee [TLC] 1955b: 7). The National Unity Association and the Toronto Joint Labour Committee for Human Rights, with the support of other organizations such as the BSCP, had to pressure Daley to charge the defendants, who were then convicted and fined $50 each plus costs (TLC 1955a: 1; 1956). These endeavours ultimately helped in the formation of the Ontario Human Rights Commission in 1960–1.

The Montreal Negro Citizenship Association's main objectives included pressuring the province to enact human rights legislation and establish a Human Rights Commission and providing education for blacks in such areas as black history and culture. In addition to collecting data on discrimination and presenting briefs to the state, they took up the struggle against racism in the taxi associations, and in 1964 were instrumental in effecting the hiring of black drivers in two of Montreal's largest taxi associations, Diamond and La Salle (NCA n.d., 1964). In 1965 the association raised funds to help Gloria Bayliss, a registered nurse from Barbados, hire a lawyer in a case against Hilton of Canada, operators of the Queen Elizabeth Hotel, for discrimination in hiring. Hilton was convicted and fined $25 and costs in 1966 (Gilliece 1965, *Montreal Gazette* 1976), the first conviction for racism in employment in Quebec and probably in Canada.

In sum, in the period from 1940 to 1967 black organizations and individuals in Halifax, Montreal, Toronto, and other urban centres across Canada collected evidence on racial discrimination in employment, education, housing, and public facilities. With the support of such mainstream organizations as churches and the National Labour Committee on Human Rights, they pressured local, provincial, and federal governments to enact and enforce anti-discriminatory legislation. They also exposed racism in school curricula – for example, use of the book *Little Black Sambo* – and demanded balanced curricula which would represent the lived experiences and contributions of people of African descent (Calliste 1994; *Contrast*, 19 December 1969).

Blacks' activism tended, however, to be politically ineffective. Its attacks on specific areas of complaint, rather than general attitudes, were not eliminating systemic racism (Walker 1981). Moreover, the weak anti-discriminatory laws were not very effective. In the late 1960s blacks realized that more militant organizing and broader strategies were needed to transform Canadian society.

Politicization of Racial Consciousness, 1968 to the early 1970s

The civil rights and Black Power movements in the United States had a tremendous impact on the mobilization of African-Canadians, increasing their militancy, political consciousness, and identity. Many black youths were members of the Student Non-violent Coordinating Committee (SNCC) which adopted the slogan 'Black Power' in 1966 and whose ideology and programs emphasized full equality and black self-determination and self-identity (Ture and Hamilton 1992). SNCC members in Canada organized black communities; for example, Burnley 'Rocky' Jones returned to Halifax from Toronto in 1965 to organize the black community politically (Burrows and Seese 1965; J. Jones, personal communication, 2 August 1994).

An important factor leading to a transformation in the politics of the black community was the influx of black immigrants to Toronto and Montreal after 1967. For example, in the period from 1963 to 1967, 23,316 Caribbean immigrants entered Canada compared with 86,981 from 1968 to 1973,[7] many of whom were skilled and professional (Canada, Department of Manpower and Immigration 1974, 34–5, 40–3). This significantly enlarged and diversified the leadership and membership base for political organization and made more salient the designation of racism as a collective black problem.[8]

In 1968, the international year of human rights, two conferences in Montreal – the Conference of Caribbean and Other Black Organizations and the Black Writers' Conference – and a visit to Halifax by Stokely Carmichael and a delegation of the Black Panther Party mobilized blacks in Canada towards a more acute awareness of their oppression. The Montreal conferences reflected an ideological shift between the moderate and militant university students who respectively organized them.[9]

The 1968 theme of the conference of Caribbean and Other Black Organizations, 'Problems of involvement in the Canadian society with special reference to the Black peoples of Canada,' indicated a decisive shift in focus from the 1965–7 theme, 'The Future of the Caribbean.' The conference program explained that the change in focus represented 'an awakening of the West Indian groups in Canada to the fact that whether they are here as students, domestics, or immigrants, their development is greatly affected by the fact that they live in [the] Canadian society' (Conference Committee 1968: 2).

Before the late 1960s many Caribbean students wanted to keep their social distance, at least publicly, from domestics; for example, Caribbean students at McGill wanted to ban domestics from attending their parties (Calliste 1991, Handelman 1964). Thus, the conference committee's acknowledgment of the oppression of all blacks regardless of class indicated a shift from previous students' biases against associating with domestics. The year 1968 also marked a radical departure in the administration of the conference. Montreal's black organizations formed the core of the organizing committee, and so the conference was directly responsible to the community rather than only the student group (Conference Committee 1968: 1–2).

The conference emphasized the need for equity in education and employment and for a national housing policy to eliminate housing discrimination. It argued that economic power was the only means to political power and called for the formation of a black national coordinating organization. This led to the founding of the National Black Coalition of Canada (NBCC), which included twenty-eight organizations by 1969 and whose objectives were ensuring structural integration of blacks in Canada, eradicating all forms of discrimination in Canadian society, developing self-identification through the inclusion of Black Studies in educational curricula, and fostering communication and co-operation with blacks of other nations in matters of common interest (such as Pan Africanism and the struggle against apartheid in South Africa) (Bayne 1969, States 1980).

The Black Writers' Conference, dedicated to the late Malcolm X and Martin Luther King, Jr, was the radicalizing agent for the black population in Montreal, particularly students. The conference emphasized the ideology of Black Power and Black Nationalism. The writers argued that Blacks in Canada were a colonized people who must seize independence partly through self-identification, self-determination, and economic self-sufficiency, and they called for power-sharing, equity, and a commitment to struggle for a non-racist society without 'class distinctions and privileges' (Forsythe 1971).

The writers did not, however, discuss patriarchy and the circumstances of black women (and may have assumed that the elimination of racism would result in black women's liberation). This is hardly surprising given the fact that the second wave of feminism had only just begun. Many black men still argue that racism is the major problem blacks experience in Canada and that any discussion of sexism in the community is divisive. However, some black feminists who have been active in women's organizations – for example, the Congress of Black Women of Canada – in the 1980s and 1990s were also activists in the 1960s and 1970s black liberation struggle. Apparently, the ideological focus and organizing of the latter activity helped prepare them for their role in the women's movement.

The Black Writers' Conference had two immediate significant effects in Canada. First, Carmichael and a delegation of the Black Panther Party visited Halifax and had a tremendous impact on increasing African–Nova Scotian militancy, political consciousness, and identity, a process which had begun with Halifax's destruction of the community of Africville. In the period 1964 to 1968 residents of Africville were cajoled into relocating as part of urban renewal. They were compensated inadequately for their property, many of them moved into public housing in Halifax and some who bought houses lost them through foreclosure (Africville Genealogical Society 1992, Clairmont and Magill 1987, Wedderburn 1970).

The second effect of the Black Writers' Conference was a students' illegal sit-in at the computer centre of Sir George Williams University in February 1969 to protest a long-smouldering case of alleged racism by a white professor. Subsequent confrontation between the students and an armed Montreal riot squad resulted in the arrest of ninety-six students, forty-five of whom were black. Three of the black students were sentenced to prison terms, and one was also ordered deported (Eber 1969, Forsythe

1971). This situation increased student militancy and heightened social awareness and sensitivity in the black community.

In Halifax the Panthers emphasized the necessity of organizing a militant black association and established communication with younger, more militant black leaders such as Burnley 'Rocky' Jones. The black community was polarized over the value of the 'American strategies.' Some blacks, suspicious of the Panthers' visit, rejected both their assessments of the Nova Scotian situation and of violent and segregationist black politics as appropriate solutions to Canadian racism. However, some young militant blacks agreed with the Panthers' analysis and felt they would heighten blacks' awareness of their common problems (Hinds 1969; *Chronicle Herald*, 6 December 1968). The visits did convey a sense of strength and universality to the Nova Scotian struggle and stimulated an ameliorative governmental response to blacks' economic marginality (Clairmont and Magill 1970).

The formation of two black organizations in Nova Scotia, the moderate Black United Front (BUF) and militant Afro-Canadian Liberation Movement (ACLM) in 1969, reflected the polarization of the community. BUF and ACLM called on blacks in Nova Scotia to unite in creating a black identity in combating racism and in community development. However, the now-defunct ACLM also cried for 'freedom now' and wanted the 'elimination of all forms of racial oppression, social and economic injustices against Black People ... by whatever means' (*Aclam*, 1 March 1969: 4).

BUF's dependence on state funding provided the Canadian state with the opportunity to influence the direction of the black struggle. In 1969 the federal government assured BUF funding of $515,000 over a five-year period, ostensibly trying to alleviate 'deplorable conditions' in Preston, Nova Scotia. However, it also ensured that moderates such as Reverend William Oliver, rather than militants, remained in charge of the organization. A memorandum to Cabinet from the Cabinet Committee on Social Policy and Cultural Affairs had stated in June 1969: 'There was a possibility of violence in the black community of Nova Scotia and a possible disruption of the Canadian Games this summer by black militants. A grant now might alleviate this situation. Absence of support might enable black militants to take over the moderates now in charge of the Black United Front' (*Mail Star*, 18 June 1969, quoted in Pachai 1990: 252). Thus, the state used funding of BUF as a form of social control.

Nova Scotia also contained the black community by creating, in December 1968, the Human Rights Commission. Some blacks described the Commission as 'tokenism,' particularly since its first coordinator was a white journalist and social worker from Ontario (*Globe and Mail*, 9 December 1968). Thus, the state helped to encourage the demise of black protests and allayed Nova Scotians' fear of social unrest through funding and the creation of the commission. This was followed in 1971 by multicultural programs to promote the cultural activities of different ethnic groups, and by RCMP surveillance of 'black activists' (Conrad 1968; *Chronicle Herald*, 5 December 1968; Moore 1980; Wedderburn 1969). The RCMP credited BUF and the Human Rights Commission as important agents in maintaining 'social and civil stability' and suggested that the federal and provincial governments give them more support. In 1974 the RCMP stated that BUF's dedication to solving regional problems (such as providing legal assistance in cases of arrest and property conflict) as well as its social and sports programs 'have been markedly successful in giving Black activism legitimate forward movement, and in the process, has served as a buffer between the White establishment and Black militants. Similarly, the presence of the Human Rights Commission has ... infused a more positive outlook in the Blacks with respect to them being able to be in control of their own human condition' (RCMP 1974).

The youth groups' militant ideology and innovative activities left an indelible mark on black organizational structures and on the orientation of anti-racist activities of the black community. Given the publicity of the youth groups' activities, the moderate leaders in BUF, NBCC, and NSAACP were pressured to become more politically forceful. For example, after refusing to discuss the Sir George Williams computer affair at the NBCC founding conference in 1969, the organization's leadership made an announcement on television in 1971 condemning the manner in which the trial of Black students had been conducted (*Contrast*, 17 March 1971). Similarly the youths' militancy forced the NSAACP's presentation to the premier on 25 October 1968 to emphasize the need for change (Conrad 1968).

Black students and youth organizations decided to attack racism by mobilizing support for Pan-African and anti-imperialist movements in the Third World and by developing within Canada tightly knit, black-consciousness organizations working for economic and cultural self-sufficiency. They said that they wanted to develop 'a revolutionary concept to replace the attitude of those who expect change to come from Ottawa' (*Contrast*, 14 February 1971). As Roosevelt Douglas put it, 'Our only salvation is to work collectively towards building co-operative institutions within our community controlled democratically by ourselves. Through them we can harness and develop our resources, escalate our support to liberation movements in Southern Africa and the Caribbean, work towards meaningful revolutionary Pan African unification and identify functionally with the global movement against imperialism' (Douglas in Tullock 1975: 140).

Black students and youths organized self-help associations such as the Black Education Project (BEP) in Toronto and adopted a policy of striving to be self-supporting and not applying for state funding (*Contrast*, 27 May 1972). BEP focused on teaching black cultural heritage to black children and youth and providing them with tutorial assistance in regular academic subjects. It also was involved in more direct political organizing – for example, in calling community meetings to address such issues as police-community relations, the activity of the neo-Nazi Western Guard, and African liberation struggles (BEP 1976, Mercer 1977).

The relative poverty of the black community, however, and the growing intervention of the state in funding organizations in the early 1970s militated against the continuation of self-support militant black organizations by side-tracking their energies and stifling protest. Most of the state's criteria were incompatible with the organizations' goals because the former involved supporting the status quo. The state's emphasis on cultural programs or multiculturalism served to control the movement and steered blacks away from economic and political power (see Loney 1977, Peter 1984, Stasuilis 1982). Dependence on state funding led to the demise of some black militant organizations such as BEP in 1978–9 when the federal government reduced spending on social and community-oriented projects during economic recession.

Conclusion

This study on urban blacks' activities to organize and to resist racism in Canada in the 1940s to early 1970s has for the most part supported the new social movements perspective. Some blacks organized and mobilized their economic and political power resources in order to eliminate racism in state institutions, the economy, and civil society, and they focused on material interests, needs, black identity, and solidarity. Some black struggles were carried out by community-development organizations led mainly by the middle class, blue-collar workers and students. From the 1940s to 1967 black anti-racist struggles were aimed at reforms to ameliorate blacks' social and economic conditions. In 1968 to the early 1970s black communities were polarized between some older and middle-class members who wanted liberal reforms and student activists who wanted societal transformation and power-sharing. However, the status quo resisted blacks' demand for institutional transformation at the height of black protests. The state co-opted and regulated the Black Power movement in multiple ways: through the appointment of the Nova Scotia Human Rights Commission, increased police surveillance, an appeasement policy of multiculturalism, by funding some black organizations, and by employing some of its leaders. Given the current emphasis on anti-racism organizing and resistance, further research is needed on blacks' contemporary anti-racist struggles.

NOTES

1 Funding from the Social Sciences and Humanities Research Council and the University Council for Research, St Francis Xavier University, is gratefully acknowledged. The author would like to thank the two anonymous reviewers and the editors for their helpful comments and Debbie Murphy for typing this manuscript.

2 In the 1940s and 1950s most porters were black (Calliste 1987; *Winnipeg Tribune*, 4 January 1969).

3 The Canada Fair Employment Act in 1953 prohibited racial and religious discrimination in employment and membership in trade unions (Canada 1953: 27–9).

4 Blacks in Nova Scotia are poorer than in other parts of Canada partly because they reside in a low-income region and partly because of more intense racism due in part to the greater competition for jobs, particularly in the high-wage, monopoly sector of the economy (Shadd 1987).

5 The Negro Citizenship Association has been criticized as being supportive of the Caribbean Domestic Scheme and thus the oppression of black women (Harris 1988). Under the scheme, which began in 1955, an annual quota of Caribbean women were recruited to work as domestics. These women were expected to have at least Grade 8 education, to be young, of good character, single, and without children. They were admitted as landed immigrants, and were required to work as domestics for one year. The domestic scheme provided almost the only opportunity for many black women to enter Canada, and some of the women who came were civil servants, nurses, and teachers. Some blacks criticized the scheme as a form of indentured labour in which Caribbean domestics were expected to work harder at much less pay than their Canadian and European counterparts (Calliste 1991). The NCA encouraged the scheme as part of its practice of using all the opportunities which were available at the time to get Caribbean blacks admitted to Canada. For example,

Donald Moore, the NCA president, made representations to the Immigration Department to admit Caribbean men and female nurses and encouraged hospitals in Ontario and Quebec to employ Caribbean nurses (Calliste 1993a, Moore 1985). And so another view is that the NCA was justified in supporting the scheme which many Caribbean women used to enter Canada in order to improve their economic and social position.

6 The term 'cases of exceptional merit' was defined as Caribbean immigrants who were admitted on humanitarian grounds or by executive direction (for example, the domestic scheme) or in the public interest (that is, those who would 'contribute appreciably to the social, economic or cultural life of Canada') (Smith 1954).

7 The data on Caribbean immigrants are underestimated given they do not include those who came to Canada from England.

8 The black community in Canada is diverse in terms of national and ethnic origins, social class, language, and religion. Disunity in the black movement based on social class, age, and ideological differences was evident (*Chronicle Herald*, 6 December 1968; Douglas in Tullock 1975). Undoubtedly, the diversity in national origins had implications for black unity. For example, at the national black Symposium in Windsor in 1977, Burnley 'Rocky' Jones, an indigenous Black Canadian, argued that Caribbeans were dominating the NBCC and were neglecting the needs and concerns of indigenous black Canadians.

9 In 1965–7 a group of Caribbean students in Montreal and Ottawa organized an annual conference on Caribbean political and social development. There was a political split between the moderates and militants within the organizing committee in 1967. The moderate wing organized the conference of Caribbean and Other Black Organizations in 1968 and the militant wing initiated the Black Writers' Conference (Douglas in Tullock 1975: 136).

REFERENCES

Aclam. 1969. 1(1), 4. Public Archives of Canada (PAC), Jewish Labour Committee Papers, MG28, V75, vol. 1, file 1, March

Acting Chief, Admissions. 1956. Memo to the Acting Director, Immigration. PAC, Immigration Branch Records, RG76, Vol. 847, File 553–110, 9 May

Africville Genealogical Society. 1992. *The Spirit of Africville.* Halifax: Formac Publishing

Bayne, C. 1969. 'A report on the Canadian Conference of Black Organizations.' *Umoja* 1(1), 30 Oct.

BEP. 1976. *The Black Education Project, 1969–1976.* Mimeo

'Blacks need better deal 1970.' *Contrast,* 15–30 Nov.

Blum, S. 1961. 'Inquiry into charges of racial discrimination against the CBRT by Mr Lee Williams, Chairman, Local 130, CBRT.' PAC, Jewish Labour Committee Papers, MG28, V75, vol. 34

Bonacich, E. 1972. 'A theory of ethnic antagonism: The split labor market.' *American Sociological Review* 37: 547–59

– 1976. 'Advanced capitalism and black/white relations in the United States.' *American Sociological Review* 41: 34–51

Bruner, A. 1979. 'The genesis of Ontario Human Rights Legislation.' *University of Toronto Faculty of Law Review* 37(2): 234–55

BSCP, Toronto CPR Division. 1956. Resolutions to the First Constitutional Convention of the CLC. Library of Congress (LC), BSCP Papers, box 104, 23 April

BSCP, Vancouver Division. 1947. *The Black Worker*, Jan.

Burrows, D., and L. Seese, 1965. Letter to SNCC friends, 10 June

Calliste, A. 1987. 'Sleeping car porters in Canada.' *Canadian Ethnic Studies* 19(1): 1–20

– 1988. 'Blacks on Canadian railways.' *Canadian Ethnic Studies* 29(2): 36–52

– 1991. 'Canada's immigration policy and domestics from the Caribbean.' *Socialist Studies* 5: 136–68

– 1993a. 'Women of "exceptional merit."' *Canadian Journal of Women and the Law* 6(1): 85–102

– 1993b. 'Race, gender and Canadian immigration policy.' *Journal of Canadian Studies* 28(4): 131–48

– 1994. 'Blacks' struggle for education equity in Nova Scotia.' In V. D'Oyley, ed., *Black Innovations in Education*, 25–40. Toronto: Umbrella Press

– 1995. 'Struggle for employment equity by blacks on American and Canadian railroads.' *Journal of Black Studies* 26(3): 297–317

Canada. 1953. *Prefix to Statutes 1952–53*. Ottawa: Queen's Printer, 27–9

Canada, Department of Manpower and Immigration. 1974. *Canadian Immigration and Population Study*, Vol. 3. Ottawa

Canada, House of Commons. 1953. *Debates*, 13 April

'Canadian blacks fight for civil rights.' 1945. *The Black Worker*

'CNR porters to battle racial discrimination.' 1962. *Winnipeg Tribune*, 4 Jan.

Census of Canada. 1961. Catalogue 92–545, vol. 1, part 2

'City negro veterans' association.' 1947. *Campus*. Toronto: University of Toronto, 10 Oct.

Clairmont, D., and D. Magill, 1970. *Nova Scotian Blacks*. Halifax: Institute of Public Affairs, Dalhousie University

– 1987. *Africville*. Toronto: Scholars' Press

Cohen, J. 1983. *Class and Civil Society*. Oxford: Martin Robertson

Conference Committee. 1968. *Program*. Montreal

Congress of Black Women of Canada, Preston Chapter. 1991. *First Annual Celebration for Black Women who have made a Difference.* Dartmouth: n.p.
Conrad, D. 1968. 'The negro in Nova Scotia.' *Globe and Mail*, 9 Dec., 7
Coward, V. 1942. Letter to A.P. Randolph. LC, BSCP Papers, box 73, 23 Nov.
– 1943. Letter to A.P. Randolph. BSCP Papers, box 73, 5 March
– 1944. Letter to A.P. Randolph. LC, BSCP Papers, box 73, 27 Sept.
Davis, M., and J. Krauter. 1971. *The Other Canadians*, 42. Toronto: Methuen.
Eber, D. 1969. *Canada Meets Black Power.* Montreal: Tundra Books
Emply, C. N.d. *Remedial Education Project Threatened.* Toronto: Mimeo
Epstein, B. 1990. 'Rethinking social movement theory.' *Socialist Review* 20(1): 35–65
Forsythe, D., ed. 1971. *Let the Niggers Burn!* Montreal: Black Rose Books
Gilliece, R. 1965. 'Charge of discrimination presented.' *Montreal Gazette*, 13 April
Handelman, D. 1964. 'West Indian Associations in Montreal.' MA thesis, McGill University
Harris, R. 1988. 'The transformation of Canadian policies and programs to recruit foreign Labour.' PhD dissertation, Michigan State University
Hill, D.G., and M. Schiff. 1985. *Human Rights in Canada*, 2nd ed. Ottawa: Canadian Labor Congress and the Human Rights Research and Education Centre, University of Ottawa
Hinds, B. 1969. 'Black power.' *Atlantic Advocate*, Jan., 9–15
'Immigration by discrimination.' 1952. *The Black Worker*, March, 1
'In search of a sense of community.' 1970. *Time*, April
Kauffman, L.A. 1990. 'The anti-politics of identity.' *Socialist Review* 20(1): 67–80
Khan, I. 1972. 'Look at black power and white racism.' *Contrast*, 1 May
Laclau, E., and C. Mouffe, 1985. *Hegemony and Socialist Strategy.* London: Verso
'Law leaves discrimination fighters in limbo.' 1976. *Montreal Gazette*, 13 April
Lee, P. 1991. 'Entire community must shoulder blame – leaders.' *Chronicle Herald*, 20 July
Loney, M. 1977. 'A political economy of citizen participation.' In L. Panitch, ed., *The Canadian State*, 446–72. Toronto: University of Toronto Press
Magnus, D. 1961. 'Negro porter calls CLC rights report a union whitewash.' *Winnipeg Free Press*, 25 Sept.
Melucci, A. 1980. 'The new social movements.' *Social Science Information* 19(2): 199–226
Mercer, E. 1977. 'Black education project.' In Urban Alliance on Race Relations, ed. *Readings in Community Involvement.* Toronto: Urban Alliance on Race Relations
Milner, J.B. 1947. 'Civil liberties.' *Canadian Bar Review* 25(8): 915–24, Oct.
Mooers, C., and A. Sears. 1992. 'The "new social movements" and the withering

away of state theory.' In W. Carroll, ed., *Organizing Dissent*, 52–68. Toronto: Garamond Press

Moore, D. 1985. *Don Moore.* Toronto: Williams-Wallace

NBAACP. 1970. 'Report to City Council of Saint John, 4.' PAC, Daniel G. Hill's Papers, MG31, H155, vol. 18

'NBAACP protests discrimination.' 1964. *Saint John Evening Times*, 12 May

'NBC (National Black Coalition): After the big conference in Montreal. 1970. *Contrast*, 11 Oct., 16

NCA, Toronto. 1954. Brief Presented to the Prime Minister. PAC, RG76, vol. 839, file 552–1–644, 27 April

– 1955. Resolution to the Canadian State and the Press. PAC, RG76, vol. 830, file 552–1–644, 13 Feb.

NCA, Montreal. N.d. *Objectives and Achievements.*

– 1964. *Secretary's Report*, 13 Jan.

'Negro defence fund started.' 1968. *Chronicle Herald*, 5 Dec., 6

Newman, L. 1978. 'Profile of a black Canadian organization.' PAC, Wilson Head's Papers, MG31, D148, vol. 4

Nicoll, C. 1991. 'Violence flares for second night.' *Daily News*, 20 July

NSAG – Nova Scotia Advisory Group on Race Relations. 1991. *Report.* Halifax, 1 Sept.

'N.S. premier accused of tokenism in negro rights bill.' 1968. *Globe and Mail*, 9 Dec.

Offe, C. 1985. 'New social movements.' *Social Research* 52(4): 817–68

Oliver, J. 1968. *Final Report on the Problem of Unemployment for the Negro.* Halifax: Negro Employment Interim Committee

O'Malley, M. 1972. 'Blacks in Toronto.' In W.E. Mann, ed., *The Underside of Toronto*, 136. Toronto: McClelland and Stewart

Omi, M., and H. Winant 1983. 'By the Rivers of Babylon: Part one.' *Socialist Review* 13(5): 31–65

Pachai, B. 1990. *Beneath the Clouds of the Promised Land.* Halifax: Black Educators Association

Peter, K. 1984. 'The myth of multiculturalism and other political fables.' In J. Dahlie and T. Fernando, eds., *Ethnicity, Power and Politics in Canada*, 56–67. Toronto: Methuen

Poronovich, W. 1968. 'Blacks agree Canadians hypocritical.' *Montreal Star*, 7 Oct.

Potter, H. 1949. 'The occupational adjustment of Montreal Negroes.' MA thesis, McGill University

Pratt, S. 1972. 'Black education in Nova Scotia.' MA thesis, Dalhousie University

'Progress not violence negro aim.' 1968. *Chronicle Herald*, 6 Dec., 17

'Racial violence planned for Canada?' 1968. *The Canadian Intelligence Service*, April

'Racism inherent in our educational system.' 1969. *Contrast*, 19 Dec., 5

Randolph, A.P. 1942. Letter to H. Brydon-Jack. LC, BSCP Papers, box 37, 24 Nov.

RCMP. 1974. *General Conditions and Subversive Activities among Negroes*, 23 Oct.

Roscigno, V. 1994. 'Social movement struggle and race, gender, class inequality.' *Race, Sex & Class* 2(1): 109–26

Ruchames, R. 1953. *Race, Jobs, and Politics*. New York: Columbia University Press

Shadd, A. 1987. 'Dual labour markets in "core" and "periphery" regions of Canada.' *Canadian Ethnic Studies* 19(2): 91–109

Sitkoff, H. 1981. *The Struggle for Black Equality 1954–1980*. New York: Hill and Wang

Smith, C. 1954. Memorandum to the Director of Immigration. PAC, RG 26, vol. 123, file 3–32–24, 26 May

Stasuilis, D. 1982. 'Race, Ethnicity and the State.' Ph.D. dissertation, University of Toronto

States, R. 1980. NBCC. PAC, Dorothy Wills' Papers, MG31, H179, vol. 13

Toronto Board of Education. 1987. *Draft Report of the Consultative Committee on the Education of Black Students in Toronto Schools*

TLC. 1955a. 'Report of activities.' (p. 1). PAC, MG28, I173, vol. 1

– 1995b. 'Report of activities.' (p. 7). *PAC*, MG28, I173, vol. 1

– 1956. 'Report of activities.' PAC, MG28, I173, vol. 1

Tullock, H. 1975. *Black Canadians*, 136. Toronto: N.C. Press

Ture, K., and C. Hamilton, 1992. *Black Power*. New York: Vintage

Urry, J. 1981. *The Anatomy of Capitalist Societies*. London: Macmillan

Vancouver Division. 1947. *The Black Worker*, Jan.

'Violence not the answer.' 1968. *Chronicle Herald*, 6 Dec., 16

Walker, J. 1976. *The Black Loyalists*. Halifax: Dalhousie University Press

– 1981. *A History of Blacks in Canada*. Ottawa: Ministry of State-Multiculturalism

Wedderburn, H.A.J. 1969. Letter to D. Orlikow. PAC, MG28, V75, vol. 41, file 1.

– 1970. 'A report of Halifax City.' *PAC*, MG28, V75, vol. 41, file 1, 14 April

Winks, R. 1971. *Blacks in Canada*. Montreal: McGill-Queen's University Press

Wood, E. 1986. *The Retreat from Class*. London: Verso

Woolmer, L. 1951. 'Fifty years of labour legislation in Canada.' *Labour Gazette* 50: 1412–29, 1432–59, Sept.

14

Challenging Spatial Control of the City: Capitalism, Ecological Crisis, and the Environmental Movement

FRANZ HARTMANN

Canadians at present face two realities. First, more people than ever before live in cities (Ley and Bourne 1993: 5), and the development of these cities seems dependent on escalating environmental destruction (Roseland 1992: 22–3). Second, since 1989 a majority of Canadians have said they are very concerned about environmental issues (Gallup 1994); the environmental – or green – movement may have anywhere between one to two million members (Wilson 1992: 111), most of whom live in cities.[1]

This chapter addresses two questions that arise from these realities and are of interest to people concerned with understanding the future of cities and the forces that will shape their future: why does urbanization seem so environmentally destructive, and what impact might urban-based environmentalists have on the contemporary city? Regarding the first question, the chapter argues that the cause of environmental degradation is not the city itself but rather a system of domination that is organized to facilitate capitalism and that leads to the specific spatial form of the capitalist city. Regarding the second, it argues that the environmental movement has the potential to challenge the reproduction of the capitalist city and transform it; this is illustrated by looking at two specific campaigns of urban environmental groups.

Urban Form and the Ecological Crisis

To explore the complex relationship between urban form and environmental degradation, we must first define the meaning of the latter term; for most people, it connotes degradation of the 'natural' environment. There is much debate about what constitutes the natural environment

(Harvey 1993, Castree 1995, Dickens 1992, Haraway 1991, Hartmann 1994). If 'nature' means those areas and life forms unaffected by human beings, then there is no such thing as the natural environment; even the most remote ecosystems on earth have been affected by humans (Smith 1984). Another approach is to think of the natural environment as something produced by the relationships among people and 'nature'; from this perspective, we can say that the natural environment arises from the interaction among all life forms on earth – including people – in combination with such forces as climate, hydrological cycles, and geological forces, and with the physical manifestations of these relations (such as rocks, soil ecosystems, and so on). Accordingly, environmental degradation means impairing the reproduction of the relationships among the organisms and non-organic forms and forces that constitute the natural environment.[2] Ensuring the reproduction of these relationships is one way of defining 'sustainability.'[3]

With this understanding of the natural environment, environmental degradation, and sustainability, we can turn to the issue of whether cities cause environmental degradation. The first response may be that cities cannot help but cause environmental degradation because they destroy natural habitats and displace other organisms in order to accommodate large numbers of people. Put differently, high population density – one element of Louis Wirth's definition of 'urban' (1938) – must necessarily cause environmental degradation. This Malthusian response has much intuitive appeal, but it is problematic on various counts. First, it suggests that all high-density spatial patterns have a negative impact on the natural environment. Yet, although many pre-industrial towns did harm ecosystems, their effects were generally localized in comparison with contemporary cities, whose impacts are sometimes global (Simmons 1989: 185). Moreover, as Hough notes (1984: 10), many pre-industrial, high-density towns had no significant harmful effect on the environment. Another problem with the Malthusian response is that major environmental degradation often occurs in non-urban areas for reasons unrelated to simple population density; for example, the destruction of forests and the contamination of water bodies and coastal areas are often the consequence of such economic motives as profit-seeking. This suggests that one cannot blame high-density spatial forms in themselves for serious environmental degradation – that to understand the degradation linked to contemporary cities we should look to factors other than density.

If only certain types of high-density spatial forms are responsible for environmental degradation, this raises the question of what types these are, an issue which points us in the direction of understanding the forces that shape cities. There are a number of approaches to this topic. My own, which will inform this chapter, is most akin to radical political economy (Soja 1989, Harvey 1993, Gottdiener 1985), an understanding of urban forms that begins with the insight that built environments are not ahistorical but products of the societies they help constitute. This perspective, which radical political economy shares with a number of other approaches, views societies as the product of myriad relationships both among people and between people and their natural environment; as these relationships change, so will society and its spatial forms. What distinguishes radical political economy is its view that the most effective way of analysing different types of societies and their spatial forms is in terms of their modes of economic production. Thus, the capitalist cities that dominate Canadian society are viewed as different from mercantilist cities, which are different from communist cities, and so on. Each of these kinds of cities is the product of a society with a distinct mode of production.

For student readers, a brief sketch of a key aspect of the nature of the capitalist mode of production may be useful. One characteristic of capitalist cities is that economic activity is controlled and organized by a class of people who predominantly own the businesses, materials, and land required for the production of goods and services. By returning to workers only a portion of the value they actually produce, the capital-owning class makes a profit. Its goal is to accumulate as much profit as possible, and to facilitate this, it has developed an urban form that promotes accumulation through, for example, shopping malls, commercial real estate markets, and the production of single-family homes. Meanwhile, people who are not part of the capitalist class seek to secure a decent wage that will allow them to have sound housing, the necessities of daily life, and a place in the community. Their interests often collide with those of capital leading to conflicts that materialize in such forms as labour strikes, opposition to property developments that threaten people's communities, and other kinds of political struggles. Radical political economy views the city as first and foremost the outcome of the activities of, and conflicts between, the different social classes.

To be sure, this perspective does not view other realms of social life apart from social class as unimportant in shaping urban forms. For example, gender relations also influence the production of urban space (Rose 1993, Peake 1993); an ideology of domesticity that promotes the view that a woman's place is at home while a man's is at work helps create particular and patriarchal community forms, such as the suburban subdivision (MacKenzie and Rose 1983, Fishman 1987). Or race relations may influence the creation of urban forms; for example, race has been found to have a key impact on women's mobility and, hence, their influence on the production of space (Peake 1993: 425). Likewise, subculture – among, say, urban 'ethnic' communities or within the gay community – may also affect urban form, as do political institutions (see note 4), religious beliefs, and activity in other realms of social life. But while cities are a consequence of multiple interacting forces, political economists argue that the most influential are the mode of production and social class.

Before turning to the relationship between capitalism and Canada's environmental crisis, two further points need to be made about urban space and how it is produced. The first is to take account of the social role of space. Space is a concept that describes one element of the physical relationships among all matter: the distance between and the relative location of objects, which are reckoned in such units of measurement as kilometres or in such less precise language as 'far,' 'close,' or 'next to.' Space is not 'out there' but is part of the relationships of everything physical. In social science, an increasing number of theorists argue that people are affected by the space they produce – that space and spatial relations not only arise from, but also influence, the social relations that create them; Edward Soja refers to this as the socio-spatial dialectic (1989: 76–93). The spaces we construct act back on us (sometimes in ways that are totally unexpected; see Massey 1992: 84), and for this reason, space – or more specifically the control of space and its production – is an important force in society's everyday life and ongoing reproduction.

Henri Lefebvre was among the first theorists to realize the importance of space in this context. He argued that when we consider space in relation to the conflicts in which social groups engage, we see that social struggle is also spatial struggle; particular groups seek to control space and produce spatial relations that help them reproduce. Gottdiener (1985) succinctly explains how Lefebvre applied this insight to an understanding of the reproduction of capitalist social relations. The capitalist class controls and (re)produces certain types of spaces that allow capital accumulation to occur; this involves both ownership of land and also control of the built environment and the activities that occur there. For example, without large shopping malls and other retail 'spaces,' it would be difficult for corporate capital to sell its products and realize an acceptable profit.[4]

In sum, spatial relations are vital to the dynamics of urban areas. They not only reflect various social forces at play in the city but also help reproduce and alter these social forces. For this reason, understanding spatial processes is vital in theorizing and transforming the city.

A second point combines the above insight with the earlier discussion about the natural environment. In considering the production of space we must look to both ecological and social forces (Hartmann 1994). Just as people create social space, the relations that constitute the natural environment – ecological forces – create ecological space; that is, they create spatial relations which become concretized in the physical environment. However, these ecological forces and spaces are never separate from nor unaffected by social relations. Similarly, social forces and spaces are never separate from nor unaffected by ecological relations; the two kinds of forces always permeate each other. In this way, human spatial production is the outcome of both ecological and social forces. For example, a building in the city is shaped partly by social forces, such as architectural taste and the owner's desire to maximize profit, and partly by such ecological forces as topography and climate. This means that understanding urban form requires taking ecological forces into account – the spaces they produce and the impact that they have on urban social space.

As we will see below, the ideas outlined here better allow us to explore linkages between contemporary spatial forms and environmental degradation. They suggest that the answer to why contemporary cities cause environmental degradation lies in social forces interacting with ecological forces. In keeping with the political economy approach, the focus is on class forces and the impact they have on spatial forms.

Capitalism and the Ecological Crisis

Much work has been done in the past decade in trying to understand the relationship between capitalism and ecology. Most of this work focuses on the extent to which current economic and political practices contribute to environmental degradation, and the main point of contention centres on how significantly our political and economic practices need to be altered in order to stop environmental degradation. Some argue that a private sector economy, based on profit and competition in a 'free' market is the best approach (D'Aquino 1992). They argue that all that needs to be done is to incorporate environmental costs into economic equations, creating what is sometimes termed 'green capitalism.' Others argue that not only is capitalism the main cause of environmental degradation but that the logic of capital necessitates environmental degradation

(O'Connor 1988). The latter approach, generally termed eco-Marxism or eco-socialism, is the perspective of this chapter.

The eco-socialist analysis of capitalism can be broadly summarized by what James O'Connor (1988) calls the second contradiction of capitalism: the tendency of capitalist forces and relations of production to destroy the conditions necessary for ecological (re)production.[5] This destruction occurs in at least three related ways.

First, in a capitalist economy, production is organized by owners of capital primarily to realize ever greater profit. This is accomplished by the circulation of capital, which requires constant increases in production and consumption. From an ecological perspective, this need for constant growth, driven by profit, leads to ever-increasing resource use and pollution.[6] Whenever something is made and consumed, resources are used, energy is consumed, and pollution is created; the faster the rate of production and consumption, the more the environmental disruption that occurs.

This drive for accumulation – at the heart of capitalism – eventually leads to ecological crisis and consequently to human crisis. Ecological space is vital to human reproduction; we depend, for example, on the continuation of existing species, on certain types of climatic conditions, and on particular geological forces to create ecological conditions that enable us to survive. But capital accumulation increasingly disrupts these ecological spaces and the ecological forces that create them through its need for an ever-increasing supply of resources and from the pollution that results from production and consumption.[7] Over time, the ecological relations necessary for human reproduction – as well as for further capital accumulation – are destroyed.

To illustrate this point, let us look at a green-capitalist initiative. In response to depletion of the ozone layer, a disposable cup manufacturer in Canada stopped using the chemical CFC in making styrofoam cups. This change has not only reduced the amount of CFC entering the atmosphere but has also saved the manufacturer money. On the surface, this suggests capital accumulation can occur without disrupting or destroying ecological forces and space; but, in reality, all the cup manufacturer did was moderate an increasing rate of environmental disruption. The manufacturing and consumption of a styrofoam cup has many negative environmental consequences; a partial list includes resource depletion of fossil fuels for energy and for materials used to make the cup, habitat destruction when extracting fossil fuels, reliance on a polluting chemical industry to produce synthetic materials to be turned into styrofoam, and pollution created from waste produced during the manufacture and after the use of the cup.

For the cup manufacturer to remain a viable corporation, it must make and sell an increasing number of disposable styrofoam cups; and so while the manufacturer is no longer contributing to ozone layer depletion, the very nature of disposable styrofoam cups and the drive for accumulation necessitate increasing ecological disruption. The only way to stop this disruption would be to produce durable cups – which are not discarded after a single use – with renewable resources. But this alternative would soon bankrupt the cup manufacturer by, among other things, removing demand for its product. This example illustrates how capital accumulation – even under an ideal 'green' scenario – damages ecological space; profit from pollution prevention only moderates the increase in environmental degradation, while keeping intact the accumulation logic that necessitates increasing environmental degradation.[8]

A second aspect of how capitalist production destroys the conditions necessary for ecological reproduction is through the commodification process. For capital accumulation to occur, natural resources must be assigned a money value and turned into commodities; this allows them to be traded like other commodities, such as labour, for money. Once this commodification occurs, natural resources can be used to accumulate capital.

Believers in green capitalism see commodification as the means by which to divert the ecological crisis. They argue that the reason capitalism created environmental problems in the first place was that no money value (or too low a value) was assigned to 'nature' – that we need to figure this 'cost' into the production of goods. But while this idea of commodifying ecological resources seems initially attractive, it is full of problems. For example, how does one put a real price to a natural resource? A 500-year-old redwood tree has a 'price,' but it reflects market forces, not the ecological labour that went into producing the tree nor the non-monetary value the tree has to other living species. In other words, the commodification of natural resources is a product of social forces that are primarily concerned with accumulation, not with the non-economic needs of human beings or the reproduction needs of other living species. The commodification process represents acceptance of and entrance into capitalist production practices and social relations because it means the natural resource becomes committed to the accumulation process; eventually, this continuation of the capitalist logic of production will lead to ecological crisis.

The third manner in which capitalist production destroys the conditions necessary for ecological reproduction involves capitalist relations of production. In these relations, owners are dependent on workers for labour power and for consumption of their products; workers, meanwhile, are dependent on owners of capital for the work that gives them the money they need to survive. This suggests that there is some degree of balance of power between capitalists and owners; but these relations of production give capitalists material and ideological powers that workers do not have. As owners, they control what is produced and how it is produced, and they have a formidable influence on workers' consumption patterns through publicity and advertising. In addition, as the managers of the economy, the capitalist class has the ideological and material clout to define economic 'success' in ways that suit its agenda. Increasing circulation of capital (measured as steady economic growth) is portrayed as good for the economy and presented as the only means of creating new jobs and increasing living standards. This combination of owning the sites of production, managing the economy, and holding the power to define the meaning of economic 'success' and to purvey the image of desirable consumption habits, has laid the foundation for the capitalist class to 'persuade' most people that capital accumulation is in everyone's best interest.

One way of countering capitalist relations of production is through such workers' organizations as unions. Through the union movement, a potential exists to wrestle away some of capital's power. In Canada, for example, unions sometimes provide alternative ideas about what constitutes economic success, occasionally gain some control over the production process, and in some cases enter into arrangements in which workers become part-owners of production sites. The union movement in Canada is also beginning to use its power to promote alternative economic activity that does not lead to ecological degradation (Canadian Labour Congress 1991). To be sure, there are still many examples of unions accepting the logic of accumulation and siding with owners against attempts to stop ecological degradation (Tatroff 1993). But a powerful union movement also might take collective action aimed at countering capital accumulation and promoting ecological sustainability.

This brief overview of the eco-socialist understanding of capitalism and its inherent tendency to produce an ecological crisis suggests that capitalist forces and capitalist space are in contradiction with ecological forces and ecological space; and it outlines the logic of the eco-socialists' view that the main reason why contemporary cities cause environmental degradation is not that they are high-density spatial forms but that they are predominantly capitalist forms. Shopping malls, expressways, bank towers, and suburban subdivisions are good for business, but they damage the environment. They are a product of, and a means to reproduce the capitalist mode of production, but they destroy ecological space necessary for the reproduction of the natural environment and for human survival.[9]

To summarize, cities are products of social and ecological forces that change over time. The social forces in question arise from a range of social realms – for example, gender, race relations, and state institutions – but among which, from an eco-socialist perspective, the most important are economic relations, social class, and modes of production.

The Environmental Movement and Urban Form

This understanding of contemporary cities and their relationship to the natural environment may paint a bleak picture, and so it is important to note that cities are not simply spaces of ecological and social domination by capital. In respect to ecological forces, various types of plant and animal life attempt to reclaim ecological space in such places as cracks in the pavement and abandoned lots – birds, raccoons, and insects adapt to the human-built environment – while earthquakes, storms, and other natural 'disasters' also modify cities. In respect to social forces, organizations concerned with a wide range of social-justice and ecological issues attempt to (re)produce spatial forms that promote equitable social and ecological relations among people and between people and the natural environment. Organized around a host of interests – class, gender, race, community – these urban groups constantly challenge the extension of capitalist-dominated spatial forms. Leading the promotion of sustainable ecological relations is the environmental social movement.

There has been much debate about the importance of social movements and the impact they have on contemporary life (Castells 1983, Offe 1985, Magnusson and Walker 1988, Carroll 1992, Wier 1993). Analysts who believe social movements can be effective agents of social change note the importance that the role of creating new spaces has in transforming civil society (Canel 1992: 33, Magnusson and Walker 1988: 63). Here, the environmental movement provides an excellent example; it represents a critical spatial challenge to capitalist urban form by promoting ecological space where natural species and ecological forces can reproduce and, in doing so, help ensure human survival.

As noted at the outset, the Canadian environmental movement is predominantly composed of city-dwellers. While it is not solely an urban movement – insofar as it wants to transform human relations with nature on a global scale – urban areas have, over the past decade, become the focus for an increasing number of environmentalists who seek to transform their cities into 'green' cities (Hough 1984, Gordon 1990, Girardet 1992, Gerecke 1991). The global and local transformations that environmental groups hope to engender are based on a set of values oriented to minimizing human impact on the environment (Paehlke 1989: 143–76). The campaigns emanating from these values have a two-pronged impact on the capitalist urban form that may inadvertently lead to a systemic challenge of capital.

First, groups attempt to (re)create ecological spaces. Most often, these spaces are 'natural' habitats which are threatened by urban development or resource extraction industries. Within cities, the (re)creation of ecological spaces occurs by reclaiming watersheds, practising organic gardening, and developing a built environment that minimizes waste, pollution, and energy consumption. Most of these ecological spaces are consciously constructed to ensure capital accumulation cannot occur in them; in this way, these spaces impair the ability of capitalists to reproduce by cutting off access to resources and land that can be commodified or by reducing the need for commodity consumption.

Second, environmentalists affect urban spatial form by challenging the capitalist production process in anti-pollution campaigns. These campaigns argue that products and production processes that cause environmental damage should be banned or at least heavily regulated. This directly affects accumulation strategies by introducing an environmental logic into the production process which supersedes and often negates profitability (Schrecker 1990). For example, campaigns to stop the destruction of the Great Lakes' ecosystems demand the elimination of toxic discharges into the lakes. One group has called for the eventual ban of a significant number of chemicals responsible for ecosystem destruction (International Joint Commission 1992). Were this to occur, chemical manufacturers would be denied access to profits earned through the production and consumption of toxic chemicals. In other words, a specific instance of accumulation – and the logic that supports it – would be undermined by an environmental logic.

While these manufacturers might switch to earning profits by making other industrial products, these profits might also become vulnerable if an environmental logic were again applied.[10] Thus, anti-pollution campaigns not only challenge specific instances of accumulation but, inch by inch, also the logic of accumulation.

In spatial terms, successful anti-pollution campaigns result in reduced capitalist space in two ways: by removing space needed for production (for example, bodies of water that receive pollution) and by attempting to create production spaces that follow an ecological as opposed to an accumulation logic (for example, green factories). Within urban areas, these altered spatial forms are visible in the form of shut-down manufacturing sites, rivers transformed into recreational places instead of toxic sewers, and workplaces designed to minimize environmental impact.

In sum, the contestation of capitalist space arising from the environmental movement leads to alterations in city form that challenge capitalist production by reducing the space and resources necessary for accumulation. Still, it is important not to overrate the impact the environmental movement has had on contemporary cities and capitalism. Although it has been successful in introducing widespread municipal recycling and other fairly simple household-led environmental improvements, it has only sporadically succeeded in transforming sites of capitalist production and in producing substantial areas of ecological space within cities. It is far from defeating capitalism.

This is partly the result of environmentalists' general avoidance of implicating capital as a cause of environmental degradation. As Adkin (1992) notes in her review of various environmentalists' activities in Canada, only a minority consciously struggle directly against capital; eco-socialists who share the perspective outlined in this chapter are only a fraction of the movement. Nevertheless, the lack of winning big struggles and the apparently implicit acceptance of capitalism by many environmentalists does not diminish the potential of the movement to transform contemporary cities and challenge capital. Although it has not worked head-on against the logic of capitalist production, it has introduced a set of ecological values into public discourse that lead to indirect confrontations with capital about its 'right' to maximize accumulation. As well, the movement is making ties with other social-change groups whose values may also lead to inadvertent challenges to capital.

To illustrate the assertion that the environmental movement can change capitalist urban form, albeit indirectly, I will turn to two movement campaigns in Toronto. Both were successful in stopping specific forms of accumulation by appealing to an environmental logic; in the process, they helped in small but real ways to change the shape of the city. The objective of the first campaign was to stop the use of toxic household substances (denoted Household Hazardous Waste, HHW). In the summer of 1993 a grassroots environmental group called Toronto Environmental Alliance (TEA) received funding from state and private sources to run 'Toxic Challenge 93.'[11] Eleven students were hired and taught about the dangers of such household toxics as paints, cleaning solvents, and garden pesticides and herbicides, and about environmentally sustainable alternatives. TEA then organized an intensive outreach program in North York, a suburb in Metro Toronto. The first step involved a Park Party where community members were invited to get together and discuss household toxics with each other and with TEA representatives. The second step involved the eleven students going to almost 4,000 households and asking them to sign on to the Toxic Challenge, a pledge to stop using household toxics for 1993. Over 1,100 households signed the pledge and received information and support kits. Concurrently, canvassers identified potential Block Leaders – people interested in receiving further training about household toxics – to act as community-based information and resource people. Telephone support was provided by the canvassers to participating households, and extensive local media coverage exposed the campaign to an even wider audience.

The rationale and the outcome of the campaign is best described in the final report to project funders:

> The environmental movement has never been just about the environment; as with any social movement, in order to make and sustain significant improvements, we have to stimulate social change. That's why when the Toronto Environmental Alliance launched its Toxic Challenge campaign ... it looked at a community development approach to toxic waste reduction. The multi benefit program that followed not only resulted in a commitment to keep 3.8 million square feet of North York pesticide free, it also put eleven young people to work, allowed face-to-face contact with just under 4,000 householders, and through its Block Leader program leaves in place a process for continuing education and neighbourhood action. (TEA 1994: 4)

The impact of the campaign on urban spatial formation is of course not dramatic. Still, 4,000 households were introduced to a new approach to household tasks that was based in an environmental logic.[12] Over 1,000 households agreed and stopped allowing their space to be used to reproduce the chemicals industry. In addition, the campaign employed eleven students in an organization dedicated to improving the social and environmental health of Toronto through community activism and in a manner that actively promoted non-capitalist space. In this way, the campaign challenged the dominant environmental logic of the city.

The second campaign had a more direct impact on urban spatial form. Spearheaded by an east-end Toronto environmental group, Citizens for a Safe Environment (CSE), community members were instrumental in stopping the development of two garbage incinerators and shutting down an existing incinerator. Without this campaign, the old port area in Toronto's east end might now be the site of three major incinerators burning over 600,000 tonnes of garbage a year. One of the proposed new incinerators was the initiative of a private sector consortium; the other was a municipal government initiative that might have been either publicly or privately run. Capital accumulation would have been enhanced not just through operation of the incinerators but also by providing a convenient waste disposal site for businesses and industry.

This did not occur. In 1983 CSE was formed by a host of community members and groups in the Riverdale area.[13] In January of that year, Toronto city council had authorized the development of a refuse-fired steam plant (incinerator) in south Riverdale. The incinerator was to provide steam needed for the recently formed Toronto District Heating Corporation (TDHC) which provides heat for commercial and institutional buildings in the downtown core. As well, the incinerator would reduce the volume of garbage from the city that was dumped at landfills. The capital cost of the facility was calculated at $155 million; the city considered both public and private ownership models.

While the CSE was busy campaigning against this proposal, another incineration plan arose. In May 1986 a private sector consortium, Trintek Systems, applied to the Ontario Ministry of Energy to construct a further incinerator in south Riverdale. Trintek wanted to develop a facility that would burn approximately 150,000 tonnes of garbage a year and provide a convenient, modern waste-disposal facility for downtown customers. To build the plant, the firm needed Toronto city council to amend a zoning by-law.

The CSE campaign expanded to include opposition to the development of the Trintek proposal. As well, the CSE lobbied to shut down the Commissioners Street Incinerator, operated by Toronto's metropolitan level of government. Built in 1955 and also located in south Riverdale, this incinerator was burning over 100,000 tonnes of Metro waste each year and was responsible for dumping tonnes of toxic emissions on residents of Riverdale and the rest of Toronto.

The CSE anti-incineration campaign was multi-faceted. Within the community, CSE held monthly meetings – or weekly when important city council decisions were approaching – and had the support of hundreds of active volunteers. Community events were held to highlight the environmental and health problems associated with incineration. The CSE collected over 8,000 signatures for a petition opposing incinerators and produced a quarterly newsletter. At city hall, the CSE made deputations to committee and council meetings dealing with incineration and waste management issues. They also worked with larger environmental groups such as Pollution Probe and the Canadian Environmental Law Association to fight incineration throughout Ontario.

Throughout its campaigns the CSE produced a simple and compelling message. Incineration is dangerous to the environment and to human health; waste can be more effectively dealt with by using the 3 Rs – recycle, reuse, and reduce. In the case of the city's proposal, CSE argued that the heating and cooling needs of TDHC's customers could be met through energy conservation strategies, not by producing more steam.

The CSE claimed its first victory in 1987 when the Ontario minister of environment decided that all proposed incinerator facilities that were to burn more than 100 tonnes per day were subject to the Environmental Assessment Act (CSE 1991). The Trintek proposal would have to go through an environmental assessment process that would involve the public in planning and evaluating the proposal. This meant community groups now had an opportunity to convince the government to rule against the Trintek proposal.[14]

A second and more substantial victory came in May 1988 when Metropolitan Toronto Council passed a motion that called for the immediate closure of the Commissioners Street Incinerator. The council cited health concerns as one reason for the closure, suggesting that CSE had an impact on the decision; raising health concerns had been one of the major points in its message.

A third victory offers more substantial evidence of CSE's influence. Toronto city council not only rejected the Trintek proposal – citing community opposition as one reason for their decision – but also passed a motion to 'co-operate with "Citizens for a Safe Environment" and their counsel, in order to assist the community with a comprehensive rebuttal of the TSI Trintek proposal' at the provincial environmental assessment hearing (City of Toronto 1988b: 1698). This was a direct acknowledgment of the leadership role of CSE and of the power of the community in stopping the project.

This success continued when Toronto city council decided in February

1989 to scrap its own proposed incinerator, a decision influenced by the CSE and the public support it had developed in Riverdale. In November 1988 the community had elected one of the original founders of CSE, Marilyn Churley, to city council where she became instrumental in rallying support within city hall against the TDHC incinerator. As well, public concern with waste management issues had mushroomed, and recycling was increasingly seen as a preferred option to incineration. Other factors besides public sentiment also helped bring about the demise of the project; the proposed railway-lands development around the CN Tower included plans to build a fossil-fuel fired steam generator that would meet TDHC steam needs, making an incinerator unnecessary. But it is also likely that this option was partly developed in response to the constant pressure of the CSE campaign against incineration.

This account suggests that concerted public opposition can influence urban environmental policies. In the case of Trintek, the citizens of Riverdale worked together to stop the development of a facility – a space – where capital accumulation would have occurred in an ecologically malignant manner. They also stopped the development of a waste management option that is most amenable to continued accumulation.[15] What drove this opposition was a desire by residents for a space in their city that was not destructive to the environment and human health. In the process, they attacked proposals for spaces that facilitated capital accumulation, and the result was a small but real transformation of the capitalist city.

Conclusion

Whether these kinds of campaigns from the environmental movement will continue to bring about critical societal and spatial transformation is hard to predict. Government and business support for many environmental campaigns suggest that, in spite of their occasional victories, they are not perceived as a threat to the status quo; indeed, the capitalist class sees members of the environmental movement as potential consumers to be tapped through the development of environmentally 'friendly' products. Meanwhile, radical critics of social movements politics would probably argue that most environmental campaigns are not to be taken seriously because they are amorphous social formations that seem to abandon class politics. Both of these perspectives, however, may underestimate the potential of the environmental movement.

Capital requires the control of urban space and the destruction of ecological space. Most environmentalists, on the other hand, want to develop sustainable relationships between people and the natural environment – to produce ecological spaces where, as it happens, capital accumulation either generally cannot occur or is at least impeded. Hence, though environmental campaigns are most often not initiated as an attack on capital, those that replace capitalist space with ecological space will hinder capitalist reproduction. In this way, the environmental movement may play an important role in the future production of urban space. More importantly, the cases discussed here suggest that city-dwellers are not simply powerless puppets of capital but that they may become conscious agents who seek to transform their spaces into environmentally and socially sustainable cities.

NOTES

1 According to staff at Greenpeace and Pollution Probe – two large environmental groups – most members sign up during canvassing, and almost all canvassing is in urban areas.
2 For example, this includes destroying the habitat of wolves and deer so that they can no longer reproduce their relationship. It also applies to such non-living forces as the ozone layer – that is, environmental degradation occurs whenever we impair the relationships between organic and non-organic matter that help constitute what we call the ozone layer.
3 The terms 'sustainability' and 'sustainable development' are highly contested, which is not reflected in the rather simple definition given here; the debate focuses on the type and quality of relations that should be sustained (for example, see Roseland 1992).
4 Lefebvre also noted how important space is to the reproduction of the state (Gottdiener 1985: 143–7). Through activities such as city planning, the state reproduces itself in two ways: first, it extends its power directly by controlling what goes on in (city) space; second, it facilitates capital accumulation, thus ensuring tax revenue. In capitalist society, the state is a product of class and other social struggles, and currently the capitalist class and other dominant social groups – such as white males – have their interests effectively represented by the state. However, the state also develops its own interests reflecting the influence of state actors. Historically, the capitalist state has promoted private capital accumulation not only because of the dominance of the capitalist class but also because capital accumulation created jobs demanded by the working class and secured tax revenue that the state could transform into state power. See Albo and Jenson (1989) for a good overview of Canadian state theory.

5 Merchant (1992: 148) offers a good diagram representing the second contradiction of capital. This section provides a brief overview of some of the arguments made by eco-socialists. For more detail, see Harvey (1993), the journal *Capitalism, Nature, Socialism* and McLaughlin (1990).

6 This suggests all economic systems predicated on constant growth may be ecologically destructive, which helps explain why Soviet-style communism, obsessed with economic growth, was so environmentally destructive. However, this does not suggest that industrialization, per se, is necessarily ecologically destructive but only those forms requiring constant material growth.

7 Young and Sacks (1995: 80) provide data showing that global materials consumption increased by 38 per cent between 1970 and 1991; they also outline the devastating effect of materials extraction on ecosystems.

8 The only way in which continued accumulation could occur without increasing ecological destruction is if profit were made solely through non-material 'production,' such as the buying and selling of financial instruments. Material production, such as food and consumer items, would have to be separated from non-material production, the former being organized by relations other than capitalist and according to a logic of sustainability. Were this to occur, a radically different form of capitalism might become sustainable. However, the push towards global competition and trade liberalization makes this possibility highly unlikely. In reality, capitalist forces are currently reducing – not facilitating – instances where material production occurs outside a capitalist framework.

9 While eco-socialists focus on capitalism as the major cause of environmental degradation, other green critics point to additional factors, such as the kinds of systems of domination that characterize social life, or anthropocentric thinking (Bookchin 1989, Merchant 1992, Eckersley 1992). As well, it is essential to stress that ecological destruction is not unique to capitalist cities; as noted above, other economic systems based on constant growth – such as Soviet-style socialism – also cause vast environmental degradation.

10 As noted above, the sole exception in which capital-accumulation logic and environmental logic are not in conflict is the production of non-material commodities. For example, accumulation driven by the production of financial instruments requires relatively little resource use – no more than the material and energy needed to construct and operate computers. Chemicals manufacturers might conceivably switch to this type of accumulation strategy.

11 This account is based on information provided by TEA (1994); the author has worked with TEA but was not directly involved in the Toxic Challenge project.

12 The accumulation logic for toxic chemicals partly works through manufacturers' exploitation of people's aversion to bugs, unpleasant odours, and germs;

for example, pesticide ads typically depict bugs as nasty, harmful, and dangerous creatures whose eradication requires application of the manufacturer's product.

13 The information in this part of the chapter is from a variety of sources that include City of Toronto (1983, 1988a, 1988b, 1989), Metropolitan Toronto (1988), Citizens for a Safe Environment (1988, 1989, 1990, 1991, n.d.), and Suttle (1995).

14 CSE claimed that it was its campaign that had persuaded the provincial government to subject large incinerators to the Environmental Assessment Act. This is difficult to substantiate; more probably, environmental groups working on incineration throughout Ontario were responsible – a process in which CSE was an important force.

15 Incineration reduces the volume of waste by 90 per cent and therefore reduces the need for large landfill sites. For businesses, this means that the only constraint on accumulation is the cost of disposal at the incinerator facility. In contrast, the 3 Rs option (reduce, reuse, recycle), which argues against the manufacture of products which are disposable, unnecessary, or wasteful, and which is advocated by most environmentalists, would impede accumulation. The landfill option, meanwhile, becomes problematic when landfill space is scarce, as it appears to be in Ontario; for example, Metropolitan Toronto has had a difficult time finding communities willing to accept its garbage in recent years, a situation that is likely to lead ultimately to constraints on capital accumulation.

REFERENCES

Adkin, L. 1992. 'Counter-hegemony and environmental politics in Canada.' In W. Carroll, ed., *Organizing Dissent: Contemporary Social Movements in Theory and Practice*, 135–56. Toronto: Garamond Press

Albo, G., and J. Jenson. 1989. 'A contested concept: The relative autonomy of the state.' In W. Clement and G. Williams, eds., *The New Canadian Political Economy*, 180–211. Kingston: McGill-Queen's University Press

Bookchin, M. 1989. *Remaking Society*. Montreal: Black Rose Books

Canadian Labour Congress Environment Committee. June 1991. *Policy Statement on the Environment*. Toronto

Canel, E. 1992. 'New social movement theory and resource mobilization: The need for integration.' In W. Carroll, ed., *Organizing Dissent: Contemporary Social Movements in Theory and Practice*, 22–51. Toronto: Garamond Press

Carroll, W., ed. 1992. *Organizing Dissent: Contemporary Social Movements in Theory and Practice*. Toronto: Garamond Press

Castells, M. 1983. *The City and the Grassroots.* Los Angeles: University of California Press

Castree, N. 1995. 'The nature of produced nature: Materiality and knowledge construction in marxism.' *Antipode* 27: 12–48

CSE – Citizens for a Safe Environment. 1988, 1989, 1990, 1991. *Eco-Logic: A Monthly Newsletter Published by the Citizens for a Safe Environment*

– N.d. *Citizens for a Safe Environment.* Pamphlet

City of Toronto. 1983. City Service Committee Report No. 7. *City Council Minutes Toronto.* Toronto

– Department of City Clerk. 1988a. *Clause Embodies in Report No. 3 of the City Services Committee which was amended by City Council at its meeting held on 11 January.* Toronto

– 1988b. Minutes of Toronto City Council, 3 October 1988. *The Proceedings of Toronto City Council, 1988,* vol. 1. Toronto

– 1989. City Services Committee Report No. 4. *The Proceedings of Toronto City Council, 1989,* vol. 3. Toronto

D'Aquino, T. 1992. 'Trade-environment links: Issues for Canadian industry.' In J. Kirton and S. Richardson, eds., *Trade Environment and Competitiveness,* 21–34. Ottawa: National Round Table on the Environment and the Economy

Dickens, P. 1992. *Society and Nature: Towards a Green Social Theory.* Philadelphia: Temple University Press

Eckersley, R. 1992. *Environmentalism and Political Theory: Towards an Ecocentric Approach.* Albany: State University of New York

Fishman, R. 1987. *Bourgeois Utopias: The Rise and Fall of Suburbia.* New York: Basic Books

Gallup Canada. 1994. 'Water Quality Tops List of Environmental Concerns.' Monday, 11 July, 1994

Gerecke, K., ed. 1991. *The Canadian City.* Montreal: Black Rose Books

Girardet, H. 1992. *The Gaia Atlas of Cities: New Directions for Sustainable Urban Living.* London: Gaia Books

Gordon, D., ed. 1990. *Green Cities: Ecologically Sound Approaches to Urban Space.* Montreal: Black Rose Books

Gottdiener, M. 1985. *The Social Production of Urban Space.* Austin: University of Texas Press

Haraway, D. 1991. *Simians, Cyborgs, and Women: The Reinvention of Nature.* New York: Routledge

Hartmann, F. 1994. 'Towards a social-ecological theory of the production of urban space.' Paper presented at the annual meeting of the Association of American Geographers, Merriot Hotel, San Francisco

Harvey, D. 1993. 'The nature of environment: Dialectics of social and environmental change.' In R. Miliband and L. Panitch, eds., *Socialist Register 1993: Real Problems False Solutions*, 1–51. London: Merlin Press

Hough, M. 1984. *City Form and Natural Process.* New York: Van Nostrand Reinhold

International Joint Commission. 1992. Sixth Biennial Report on Great Lakes Water Quality. Ottawa

Ley, D., and L. Bourne. 1993. 'Introduction: The social context and diversity of urban Canada.' In L. Bourne and D. Ley, eds., *The Changing Social Geography of Canadian Cities*, 3–30. Montreal: McGill-Queen's University Press

MacKenzie, S., and D. Rose. 1983. 'Industrial change, the domestic economy and home life.' In J. Anderson, S. Duncan, and R. Hudson, eds., *Redundant Spaces in Cities and Regions: Studies in Industrial Decline and Social Change*, 155–201. London: Academic Press

Magnusson, W., and R. Walker. 1988. 'De-centring the state: Political theory and Canadian political economy.' *Studies in Political Economy* 26: 37–71

Massey, D. 1992. 'Politics and space/time.' *New Left Review* 196: 65–84

McLaughlin, A. 1990. 'Ecology, capitalism and socialism.' *Socialism and Democracy* 10: 69–102

Merchant, C. 1992. *Radical Ecology: The Search for a Livable World.* London: Routledge

Metropolitan Toronto. 1988. 10 May Item 220. *Metropolitan Toronto Council Minutes, 1988*, vol. 1. Toronto

O'Connor, J. 1988. 'Capitalism, nature, socialism: A theoretical introduction.' *Capitalism, Nature, Socialism* 1: 11–38

Offe, C. 1985. 'New social movements: Challenging the boundaries of institutional politics.' *Social Research* 52(4): 817–68

Paehlke, R. 1989. *Environmentalism and the Future of Progressive Politics.* New Haven: Yale University Press

Peake, L. 1993. '"Race" and sexuality: Challenging the patriarchal structuring of urban social space.' *Environment and Planning D: Society and Space* 11: 415–32

Rose, G. 1993. *Feminism and Geography: The Limits of Geographical Knowledge.* Minneapolis: University of Minneapolis Press

Roseland, M. 1992. *Toward Sustainable Communities.* Ottawa: National Roundtable on the Environment and the Economy

Schrecker, T. 1990. 'Resisting Environmental Regulation: The Cryptic Pattern of Business-Government Relations.' In R. Paehlke and D. Torgerson, eds., *Managing Leviathan: Environmental Politics and the Administrative State.* Peterborough, ON: Broadview Press

Simmons, I.G. 1989. *Changing the Face of the Earth: Culture, Environment, History.* Oxford: Basil Blackwell

Smith, N. 1984. *Uneven Development: Nature, Capital and the Production of Space.* Oxford: Basil Blackwell

Soja, E. 1989. *Postmodern Geographies: The Reassertion of Space in Critical Theory.* London: Verso

Suttle, A. 1995. Personal interview

Tatroff, D. 1993. 'Clear-cut thinking: B.C. unions at loggerheads.' *Our Times* 12: 26–9

TEA – Toronto Environmental Alliance. 1994. *Hazardous Waste Reduction and Social Change: The Residential Pollution Prevention Project,* Toronto

Wier, L. 1993. 'Limitations of new social movement analysis.' *Studies in Political Economy* 40: 73–102

Wilson, J. 1992. 'Green lobbies: Pressure groups and environmental policy.' In R. Boardman, ed., *Canadian Environmental Policy: Ecosystems, Politics and Process,* 109–43. Toronto: Oxford University Press

Wirth, L. 1938. 'Urbanism as a way of life.' *American Journal of Sociology* 44: 1–24

World Commission on Environment and Development. 1987 *Our Common Future.* Oxford: Oxford University Press

Young, J.E., and A. Sachs. 1995. 'Creating a sustainable materials economy.' In L. Brown et al., *State of the World 1995,* 76–94. New York: W.W. Norton

15

Victoria Regina: Social Movements and Political Space

WARREN MAGNUSSON

A century ago Victoria was the centre of Canada's drug trade (Baskerville 1986: 53–4). However, in this as in much else the city has had to cede pride of place to Vancouver. In those days the drug of choice was opium, and it was manufactured in large quantities in Victoria's bustling Chinatown. The principal markets for the drug were in the United States, which had banned opium production. The supplies of raw materials came through Chinese commercial networks recently extended across the Pacific. As is well known, Chinese labour was welcomed in Canada for a time, partly because of the need for people to construct the railways. However, the trans-Pacific immigration began much earlier, when Kanaks from the Sandwich Islands came to work at what was then the major British entrepôt in the Pacific Northwest. That entrepôt had been established in 1843, when the Hudson's Bay Company moved its centre of operations from Fort Vancouver on the Columbia (across the river from what is now Portland, Oregon) to a more secure position on British territory at the southeastern tip of Vancouver Island. The island and its capital developed as the major British colony west of Winnipeg, and Victoria held its position as the Pacific entrepôt of British North America until almost the end of the nineteenth century. When the opium trade was at its height in the 1880s, Victoria was Canada's fifth largest manufacturing centre (Baskerville 1986: 46). Of course, most of its exports were more respectable than opium, and more dependent on the extraction of local natural resources: seal-fur, whale-oil, tinned salmon, coal, and lumber. The city existed by virtue of Britain's sea-borne empire, and indeed it harboured at nearby Esquimalt the North Pacific Squadron of the Royal Navy. As an imperial trading, shipping, and manufacturing centre, Victoria brought labourers, merchants, and seamen from British outposts on the China coast, the South Pacific, and South East Asia. It stood between the land-based American and Russian empires, a centre of trade with the once rich and powerful coastal Indian peoples, connected to Britain and the Far East, but only distantly related to the British colonies on the Atlantic coast and its tributaries.

This Victoria – a Pacific entrepôt with global pretensions – figures little in Canadian consciousness because it owed so little to Canadian enterprise. Although the most celebrated Canadian venture of the late nineteenth century – the CPR – was promoted from Victoria as well as from Montreal, the railway's arrival at its new Vancouver terminus in 1886 spelled the end of Victoria's commercial ascendancy in the region. The older city remained the capital of British Columbia (itself a union of the mainland and island colonies), but it was rapidly overshadowed economically and settled slowly into its new image as a fusty retirement town, with a naval base, some provincial civil servants, and a rather British demeanour. This image of Britishness was carefully cultivated, because it proved appealing to tourists seeking a respite from the rampant Americanism of the West. In fact, the city entered into a postmodern, postindustrial phase very early, as it adjusted itself to the demands of the pleasure-seekers and retirees brought by steamship and railway from Europe, the British Orient, and the rest of North America. From early in this century Victoria began presenting itself as a 'bit of Olde England' in the North Pacific, with gracious houses, lush gardens, cricket on the lawns, and tea in the afternoon (Baskerville 1986: 90). Maintaining this imagery meant pushing the city's other realities to the margins: its continued functioning as a fishing, whaling, sealing, and lumber port; its business as a milling, ironworking, and shipbuilding centre; its importance not only as an army and navy base, but also as capital for the country's third largest province; and its ethnic diversity, as site of Canada's oldest (and long its biggest) Chinatown (Lai 1991) and as home to no less than six bands of Coast Salish (to say nothing of the other First Nations people who came to trade, look for work, and explore the supposed advantages of the city).[1] Thanks to the tourist and retirement industries, Victoria had and still has an interest in concealing its diverse, metropolitan character. This makes it difficult for mainlanders to take it seriously as a centre for urban politics.

We should not be deterred by such ignorance, however, for Victoria is now part of a huge urban agglomeration that overshadows Montreal and rivals Toronto in population and economic power. This is the region around Puget Sound and the Georgia Basin, which forms an oval of about

300 by 100 kilometres extending across the international border. It contains over five million people in a chain of cities and towns stretching from Olympia (the Washington state capital) in the south to Nanaimo (on the east coast of Vancouver Island) in the north. Seattle and Vancouver (just over 200 kilometres apart) are of course the major centres, but Victoria is at a key location at the opening of the Strait of Juan de Fuca, just about halfway between the two larger cities. The strait leads out to the open ocean, away from the great protected bay (of the sound and basin) where most people in British Columbia and Washington live. The cities of Nanaimo, Vancouver, Victoria, Bellingham, Everett, Seattle, Tacoma, and Olympia share a common setting, with mountains to the east and west and dozens of rocky, forested islands scattered in the tranquil waters between them. There is a common, but distinctive coastal climate, everywhere mild, in some places wet, but elsewhere (especially in Victoria) surprisingly dry, especially in summer. This contributes to a regional consciousness marked by a smug pride in the quality of the environment and a nervous fear of excessive immigration. It is not just British Columbia that has drawn immigrants in recent years. Washington, particularly in the Seattle area, has been one of the American boom states, attracting more and more people north from California. What is more, there is a sense that the whole region, which already has an important place in the knowledge-based industries – Seattle is headquarters to both Boeing and Microsoft – and is well located in relation to the new Asian centre of the global economy, is bound to develop rapidly in the coming decades. There is a fear that the superior environment, itself an attraction to investors, will be damaged by over-intensive urbanization. Thus, the feeling that there is too much city, even in Victoria – recently expressed by an American travel writer who complained that a town of 300,000 was too big for an island – is not to be taken lightly.

In some respects Victoria functions as a suburb of Vancouver, less than 100 kilometres north (further than Hamilton from Toronto, but much closer than Ottawa to Montreal). The land-sea journey from downtown to downtown takes three hours each way – too far for daily commuting – but seaplane and helijet connections can reduce the time from office to office to less than half an hour, which obviously facilitates high-level business and government contacts. Important agencies of the provincial government are located in Vancouver, and this ensures steady traffic. Increasingly, Victoria is oriented on an axis that links the downtown, on the Inner Harbour opening south into the Strait of Juan de Fuca, with Swartz Bay, about thirty kilometres north at the top of the Saanich Peninsula, where the ferries leave for Vancouver. The peninsula was traditionally agricultural, but it has been the favoured site for suburban development for decades. Thanks to the Agricultural Land Reserve, established by the provincial government in 1974 to protect the province's limited farmlands, a significant part of the peninsula is still reserved for agriculture. This measure has helped push development into the so-called Western Communities, on the other side of Victoria from the naval base at Esquimalt. This has also put pressure on the highlands that lead up into the Sooke Hills – the range that protects Victoria from the Pacific storms and physically separates the capital region from the rainforests on the island's west coast. Again, much of the former area has been protected by parks and water management districts, and this has stimulated development 'over the Malahat' – that is, on the other side of the pass that connects the region with the towns to the north, along the milder east coast of the island. The most dramatic of contemporary development proposals is for a new town at Bamberton, just over the Malahat and within relatively easy commuting distance of downtown Victoria. Although this development has been presented as a model of ecological sensitivity (Freedman 1994), local environmentalists have been extremely sceptical.

Except for the strip along the east coast from Duncan to Courtenay, which has been the object of much retirement/resort/cottage development, most of Vancouver Island – which is about the size of Belgium – is still given over to logging. This leads to a sharp division of sensibilities between people in the Georgia Basin and those who live in the logging and milling towns in the 'frontier' beyond. For most city residents, the logging roads through the forests are an abstract presence – an ugly feature of the terrain that separates them from the ski hills, campsites, hiking trails, and seaside cottages that mark the urbanites' wilderness. As environmental sensitivity has increased, the idea of preserving in a natural state whatever is beyond the urbanites' use has gained in popularity. As the economy of the basin and the sound has matured, the claim that it all depends on logging and mining for its prosperity has lost credence, even though that notion is constantly promoted by the resource companies. Thus, Victoria, like the other urban communities, is increasingly at odds with its rural hinterland, in terms of its attitudes towards forestry and the other traditional resource industries of British Columbia. This sensibility reinforces the physical barriers between the capital region and the rest of the island. Although the city still functions as the island's metropolis, in most respects it is more closely linked to the lower mainland.

In terms of private business, Victoria is much more obviously dependent on tourism than on logging or mining for its prosperity.[2] The image of Beautiful British Columbia – of the unspoiled land of forests, mountains, and wondrous waters – is crucial in this regard, and can easily be harmed by pictures of unsightly clear-cuts. Closer to home was the damage done by widely publicized stories – one a feature in the *New York Times* (Egan 1991) – about the city's practice of dumping its raw sewage into the Strait of Juan de Fuca.[3] When the voters of the region turned down a proposal for sewage treatment facilities, they tarnished a carefully cultivated image of tidiness, cleanliness, and environmental sensitivity. The Chamber of Commerce, the Tourist Bureau, and the area municipalities were forced into an awkward propaganda campaign to prove – especially to potential visitors from the state of Washington – that Victoria had no need in its circumstances to treat its sewage. Despite considerable scientific support – it seems that a non-industrial city of moderate size, which can put its sewage into a strong, cold ocean current, is just as well advised to recycle its liquid wastes in that way as to extract the organic solids and spread them on the land (Capital Regional District 1993, Anderson 1992) – the authorities have had a difficult time selling their message, especially since American federal law has required neighbouring municipalities in Washington to install the sort of treatment systems that Victoria has avoided. The city – and ultimately the province, which is requiring the city to commit itself to a future treatment system – are obviously part of a wider community that imposes its own (in this case rather abstract) environmental standards.

Maintaining the flow of tourists is also a matter of creating the proper ambience in the downtown and at the outlying tourist attractions. From the provincial legislature on the harbour – lit up like a fairy castle at night – to the dressed-up Victorian buildings of the Old Town, the friendship gate at the entrance to Chinatown, the caleches and rickshaws peddled by eager students, the Indian canoes and motor launches carrying people around the harbour, and the cobblestoned streets lined with flower baskets, the town provides a Disneyland experience without the formal admission fees.[4] The museums and galleries are supplemented by street entertainers, music and theatre festivals, and the occasional extravaganza like the Commonwealth Games of 1994. This concentrated effort is intended to make Victoria into a place that can be consumed as an entertaining spectacle – and held in the memory as a place for future retirement. The consumption is organized in such a way that merchants can profit from selling a wide range of goods and services. One of the great political conflicts of the mid-1980s concerned a proposal to create a miniature Eaton Centre, on the Toronto model, in the downtown.[5] A large section of the business community aligned with heritage preservationists and other urban activists in opposition to the downtown mall. Although their fight was ultimately unsuccessful, the mall opponents, like a previous generation of activists in the early 1970s, gave strong expression to a conception of Victoria as a unique city, without need of the homogenizing artefacts of corporate urbanism.

If there is a conflict among the burghers of Victoria, it is between those who value the peculiarities of the place and those who do not. As Disney has shown, a particular ambience can be created anywhere, and there is no necessity that the historical reconstructions and architectural fantasies presented in Victoria should recall that city's past any more than New Orleans' or Rome's. The modern suburb or shopping mall can be formed as a dream of New Spain or Shanghai, according to the tastes of the consumer (cf. Zukin 1991, Shields 1989). The suburban sensibility reflects this sense of the arbitrary character of historical allusions. Insofar as it imposes itself on the downtown, the actual historical relics are threatened. Those who value these relics – which create the illusion of a past that was better than it was – tend to resist this pressure in the name not only of historical preservation, but also of communal autonomy. A city that celebrates its own past, maintains what it can of its original streetscape, and favours local businesses is frequently considered more autonomous – more of a real place – than one that capitulates entirely to the homogenizing forces of external capital. This rather nostalgic view of things is inevitably appealing to those of us who are interested in cities, but we should not imagine that the triumph of such a localist sensibility has a huge effect on the fabric of a city or that it reflects a more generous and egalitarian understanding of whom the city is for.

Clearly, to most Victorians and most visitors, the city is not for the homeless who congregate under the Johnson Street bridge, sleep under the trees in Beacon Hill Park, or panhandle on the streets. Nor is it for the pimps, prostitutes, and street-kids who idle around Government and Yates Streets. Victoria, like Vancouver, is an attractive place in winter for people with nowhere else to go, and in any case it produces its own share of misery (Community Council of Greater Victoria 1988, Baxter 1991, Mullens 1992, Whysall 1993). The cost of living is high and economic opportunities for the young are limited, so that there is an undercurrent of desperation typical of even the most prosperous of contemporary cities. Many local leaders look enviously at Seattle, Portland and other cities that have effective vagrant removal programs.[6] The hope, as elsewhere, is to push the undesirables out of the way, as most high-class suburbs have succeeded in doing. A city cleansed of its social problems is supposed to be able to realize either the corporate or the localist version of the postmodern dream – with trolley cars gliding carelessly along cobblestoned streets, past the Olde English pubs and shops full of tourists, with baskets of flowers to adorn their way. Idylls of this sort are being pursued in one city after another across the country and around the world (Harvey 1989, Zukin 1990). The question is whether anything can disrupt the process, especially in a city as favoured as Victoria.

The Displacement of Urban Politics

In a place like Toronto, with a monumental centre and large studios for the news media, it is easy to imagine that urban politics is fixed to the site. Such a belief is more difficult to sustain under the postmodern conditions that typify Victoria and indeed most of what we call 'urban Canada.' Canadian urbanites generally live far from the monumental centres and have little to do with them. The municipalities that most people inhabit – places like North York, Nepean, Richmond, or Saanich – have little historical resonance for us or for anyone else. People are linked by road, air, and telecommunications to wider urban regions, and may feel as connected with Los Angeles or Chicago as with any closer urban centre. This abstraction of urban space leads to an abstraction of urban politics, so that an issue like 'crime in the cities' becomes a matter of debate anywhere and everywhere regardless of local conditions. Similarly, 'the environment' or the threat to it from human settlement becomes a free-floating issue that can be as well played out 'there' as 'here.'

This is illustrated by the recent battle over Clayoquot Sound.[7] Clayoquot, which is on the west coast of Vancouver Island near Pacific Rim National Park, a few hours drive from Victoria, is one of the centres of environmental controversy in British Columbia. South Moresby, Meares Island, the Carmanah, the Walbran, Clayoquot – these read like an honour role of recent sites of struggle for environmentalists who seek to preserve what remains of the ancient temperate rainforests. From the loggers' perspective, it seems that every stand of old-growth timber now attracts a band of protectors, not only from Victoria and Vancouver, but also from the other cities that generate environmental activism. Perhaps typically, the most publicized leader of the Clayoquot Sound 'Peace Camp' – from which protesters bore witness to what they regarded as environmental degradation, or took direct action to impede the construction of logging roads into the area – came not from British Columbia but from Toronto (Coull, Dyment, and Kleiman 1993). The Peace Camp was supposedly organized on eco-feminist principles, and so it appealed simultaneously to environmentalists, feminists, and pacifists. Such a working together of major social movements is typical of contemporary progressive politics. Not so much coalitional, as ad hoc and action oriented, activity of this sort depends on a sharing of sensibilities among people who identify with different, but not mutually exclusive social movements. For the most part, these movements are generated within a free-floating urban culture, whose space is defined cybernetically. Once oriented to the cause, an environmental activist in Toronto may find the issue of rainforest destruction in British Columbia or Brazil more pressing as an urban or local issue than solid waste disposal in southern Ontario. What seems local in this context will depend on one's ideological orientation and personal sensibilities.

It has long been recognized that land use struggles are at the heart of urban politics (Lorimer 1972, Magnusson and Sancton 1983, Logan and Molotch 1987, Duncan and Goodwin 1988), but contemporary urbanism has a different relation to the land than was typical even a generation ago. In the first quarter-century after the Second World War, people were struggling with the fact that automotive transportation was breaking up the old cities of the industrial era. The new metropolitan centres spread out over the countryside, absorbed old towns, and established networks of transportation that enabled people to commute freely over vast distances. In this context it still seemed sensible to dream of regional planning authorities that could span each commutershed and ensure rational urban development. However, these visions of regional integrity seem increasingly archaic in the context of the Internet, fibre optics, cellular phones, PCs, satellite dishes, and information super-highways. In the emergent global cyberspace regions are defined in an entirely different way, and the struggle for territory may have little to do with land as such. For instance, there is an urban reality that links currency and commodity traders all over the world – some in the air, others on the highway, still others in their fishing lodges or riding stables in the countryside. This exclusive, carefully guarded, hierarchically organized cyberspace is a territory unknown to most people, but one in which the key decisions about the development of physical space are arbitrated. Those who wish to challenge those decisions have little option but to organize themselves cybernetically if they are to be effective politically.

Greenpeace, the world's largest environmental organization, which began in Vancouver in 1971, is illustrative of this (cf. Harwood 1988, Ostertag 1991, Horton 1991, Spencer 1991, Livesey 1994). Beginning with campaigns against nuclear testing off the Aleutians and in the South Pacific, moving onto assaults against sealing and whaling, and gradually broadening its concerns to encompass a wider range of environmental issues, Greenpeace managed to establish itself as a major international presence. It took advantage of the media's interest in sensational encounters to stage attention-getting stunts on the seas, at factories, and in corporate offices. In some cases these stunts involved civil disobedience, and in others a challenge to the rights of people to use international waters as they pleased. Greenpeace grew by a process of nucleation, ultimately fostered by an international organization based first in England and later in Holland, which controlled the Greenpeace trademark. It thus mimicked a modern business that franchises its operations in different countries. It also developed its own information systems – notably GreenNet and GreenLink – which enabled campaigners in different parts of the world to coordinate their activities. Among other things, this has meant that when Greenpeace intervened in the Clayoquot dispute (as part of a broader forestry campaign), it was able to activate people in Europe to put pressure on the companies buying BC forest products.[8] This demand-end campaign, which led to the cancellation of important orders, has had as much or more effect on the companies and on the BC government than any of the protests in the woods themselves.

The action in Europe, however, is not unconnected to the action on Vancouver Island. Greenpeace quickly hired the Peace Camp organizer for its Vancouver office, and it has been acting along with a variety of other organizations to put pressure on the provincial government. The confrontations at the Clayoquot site have been used to generate international publicity. Midnight Oil held a concert for the protesters, Tom Hayden came up from California to remarry on the beach nearby, and Robert Kennedy, Jr, kayaked into the area to express his concern. All this combined with the arrests of protesters who were blocking the trucks to create a sense of crisis with which the companies and the government had to deal. Victoria too became a site for the drama, as the civil disobedients – many of whom lived in the city – were brought there for trial. For months there was a sort of peace encampment outside the courthouse – complete with Buddhist monk in saffron robes – and each trial was marked by a spirited demonstration. This linkage to the city and its social movements symbolized the fact that the Clayoquot dispute, like the ones on the Walbran and the Carmanah, was occurring in Victoria's 'own' wilderness – in part of the territory that Victorians used for their recreation and that formed the fabric of their local environment.

Supposedly, municipal government allows people to participate in land use planning decisions. However, the decisions in this case were and are far removed from municipal authority. The territory incorporated for municipal purposes on Vancouver Island is generally in a narrow band from Victoria north to Campbell River, along the east coast of the island. Immediately west is a large swath of land originally granted to the CPR and now held by various logging companies. Most of this territory has already been logged at least once. Finally, to the west and north are the Crown lands, which cover most of the island and contain the bulk of the remaining old growth forest. Aside from the areas reserved for parks and settlements, this land has generally been given over to the logging companies under various forms of tenure. The annual allowable cut is set by the provincial ministry of forests, and there are both federal and provincial environmental regulations – the latter to be strengthened by a new provincial Forest Practices Code. However, the companies have definite and extremely valuable cutting rights on the lands that they use. Historically, land use planning has meant planning by the companies, which have gradually been liquidating the old growth forests and replanting them with trees that can be harvested on a regular cycle. Although the province remains the ultimate landlord and extracts revenues from the companies in the form of stumpage fees, it tends to put itself at one remove from the actual management of the land; it has had neither the will nor the means to police the logging companies closely. The municipal councils have no control over the neighbouring forests, even though there are six regional districts on the island which cover both incorporated and unincorporated territory. To the extent that the regional districts are involved in land use planning on unincorporated lands, their focus is on settlement-related issues, rather than on forestry.

When the New Democratic party came to power in BC in 1991, with a mandate to deal with the developing War in the Woods, the assumption was that different structures would have to be developed to allow for a resolution of the conflict between logging and environmental interests. The key move was to create a Commission on Resources and Environment (CORE) with a mandate to develop regional planning processes for areas where the conflicts were particularly acute. Vancouver Island was immediately designated as one of the three priority areas. The commission established a planning system that was premised on the representation of all 'stakeholders' throughout the process. The municipalities were ultimately identified as one of *fourteen* groups of stakeholders, in a process that, according to the commission, represented 'the most direct public participation in land use decision-making ever offered to British Columbians' (British Columbia 1994: 32–3). Clearly, it was assumed that the normal processes for public participation in land use decision-making – the ones that flowed through the municipalities and the regional districts – were of minor consequence and that the commission was for the first time offering people a part in the really important planning that was occurring. Although the municipalities complained afterwards that the CORE process had marginalized them, the general perception was that the real political conflict was between the environmental organizations and the logging interests, with the aboriginal groups standing to one side ready to assert their own interests. Generally, in the small resource towns on the north and west island, there was massive support for the logging interests, expressed partly through municipal resolutions, but more dramatically in a massive loggers' demonstration in front of the legislature in downtown Victoria. The urban-based environmental organizations were able to generate their own, somewhat less effective counter-pressure without appealing to the municipal councils where they had influence.

After a year's deliberations CORE was unable to generate the consensus it sought, and the commissioner finally proposed a compromise regional plan that was intended to give each side its due. That plan was in turn modified by the provincial government, which responded especially to complaints that the controls on logging were too severe. Significantly, the whole issue of Clayoquot Sound – the most immediately pressing dispute – was handled by a different process, outside CORE's jurisdiction, ostensibly because the need for a final decision was more urgent. Thus, the formal resolution of the region's most vexed problem in land use planning was doubly displaced from the formal institutions of local democracy: first from the municipalities, and then from CORE, the ad hoc regional commission. It is small wonder in the circumstances that people treat these institutions with considerable scepticism. There is a recognition that ultimate decisions on matters of such import are not made by subordinate agencies of the state (like the municipalities) and that effective oppositional movements have to be prepared to operate on a different terrain. Thus, the environmental groups tried to generate negative publicity about BC clear-cuts in Europe, the United States, and Eastern Canada, knowing that this could have an effect on tourism and urban-oriented investment. At the same time, they tried to mobilize 'green' market power to put pressure on the forest companies. Among the forestry workers and their supporters in the logging towns, environmental groups tried to make the case that ecologically sensitive forestry would in the long run be more productive of jobs in the woods (M'Gonigle and Parfitt 1994). Somewhat more successfully, they put the case to aboriginal leaders that their land claims, which were still unsettled, would be of much less value if logging continued at its present rate.[9] In all of this activity, the environmentalists were marking out a terrain of urban politics far removed from the one that we have normally conceived.

The Fixations of Municipal Government

It is a comforting illusion to suppose that municipal institutions were designed to provide for local democracy. Almost the opposite is the case. Precisely because city hall or the town council is more accessible than the senior governments to the poor and the dispossessed, local authority has always been organized in a way that insulates it from unwanted popular influences (Magnusson 1981, 1986). Traditional restrictions designed to prevent the 'rootless poor' from voting were maintained at the municipal level long after they had disappeared elsewhere. In the industrial era, the mass meetings that had characterized early forms of local democracy rapidly gave way to elective authorities, which in turn yielded much of their power to professionalized bureaucracies and appointive boards drawn from the 'respectable classes.' The respectability, caution, and conservatism of local governments were reinforced by legislative measures and judicial decisions that severely limited both the fiscal capacity and the regulatory authority of bodies at the municipal level. Progressive activists who were influenced by socialist ideas gradually discovered that their capacity to effect change through purely local institutions was severely restricted. As a result, much of the democratic political energy that might have gone into local government has been directed elsewhere – especially into the political parties that contest for control of the 'senior' governments. For most of this century, municipal politics has played only a minor part in people's efforts to gain control over the conditions of their own lives.

Victoria is typical in this respect. As noted above, the city proper is only a small part of the Capital Regional District,[10] which in turn is only a suburban region of the transnational metropolis centred on Seattle and Vancouver. There is no metropolitan government in the larger sense, and the CRD is just an indirectly elected authority with little political presence and very weak systems of democratic accountability. As elsewhere in Canada, much of the local state is under the direction of school boards, hospital societies, and other agencies at arm's length from the general-purpose local governments.[11] These bodies tend to have even less autonomy in relation to the provincial government than do the municipalities. With the powers of local government dispersed, displaced, contained, and controlled in this way, it is hardly surprising that purely municipal elections attract only limited public attention. The usual cast of characters run for municipal office – realtors, merchants, lawyers, and others associated with the local business community, together with a scattering of teachers, social workers, and community activists. Generally, as elsewhere, the business-oriented candidates – well connected, better funded, and benignly regarded by the local media – have the electoral advantage and end up dominating the municipal councils. The stiffest opposition to these people comes from community activists who can appeal to public concerns about insensitive and over-rapid urban development.

Development concerns do not necessarily generate an innovative, wide-ranging approach to local issues, but some activists have been trying to expand the agenda of municipal politics, especially in the city proper. Since 1990 there has been an effort to use the NDP to organize a 'progressive' opposition. This followed a period in which progressives contested local elections as unaffiliated independents. In 1990 the Victoria Civic Electors (VCE) was formed as a local branch of the NDP, and it put a slate of candidates forward for the city council (Walsh 1994). (This was a controversial step within the party, which has usually found that a significant portion of its supporters oppose partisan intervention in municipal affairs.) The VCE captured four of the nine seats, including the mayoralty – which was taken by a narrow margin in a three-way race – and thus established what appeared to be an unprecedented 'left' presence in civic affairs. This presence was sustained in the 1993 elections, although the mayoralty was lost when the 'right' put up a single credible candidate. A parallel organization had considerable success in the school board elections, and some NDP-affiliated candidates were elected in the suburbs. Thus, NDP partisans had some reason to take comfort in what was otherwise a disastrous year for their party.

Nevertheless, this electoral toe-hold can hardly be taken as a sign of mass popular mobilization. The 1993 municipal elections were marked by exceptionally low voter turn-out, rather than by the surge of interest one might associate with bold municipal initiatives and vigorous public debate. Many attributed this to voter exhaustion, since the elections were held just after the federal ballot. However, the truth is that the VCE had had little impact on the public consciousness and had failed to develop anything resembling a grass-roots political movement. This was ironic, since one of the initiatives that did distinguish the now-defeated VCE Mayor, David Turner, was an effort to broaden the base of public participation in municipal affairs. A host of civic advisory committees were established at his instance, and considerable effort was made to open these bodies up to volunteers from all sectors and levels of society (Wilson 1992, MacDonald 1992). Unfortunately, this open, participatory structure was not mirrored in the VCE itself, which (according to its constitution adopted on 26 June 1990) remained closed to anyone who was not a member of the NDP. There was no serious effort to develop a party platform on the basis of widespread community involvement, and in fact the candidates elected under the VCE banner were not committed to any form of unity on matters of policy. (This was demonstrated dramatically just before the opening of the Commonwealth Games, when the VCE councillors split on the issue of a settlement with the city's unionized workers.) The VCE's main focus seemed to be to encourage New Democrats to run for local office and to provide them with organizational and financial support. The party's limited electoral success was the result not of innovative policy-making and vigorous community organizing, but of very traditional efforts to signal to NDP voters 'who their friends were.' This may have done something to redress the partisan balance on council, but it was hardly a revolution in civic politics.

A local party that is not a movement, that confines itself strictly to its own turf, and that defines its purposes in purely electoral terms is not likely to generate much public enthusiasm – especially when it presents itself as a local branch of some other political organization. Although it is easy to blame the leaders of the VCE for the particular approach they adopted, it is hard to point to many more successful examples of enduring popular mobilization at the municipal level. It seems that the 'fixations' of municipal government – its functional and geographic limitations, its administrative subordination to the higher authorities, and its commitment to a particular model of democratic representation – make this political space relatively unattractive. Many observers assume that the spaces for popular political organization should reflect the structure of the state: that is, that people should organize politically at each of the levels of government. However, the 'lowest' level of government has comparatively little power, and so, insofar as political attention comes to be focused on a municipality or some other local authority, it gets fixed at a place where little can be done. Ordinary people are not so dull or unsophisticated that they do not realize this. They sense that serious politics – including serious urban politics – goes beyond the borders and beyond the jurisdiction of any particular municipality. As a result, they operate with a sense of political space that tends to disrupt the neat hierarchies of government.

Increasingly, ordinary people are coming to recognize that even the higher levels of government lack the power commonly attributed to them. There is always a 'beyond' that cannot be reached. The Capital Regional District has wider geographic authority than the City of Victoria, but the new Town of Bamberton, the most important development project in the Victoria region, is just outside its jurisdiction. Even on a matter like sewage disposal, the CRD finds that its freedom of action is severely constrained by federal legislation, provincial directives, and the need for maintaining the city's image for purposes of tourism. The Province of British Columbia has wider jurisdiction and more resources, but its effort to manage the island's forest lands in a way that meets local political needs has been constantly disrupted by pressures that come from the global environmental movement. The government of Canada is likewise vulnerable to external pressures, most of which, of course, have little to do with environmentalism. For the past two decades all the major industrialized countries have been scrambling to adapt their economic and social policies to the changing requirements of international investors. It seems that what ordinary people want is far less important to the governments concerned than what 'the market' requires: although Canadians may want to maintain the welfare state, the investors have made it clear that such an arrangement is simply intolerable. As a result, successive Canadian governments (federal and provincial) of all political stripes have been retrenching on the services that people came to expect in the 1960s and 1970s. There is every reason to suppose that this process will continue.

One of the common insights of contemporary social movements[12] is that the space for political action has to be as extensive as the one occupied by the forces with which the movements contend. Thus, if the capitalist market economy is problematic for workers or environmentalists, then the workers' movement or the environmental movement has to create a political space for itself that is as global as capitalism itself. This means that the movement cannot be confined to a particular state, or kept strictly within the public sector. Somehow, it has to mobilize people to change things at the workplace, in the home, on the streets, in the shopping centres, and out in the wilderness. From the perspective of the most innovative movement activists, the space of struggle is everywhere, and each location has to be conceived as one node in a global network. To create a space for the workers' movement is a matter of raising people's consciousness of themselves as workers, deepening people's understanding of their needs as workers, and translating this understanding into enforceable social claims. Creating a space for the environmental movement, or the feminist movement, or the aboriginal rights movement, or any other major social movement involves a similar process. To the extent that the process is democratic, it will be a matter of self-activity in response to the concerns of everyday life. And, as we know, everyday life even in the most remote places is increasingly urban.

This suggests that an urban politics invested with the energy of critical social movements will inevitably burst the bounds of its municipal containers. It will also override the boundaries between one country and the next, because territorial states are ultimately inadequate to the purposes of the major social movements. The urban politics occurring in the woods near Victoria, in the city's courthouse, through the Greenpeace networks, outside Canadian embassies in Europe, in the boardrooms of the paper-purchasing companies, and in broadcasts of MuchMusic is typical of the explosiveness of the global city. The space for political action is defined by global market relations, cultural networks, and social movements that link people with common sensibilities in different parts of the world. This space is not the space of cities as distinct entities, but rather of the global city – the encompassing network of urbanity – as such.[13]

The Politics of the Global City

The World Bank reports that, by the end of the century, most of the people in the world will be living in cities of more than a million, and that a large proportion will be in the mega-cities of ten million or more. Hardly any of these mega-cities will be in the advanced industrial countries. In fact, one of the signs of power in this new world order will be a capacity to evade population growth and its attendant problems. Victoria (and the larger metropolitan region of which it is part) will no doubt continue to display this kind of power in maintaining the quality of life to which we alluded at the beginning of this chapter.

This suggests that in speaking of Victoria Regina (Victoria the Queen) we are talking about a kind of imperial order that enables some people to displace urban problems onto others. Viewed holistically, the barrios of

Manila and Mexico City are the far suburbs of Los Angeles, Toronto, and Puget Sound/Georgia Basin. They are containers for the people who are as yet of little value for the capitalist economy: that vast 'reserve army of the proletariat' that Marx referred to more than a century ago, and that Engels tried to describe in his classic study of Manchester in 1844 (Engels 1987). What was an emergent localized reality in the nineteenth century has become pervasive globally. In this context the decisive moves in the politics of domination, repression, and exploitation are the ones that separate 'here' from 'there' – that create fortresses and highways and safe spaces that protect the 'tame' from the 'wild' (cf. Luke 1993). Victoria, like Santa Barbara or Monte Carlo, is a privileged space within the privileged space and as such is defended by barriers, within barriers, within barriers. However, its condition is symptomatic of a more widespread organization of privilege that depends on access to capital, cultural resources, and state power. Thus, the symbolic truth of 'Victoria' is expressed not only in its name and in its past as an imperial outpost, but in its presence as a destination for tourists and retirees, an assembly point for 'peacekeepers' who go out from Canada to patrol the wild lands of the world, a site for cultural production and conspicuous consumption, and a locus for private and public administration.

In this context it becomes clear that a critical urban politics for Victoria (or anywhere else) is necessarily excessive, in the sense that it must exceed the given boundaries of the capitalist economy, the bureaucratic state, and contemporary consumer culture. Those boundaries are, in their statist guise, both geographic and functional. They distinguish 'the municipal' – what is definitely within the jurisdiction of the local government – from 'the urban' – what brings people together and connects them with the wider world. Although the municipal is necessarily contained and limited, the urban explodes outward. It is in the urban that the local becomes the global, and the global becomes the local. There are both dangers and opportunities involved in this. Urbanity implies a double relation, because cities are places where things are concentrated and where complexity is the rule. If concentration involves hierarchy, domination, and stability, complexity entails flux, change, and unpredictability. Although urban life implicates people in many forms of domination, it also poses new possibilities. It is in this latter aspect of the urban – its boundary-breaking excessiveness – that we can find hope for a critical politics. It is there that the possibility is raised that we can reconstitute our relations of ruling in more egalitarian and less exploitative terms.

Certainly, if we are looking for a critical urban politics, we are likely to find it in a space that transcends municipal government. If we look carefully in most cities, we will discover people inventing new forms of housing, assisting the homeless to organize themselves (Victoria Street Community Association 1993a, 1993b) creating new facilities for battered women (Kenny and Magnusson 1993), establishing forums for intercultural communication, building bicycle paths, developing urban gardens, and, of course, protecting the nearby wilderness. Activities of this kind (and there are many others, see Fowler 1992) occur in the public space that some would conceive as the domain of 'civil society' (Cohen and Arato 1994). However, the people concerned come together to support more explicitly political campaigns and movements. This gives wider effect to a developing consciousness. The social movements and the activities they generate thus mediate the relation between the local and the global. This process of mediation, which brings the world into us and takes us into the world, is not something that excludes the municipal as a venue for action. In fact, it might be argued that the abandonment of the municipal field is a sign of political decay.

Municipal politics has been extraordinarily creative in many cities,[14] but this creativity depends on a willingness to challenge the political assumptions and the constitutional restrictions that limit municipalities to a narrow range of activity. The Victoria Civic Electors are typical in their timidity in this respect. The city as we know it in Victoria and elsewhere is largely a product of the greatest, but in many ways most pernicious 'social movement' of modern times: capitalism (Magnusson 1994). Confronting that movement with open eyes – recognizing its pervasiveness, its complex effects, manifold repressions, exclusions, and exploitations, and, most importantly, understanding that capitalism is 'in here' as well as 'out there' – is probably the key to recognizing the possibilities for critical political action (Magnusson and Walker 1988). For most of this century progressive activists have allowed a crude understanding of the nature of capitalism and its relation to the state system – one developed in the years leading up to the First World War and revised in the wake of the Second – to guide their theory and practice. This is the understanding that informed a variety of statist projects, from the American New Deal and the Great Society programs of the 1960s to postwar European social democracy and Soviet communism. Progressive activists have been moving away from this statist model for the past thirty years, but they have been unable to conceptualize the space for their actions in a way that takes account of the complexities of the contemporary world. This is why the urban is such a crucial focus for our political attention. Thinking about the global city (which is at once an effect and a cause of the capitalist world economy) and the social movements that characterize it – both the ones we like (feminism? environmentalism?) and the ones we do not like (religious fundamentalism? ethnic chauvinism?) – is essential for understanding and responding effectively to the processes that are actually making the world in which we have to live.

It is easy to say that we should 'think globally and act locally,' but we have a long way to go before we can understand how to do that. In focusing on Victoria in this chapter, we have actually been looking at a global reality, which might as well have been approached from any other location. We have found a city that is now and always has been beyond itself: a city that is neither contained within its immediate environment nor governed by its local government. It is a city remote and unnoticed in the Canadian context and yet part of an urban complex that is as great as or greater than the one centred in Toronto. Both Victoria and Toronto are nodes in a global city whose hierarchies we have hardly begun to comprehend. These nodes are also the locales for social movements that disrupt those hierarchies. Whether we like it or not, it is in these confusing urban spaces that the politics of the twenty-first century will be practised.

Acknowledgments The author thanks Sandra Kahale, Michael Lancaster, and Catherine Walsh for their research assistance and the Social Sciences and Humanities Research Council of Canada for its financial support.

NOTES

1 In recent years, Victoria's marketing strategy has shifted somewhat to take advantage of its 'native heritage.' This reflects the fact the city is now being marketed in Asia and Europe, where Britishness is not a particular selling point. See Fotheringham (1994) for critical commentary on the exploitation of the native theme during the 1994 Commonwealth Games.

2 However, the major employers are in the public sector. For data, see Capital Regional District (1993). There is a comparative analysis of the 'three economies' of British Columbia – Victoria, Vancouver, and the Interior – in Davis (1993). For somewhat dated but still useful historical and geographic data on the region, see Foster (1976).

3 Compare Wilson (1991), 'U.S. points environmental finger at B.C.' (1991), 'Thy neighbour's drains' (1991), 'Victoria sewage raises stink' (1991), Hunter (1992), 'A dirty business' (1993), Brown (1993), Daniels (1993).

4 See Hamilton and Simard (1993) for a useful discussion of the setting for the downtown tourist industry. Compare Murphy (1992) on the results of a survey on Victoria tourism.

5 There was extensive and informative coverage of this issue in the Victoria weekly, *Monday Magazine*, especially in the issues between 4 and 10 September 1986, and 12 and 17 March 1987. See also Williams (1991).

6 In his inaugural address in December 1993, the new conservative mayor, Bob Cross, spoke admiringly of Seattle's tough approach towards 'aggressive panhandling.' Compare 'Taking it to the streets: Portland cleaned up its inner city, Vancouver can too' (1992).

7 Compare 'Tree mischief' (1993), Levin (1993), Nichols (1993). See Hatch (1994) and MacIsaac (1994) for the protesters' views.

8 Ward (1994). Compare Hamilton (1993); 'A global war with Cold War techniques' (1993); 'British supplier drops BC paper hankies' (1994). See also Williamson (1993) and Langer (1993). The industry/government counter-attack is discussed in Nelson (1994).

9 The province responded to this challenge by offering a deal to the local First Nations: Leyne (1993). However, compare Watts (1994).

10 On the regional district system, see Bish (1990).

11 The term, 'local state' is confused and contested. I have discussed some of the conceptual difficulties in Magnusson (1985).

12 For helpful discussions of the theory and practice of social movements in the 1980s and onwards, see Boggs (1986), Eyerman and Jamison (1991), Carroll (1992), Tarrow (1994).

13 Thus, I use the term differently than Sassen (1991) or Fainstein (1994).

14 See, for instance, Clavel (1986), Blunkett and Jackson (1987), Mackintosh and Wainwright (1987), Conroy (1990), Kling and Posner (1990), DeLeon (1992). Compare Harris (1987), Caulfield (1988) and Magnusson (1990).

REFERENCES

Anderson, D. 1992. 'Victoria Responds: "We're not as bad as you think,"' *Seattle Post-Intelligencer*, 20 Dec.

Baskerville, P.A. 1986. *Beyond the Island: An Illustrated History of Victoria*. Burlington: Windsor Publications

Baxter, S. 1991. *Under the Viaduct: Homeless in Beautiful BC*. Vancouver: New Star Books

Bish, R.L. 1990. *Local Government in British Columbia*, 2nd ed. Victoria: University of Victoria School of Public Administration

Blunkett, D., and K. Jackson. 1987. *Democracy in Crisis: The Town Halls Respond*. London: Hogarth Press

Boggs, C. 1986. *Social Movements and Political Power: Emerging Forms of Radicalism in the West.* Philadelphia: Temple University Press

British Columbia. 1994. Commission on Resources and Environment, *Vancouver Island Land Use Plan*, vol. 1, Feb., 32–33

'British supplier drops BC paper hankies.' 1994. *Vancouver Sun*, 1 March B1

Brown, N. 1993. 'Sewage issue "taking toll" on tourism.' *Victoria Times–Colonist*, 8 Jan., C8

Capital Regional District. 1993. *Victoria's Capital Region: A Statistical Guide.* Victoria: CRD Regional Information Service, Dec.

Carroll, W.K., ed. 1992. *Organizing Dissent: Contemporary Social Movements in Theory and Practice.* Toronto: Garamond Press

Caulfield, J. 1988. 'Canadian urban "reform" and local conditions: An alternative to Harris's "reinterpretation."' *International Journal of Urban and Regional Research* 12: 477–84

Clavel, P. 1986. *The Progressive City: Planning and Participation, 1969–1984.* New Brunswick, NJ: Rutgers University Press

Cohen, J.L., and A. Arato. 1994. *Civil Society and Political Theory.* Cambridge: MIT Press

Community Council of Greater Victoria. 1988. 'The "hard to house" in Victoria: The downtown inter-agency meeting, October 1988'

Conroy, W.J. 1990. *Challenging the Boundaries of Reform: Socialism in Burlington.* Philadelphia: Temple University Press

Coull, C., M. Dyment, and C. Kleiman. 1993. 'The women of Clayoquot.' *Focus on Women* [Victoria], Nov., 16–21.

Daniels, A. 1993. 'Tainted tourism.' *Vancouver Sun*, 25 Feb., D1–2

Davis, H.C. 1993.'Is the metropolitan Vancouver economy uncoupling from the rest of the province?' *B.C. Studies* 98 (Summer): 3–19

DeLeon, R.E. 1992. *Left Coast City: Progressive Politics in San Francisco, 1975–1991.* Lawrence: University Press of Kansas

'A Dirty Business.' 1993. *Maclean's*, 25 Jan., 7

Duncan, S., and M. Goodwin. 1988. *The Local State and Uneven Development.* Cambridge: Polity Press

Egan, T. 1991. 'Waves of sewage and auto traffic sweep down on U.S. from Canada.' *New York Times*, 19 May 114

Engels, F. 1987. *The Condition of the Working Class in England.* London: Penguin

Eyerman, R., and A. Jamison. 1991. *Social Movements: A Cognitive Approach.* Cambridge: Polity Press

Fainstein, S. 1994. *The City Builders: Property, Politics, and Planning in London and New York.* Oxford: Blackwell

Foster, H., ed. 1976. *Victoria: Physical Environment and Development.* Victoria: University of Victoria Department of Geography

Fotheringham, A. 1994. 'A guilt complex at the Games.' *Maclean's,* 29 Aug., 56

Fowler, E.P. 1992. *Building Cities That Work.* Montreal: McGill-Queen's University Press

Freedman, A. 1994. 'Will this "virtual" town ever get real?' *Globe and Mail,* 3 Sept., C2.

'A global war with Cold War techniques.' 1993. *Vancouver Sun,* 30 June, A1–2

Hamilton, G. 1993. 'Environmentalists call for boycott: Clayoquot wood goods target in Europe.' *Vancouver Sun,* 11 May, D1

Hamilton. W.G., and B. Simard. 1993. 'Victoria's inner harbour, 1967–1992: The transformation of a deindustrialized waterfront.' *Canadian Geographer* 37(4): 365–71

Harris, R. 1987. 'A social movement in urban politics: A reinterpretation of urban reform in Canada.' *International Journal of Urban and Regional Research* 11: 363–79

Harvey, D. 1989.'From managerialism to entrepreneurialism: The transformation in urban governance in late capitalism.' *Geografiska Annaler* 71B: 3–17.

Harwood, M. 1988. 'Daredevils for the environment.' *New York Times Magazine,* 2 Oct., 72–5

Hatch, R., et al. 1994. *Clayoquot and Dissent.* Vancouver: Ronsdale

Horton, T. 1991. 'The green giant.' *Rolling Stone* 612 (5 Sept.): 42–8, 108–12

Hunter, J. 1992. 'Washington officials threaten tourism boycott of Victoria.' *Vancouver Sun,* 24 Nov., B1

Kenny, L. and W. Magnusson. 1993. 'In transition: The women's house saving action.' *Canadian Review of Sociology and Anthropology* 30(3): 359–76

Kling, J.M., and P.S. Posner, eds. 1990. *Dilemmas of Activism: Class, Community, and the Politics of Local Mobilization.* Philadelphia: Temple University Press

Lai, D. C. 1991. *The Forbidden City within Victoria.* Victoria: Orca

Langer, V. 1993. 'Clayoquot international campaign.' *British Columbia Environmental Report.* Oct., 25

Levin, B. 1993. 'A forest fable.' *Maclean's,* 16 Aug., 1993, 20–7

Leyne, L. 1993. 'Bands get limited control of logging.' *Victoria Times-Colonist,* 11 Dec., A1–2

Livesey, B. 1994. 'Greenpeace exposed.' *Canadian Dimension* 28(4): 7–12

Logan, J., and H. Molotch. 1987. *Urban Fortunes: The Political Economy of Place.* Berkeley: University of California Press

Lorimer, J. 1972. *A Citizen's Guide to City Politics.* Toronto: James Lewis and Samuel

Luke, T. 1993. 'Discourse of disintegration, texts of transformation: Re-reading realism in the new world order.' *Alternatives: Social Transformation and Humane Governance* 18: 229–58

M'Gonigle, M., and B. Parfitt. 1994. *Forestopia: A Practical Guide to the New Forest Economy.* Madeira Park, BC: Harbour Publishing

MacDonald, G. 1992. '"Real people" at city hall.' *Monday Magazine,* 19–25 March, 13–15

MacIsaac, R., ed. 1994. *Mass Trials: Defending the Rainforests.* Vancouver: New Society

Mackintosh, M., and H. Wainwright. 1987. *A Taste of Power: The Politics of Local Economics.* London: Verso

Magnusson, W. 1981. 'Community organization and local self-government.' L.D. Feldman, ed., *Politics and Government of Urban Canada,* 4th ed., 61–86. Toronto: Methuen

– 1985. 'The local state in Canada: Theoretical perspectives.' *Canadian Public Administration* 28: 575–99

– 1986.'Bourgeois theories of local government.' *Political Studies,* 34: 1–18

– 1990. 'Progressive politics and Canadian cities.' In D.S. King and J. Pierre, eds., *Challenges to Local Government,* London: Sage 173–94.

– 1994. 'Social movements and the global city.' *Millennium: Journal of International Studies* 23(3): 621–45

Magnusson, W., and A. Sancton, eds. 1983. *City Politics in Canada.* Toronto: University of Toronto Press

Magnusson, W., and R. Walker. 1988. 'Decentring the state: Political theory and Canadian political economy.' *Studies in Political Economy: A Socialist Review* 26: 37–71

Mullens, A. 1992. 'Homeless population doubles: Warm climate makes city a natural destination.' *Vancouver Sun,* 21 Jan., A3

Murphy, P. E. 1992. 'Urban tourism and visitor behavior.' *American Behavioral Scientist* 36(2): 200–11

Nelson, J. 1994. 'Pulp and propaganda.' *Canadian Forum* 73(831): 14–19

Nichols, M. 1993. 'The whole world is watching.' *Maclean's,* 16 Aug., 20–7

Ostertag, B. 1991. 'Greenpeace takes over the world.' *Mother Jones* 16(2): 32–7, 84–7

Sassen, S. 1991. *The Global City: New York, London, Tokyo.* Princeton, NJ: Princeton University Press

Shields, R. 1989. 'Social spatialization and the built environment: The West Edmonton Mall.' *Society and Space* 7: 147–64

Spencer, L., with J. Bollwerk and R.C. Morris. 1991. 'The not so peaceful world of Greenpeace.' *Forbes Magazine,* 11 Nov. 174–80

'Taking it to the streets: Portland cleaned up its inner city, Vancouver can too.' 1992. *Vancouver Sun*, 5 Dec., A21

Tarrow, S. 1994. *Power in Movement: Social Movements, Collective Action and Politics.* Cambridge: Cambridge University Press

'Thy neighbour's drains.' 1991. *Economist*, 6–12 April, 29

'Tree mischief.' 1993. *Economist*, 1 May, 41

'U.S. points environmental finger at BC.' 1991. *Toronto Star*, 26 April, A23

'Victoria sewage raises stink.' 1991. *Calgary Herald*, 10 June, A9

Victoria Street Community Association. 1993a. *Street Meet 93: The Poor People's Conference*, April

– 1993b. *When Housing Is Not a Home: Tenants Speak Out on Victoria's Housing Crisis*, June

Walsh, C.S. 1994. 'Partisanship in Victoria – A critical analysis of the VCE experience.' Honours Paper, Department of Political Science, University of Victoria, April

Ward, S. 1994. 'Pressure mounting in Europe to stop clearcutting in BC' *Victoria Times–Colonist*, 1 March, A2

Watts, R. 1994. 'Clayoquot: A political fiasco,' *Victoria Times–Colonist*, 4 Jan., A8

Whysall, S. 1993. 'Trouble in the garden: Behind Victoria's grand facade lies a crisis in affordable housing.' *Vancouver Sun*, 2 May, A7

Williams, J.-A. 1991. 'The Victoria Eaton Centre and the discursive construction of local politics.' MA Thesis, Department of Political Science, University of Victoria

Williamson, R. 1993. 'Glitz is the winner in the logging war.' *Globe and Mail*, 7 Aug., B1–3

Wilson, C. 1992. 'Community takes major role in year of change in Victoria,' *Marketplace* [Victoria *Times–Colonist*], 2 Jan., A3

Wilson, D. 1991. 'Washington steams over fair city's waste.' *Globe and Mail*, 4 March, A3

Zukin, S. 1990. 'Socio-spatial prototypes of a new organization of consumption: The role of real cultural capital.' *Sociology* 24(1): 37–56

– 1991. *Landscapes of Power.* Berkeley: University of California Press